D0287877

A MANUAL OF CLASSIFICATION

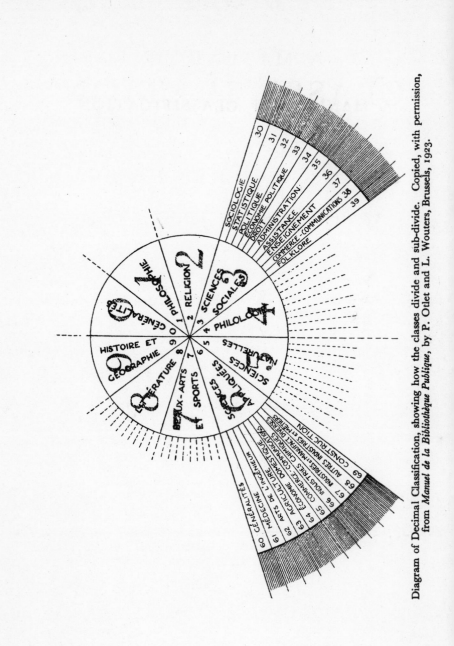

Diagram of Decimal Classification, showing how the classes divide and sub-divide. Copied, with permission, from *Manuel de la Bibliothèque Publique*, by P. Otlet and L. Wouters, Brussels, 1923.

Frontispiece

A MANUAL OF
CLASSIFICATION
FOR LIBRARIANS AND BIBLIOGRAPHERS

By
W. C. BERWICK SAYERS

THIRD EDITION—REVISED
WITH SOME CORRECTIONS

WITH ILLUSTRATIONS AND BIBLIOGRAPHY

LONDON HOUSE & MAXWELL, Publishers

122 EAST 55TH STREET • NEW YORK 22, N. Y.

"As I pondered thus upon the unified nature of library service, I discovered that classification could be thought of only in relation to the part it contributed to a final goal. Again it resumed a kind of central position; but this time, instead of resuming also to separate entity, it seemed to radiate throughout the structure shafts of illumination, lighting up and strengthening all library service. It seemed to me that classification could be made to reinforce the framework of our service and prevent the whole from collapsing into a formless and undirected tangle."—GRACE O. KELLEY.

First Edition 1926
Second Edition 1944
Third Edition 1955
Reprinted with corrections 1959
Reprinted 1962
Reprinted 1963
Copyright © 1959 by W. C. Berwick Sayers

REPRINTED BY LITHOGRAPHY IN GREAT BRITAIN BY
JARROLD AND SONS LIMITED, NORWICH

PREFACE

I. When I began work as lecturer on classification at the University of London School of Librarianship in 1919 I soon became of opinion that there was need for a comprehensive statement of the whole field of classification, as the librarian was concerned with it. That expresses my purpose and the limitations I necessarily set myself then and now. The pages that follow can have no special interest for the logician as classifier, or the scientist or philosopher in the same rôle. A treatise for them would be a theoretical and historical description and exposition of all the namings and groupings of knowledge that have been attempted since the beginning of the world; a book of which the late Professor Robert Flint's *History of the Classification of the Sciences* may be considered to be an outline; and for the writing of such a work I need scarcely say that I have not the necessary equipment. What I have attempted is (1) to set out the cardinal principles which appear to have actuated classifiers when devising their systems; (2) to glance rapidly, but I hope sufficiently, across the schemes which have directly influenced, or have been designed for, the classifying of books, catalogues or other literary or cognate material, avoiding the too frequent tendency·to confuse the student by cramming him with schemes which have, it may be, an antiquarian interest, but which he is not in the least likely to use; but emphasizing and explaining at some length the great systems of Brunet, Dewey, Cutter, Brown and the Library of Congress—the only systems which have now any considerable number of adherents, in Anglo-Saxon, Latin and Slavonic libraries at any rate, and adding to these, for this second edition, accounts as full as space allows of the new challenging system of Bliss and the intriguing novel one that comes to us from Madras from Ranganathan; and (3) to explain how classification affects library methods, how it is applied to shelf-arrangement, book display, catalogues, files, clippings, illustrations, maps, deeds, and the other materials and operations of libraries.

II. While thus in purpose and manner the book has been written for librarians, the subject is one that has a much more universal appeal and application. I believe experience proves that workers in almost every sphere in which organization of materials or time is involved would derive some benefit from a study of the subject; for, in the examples which the use of classification in libraries offers, we have organizing method severely applied to severely practical ends—to the exploiting of the library stock,

v

which phrase may stand as a sound, if seemingly unromantic, definition of the occupation of ninety-nine out of every hundred librarians.

III. To the beginner in the study of classification few things are more apparent and puzzling than the simplicity of the problem which faces the librarian and the complexity of the solutions of it that have been proposed. In brief, his problem is to arrange the books on library shelves and entries of them in catalogues in the manner which shall be most convenient for the users of the library and shall best reveal their contents. Years of study, observation and discussion have convinced him that in most cases this most convenient order is an arrangement of books by their subject matter. Out of that conviction has arisen the complexity. The questions arise:

When subject-matter has been discovered and defined, what is the order of the subjects?

What is to be done with the book which is in itself a complexity of subjects, or has no real value from the point of view of its subject?

What provision is to be made to accommodate in the order a new subject, or the new version of an old subject; in short, how can the classification keep pace with that most fluid of things, human thought?

How is the book to be retained in its proper place in the classification on the shelves, and how recorded in catalogues?

IV. Perhaps these are the main questions, but they give rise to many subsidiary ones, and on each of these main ones there has been a flood of discussion and controversy. From the birth of libraries to the present, persistent attempts to settle them have been made, with varying success, but in no case with complete satisfaction to everybody concerned. Albert Cim, in his *Le Livre*, quotes H. le Soudier as the authority for the statement that 130 systems existed in 1907, of which 46 were German, 41 French, 14 English, 14 Italian, 4 Spanish, 2 Belgian, 2 Arabian, 2 Russian, 1 Swiss, 1 Dutch, 1 Danish, and 2 American—a survey which must be very incomplete, as the figure for America clearly indicates.

V. In our early text-books the method was to give numerous brief outlines of schemes such as this:

Classification of Naudé.

Theology.	Geography.
Medicine.	History.
Bibliography.	Military Art.
Chronology.	Jurisprudence.
Council and Canon Law.	Politics.
Philosophy.	Literature.

But such outlines are of small value to the student. They certainly do show that the sum of being which we call knowledge may be split up into this dozen or so of vast groups; but library classification in its modern sense is a matter of very minute detail being fitted into larger and larger groups in progressive order: the synthesizing of detail to form the main classes and the analysis of the classes to make the detailed sub-classes for specific placing of books. The problem is not to classify a book on Science or History as a whole, but to place correctly Freud's *Beyond the Pleasure Principle*, Einstein's *Relativity*, a pamphlet on the nerve ganglia of the wasp, or a newspaper cutting on Epstein's *Rima* panel. The outline cited does not further the solving of this problem much, if at all.

VI. The first part of this book consists of a discussion of logical principles that may govern the making of a classification. It is based on a course of lectures which I gave in 1920 to classes in the University of London School of Librarianship; these have now been revised and amplified and there is much new matter; but I fear the "lecture" style still remains, it may be at the expense of literary quality, but I hope this will not offend. There is also, as happens in teaching, a good deal of repetition, even of words, but I conceive that this is not be to deplored. At the base of these lectures, in spite of efforts to be impartial and to give due credit to other views, lies the theory that there is an order of things to be discovered, recorded and applied, and that a true classification for books is based on that order. What differentiates the library from the philosophical and science classification is its special purpose of arranging *books* which have an individuality and complexity which are reflected in the provision of classes for such groups of books as De Quincey connotes by the term the Literature of Power (form classes), such works as are too composite in character go into a single subject class (generalia classes), and mnemonic aids in order to show points of view and methods of treatment (common sub-divisions). To these are added the mechanical devices of short signs for terms (notation), and indexes of the terms used throughout the classification system, as well as other features. In this view I am in a large measure the disciple of Professor Ernest Cushing Richardson, to whose little book, *Classification*, every student of the subject is indebted, although I agree that some of his pioneer theories are now unacceptable.

VII. I venture to quote what Richardson calls his "main propositions":

"(1) That the order of classification is the order of objects. (2) That this order forms a series of growing complexity from the simplest to the most complex. (3) That this order is at the same time the logical, chronological, and generally the genealogical order. (4) That this order concerns the sub-human, the human, and the superhuman, and (5) That the human has to do with (*a*) ideas of natural objects (images of things that are or have been, including human or superhuman objects), and (*b*) ideas of artificial objects (images of objects produced or modified by the human mind or which represent objects having no counterpart in the outer world except as figures or what might be). (6) That practical classification is the putting together of books most used together. (7) That in case of conflict in book classification the practical always prevails over the theoretical."

I have indulged in thus much plagiarism in order to acknowledge what has been a very great obligation. The most controversial part of Richardson's summary is contained in its first three statements. He declares that there is an order of things ordained by Nature and that the classifier's relation to it is one of inquiry and discovery. Other schools of thought reply that there is no such order apart from its apprehension by the human mind. Whichever way we may decide this, there still remains the inquiry: is the order of things necessarily the order which the classifier must adopt for the most satisfactory arrangement of books? I accept the view that in general this is so; that, where the sciences and the arts are concerned, the librarian will succeed in so far as his arrangement of books on these sciences and arts corresponds to the arrangement of their material made by the workers in them. Thus the classification of plants made by the botanist is the best basis for the arrangement of books on botany, and so with the other branches of knowledge; we have exemplification of this in the divisions of botany in the Dewey scheme; in short, bibliographical classification, if not merely scientific and philosophical classification conditioned by adjustments which are consequent upon the form of books, is derived from the same order of concepts. Bliss does not accept Richardson's "natural order," and substitutes for it arrangement "in accordance with the educational and scientific consensus," which appears to me to be in accord with what I have just written.

IX. The contrary view is that philosophical and science classifications are unsuitable for library use, being classifications of ideas only, and in consequence providing multitudinous divisions and sub-divisions of subjects upon which literature is improbable or even impossible. A book classification consists of the grouping together of books which are commonly used together, the naming of such groups, and the fitting of the groups into some sort of pattern in much the manner in which the pieces are fitted into a jig-saw puzzle. A book classification is therefore built up, bit by bit, from an examination of the books themselves, a sub-division being made for any new subject whenever a distinct monograph upon it appears. Examining this theory critically, it would seem that the only real justification for this exceedingly difficult form of synthesis is the fact that pure classifications are too minute; and because of this admitted fact, which to a qualified classifier is no difficulty at all, the advantages of relating library classifications to the classifications of thinkers in all branches of knowledge are to be sacrificed. Such a reason does not seem to be adequate. It is admitted that bibliographical and library classification can never be perfect according to the Order of Things, must always be artificial in a large measure, but there is more satisfaction in trying to make them approximate to it than the alternative method supplies.

X. The method of the second, or historical, part of the book is explained in the chapter on Preliminary Considerations. I have attempted to give a glimpse of the antiquity and perennial interest of the classification problem; but I have been much more concerned to give an account of the classification systems which are in actual use in most libraries to-day, sufficient for the reader to understand the general scope, method and qualities of each. One cannot go further or even do so much perfectly, because full appreciation of a system can only be gained by applying and testing it for some considerable time.

XI. The third part is severely practical. It faces the position of a librarian who has been placed in charge of a library; and endeavours to show the effect of classification on the planning and working of his library, as well as giving the more general methods of classifying books, entering them in classified catalogues, marking them for shelves, and supplying guides to their arrangement.

XII. I have not attempted to supply here the "drill" in the classifying of books which is as essential to the student librarian as is the drill in his paradigms to the student of Latin or Greek. That I have already endeavoured to do in my *Introduction to Library Classification*, which may be regarded as both preliminary and supplementary to this book.

1926 (reduced).

XIII. This introduction has been revised in the light of the twenty years' experience this book has endured in the rough and tumble of the limited but critical world of librarians. As I have already said, it was as to its greater part a reprint of lectures. The conditions under which it was written gave a certain character to its style which I have, in a measure only, eliminated in this edition.

XIV. A conservative method has been employed. As one of my much appreciated critics tells me with a frankness which does him credit, "You were unfortunate in that your book appeared just before the creative work in classification was done." I was, no doubt; Bliss and Ranganathan were hard on my heels, but the first of them had not then caught me up and the second was a listener, one of the most remarkable I had, to these lectures at the School of Librarianship. Both have done work which makes the workers previously in the field seem as amateurs. But E. C. Richardson and I have both contributed in a humble way to the work of these excellent librarians, and one of us lives to feel some pride and pleasure in the fact. And, after all, this book was my own, written my own way, presenting my own ideas. Others have felt with me, strangely enough, perhaps, that it has a place which the books of my more learned friends do not occupy. I realized, however, that if it was to survive, drastic re-writing of some parts was essential, because I admit that the researches of Bliss had outmoded many of our notions, especially in the realm of order, and the older rules of division now seem too rigid. The essential parallelisms between the order of knowledge classifications and book classifications and the main principles of construction and application held by all of us coincide to a remarkable degree. But if Bliss and Ranganathan owe some trifling things, handsomely acknowledged, to me, I owe more to them than I am able to express here.

XV. From this the extent of revision may be guessed. The whole has been reviewed, the first part with the exception of a page here and there entirely re-written; in the second part the chapters on Cutter, Brown and the Universal Decimal Classification have been entirely re-written, and all the others have been completely revised; that on Ranganathan is new; and I have had the valued assistance of Lawrence A. Burgess, who has remodelled the chapter on Bliss, while A. J. Hawkes has done a like service for that on the Library of Congress. Mr. Burgess knows the new classification well, has contributed the British section to its geographical tables, and is our foremost enthusiast for its order; Mr. Hawkes has applied the Library of Congress classification in two libraries, one of them a national one, and has possibly done more practical classing of books than any of us. The third part, which concerns practice, has been less susceptible to change, but it has been revised. The question of Book Display, which is essential to library missionary work and is good business, is touched upon, but not extensively, as its practice is a matter of the use of common perception rather than of technique; and I have considered some of the most often heard objections to classification in a final chapter which is new to this volume. The Bibliography has been completely rehandled.

XVI. I have found the revision a most strenuous task and the imperfections of the result are to me most obvious. Except in the chapters mentioned in the last paragraph no one but myself is responsible for the ideas here except those which are expressly quoted. The delay in the work has been due to many circumstances, amongst them a Nazi bomb which put me out of action for the best part of a year. The bibliographical references and citations throughout may be regarded as the acknowledgment of my obligations to previous writers. Mainly, I was originally indebted to Ernest Cushing Richardson, James Duff Brown, E. Wyndham Hulme and L. Stanley Jast. Now I gratefully add the names of Henry Evelyn Bliss and S. R. Ranganathan; my collaborators; John L. Thornton, who, after a thorough re-reading of this book, wrote me a most useful letter with some suggestions I have been happy to adopt; and the lively critics whose work makes *The Library Assistant* a stimulating companion. But my debt is legion, and can only be expressed in a general manner.

I have been sometimes critical of the excellent work done by Dr. Grace O. Kelley, who has been equally critical of mine, as she has every claim to be. The quotation from her pen on the back of my title page represents a sentiment where we, and I hope every maker and user of classification, meet in entire harmony.

October 1943

XVII. Only a few words need saying about this new issue of the Manual. The first is that no work of its character could keep pace with the fermenting processes that are being created or studied in the art of arranging the manifold records, in manuscripts, books, periodicals, clippings, pamphlets, circulars, catalogues, maps, prints, films, sheet music, sound records disc or other, and whatever else may form permanently or transiently part of the stock of such repositories as libraries have become today. More discussion and experiment have been and are being devoted to the study of these than at any previous time. Meanwhile a demand for this simple work persists, strange as that may seem to those to whom the current conception of what is called depth classification, of the inductive, self-perpetuating type, prevails over all others. I have therefore left the book substantially as it was in 1944, but I have rewritten some chapters in the light of these prevailing conceptions. These are confessedly not adequate.

XVIII. The chapter on the Dewey Decimal Classification has been rehandled and I have attempted to show not only the defects in it that obsess its critics, myself included, but also to do justice to its surprisingly capital virtues as a scheme which introduced general classification into libraries and, as its use developed, taught all subsequent classificationists the main possibilities of a synthetic scheme. The fifteenth edition, 1951, is studied briefly from three points of view: as an elementary scheme suitable for smaller popular libraries; or, for larger ones with sufficient classing power to make their own necessary subdivisions; or, again, as a modernized version of the skeletal main features of the original Dewey upon which there is fairly general agreement amongst us, and preliminary to a necessarily fuller sixteenth edition.

XIX. I have retouched some other pages, but in bulk the book is unchanged. Whatever may be the ultimate optimum classification, it is clear that the coral-like structure of a library *shelf* scheme which begins with only uniquely defined science subjects, as the ingenious J. E. L. Farradane proposes, but for indexing, must be a tremendously long process; Science, vast as it is, is only a fragment of Being, past, present and future, which may be recorded in books; to cover that, even approximately, would seem to demand by this method a corps of specialists perpetually in session such as Ranganathan suggests in the last chapter of his *Philosophy of Classification*. One may hope such a corps can be organized and perpetuated; perhaps the Committee on Classification, set up as a suggestion of the Royal Society (see paragraph 323), of which Brian C. Vickery, one of the best-equipped recent writers on the new methods, is honorary secretary, may be preliminary to this. The fact that the Fédération International de Documentation has confided the study of important aspects of classification to Indian librarians is another portent worthy of note.

XX. Meanwhile, although such work must influence all libraries, the general librarian, and especially the public librarian using open shelves, will be more than fortunate if he has the time and staff to work out his own classification. Down-to-earth common sense suggests that for the present, perhaps for many years to come, most of us must use one of the great so-called "enumerative" schemes that have been tried and have established their claim to be workable; and those are the schemes of Dewey, the

Library of Congress, the U.D.C., Brown and Bliss. The student needs to know here and now how these schemes came to be and their construction and application. This I have endeavoured to provide and is the sole justification for this book.

W. C. BERWICK SAYERS

Croydon 1954

CONTENTS

DIVISION THREE

THE PRACTICAL WORK OF CLASSIFICATION

LIST OF ILLUSTRATIONS

NOTE.—Illustrations numbered 1 and 2 were taken from *Open Access Libraries*, and 13 from Brown's *Library Classification and Cataloguing*. All three were originally drawn by Mr. James Douglas Stewart. Numbers 14–15 are from blocks lent by Libraco, Ltd. The rest were re-drawn from my own crude sketches, as follows: numbers 4–5 by Mrs. K. M. Crosby, 14 by Miss Beryl M. Clarke, and numbers 1, 3, 6, 7, 8, 9, 10, 11, 12 by Miss Nancy Leechman. To all concerned I offer my thanks.

LIST OF FOLDING TABLES

NOTE.—Tables I–II are from Edward Edwards's *Memoirs of Libraries*, v. 2, 1859.

DIVISION ONE
THE THEORY OF CLASSIFICATION

CHAPTER I

THE NATURE AND PURPOSE OF CLASSIFICATION

1. *Preliminary Definitions*. From the day when a man first assembled books of any kind or form, men have been interested in the ways of arranging them. It is merely a part of the divine instinct that "order is Heaven's first law"; for arrangement, or classification as we call it, lies at the base of every well-managed life and occupation. As we shall see later, the clay tablets which formed the books of the library of the Assyrian, Assur-ban-i-pal, were placed on their shelves in a considered order; and in the record of libraries throughout the ages, wherever we have any details of them, we have also evidences of the preoccupation of their librarians with this question. It is one of much interest and is simple in its essentials, but in the course of years has assumed a complexity which is the outcome of the general tendency of men to seek scientific or philosophical reasons for the processes they employ. The classification of libraries may be defined as: *The arrangement of books on shelves, or descriptions of them, in the manner which is most useful to those who read.* Classification, then, is a tool for a very simple but infinitely important purpose. If, however, a preliminary definition is easy, its full explanation and application are not so; but it is essential from the outset that we keep clearly in mind this one end: to be useful to our readers with the smallest complication of search or other effort for them or for ourselves. The studies and theories of librarians deal drastically with our definition, developing all its terms and applying them with all sorts of enlargements, reductions and conditions. Thus the subject often presents an appearance of difficulty which has little warrant in the facts.

2. This prelude is desirable, as younger students are often repelled from what is one of the attractive and useful studies in our work as librarians by its jargon. "There are few subjects about which it is so possible to weave a web of philosophical moonshine as classification, and this, I suppose, arises because every science and art has a tendency to acquire a phraseology of its own which becomes a real veil between the uninitiated and

the subject." These words, written twenty-five years ago, have an even greater applicability to-day; the successive writers on the subject, who indeed have added greatly to its boundaries, have provided us with a vocabulary which is truly formidable. By the sheer weight of their authority I must adopt, and with gratitude, some parts of their doctrines. They are of much value. Nevertheless, throughout this book the simplest words are used that are believed to be capable of conveying the right meaning, and so, I hope, some of the alleged difficulties will at least be reduced.

3. Before we come to the study of library classification as such, it is necessary, or at least desirable, that we should form some elementary notions of the mental processes involved. This chapter, and the three that follow, are therefore devoted to the simple principles drawn from formal logic which tell us what a classification is and what are its uses. These chapters are not intended for those who have had a training in logic and especially in the more modern phases of it, which all such persons know to reject many of the positions of scholastic logic and to extend others greatly. The simple notions here insisted upon have their own use as showing the approach that most men who have constructed general library classification systems have made to their subject.

4. We cannot reason, even in the simplest manner, unless we possess the power of being able to classify things; indeed we cannot live at all. A Wellsian picture is easily conjured up of an inhabitant of another planet, who possesses every human faculty but has had no human experience, who finds himself set down suddenly on one of our country roads. The world he has come from has none of the features of this; everything therefore before and around him is new. He walks along the road. The first object of consequence that he notices is a tree. He sees that it has a perpendicular trunk, covered with a corrugated substance, that it branches off above his head, and on these branches are rustling extremities which we call leaves. With no knowledge to aid, his eyes do not awaken in his mind memories of something like it seen elsewhere which will tell him what it is. He proceeds to experiment; he feels the trunk, and finds it solid; he plucks a leaf, somewhat surprised to find it is easily detachable; greatly daring, he tastes the leaf, and finds it has a sweet, acid, not pleasant or unpleasant, flavour. He goes on his way, and meets another such object, but different in shape—in an accidental particular—and he repeats the experiments he made with the first tree. His impressions of solidity of the trunk, detachability and the flavour of the leaf are repeated. He is on the way to

classification; he decides that this second thing must have a definite *likeness* to the first thing. Repeated experiments with other trees strengthen and confirm this inference. So, by gradual and sometimes painful processes, he arrives at the notion that there is a group of things every member of which is like every other in all essential particulars. If he live long enough he may learn from man that the group has a name, Trees; but in any case he has formed an idea to which he will attach some label or name of its own in order to distinguish it. This is classification, in a broad sense. It becomes more advanced classification, when from repeated experiences he learns that while all trees resemble one another in their main characteristics, some trees have darker leaves than others, some have oval leaves, others bifurcate or double leaves, some have smooth edges, some are serrated or tooth-edged; and his recognition of these differences enables him to make groups within the greater group of trees; to separate mentally the pine-tree from oak, the alder from elder and birch from beech; and later he will find that fir, larch and cedar very closely resemble the pine, although they have differences, but differences not nearly so marked as the difference between the oak and pine. Later, if his observations are continued, he will discover that even the pine-tree has several kinds, the Weymouth, the Norwegian, the Italian Stone Pine, and so on. When he has reached this stage, he has co-ordinated a series of observations by the use of memory—and also by what the psychologists call the Law of Association—in such a way that the sight of one pine-tree calls into his mind the characteristics of all pine-trees as distinct from other kinds of tree. He can *classify* them.

5. I doubt if a man would survive for twenty-four hours if he were entirely without this power of classifying. Imagine a man in a London street, who beheld a car knock down and injure a man, and yet was unable to infer from the incident that any other car would behave similarly in similar circumstances—who could not recognize that any swift-rolling vehicle (and "swift-rolling vehicle" constitutes a *class* of things) was a dangerous thing with which to collide. From a single incident of this kind a man with classifying power but without experience might make the error, but a second would teach him to avoid it, and the first would make him cautious. But the man without the power would be unable to relate one car to another; experience would be of no use to him; he would probably walk quite carelessly in front of any car he saw. The example seems ridiculous enough, but were we deprived of classifying power the circumstances might be precisely as suggested.

6. It is commonly understood that animals are lacking in

reasoning powers. Science is divided upon the point; but there is no doubt that they possess classifying powers, if only in a modest measure. Richardson, in his pioneer little book on *Classification*, has said picturesquely: "classification made the ape a man," meaning, of course, that when in the process of evolution the ape, or whatever form of animal was man's ancestor, reached that stage of reasoning which enabled him to distinguish the likenesses and differences existing between things, he became possessed of a power which is peculiar to man—the higher reasoning power. The statement is only roughly accurate, and may be largely untrue; we do not yet understand the mental powers of animals sufficiently to say that they are without reason. There is much evidence that they possess something which resembles it very closely. For example, the lower animals certainly have the power of distinguishing two classes of things: those that are eatable, and those that are not. The beaver in his architecture shows a power which may be instinct but is very like reason. So, too, the eagle in choosing a nesting-place on great heights, usually over precipices, must in some way be aware that precipices are inaccessible; and the cuckoo, as E. C. Stuart Baker has demonstrated,[1] is able to distinguish colour in choosing the fosterers of its eggs and, to some extent, size—all this is probably a primitive reason. It is probable also that the animal or bird has no consciousness of the reasons at the back of its doings; and in that respect man alone may be pre-eminent; in any case, these powers which seem to be merely rudimentary in animals are developed in man to a high degree; they are so even in the uneducated man; and on these considerations may rest the validity of Richardson's saying.

7. All this may enable us to reach another useful definition of classification. It is that exercise of the powers of perception and reason which enables us to assemble things in an order of likeness, and to separate them according to an order of unlikeness. There is rather more in this than may appear on the surface. The definition means not merely the grouping of things which resemble one another, but the arrangement within each group of its components according to their degrees of resemblance. To take a rough unscientific example, which will, however, illustrate our point sufficiently. A group of dogs will contain (let us say) greyhounds, foxhounds, wolfhounds, terriers, Irish terriers, and Scotch terriers. All these have the general resemblance implied in their common name—dogs. But all hounds are more like other hounds than they are like terriers; all terriers more like other terriers than they are like hounds. So these would form

[1] *Cuckoo Problems*, Chapter IV, etc., 1942. Witherby.

sub-classes within the class, dogs; but, again, a bull-terrier is more like a mastiff (probably) than it is like a hound; and this relationship must be shown in our arranging of the class, dogs. Classification, then, is not only the general grouping of things; it is also their *arrangement* in some sort of logical order so that the relationships of the things may be ascertained.

8. Classification is merely the power of observation applied; and we have to apply it to all things. The simple process of emptying the pocket in which you keep your money is a good example.[1] To enable you to know its value, you must first classify that money. You will first place into heaps your notes, gold, silver, and copper respectively. That is arrangement into main divisions. You will next divide each of these groups into pound and ten-shilling notes; into sovereigns and half-sovereigns; into crowns, half-crowns, florins, shillings, sixpences, threepenny pieces, pennies, half-pennies and farthings. The process illustrates roughly a principle upon which classification depends. The money has been arranged in two ways, or by two principles. In the first grouping—notes, gold, silver and copper—it was by the *material* of which the money is made. In the sub-division of these groups the arrangement was by *value*. If one principle of division were used throughout—that of value—sovereigns would fall into the same group as pound notes, and half-sovereigns into the same group as ten-shilling notes—the normal currency value of these respective things being identical. Classification is not merely grouping, and the arrangement of things into groups and within groups—it is arrangement according to a principle. Here we have the most complex problem in classification theory; one that we must return to again and again.

9. In his little book entitled *A Manual of Library Classification* the late James Duff Brown gave another simple example which is worth a passing mention. You may see, he says, a practical demonstration of classification on any coster's fruit barrow. That intelligent merchant does not mix all his fruit together indiscriminately on his barrow and label the result comprehensively "Mixed Fruit." He separates the various fruits carefully into compartments. Indeed, he does more. If you could investigate his arrangement thoroughly—an investigation which he would probably not welcome cordially—you would possibly find that (say) in the group strawberries, the best and ripest fruit were placed on top and facing towards the public. The inferior fruit would be hidden by the better—not to the benefit of the buyer, be it remarked.

10. Enough has been said to emphasize the truth that man's

---

[1] This example is borrowed from E. C. Richardson.

universe is so great and complex that on first appearance it is a chaos, a tangle of things to which he has no clue and of such extent that he can obtain no grasp of it unless he provides himself with some sort of a map. This *map of things* is a convenient expression for a scheme of classification. The whole universe of thought and things must be put into some order by the mind and that order must be recorded. Not only the whole universe, which means everything; even the single sciences are far too extensive for our comprehension until we have made some sort of map of their territories. Much of the study of men has been of what may be called a classificatory kind; that is to say, it has been concerned to observe and to record the appearance, structure, habits and purposes of things with a view to their accurate description; so that we may name them adequately and understand them. Indeed, it has been well said that the greater part of *knowledge consists in the giving of right names to things.*[1] Such research reveals the various likenesses which things have, and by these the things tend to be assembled into classes. Richardson asserts, without qualification, that "the things in nature are already classified," and from this we may infer that what man has to do is only to trace out the order of that classification and to record it. There are not wanting those who declare that there is no order in nature apart from the human mind that conceives it, but this is a vain speculation of Berkeleyan sort which declares that things only exist because the human mind perceives them to exist. We do know that in the natural world animals with a backbone form one group and those without another; that plants with flowers are one group and flowerless plants another; that some birds live mainly in the water and some are exclusively land creatures, and so the process may be extended. The mere recognition of such likenesses and differences as these is an act of classification; the commonness of the process is patent It may be well, however, to say that while classification is necessary to knowledge, it is only a method of approaching it. Much of the difficulty that is found in classifying, and especially in the classifying of books, arises from want of knowledge of the subjects we endeavour to arrange. We cannot classify a thing without knowing at least some of the qualities of the thing—what it is—and we cannot classify accurately or with any degree of finality without knowing most of, or all of, its qualities. We could not, for example, classify dogs without knowing what dogs are, and still less could we sub-divide them into their many species. Observation must first tell us the main characteristics of dogs: and having some view of these the classifying process is to arrange them.

[1] Carlyle.

In like manner, we cannot classify books by subjects unless we know what they are about. That seems trite enough when thus stated; but the statement is not at all unnecessary.

11. *A Further Definition.* Our rough definition of classification as the arrangement of things according to their degrees of likeness has served to lead up to a much more extended and now classic definition. It was first enunciated by Huxley, has been modified by Jevons and added to by Jast:

> By the classification of any series of objects is meant the actual or ideal arrangement together of those which are like and the separation of those which are unlike; the purpose of this arrangement being, primarily, to facilitate the operations of the mind in clearly conceiving and retaining in the memory the characters of the objects in question, and the recording of them that they may be conveniently and quickly referred to; and, secondarily, to disclose the correlations or laws of union of properties and circumstances.

This can be explained more simply perhaps. Classification is primarily a mental operation. When we say we arrange things we mean that we place them in an order which corresponds with an idea or series of ideas in our minds; we could not arrange things in an order which did not thus exist in our thought. To do this we have mental pictures of the things we are to arrange. That is ideal arrangement, indeed this mental process is the true meaning of classification. Actual arrangement is the placing in order of objects that we can see or touch, such as mineral or botanical specimens or coins.

12. It will be seen, we think, that the classifier is concerned not only with external things, the manifestations of the natural universe; he has a whole universe within himself—of emotions, thoughts, precepts, concepts, ideas—which he must also reduce to order. Some of man's thought is really external to himself, having been derived from others; his thoughts, for example, on current happenings are too often merely the reflection of the leading article in the newspaper he reads; but for most useful purposes we may regard them as his own. This subjective, intangible matter, we repeat, is equally to be controlled and set in order. A moment's reflection will show that when their inner phenomena is described—is represented by manuscript or printed signs on paper—the representation is something that must be arranged, and this cannot be done adequately unless the ideas represented are first arranged in the mind. So the definition might read, "Classification is the arrangement of things themselves or of our mental pictures of things." This gives us a valuable point for consideration, which may be put in the form of a question : "What is the *material* of classification?" The reply is—*everything*.

We can classify not only tangible, objective things which we can see and touch; we can also arrange impressions, ideas, notions; we can and must arrange things which exist, have existed, or may exist. Perhaps the well-known example drawn from library classification may serve to do this. There is no such thing in reality as the philosopher's stone, no such possibility (so far as we know) as the squaring of the circle. But both were attempted by generations of mediæval alchemists and mathematicians. The things may not exist, but they have been written about, and a general book classification must find places for them. Let us return for a moment to our definition, not to exhaust it—it will require several chapters to do that—but to comment briefly on its former provisions. The purpose of our arrangement of things is to enable us to write their names in order, and so to mark the names that we have a key to the arrangement. Or, briefly, a library ought in the main to be classified by the subjects of the books. That seems simple enough. But, is it? We soon discover that we have books on the Bible, Angling, Abbeys, Coal-mining, Gardening, Architecture, Accidence, Agriculture and so on. How shall we arrange these subjects, even when we have thrown the books into them? Supposing we take, as being the readiest, an alphabetical order of those subjects. We shall get such an arrangement as

> Abbeys.
> Accidence.
> Agriculture.
> Angling.
> Architecture.
> Bible, etc.

It is a useful order; but it is obviously imperfect. Abbeys have no relation to Accidence, but they have to Architecture. All the subjects are unrelated and separated from their like subjects. The classification is imperfect in that it does not assemble according to degrees of likeness or separate according to degrees of unlikeness. A classification of books to answer the conditions of our definition must arrange the subjects of books in some such way that the relations of books to other books are made apparent. Where a rightly designed classification exists, librarian or reader may go to a definite set of shelves and see at their beginning the books dealing with subjects which are preliminary to or are the foundation of the sought subject; find, following these, the books on the subject itself; and, following them in turn, the books on the subjects which develop from that subject. If classification is applied in a systematic catalogue or bibliography the entries of books in it will be similarly in order. Thinkers are divided as to the order which will accomplish this best; and we have had fairly definite views expressed from several standpoints on this matter, with which we shall deal in due course.

13. Classification, thus perfected, has the obvious value of economizing time and energy. It is an economy in the mere finding of books; for it is clear that if all the books and other material on a subject are assembled as nearly as is physically possible at one place there will be an important saving of time in the obtaining of a general view of the literature. But classification is not limited in its use to the arranging of books on shelves. It has an even more *analysing* use, in the making of class-entries in catalogues, be these on cards or in any other form. For example, in the card catalogue, a card can be filed under every subject with which a book is in any important way concerned. That catalogue then becomes a more or less complete record of all the matters in books and these may not be indicated by the titles of these books or revealed by the places which they occupy on the shelves. The economy value of this is clear. How many a research worker, inventor, thinker, writer, has wasted an immense time in finding out and in solving for himself facts and problems with which other workers have already dealt! Were only the results of former labours recorded in class catalogues, many such men would be saved from the labour of duplicating work that has already been done, and from the vexation of discovering their waste of energy. Life is too short to allow the neglect of classification.

14. The foundation of the library is the book; the foundation of librarianship is classification. Without classification no librarian can build up a systematic library; one, that is to say, which represents adequately the field of human learning as it is recorded in books. Think of the difficulties facing him—if he is honest in his work—in an unclassified library. He must gather together temporarily all the books on any given subject from all parts or his library, every time he wants to add to the strength of that subject or—what is equally important in all but the greater libraries which aim at completeness and never discard books on account of age or for the usual reasons which prompt withdrawal in libraries of more modest size—weed out books which have become obsolete. We fear that much inefficient work has resulted from want of classification. Librarians of larger libraries sometimes advocate the close classification of book entries in catalogues, but reject it for their shelves in favour of no classification or at the best broad classification. The reasoning on which this advocacy is based is not convincing. At any rate libraries arranged upon the open-access system, which in a few

years may be the only system in popular libraries,[1] are impossible to work without adequate shelf classification. Readers would be lost hopelessly in an unclassified welter of books.

15. If, then, a library cannot be built up, or revised, without classification, and if students and readers can get no comprehensive view of the literature of subjects without it, the vital character of our subject is easily demonstrated. Our purpose in this volume is to study the methods by which the contents of a library are arranged both on its shelves and in its catalogues. The methods which the librarian comprehends as classification, are derived from a consideration of the many ingredients which go to make up the book, an enumeration of which in quite incomplete form would include the size, subject, form, mode of treatment, binding, and printing type used in it. Such classification is of distinctive character. It is specially designed for application to books as an economy in library management, enabling us to determine as rapidly as possible what the book is, to relate it to other books like it, and to enable us to house it with some permanence and to find it for service with ease. It may seem to be superfluous thus to stress this obviously purposive nature of a library classification, but in recent years writers on the subject have busied themselves to a quite unnecessary extent in trying to prove what has long since been proven. In doing so, they have protested too much, even to the extent of alleging that a classification of books is so special that it has no relation to the classification of knowledge, but is an artificial experiment of the librarian. Much in a classification system is necessarily artificial and mechanical, but the basis of the practical schemes which are most likely to endure is the order which workers in the various fields of knowledge have arrived at in their subjects; they are, as Henry Evelyn Bliss, has affirmed, "in consistency with the scientific and educational concensus."[2] It is unfair to plunge the reader at this stage into one of the controversies of modern classification method. The reader who can settle the problems involved has no need of this or any book on classification theory. The beginner, however, must become acquainted with the way in which the classifier looks at things and tries to co-ordinate them; and for him the next chapter or chapters repeat quite elementary notions which indeed are available in a hundred textbooks but which he may find it convenient to have brought together. Finally, our definition indicates that when we classify things we do so by some principle which binds them together.

[1] Perhaps, I should say, in small or moderately sized libraries. Open access to entire collections would rarely be advisable or even possible in large libraries.

[2] Bliss. *Org. of Knowledge in Lib.*, p. 42, and *Org. of Knowledge and the Syst. of the Sci.*, pp. 16, 300, 301.

This may be one of several features possessed by every member of the class we make. This constitutes the likeness in these things. This likeness is the union of properties in the class. A classification, then, by arranging objects according to their likeness, throws into relief the features which make that likeness—the unity which there is in things. This will become clearer as we proceed.

16. *Nature as Classifier.* A classifier faces the multiplicity of things in the universe, an apparent jumble of natural figures, forms, movements, causes and effects—an apparent chaos—and tries to reduce it to order. I think there is abundant scientific evidence of natural order in the universe—without relying on the Mosaic theory of creation, in which the first act of the Almighty was one of classification: the dividing of the light from the darkness, and then the seas from the dry land. Nature in her mysterious way classifies in almost everything. All vertebrates—a great class—have certain characters in common, of which the principal is the possession of a back-bone; it is this possession which is the principle which unites them into a class; and Nature provides the principle; it is there to be discovered! That discovery is an applied act of classification. A glance at a zoological classification, to be found in any good text-book, will prove not only this point, but also that there is class-order amongst every species of animal life. We may draw a rough and ready example of the classifying powers of Nature from the recent science of ecology, the science which deals with geographical distribution of vegetable life as it is influenced by geological factors. Very remarkable results accrue from this study. It is found that where there is a sand and gravel soil, heather and the birch- and pine-trees are usually associated with it; that a clay soil, on the other hand, does not produce heather, but grass and the oak and elm; and so on. The ecologist knows that a given soil as a rule produces a given vegetation; and he can make inferences from the geology of any place as to the character of its vegetation. A beautiful example of natural classification is that which controls the study of crystals.[1] Nature does, in a very discernible measure, classify her works; and man is not merely the agent who produces the classification, he is rather the explorer who discovers and applies it.

17. The use of this instrument has led to many of the discoveries of investigators. Examples are legion, but a classic one is that classification of the chemical elements known as the Periodic Law first set out by Newlands in his Law of Octaves and enunciated independently by Mendeleeff. In this the elements are arranged by their valencies and a statement of them falls into vertical and horizontal groups in such manner that any element shares the

[1] Dealt with from our point of view in Jevons's *Principles of Science*, pp. 685–9.

nature of the elements above, below and on either side of it in the table. It follows that where a gap occurs in a column it may be inferred that it represents a missing element, the character of which is approximately known. This proved to be the case when one such gap was filled by the appearance of Radium.[1]

18. *The Value of Classification in Libraries.* Classification is a key to knowledge; because it is clear that if we arrange things in a definite order, and we know what that order is, we have a very good map of, or key to, those things. What is the purpose of this and what does this mean in relation to librarianship? *Merely that classification is the basis of all order in handling literature and its record.* That is a large statement, but it is one capable of conclusive proof. Books are a class of things, when we take into our view all the objects in the universe; and when we separate books from all other things, merely as an assembly of books, we have performed an act of classification. But it is a very elementary one. A huge room full of books is, in fact, having regard to the welter of things they are written about and the many forms and sizes they take, about the nearest representation of chaos that we can imagine. That is to say, if they are not classified in some way apart from their mere separation from things which are not books. Unless they are classified we cannot discover without immense loss of time what books there are there on chemistry, history, theology, poetry, or what not. Some libraries are of this kind, or are arranged by some such accidental characteristic as the colour of the bindings of the books. When the purpose of the books is that they shall be seen and not read, this is an excellent arrangement. Some are arranged—and these are more highly organized—by the names of the authors of the books. There is a definite value in that arrangement for the private library owned or used by the student who knows all his authors, and he often prefers this arrangement. If we know, for example, that Charles Darwin was a great naturalist, we know that under his name we shall find works on natural science. But the author-order tells us nothing about naturalists of whose names we may be ignorant, and it is no disparagement of the ordinary user of a library to say that he usually is unacquainted with authors. The only order then for a general library—we shall deal with special ones later—is one which in some way reveals what the books are about.

[1] A simple account appears in E. J. Holmyard's *Inorganic Chemistry*, Chapter XV.

CHAPTER II

CLASSIFICATION METHOD: FURTHER PRELIMINARIES

19. *Classification as Order.* At this early stage we shall find our way made more smooth if we can accept a series of simple notions. Classification is the arrangement of things in classes, and when our classes are made and these are themselves arranged we have produced some sort of a classification system or scheme. The systems the world knows best are those of Francis Bacon, Auguste Comte, Samuel Taylor Coleridge, Herbert Spencer and Karl Pearson, to mention those which come readily to mind, although there were many earlier and intermediate ones; in fact the thinkers have always been concerned to find some sort of system into which to fit the parts of their universe. Classifications, we have seen, are devised for the arrangement of the materials of special studies and are improved as those studies progress. So far is this so that the main scientific studies are known as the classificatory sciences. This coincides with and may be said to explain Carlyle's famous utterance that knowledge was the art of giving right names to things, for the naming of a thing rightly implies in the name-giver the power both of understanding the thing and so relating it to other things, and the discovery of the relationship between things is the purpose of such classification as, indeed, it is the purpose of knowledge.

20. It is the classes thus made which are arranged by the students of them into a *special* system, as, for example, a system of theology, or of botany, zoology or chemistry, and after this comes the philosopher who puts these special systems into some sort of logical order, based upon his own view of their importance, their origin, or even of their moral or religious significance, and so makes a *general* system. This, with some qualifications which need not detain us now, is what Bacon and the others did. Later still, to put it quite simply, came the librarian who worked on these philosophical systems, or systems of the sciences as they are perhaps more accurately called, for the arrangement not of actual scientific notions or objects but of books, and this is done by the addition to the system of classes to accommodate works which deal, as an encyclopædia does, with many subjects and are special to none; with classes for books which are distinctive in the patterns in which they are written rather than in their subject-matter, as books of poems, dramas and essays; with a series of symbols, called a notation, which are short signs standing

13

for the names or terms in the classification; and with an index which enables the place of any subject in the scheme to be identified and fixed. There are other features of a library classification as will appear later.

21. While what we have said is true in an elementary sense, there is also a sense in which library classifications may be said to be independent of the order of the sciences as the philosophers see it, and the reason is partly in the fact which the librarian's adjustments indicate, that a book is not itself the subject of which it treats, but is a book; and partly because thinkers are by no means agreed about the order of the sciences. It has been the unrealized dream of the thinker that he might make a scheme so comprehensive and so based upon truth that it would be the final statement, or microcosm, of the universe of thought. What, indeed, he has reached is a much more temporary statement of the position of thought in his own day. Hence, of course, the varying and successive systems we have cited. The librarian's classification was declared by E. Wyndham Hulme in a series of carefully reasoned articles, which appeared in *The Library Association Record* in 1911-12 and which unfortunately were not completed, to be without any real affinity with science and philosophical classifications. He writes "all classifications may be divided into two groups, (*a*) mechanical, (*b*) philosophical. The former, to which book classification belongs, deal with the mechanical assembling of material objects into classes, while the latter are concerned with the ordering of our ideas of things. As a rule mechanical classifications are left unco-ordinated; but when, as in the case of book classification, a systematic co-ordination of classes is introduced, this operation must always be of secondary importance. If, therefore, we were in agreement with Dr. Richardson, that the co-ordination of book classifications should follow the true order of the sciences, we should still be unable to acquiesce in his dictum that the test of the efficiency and permanent value of such classifications was to be found in the degree in which the order of their classes approximated to those of the higher type."

22. Hulme brings out his results in the phrase that a library classification is like a jig-saw puzzle in which the classes are the parts to be fitted together. The example does not seem to be good as the problem of the jig-saw puzzle is to reassemble the parts of an existing pattern; it is not a design made up by the solver as he goes but a series of bits cut from the design and together forming it. A classification made in this way would therefore be the assembling of classes of things in an order which already existed. The example therefore could be used to support

the doctrine of E. C. Richardson that nature is classified and the business of the classifier is to find clues to enable him to distinguish the parts and to fit them together again—to sort them into a coherent whole.

23. Thus early the reader is introduced to a main question of classification: i.e., is there an optimum order of knowledge superseding every other and valid in all circumstances? It is not certain that an unconditioned affirmative can be given in answer, although Henry Evelyn Bliss seems to draw near to that claim for the order he has used in his *Bibliographic Classification*, 1940.

24. A great deal of misunderstanding has come from the author's own earlier assertion, already again expressed in this chapter, that knowledge classification is the basis of library classification. I do not know that anyone has taken any purely philosophical system, added notation and index and, without other alteration, straightway applied it. What was and is meant is that the method and a good deal of the class-making of the philosopher inevitably lie behind every well-constructed scheme. This must be so in the very nature of the subject which is knowledge and knowledge is one however it may be approached. A classifier, whose experience has few rivals in this country, has written to me as follows: "That book classification with certain minor additions of a practical nature is an *a priori* doctrine experience shows to be wholly false. Experience shows that books are most usefully arranged when the order of their arrangement corresponds most closely with the scheme and mesh of man's vocational associations." If I understand this aright, it is what is intended by Bliss when he requires that a scheme be in accord with the educational and scientific consensus, and is a part of what the present writer means when he says that "characteristics chosen as the basis of the classification shall be essential to the purposes of the scheme." In short, it can be demonstrated that while every well-devised scheme has necessarily a philosophical—a thought—background, to be practical it must have an order of classes that is useful to those for whom it is devised. Librarians therefore have made their schemes to meet the needs of readers, and just as scientists and philosophers have made "systems of the sciences" in order to arrive at the final and unalterable system, and have so far failed, so librarians have contrived successive schemes for books with a like intention. Those best known to the English-speaking world, although by no means confined to it, are studied in some detail in the second part of this book; those that come most readily to mind are the Baconian Chart of Learning, 1623, and the classifications known as Dewey's Decimal, 1876–, Cutter's Expansive, 1891-93, Brown's Subject, 1906, Bliss's

Bibliographic, 1935–, Ranganathan's Colon, 1933, the scheme of the Library of Congress, 1909–, and the expanded adaptation of Dewey's Decimal scheme known now as the Universal Decimal Classification, 1905–. The existence of so many major schemes of book classification is evidence of the interest and importance of the subject, and our apparent failure so far to make a system which secures common acceptance.

25. *Classification as a Map.* We have proceeded so far without going into the simple truths which underlie the making of a classification. It seemed, however, best to face the problems inherent in making any form of classification before defining our terms. The act of classification, as already asserted, is expounded in different ways in many text-books and treatises on logic and it may for some readers be a work of superfluity that we set it out again here. These, however, can skip the remainder of this chapter. To those new to the study it is desirable that the ground should be covered as this should make clearer what follows.

26. We may extend an earlier statement by considering the expression: *A classification is a map of things which cannot be drawn graphically, but is set down in words.* The task is to provide for the field of knowledge, or part of it, as comprehensive and clear a statement as the cartographer is able to make of a territory of the earth. The untutored person has no connected view of the subjects which occupy men's minds; his knowledge is unrelated; but the educated man must at least have some notion of such a view, although only those who have looked at the question carefully have any definite one. Our conception of a country of which there were no maps would be much the same as that of the ordinary man in face of any branch of knowledge which he had not examined, and the place of that branch in relation to other branches would be as indefinite to him. The purpose of classification as a process of thought is by an examination of the qualities of things to bring them into relation with one another and so to increase the knowledge of them that they can be named accurately. A verbal description of a country, unless we have prior accurate knowledge of it, will I think fail to convey the relationship of place with place. If, however, we study an accurately drawn map of it, we can see the relationships of place and distance, and by the use of such symbols, for example, as are employed on maps of the Ordnance Survey see the physical and economic character of the territory.

27. From this example of the map we can illustrate the qualities of a *general* classification and of a *special* classification. A map of England is the graphic description of a special territory; some of its relations to the British Isles and to the European coastline

may be indicated, but not its relation to the whole earth. On the other hand, a terrestrial globe also shows the map of England but it shows in addition every other part of the world and, what is important in this connexion, shows the exact relations of every land and sea to every other. The map of England does the work of a special classification limited to one subject; the globe that of a general classification which embraces all subjects. That is to say, if we substitute a science, say Zoology, for England, and Knowledge for the terrestrial globe, we gain some impression of what it is the task of the classification of knowledge to do and that, to repeat, is to describe accurately the extent and content of each part of knowledge and then to set it in its place in the general order of knowledge. The process is of the same nature as that of the map-maker but more complex, because the globe of the earth is, as it were, fixed; the countries may change hands indeed, but they do not change position; while, in a knowledge or a book classification, owing to our imperfect knowing, the positions of subjects may change or seem to change and the globe itself is therefore a rather different one for each classification scheme maker.

28. Incidentally, there is another important way in which our map may illustrate a classification principle; and that is in demonstrating that a scheme is arranged according to the needs of its user. A thorough atlas may have in it several maps of England, each designed to exhibit a given set of facts; thus, we have physical, orological, geological, meteorological, economic, botanical maps and maps showing communications, local government divisions, surface utilization and other characteristics of the land. It is the same land that is dealt with and in the main the same things in it, but the arrangement is in each case by the characteristic most useful for the purpose for which the map is to be consulted. What is thus shown is required in a scheme designed for books: that it shall be in the order most convenient for the worker in the material which is being arranged. It is therefore not only possible but often desirable that the same subjects be regarded from various standpoints and then positioned most conveniently for the purpose in hand. As our geological map surveys the same total of facts as our economic one but is yet prepared from a quite different standpoint and for a different purpose, so the book classifier may take precisely the same series of subjects and arrange them in different ways according to the specialism which the arrangement is intended to serve. The two ways in which money may be arranged, as shown in paragraph 8 above, are simply another manner of expressing the principle.

29. Another conception of classification may take the form

which a genealogical table assumes. The making of a family pedigree involves many of the factors which occur in the making of a pedigree of such a subject as botany. From a common ancestor we proceed to his children, from each of these to their children, thence to theirs, and so on where the generations are known, in a perfect modulation which shows accurate subordination of the parts as well as all the collateral relationships. So in botany, from the common plant ancestor we get the two great families of cellular and vascular plants and proceed to their descendants in a similar manner. This example is given not merely to show a method of setting out a subject, but also to draw attention to a difficulty. This was indicated when we said that our map must be "set down in words." A map of knowledge in graphic form, or in the form of a genealogical table, would occupy acres of paper, be intricate in shape and too difficult to handle for ordinary work. The advantage of the map is that we can see the relation of place to place at a glance because we can read it both from top to bottom and from left to right, and the genealogical chart has much the same quality. A classification scheme, however, can be set down *only in vertical columns of terms* which we call its *schedules*; its real order is not apparent at sight and must be learned.

CHAPTER III

CLASSIFICATION METHOD: LOGICAL FACTORS

30. A classification schedule is, then, a series of words printed vertically in a column. This being so, we must understand what these words shall be. To put it another way, a scheme is a statement of knowledge in *terms*. Terms therefore are our first theme. A term is a name for a class; it may be a word or a phrase. Obviously for practical use it is better if it is a single word, merely because it is shorter, but it must be sufficiently descriptive of the class named by it. It is really a matter of indifference if it is a technical word or a popular one, so long as it is the best we can find, because a classification is for the use primarily of classifiers, and no library should be afflicted with inferior terms merely as a concession to ignorance. To take the commonest examples, *Life* is a simpler term than *Biology, Plants* than *Botany* and *Animals* than *Zoology;* yet Biology, Botany and Zoology are approved terms the connotation of which is known in the commonwealth of knowledge, while Life, Plant and Animal may each be subject to possible ambiguities in their use; and it is a condition of classification terms that they shall be used unambiguously and consistently.

31. When we speak of the consistent use of a term we mean merely that in the bringing together of things to form a class the name by which we call any thing shall represent that thing and that alone in the class. It does not mean that such a word as *engine* when used in the class Railways shall mean exactly the same thing as it means in the title *The Engines of the Human Body* where the class is Physiology and the term is used merely pictorially. A certain resemblance is admitted, otherwise the analogy the terms imply would not exist, but they are really quite different terms. We need not pursue at any length the various examples that were given formerly of inconsistency in the use of terms; they were often examples of words used analogically, metaphorically or carelessly, as when it was shown that "spring" may stand for an action, a season, a stream, or a thing; and when we use the word "sharp" of a needle, a street-arab, or a sensation of grief or pain, and so on. Intelligent people are able to detect such ambiguities from the context in which they are found. The recognition of the simple fact that such usages exist is, however, an aid to our clearer thinking.[1]

[1] I discover on re-reading that Bliss uses the examples of Zoology and Botany for

32. This emphasis we place upon the choice of class-terms is justified because they are the brief statement of the principles which we have recognized in making the class itself. Some part of the meaning has emerged already, it is hoped, but further explanations may be forgiven. Every classical reader knows that the word "class" in our sense has the same meaning that was given it in Ancient Rome when the effective nobility were arranged in six orders or ranks according to their real or supposed qualities of blood or wealth. These were the *classes* of the population, as distinct from the lower orders. A *classis*, then, was made up of a number of persons having a certain quality in common, or as we should say now, using words a little inaccurately but with a meaning we all understand, being of the same class. So in our study a class consists of a number of things which are alike in some particular, have some quality in common by which they may be sorted out from other things and which at the same time makes their own unity. It may safely be assumed from the outset that every thing in the universe is a member of some class; it cannot be affirmed with absolute certainty; but clearly if there is a thing which has no likeness to any other thing and therefore has no relationships it is unique and such things, if they exist, must be few. We can test this readily if we consider any of the common things of life—plants, animals, men, houses, streets, stones, stars, clothes and what not. The mere mention of any one of these brings to the mind not a single object but a whole series of things which have the common name. Such a name is a *class name*. The name of almost any thing is a class name.

33. A class, the definition requires, is made up of like things. This means clearly an assembly of things but as a necessary result it means also their separation from other things. The rule, stated briefly, is "*Classification assembles things according to their degrees of likeness and separates them according to their degrees of unlikeness.*" Likeness has been dealt with in admirable manner by Richardson in the introduction to his *Classification*. It is not sameness, because no two things have absolutely that likeness which would mean that they were alike in every particular and both occupied the same position in space, which is manifestly impossible. In common speech their distinction is often confused as when two men order drinks and the second after hearing the first says "I'll have the same." He could have something from the same cask or bottle but it would not be the same liquid. A better definition for us of likeness is the quality or qualities in things which enables

Animals and Plants (*Organization of Knowledge in Libraries*, p. 87, where there is an admirable discussion of terms); but I am allowing this much of unconscious debt to him to stand. His chapter should be read.

them to be substituted for each other, as, for example, the cartridges in a particular type of machine gun, the cards used in a catalogue, the letter *a* in a font of type of a given size, and pennies. Each of these resembles the companions in its class in a high degree. It is clear that there must be many ways in which things are like, as is seen in the simple example of a collection of pennies, as by the sovereigns who reigned at the time of issue, their date, their size in differing periods, their stages of wear; it is possible to arrange them by any of these likenesses, the only qualification being that the arrangement chosen serves its maker's purpose. The example may seem trivial, but as we saw in our description of the many viewpoints from which maps of an area may be drawn, the condition it implies is necessary to all practical classification, for it leads us again to the principle already emphasized that the arrangement must be that most useful to its user. We shall find that in the making of classes likeness is often interpreted with a certain looseness and some classes contain things which have minute degrees of difference which are too small or unimportant to require the further sub-division of the class. In book classification this is certainly so.

34. If, then, a class is a group of things brought together by a chosen likeness, how do we proceed to make this class and to break it up into sub-classes? It is clear that while such a term as Botany is the name of a great class, the members of which have all the likeness of insentient life, growth and decay, the class is too vast for any detailed study and must be broken up into its parts. The first process is one of assembly. A quality of likeness is chosen as the *characteristic*, by which we assemble things to make our class. The second process is to sub-divide our class into its parts. In formal phrase a classification proceeds from terms of great *extension* and small *intension* to terms of great *intension* and small *extension*. Or, more simply, it proceeds by taking class terms which connote great areas of subject-matter and divides them by gradual steps into terms less and less extensive until division is no longer possible. This definition is convenient but obviously depends upon the order adopted, because as Carveth Read shows "Classification may be either deductive or inductive; that is to say, in the formation of classes, as in the proof of propositions, we may, on the whole, proceed from the more to the less, or from the less to the more general; not that these two processes are entirely independent."[1] If a classification were in the developmental, historical or evolutionary order of a subject, it would proceed from such a term as Being, which might connote all existence past, present and possible, to the atom by gradual stages,

[1] *Logic: Deductive and Inductive*, p. 334, 3, 1924.

and there we have an excellent example of the meaning of our rule but, as we have shown, there may be as many arrangements of things as there are kinds of likeness to be found amongst them; it is therefore quite possible to reverse this order and to proceed from the special head to the general one. In usual practice, however, library, and many other, schemes of classification do proceed from great class-headings, which are terms of enormous extension, to the smallest subjects which may be reached by successive sub-divisions.

35. In this short paragraph have been used some words which an advanced worker on our subject may assume to be commonly understood, but for reasons already given I repeat a few of the simpler explanations.

Extension and Intension, Denotation and Connotation are words from formal logic representing certain powers and applications of terms. A further series of qualities which may be predicated of terms is that described as the Five Predicables and the application of all these terms is illustrated by the Tree of Porphyry or the Ramean Tree as it is also called.

By the *extension* of a term we mean all the things to which it may be applied. John Stuart Mill and some of his successors use *denotation* in the same sense. The term "Man" denotes any human being, "Animal" any living creature, and so on. By the intension of a term we mean the qualities implied in the thing named. Connotation is used as an alternative to intension. In intension "Man" connotes a mammal of upright gait who possesses reason, and "Animal" an organized living being, vertebrate or invertebrate, with sensation and capable of voluntary motion. The greater the extension of a term the smaller its intension and, conversely, the greater its intension the smaller its extension, as the Tree, below, may be used to demonstrate. The term "Being" already used is one of great extension, seeing that it covers all that is, but the term "pen" or "dog," although it has extension, is of enormously smaller extent and of much greater meaning or intension. The name of an individual, as Edward Edwards, is the example of a term of the smallest extension as it is limited to one man, but of the greatest intension for it implies every quality, racial and individual, that an English librarian of the middle of the Nineteenth Century can be known to have possessed.

The Five Predicables are a group of words which indicate qualities which may be *predicated* of terms. They were an addition to the Aristotelian Logic taken in the Third Century from Porphyry's Isagoge or Introduction to the Categories. They are *Genus, Species, Difference, Property* and *Accident.*

Genus is a group of things which may be divided into sub-groups, or *species*.

Species, then, are the group into which the *genus* may be divided.

The character which determines the division of the genus into the species is the *difference*, which may be defined as something added to the genus. The species, therefore, is the genus plus some quality or property which is over and above the unifying quality or property of the genus as a whole.

A *species*, however, may, and does in frequent cases, itself become a *genus;* that is to say, if it may be divided into sub-species; so far as these sub-species are concerned, the species is the genus; and, again, the sub-species themselves may each become a genus for possible sub-sub-species.

A *property* is some quality of a thing or class which is common to that thing or class, but which is not necessary to the definition of that class. The possession of a heart is a property of man, but is not peculiar to him since reason is his distinctive characteristic; and many things possess properties which are not exclusively the possession of the group or class to which they belong; thus, the emotions and certain physiological functions are not exclusively human although possessed by all men; they belong also to other animals.

An *accident* is a quality which is incidental to a class, may or may not belong to it, and has no necessary effect upon its other qualities. The size of a man is a mere accidental quality; so is the cut of a man's clothes; so, too, is the colour of his countenance, if we take man in general.

The Tree of Porphyry. Porphyry was also responsible for the Ladder or Tree which is usually employed to illustrate the division of a term and the uses of extension and intension as well as the predicables. Pierre de la Ramée, the French savant (1515-72), seems to have revived it in the sixteenth century with such effect that some thought him to be its creator and gave it the alternative name of the Ramean Tree. The version here is that used by Aldrich and translated by Jevons.

This is an example of what is called the bi-furcate method of classification, or classification branching in pairs, and in some ways it is a classification of broad character, but its value for us is to illustrate terms and to show the inevitable method of dividing terms. Substance is a term covering everything that exists, it is the most extensive, has the greatest extension, of any terms readily available. Conversely, it is so wide that it is impossible to indicate the multiplicity of things implied. Therefore it is a term of great extension and small intension. Corporeal Substance is still a term of great extension, but it has less extension, connotes fewer things, than Substance; it is therefore a term of greater intension, more qualities in it are definable. Animate Corporeal Substance is again of less extension and greater intension than Corporeal. The addition of the quality of Sensibility continues the process of lessening the extension and increasing the intension while the further addition of Reason completes the process by bringing us to Man who alone possesses it and who is divisible only into individuals such as Plato and you and me.

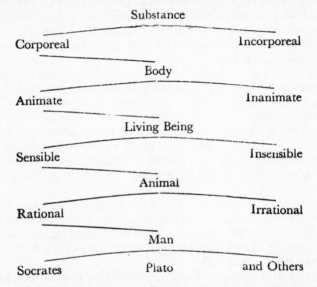

The Tree illustrates the predicables as simply. Substance is a *genus* which by the addition of the *difference* Corporeal (or possessing a body) divides the genus into the two *species*, Corporeal and Incorporeal. Leaving aside Incorporeal Substance, and, following what may be called the biological or living line of sub-division, we add the difference Animation to Corporeal Substance and break it into the two species Animate (the Living Body) and the Inanimate. Thence, adding Sensibility, we make the further species, the Animal, and leave over the living thing that is not Animal (the plant, etc.); and, finally, the difference Reason is added to the Animal to sort out the Rational Being which is Man, and the Irrational Animal is left over. *Property* and *Accident* are two predicables which are not illustrated in any obvious way by the Tree, although so far as Property is concerned words could be stretched, in a way unnecessary here, to prove that life is a property of all the left branches of the Tree and lifelessness those on the right. *Accident* it may be noted is a most important subsidiary quality in our study as every artificial classification rests upon artificial characteristics; i.e., the size of a book is an accident, as is its date of publication, its type and binding, as some of these accidents affect its important characteristic which is subject or literary mode.

It will not seem difficult to discover in what an important manner the method of division we have considered in the Tree of Porphyry affects the making of an classification. Every great class of literature is a genus which corresponds, according to its extension, with Substance in the Tree and must be divided into smaller classes by the addition of differences, as we may see if we glance at the progression of the Dewey classification in any subject; for example, if we start with Knowledge, as meaning the whole field of the classification scheme, and end with the morphology of the petals of a flower, we get this order

Knowledge.
    Science—other Knowledge.
        Biology—other Science.
            Botany—other Biology.
                Physiologic and Structural Botany—Historical and Geographic Botany, etc.
                    Morphology—other Physiological Processes and forms.
                        Generatory Organs—other Organs.
                            Flowers—other Generatory Organs.
                                Gross Anatomy—other Anatomy.
                                    Perianth—other parts of Gross Anatomy.
                                        Corolla—other parts of Perianth.
                                            Petals—Ligules.

At every step the intension of the class has been reduced the intension increased until the indivisible species, the *infima species*, is reached. We have abstracted this subject by the Porphyrian process from the scheme and the method of progression from the general heading to the most specific is clearly shown by it. As clearly, only one subject is thus abstracted and, as classification schemes, both the Tree and the example from Dewey are absurdly inadequate; not, however, because they are useless or absurd, they are indeed essential to the process, but because they are partial and limited. Classification of a subject does not divide into positive and negative terms and, following the positive, ignore all the negative. Each *pair* of branches of the Tree has to be followed. The classification must be much more gradual, must include all its parts or, in other words, be comprehensive and, so far as knowledge goes, be exhaustive. These conditions will shortly become evident.

CHAPTER IV

CLASSIFICATION METHOD: CHARACTERISTICS AND SCHEDULE-MAKING

36. *What Classification Does.* As the value of a classification scheme to its user is its cardinal quality it follows that in constructing its schedules the examination of the material to be classified must be of first importance. Librarians think this to be specially so of books, but no arrangement of books which does not follow the principles of logical classification is likely to meet general needs or to endure for long. That there are differences between the book classification and the knowledge classification is obvious to simple perception, but the resemblance between them is even greater. The purpose of knowledge classification is to assemble things in classes in order that their causes and effects may be examined, and where a cause seems invariably to produce an effect the process is regarded as a natural law of the things. Such classification clarifies thought, advances investigation, shows gaps in the sequence of knowledge and promotes discovery; revealing, as it should, the relationships of things, it enables a more or less complete survey of knowledge to be made. The variety of schemes of classifications of knowledge is a necessary condition of knowledge; it cannot stand still, it is infinite. It is doubtful if any one man can produce a scheme of all knowledge and it is certain that no scheme can ever be final and inalterably the best.

37. If that is the condition of the classification of knowledge, to some extent it is reflected in book classification which, primarily, seems to have another purpose. This is to place books in their relations to one another from the point of view of the reader. That reader must to a certain extent at least be a hypothetical person as we see when we encounter the university professor who blandly advises alphabetical author order or when we meet Jevons's statement that the classification of books is a logical absurdity—it is, of course, if we pretend that any method of book arrangement will resolve into a precise set of relations the welter of cross-classification which almost every book is. The library classifier makes no such pretence; he says that every book deals with an area or several areas of knowledge or is in a form which gives it its chief interest; in short, has a dominant character and the placing of the book by that character is a convenience and a library economy. The problem is to discover a way of

putting books on shelves in an order which will be recognizable, be in harmony with current studies and enable the finding of books together which have likeness in a greater or less degree. So we reach the condition that while an examination of books precedes the final arrangement of the classification, the scheme must first be known to the mind in outline at least. If, then, books are to follow the order of studies, by which we mean broadly what Mr. Hawkes calls the vocational activities of men, the order which the workers in the various branches of knowledge work must be the groundwork of the outline of principal divisions or main classes and their important sub-divisions.

38. *It Rests on a Theory of Knowledge.* The assembly of things into classes and the setting of classes in order to bring out their relationships has been the occupation of all creative, system-making philosophers from the earliest recorded time until now. To realize this we may revert to our analogy of the map of the world. The position of the traveller or geographer before the making of the maps of Ptolemy must have been very like that of the scientific worker in his early efforts to discover the nature and order of phenomena. In like manner he had to discover and name the continents and by gradual stages of enquiry reach to the whereabouts and character of seas, countries, rivers, mountains and so on. The parallel is a good one, for as the geographer has his divisions of the globe, so has the classifier to divide knowledge into its great classes or continents, its countries or sub-classes and its lesser parts. His task has been the more difficult, because while the geographer surveys a concrete, physical and visible set of phenomena, the scientist has much wider and less defined territories with which to deal. But as geographical maps have grown, changed and improved at every successive stage of dis-covery, so the classifications of knowledge have progressed. There the parallel may end, because there is a limit to the terrestrial globe; there is no limit to knowledge either in the physical or mental field, there is much more that is unknown, is possibly unprovable, subject to changes. No scheme of classification goes far beyond its own age, if it passes beyond it at all. Therefore we see that successive philosophers have suggested at intervals new characteristics on which to base the outline and the development of their systems. We can mix general and library classifications in our consideration of schedule-making because either form will illustrate the principles, which may be written briefly thus:

A classification is an assembly of classes in their relations.
Classes divide from the general head to the special by gradations of likeness and difference.

The gradation must bring about the subordination and co-ordination of the sub-classes.

The arrangement must be uncritical.

It must be exhaustive.

The process, either of assembly into classes or the sub-dividing of the classes when made, must depend upon some theory of knowledge. Even when we are arranging in the roughest manner a group of books, we do it by some order in our minds that must precede the act of arranging. So the classifiers in turn took some theory that we may say to be their characteristic. Thus Callimachus took the *kinds* of writer as his basis; Gesner, the order of the studies as they were pursued in the mediæval university; Bacon the products of the operation of the mental faculties memory, imagination and reason; Comte the progression of sciences from the primitive theological view through the metaphysical to the positive, the sciences increasing in specialism along or down a ladder of knowledge; James Duff Brown the operations of matter and force as they lead to the development of life, mind and the records of man; Henry Evelyn Bliss what he calls "the educational and scientific consensus."

39. *The Classifying Process.* The process may be illustrated from more limited and simpler things. Instead of the whole of knowledge, we can take clothes or domestic equipment or dwelling houses, indeed anything that is capable of assembly and of division, either in the actual objects or as mental concepts or ideas. In the clothing trade it is possible to arrange garments by their material, their purpose, sizes, prices and many other ways. In domestic equipment, purpose, material and position are some of the possible characteristics. In dwelling houses, style, size, building materials, position and so on may each serve. All such characteristics may in turn be used but only one at each stage of the classifying process. If, then, we are arranging clothes, we may begin by considering their purpose, pursuing this line until all the material is exhausted; for example, under and outer garments would possibly be two great main divisions. Each of these could then be divided by the part of the body the garment is intended to cover, and, having exhausted that, the size of the garments might be taken up and exhausted, and so on with any other characteristic which clothes will exhibit. This homely example exhibits many of the conditions of all classification schemes; thus the whole field of knowledge covered is assembled by the characteristic "that which covers and protects the individual body"; to this we add the difference "for outdoor wear" and immediately produce the two species *under* and *outer* garments which, being its parts, are subordinate to clothing generally.

They are also co-ordinates as they must range together in the mind and they are correlatives as an outer garment necessarily implies an inner one as brother implies a brother or sister and parent implies child. The two divisions thus made cover all clothes and thus far exhaust its extension or connotation. Further, it may be seen that while it was the difference "outdoor" which divided off or abstracted a sub-class of garments from clothing generally, "outdoor" is also the likeness which brings all the garments together and separates them from all others. Our first characteristic has been exhausted and on the broadest lines the classification is complete. But, for practical purposes, sub-division must proceed and a new characteristic, to be exhausted in turn, must be provided. This can be (I imagine usually is) the parts of the body to be covered by the garments: footwear, legwear, bodywear, neckwear, headwear, and again each of these is subordinate to outer or under clothing as the case may be, each is held by the likeness of the part of the body, and they are co-ordinate classes. The process may be continued by the use of the other characteristics named until the exhaustion of each. The result exhibits in the simplest manner the consistent use of characteristics.

40. *The Characteristics of Classification.* Thus we see, if we use another set of illustrations, that when we arrange a series of things, for example, money by value, animals and plants by their physical structure and functions, buildings by the uses to which they are put, the chemical elements by their atomic weights, we have arranged each of them by a principle. The principle employed— value, physical structure or use—we have called the *characteristic* and the word, although not employed except by library classifiers in that sense, is a convenient one to indicate a definite notion. A brief study of characteristics is desirable, because the first rule in the constructing of the schedules of a classification is that *characteristics* employed shall be *essential* to the purpose in view, as has already been said (paragraph 28). It is common sense that, if I make an arrangement of my possessions, it is because I want them in the order that will make them most useful or agreeable to me, and that condition governs all classification-making. I imagine a butcher would classify animals by some other principle than the zoologist if his purpose were to serve his business as a member of the meat trade, that an artist's arrangement of flowers may be different from a botanist's, that a printer may arrange books differently from a librarian. If their arrangements are the best for their purpose, they are, of course, correct. Such considerations will prevent any dogmatizing as to what is the best characteristic to choose and it denies the assumption that there

is an optimum order for everything that is so for everybody and at all times. The most useful order is the best for its purpose, of course, but this does not necessarily mean that the order most useful to a particular person is the best for all or a majority of people, as the examples just cited prove.

The characteristic, then, is the quality, property or feature by which things are divided. The Library Association examiners have declared several times that "the characteristic is not a subject." The point involved is a fine one but is accurately made, because the subject is the thing divided or classified, and the characteristic is the likeness or quality by which the process is carried out. This now obvious principle is worth stating again since it has caused discussion and some discomfort to those who have not realized the distinction. An example may clear up the matter sufficiently. If we arrange a group of shells by their relative degrees of *whiteness*, whiteness is the characteristic, shells are the subject. On the other hand, whiteness as an abstract quality is certainly a subject of thought and itself can be arranged, because clearly there are imaginable or conceptual degrees of whiteness and therefore divisions of it; and anything that can be divided is a *subject* for classification. The fault of which the examiners complain lies in the fact that the candidate committing it had probably confused the subject with the characteristic in the application of the one to the other. Stated baldly, the examiners' remark is somewhat confusing itself: what they meant was "when we speak of a characteristic of classification we do not mean the subject we divide by that characteristic; the divisor must not be confused with what is divided."

Ever since man first realized classification, his work has been to discover the essential characteristic. And we get some very interesting results in the history of science and thought from his efforts.

41. *The Artificial Classification.* One sympathizes with Man in his early effort to reduce chaos to order; he had such a multiplicity of things with which to deal. It is not remarkable, is it, if in his earliest efforts he used his eyes, and reasoned from first perceptions? The appearances of things were there, and if two things "appeared to be like each other," he naturally brought them together. Thus, whales to him were fishes, bats were birds, spiders were insects. He reasoned in general from *analogy* which, to give a rough and ready definition, means the likeness in things which have a similar *function*, however different may be the plan upon which they are constructed. Or it may mean, in a sense sufficient for our argument, a likeness in appearance and purpose. *Homology*, on the other hand, means the likeness in things which resides in the fact

that they *are constructed* upon the same plan, however different may be their functions. These definitions are usually drawn from Biology as we show in the next paragraph. There is also the definition of analogy as any form of likeness or comparison between things which in their essence may sometimes not be alike: as when the engines of the human body and those of a motor-car are said to be analogous; or when two historic events appear to have occurred in similar circumstances; as when two cases in law seem to resemble each other. Every form of likeness, in a sense, provides an analogy, including forms which are also homologic. Homology, however, implies a more total likeness founded upon the essence of the things, which is fundamental to them and which makes them *conform in character and purpose*. And this may apply, not only to living things, as we are about to show, but it may also apply, indeed does apply, to all things man makes for his purposes. Thus chairs, to use an example, given me by A. J. Hawkes, are a homologic group assembled by the *purpose for which they exist*—their use—not by their construction. Analogy and homology are then, in a sense related. They are not interchangeable terms, and it is useful to repeat that an analogy is usually a likeness formed upon a few obvious characteristics which are not necessarily fundamental, while homology always implies the likeness based upon the vital characteristics of things.

42. Let us illustrate a little from the older classifications. We find that in the earliest animals were arranged by the element in which they lived; it was the most obvious thing about them; thus we got:

Animals.
Terrestrial.
Aerial.
Aquatic.

with the result that seals and whales and many molluscs were classed as fishes, while, as I have just said, the bat became one of the birds. This system would also naturally make such flying insects as butterflies into birds. There were variations of this characteristic for centuries, but of course men saw the inadequacy of it. Even Linnæus, who arrived at a more reasonable classifying method, arranged by *analogy*, choosing as the characteristic of classification the "general appearance and economy of the animal"; and making classes wherein the place of a creature was determined by such factors as the arrangement and number of toes, teeth, claws, beaks and scales. This leads, does it not, if we choose the number of limbs as a characteristic, to the frog and toad getting into the same class as tigers, as they evidently have four legs? Clearly these arrangements depend upon accidents and are artificial classification. Or, to put it in a more scientific manner, only one or two characters of the animal are chosen as the basis of the arrangement, and it is therefore partial, incomplete and necessarily inaccurate.

43. We had almost similar deficiencies in the early attempts to classify in the botanical sphere. The first classifier saw that some plants were larger than others, and he took size as a reasonable basis for his classing—with incomplete results. So he obtained: Trees, Shrubs and Herbs as a first outline, the inadequacy of which soon became obvious. Linnæus, again, offers us the most striking example of classification by a few qualities or properties, which often had no real relation to the nature of plants; and resembled, in some degree, the classification a child makes when he arranges flowers by their colours: everything white being a daisy; everything yellow—celandine, dandelion, buttercup, king-cup, etc.—being a "buttercup." It is worth while to consider the various Linnæan classifications with some care, as the classical examples of classification according to arbitrary factors, pursued *without a due examination of all the characters of the things classified*. Briefly, Linnæus chose the arrangement and number of the several organs of plants as the basis of his arrangement; the two main classes being

A Flowers present.
B Flowers absent (or stamens and pistils not evident).
    [Stamens are male organs, and pistils are female organs.]

These he sub-divided by certain appearances in the plants. Thus in class A we get

A Flowers present.
    I Stamens and pistils in every flower.
    II Stamens and pistils in different flowers.
    III Stamens and pistils in the same or in different flowers.

And again he sub-divided AI into

    AI Stamens and pistils in every flower.
    AIa Stamens of equal length.
    AIa I.   Having 1 stamen.
        II.   ,,   2 stamens.
        III.   ,,   3 stamens.

and so on, until he reached flowers having twenty or more of these organs. Now note the effect of such a system. It depends entirely upon the floral organs, as we have seen; but plants are in flower only at certain seasons, and if, when we went to classify them, they were not in full flower with all their stamens and styles perfect, it would be impossible to determine their class.

Moreover, in various stages of growth, as Balfour has pointed out in his *Manual of Botany*, different flowers on the same plant vary in the number of their stamens; and consequently the classifier would get like plants into quite different divisions. This sort of cross-division must always result when an accidental characteristic is chosen as the basis of the classification.[1]

44. Nearly always when we classify by number, size, or position in space, we get some such results as those with which we have been dealing. If we classified buildings by the material of which they were built, we might get villas, mansions, churches, town-halls, theatres and what not, all into one group, without any distinguishing difference between them; and I need not say how inadequate that would be as a classification. Another simple example would be the arrangement of tables by the material of which they were made; or of bottles by their colours—which would tell us nothing beyond their hue, and not even that satisfactorily. Everyone has met with the classification of the alphabet which is essential to the study of philology—especially to the study of such languages as Greek, where whole rules of phonology and speech turn upon the classification of the alphabet. In the accepted natural form the alphabet is classified according to the parts of the vocal apparatus which are brought into action in pronouncing them. But a classifier, working by analogy, by appearances, would arrange them by the often-described plan of their position in relation to the horizontal line on which they were written, which tells us one accidental thing about their quality and character.

45. Focusing the results of this mode of classification upon books, we shall see how far it would lead us astray. Some libraries, even to this day, arrange books by size. It makes the library *look* very nice, the shelves being ordered as are properly "sized" ranks of infantry; but it would mean that if we had ten editions (say) of Milton they would be in ten different places. Examples can be multiplied. Again, if we arranged the books by their printing types (typography), the results would be similarly valueless, except for the student of typography—for whom, be it remarked, it might be a perfectly "essential" arrangement (but, mark this, too, only if the books are regarded as "museum specimens," and not as having any other meaning). In a rather similar manner, if we arrange books by the language in which they are written, we get a very wide separation of *subjects*; although, again, if they are arranged for the student of language who is interested *only* in language, that would be a perfectly justifiable arrangement.

[1] A useful account of natural and artificial classification is that given by Thomas Fowler, *Inductive Logic*, Chapter 2, pt. 2.

46. All these arrangements, it will have been observed, are dependent upon one or more properties of the things classified; and those properties (or, to use our technical term "characteristics") are accidental ones. All these classifications are artificial ones; and to crystallize all we have here considered into a definition:

> *An artificial classification is one in which some accidental property of the things classified is adopted as the characteristic of arrangement.*

The incomplete and partial nature of artificial classifications can be seen, but I have also tried to show that they are not necessarily wrong; their use may in some circumstances be supremely right. What we want our classification to do—the end we have in view—must govern our choice of characteristics. This is merely repeating the rule that they "must be essential in relation to the purpose of the classification."

47. *The Natural Classification.* A natural classification is one that is made by the inherent properties in things; by those properties without which a thing could not be the thing that it is. If we return to Zoology for our examples, we shall find that one great fact cuts the animal realm into two parts. This is, the possession or absence of the vertebral column or backbone; and, although in the lowest forms of animals held to be backboned the manner in which they differ from those without backbone is not at once obvious, it is quite definite. This then is the primary natural characteristic relating all the higher animals, the vertebrates and, dividing them from the lower forms, the Invertebrates. Thus we get as the basis of all natural zoological classification:

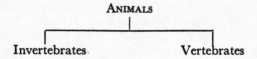

ANIMALS

Invertebrates   Vertebrates

and additional structural differences, in blood, breathing apparatus, method of propagation, etc., continue to increase the intension of this primary characteristic until we reach Mammals in the Vertebrates and Insects in the Invertebrates.

48. Take, as a further example, three different insects and examine them—a butterfly, a beetle and a blue-bottle. In the first place we shall notice that they have no vertebral column—they are not vertebrates; in the second, that their bodies are in three parts or segments, which seem as though they were hinged together; that on the second or middle segment each has three pairs of legs; and that each has two pairs of wings. In the butterfly the wings are apparent, are visibly seen to be a fore and back

pair of wings; in the beetle the fore wing has evolved into a hard shining sheath, which when the creature is at rest is an enveloping case for the hind wings; and in the blue-bottle the back wings are rudimentary, are two little button-shaped nobs, but they are still wings from a zoological point of view. Thus, when we chose the characteristic of structure for their arrangement, and reached the name *insect*, we formed a class in which all the members had this triple-segmented body, these three pairs of legs, and these two pairs of wings. The word insect connotes a whole series of qualities. A glance at the next garden-spider you meet—and the average person seems to think a spider is an insect—will show his body to be in two parts, with four pairs of legs, and no wings rudimentary or formed. He is thus outside the characteristic we have chosen.

49. So, in botany, the Natural System, as opposed to that of Linnæus, depends upon a whole series of structural characteristics, which we may reduce to very simple terms. The first thing man noticed about plants was that they had flowers or did not have them; he formed two groups in his mind, flowering and non-flowering plants. Following this clue he found that flowerless plants had forked leaves, that they grew by a peculiar method of addition to the summit of that part of the plant already existing, and that the rootlets sprang both from without and within the root-proper. On the other hand, he observed that flowering plants had parallel or reticulated leaves, that there were apparently two kinds distinguished by this particular. That one kind of flowering plant grew by additions of new internal material, and that its rootlets sprang from within the root proper. That the other kind of flowering plant grew in an opposite sort of manner, by the addition of material to its exterior and that the rootlets sprang from without the root proper. These were external, easily observed features; but when he came to dissect the plants, the two main groups he had discovered were found to correspond with a definite internal structure; that his flowerless plants were composed of cells, and his flowering plants of both cells and vessels. An examination of the plants in embryo (that is in their earliest stage) confirmed his grouping still further. He found that the flowering plants have all seed-lobes, or cotyledons, while the others are without them. He found also, in regard to the seed-lobes of flowering plants, that one group had one such seed-lobe, while the other had two or more seed-lobes. He had now a whole series of mutually dependent characteristics, inherent in the structure of plants; and he chose the structure as the basis of his arrangement. Thus the distinguishing characteristic was whether the plant was cellular or vascular; the

second whether it had seed-lobes or had them not; and so on through the series we have mentioned, in what may be supposed to be the growth-order (evolutionary order, if you like) of the plants. So we get:

    I. CELLULAR PLANTS [Non-Flowering Plants].
        Acotyledonous [no seed lobe].
           Heterorhizal [rootlets spring from without and within the seed proper].
           Acrogenous [stems spring from the summit].
           Cryptogamia [Mosses, etc.].
    II. VASCULAR PLANTS [Flowering Plants].
        I. Monocotyledons [one seed-lobe].
           Endorhizal [rootlets spring from within the root proper].
           Endogenous [grows by internal additions to its structure].
        II. Dicotyledons [two or more seed-lobes].
           Exorhizal [rootlets spring from without the seed-lobe].
           Exogenous [grows by additions to the exterior].

50. If I have made myself clear, I think you will now have a sufficient idea of what we mean when we speak of the difference between natural and artificial classification. If we bear in mind the principle that the natural characteristic of a thing is that without which it could not be what it is, its very essence, while the artificial is merely an accidental feature which does not affect its structure, purpose or intrinsic character, we shall not go far wrong in making a choice between them.

51. *Accepted Order.* The application of what we have learned of characteristics by the educationist, scientific worker and others is bound in a way to be artificial because, as we have hinted, such schemes are based upon limited knowledge; nearly the whole of them have been broken down or destroyed altogether by increasing knowledge. Nevertheless, as Bliss has shown more tellingly and with greater authority than any of his predecessors, from the successive studies of intellectual and scientific workers it has been possible to produce arrays of subjects in the order these most commonly use, and to say that though the foundations of knowledge are all axioms unproveable and liable to disproof, yet there is a certain permanency about the main pillars of knowledge and it is chiefly in the details of knowledge that change is inevitable. To alter our architectural metaphor into a surveying one, a classification scheme-maker, then, takes his field and divides it into its larger areas as we have already shown.

This seems to be the converse of the process of assembly of things into classes, but, not to make a mystery of simplicity, both processes, of assembly and division, work together in classification. Knowledge is an assembly of all things; knowledge is a genus to be divided by differences; each difference is a quality in the things divided, which the other things in the genus do not possess, and the possession of this difference is the likeness which assembles them in their own class. Thus, when we divide Science into the Physical and the Biological Sciences for ordinary purposes each excludes the things that the other contains. At the same time all the physical sciences—Mathematics, Astronomy, Physics, Electricity, Heat, etc.—are assembled by their likeness, in *not possessing life*, under the first of these terms and are thus separated from the Biological sciences which form a class in its turn comprising by their likeness—which is *life*—past and present plant and animal life. These, then, the Physical and the Biological sciences, are the primary great divisions of knowledge, and all things opening from them, because Life (Biology) naturally gives rise to the highest form of life (Anthropology) and this, which is the study of man, proceeds from his natural beginning through his ethnic development to his work in society and in nations and on to the records of his mind, his worship, morals and the products of his mind. The order may, and does, vary in its sequence according to the approach of the thinker proposing it, but the order has a wide general acceptance and, as we shall assert, a definite permanence. This question must recur frequently in our study.

52. *Choice of Characteristic.* The essential characteristic will differ for different men, as we have sufficiently stressed. Richardson says that the possible orders on which a classification may be based include (1) *Logical* order—from the complex to the simplest; (2) *Geometrical*—according to the position of things in space; (3) *Chronological*—according to position in time; (4) *Genetic*—according to likeness in origin or race, the "family" order; (5) *Historical*—according to position in space, order in time and genesis and therefore a combination of many of the preceding characteristics; (6) *Evolutionary*—the order of likeness from simple to complex, the converse and complement of Logical order; (7) *Dynamic*—order of power; (8) *Alphabetical*—according to letter-order of terms, the commonest artificial order; (9) *Mathematical*—according to numerical symbols; or order by means of a notation.

53. We may put aside alphabetical classification as not a classification order in our modern sense; it is an index order; and when Richardson defines mathematical order as "the prince

of artificial classifications and the servant of all natural classifications" he really means that whatever order we give to things we record it by means of symbols which have a mathematic aspect, fix the order and are its means of reference; in other words, it is classification or arrangement supplied with a *notation*. Many schemes of classification employ several of Richardson's characteristics: are logical, evolutionary, genetic and geographical in turn, the characteristic changing as the scheme requires.

54. These enumerations are intended to show that for the student of classification-making the modes available to him are many. That one way is better than another for this or that purpose is true enough. In knowledge classification Bacon, Coleridge, Comte, Karl Pearson, Spencer can be named again as each in turn insisting upon his own as an advance; so in library classification the only reason for the work of Dewey, Cutter, Richardson, Brown and Bliss is that each thought his order was an improvement. The student could express a preference with any assurance after the most careful study of the theory of knowledge used in each. He may find that most of the book classifiers were working, as was Comte most certainly, towards the position as stated by Bliss when he says of science order: "One study may be applied to, or introductory to, another, as mathematics to physics, physics to chemistry, chemistry to biology, biology to society, sociology to economics, linguistics to literature, and logic to philosophy";[1] and so a logical order of main classes emerges on a characteristic of progression from one science to another.

55. Continuing to study our schedule-making we revert again to the geographical map. The universe of knowledge we divide first into its continents, then into its countries, into its counties or departments, and then into its towns, villages and smaller units. These correspond to the parts of the schedule which are called alternatively

Main classes (groups of sciences).	or by Bliss who inverts the	Main divisions (groups of sciences).
Divisions (principal sciences or studies).	meaning of Dewey's nomen-	Main classes (principal sciences or studies).
Sub-divisions.	clature for	Sub-classes.
Sections.	Main Classes and	Sections.
Sub-sections,	Main Divisions	Sub-sections.

The Main Classes are naturally of great areas of knowledge, as the subjoined main classes of Dewey and Brown show:

[1] "Form in Classification"—a letter to *The Librarian*, v. 26, pp. 128–30, 1936–7.

Dewey.

Reason	Philosophy. Religion. Sociology. Language. Science. Useful Fine Arts.	Matter	Physical Science.
		Life	Biological Science. Ethnology, Medicine. Economic Biology. Domestic Arts.
Imagination	Literature.	Mind	Philosophy. Religion. Social and Political. Science.
Memory	History.	Record	Language. Literature. History.

Each of these columns in its way must comprehend the whole of knowledge.

Each term is then broken down into its divisions, as thus in Dewey:

Science.
Mathematics.
Astronomy.
Physics.
Chemistry.
Geology.
Paleontology.
Biology.

which, added up, should comprehend the whole of the Physical and Natural Sciences. [There are cross-divisions of science with philosophy in this system, but in a rough way the statement is true]. Such an arrangement should answer the rule that a schedule must show the sub-ordination, co-ordination and collocation of subjects. It is obvious that the divisions of a subject are subordinate parts of it, that Astronomy is subordinate to Science and Science to Knowledge. *Co-ordination* depends upon the placing of classes that have relations in such order that the subjects leading up to a subject come before it, and those which come out of the subject, or are next in likeness or character, come next. They are *co-related*. All schedules try to do this, and if we were tracing one line of development, as in the Ramæan Tree, or in the application of it to Petals in section 35, the co-ordination would be easily seen to exist; but it is also a rule that the process of sub-division must be gradual and must be modulated "by degrees of likeness." Nature does not leave gaps in her order of things. But in the vertical writing of a classification we cannot proceed by the method referred to; we must show in the schedules all the parts into which any genus or class divides; thus, in these Dewey divisions, while the *order* corresponds in a rough way and in part to the science order given in the Bliss quotation above, it is more convenient to regard them as a series of equal-ranking classes. To such classes Bliss has given the useful name "collocative." The difference between this practical necessity and the logical process from the general to the special head by one characteristic as shown in the example of petals is seen if we introduce the intermediate stages omitted from that example. Thus

Porphyrian method.	Dewey schedule method.
Knowledge.	PLANT Morphology.
Science—other Knowledge.	Organs.
Biology—other Science.	Circulatory.
Botany—other Biology.	Respiratory.
Physiologic and Structural Botany —Historical and Geographic Botany, etc.	Nutritory. Secretory or Excretory.
Morphology—other Physiological Processes and forms.	Generatory. Cryptogamic Generatory Organs.
Generatory organs—other Organs.	Flowers. Theoretic and Gross Anatomy.
Flowers—other Generatory Organs.	Gross Anatomy. Peduncle.
Gross Anatomy—other Anatomy.	Receptacle. Perianth.
Perianth—other parts of Gross Anatomy.	Calex, Sepals. Corolla.
Corolla—other parts of Perianth.	Petals. Ligules.
Petals—Ligules.	Corona.
	Motary.

The Dewey schedule is for only a part of the field outlined in the left-hand example and several of the minor sub-divisions and sections have been omitted, except under Gross Anatomy. It can be seen that the physiological characteristics of the plant organs, while subordinate to plant morphology and the class "organs" as a whole, are in a logical rather than developmental order; they are complements. At the Gross Anatomy stage peduncle, receptacle, and perianth, again subordinate, are themselves collateral, as in their more specific stage are Calex and Corolla, and the still more specific sub-sections, Petals and Ligules. Whenever such classes stand together, equal in the schedule and correlated and not obviously derived from one another, they are collocative classes; i.e., classes placed together, and they are properly collocated if those which have most qualities in common are arranged in proximity.

56. All classification schemes have the qualities we have endeavoured to describe, but to make the new terms somewhat clearer for the beginner we may be allowed to use Bliss's own distinctions of them. In a family there are ancestors, parents,

children, uncles and aunts, cousins, etc. Here *subordination* is illustrated by the position in time of the members of the family; *co-ordination* in placing those most nearly related by being in the direct line and in that by primogeniture; and *collocation* consists in arranging in relationship order as nearly as may be the members, not in the direct descent, as uncles, cousins, etc. But the whole process is a *co-ordination* of the family.

57. In the progress down the schedule the steps are very gradual. *The process of sub-division must exhibit, so far as possible, the hierarchy of the subject; must proceed by gradual steps; thus showing perfect co-ordination of the terms.* This can be demonstrated from the example just given. We cannot imagine that the flower developed at a jump from the primitive forms of vegetation: it is a very complex structure, the result of long-continued life with an infinite number of variations. Nature moved slowly; and so must our classification, step by step; if we made a jump we should never cover our subject fully, never reach exact definition, be continually leaving out of our reckoning whole groups of qualities; in short, it would make more or less confusion of our arrangement. What is here done for one chain of classification can be done for any subject and it is an excellent exercise to take any common thing known to us and to construct a scheme involving the principles of division from main class to sub-section, showing the whole of its *hierarchy*, or order of precedence of the various subdivisions, and how they are controlled by gradualness, subordination, co-ordination and collocation, are mutually exclusive and that the whole exhausts the subject. The method shown by the abstraction of petals is invaluable in the actual using of a scheme by one who applies it. If we can trace the subject we are classifying back stage by stage to its main class and find it fits in all the way, we shall be sure of the accuracy of our work. This, however, will be dealt with later.

58. *Classes are Mutually Exclusive.* The classes, the logical method requires, *must be mutually exclusive.* A thing cannot be itself and something else at the same time. Applied to classification schemes this means merely that when we made our main classes we separated by the class name an area of knowledge from all other classes; and as we progress with our sub-division, at each stage the difference by which we subdivide marks off the divisions from other divisions, and so with the sub-divisions. No two classes, it used to be said, can overlap. In a true and abstract classification that is actually so. The corporeal excludes the incorporeal, sensibility insensibility, and reason the irrational. What we as classification makers mean is: the divisions and subdivisions shall as far as possible be self-contained so that, wherever

a "pure" as compared with a "compound" subject is found, it
shall normally have one place only in the classification. But as
Lawrence A. Burgess pointed out in a constructive and trenchant
criticism of the Canons formerly enunciated in this Manual[1]
"books are normally written upon variable *groups* or associations
of ideas rather than upon isolated objects." Not normally, but
often, it is the case and for these cases what follows it is excellent
and agreed. "For example, when classifying a number of books
on sports and pastimes, is it really more important to have one
fixed place for, let us say, stool-ball or table tennis: than to allow
for those perverse groupings (by 'Cross-division') that writers
will use, such as 'out-door games,' 'ball games,' 'traditional
games,' 'children's games,' 'week-end entertainments'? Though
each particular game will naturally be mentioned specifically
only once in the schedules, it will necessarily be covered or implied
by quite a number of other headings. Is it not a common experience that so much approximate placing is due to just this
failure of headings to overlap? Fortunately our practical schemes
are generally more liberal in this matter of 'cross-division' than
our theories; so we are never called on to face directly the problem
of whether our duty as classifiers requires us to classify the books
that are written or to insist that authors write books to fit our
schedules! It has always seemed to me that, provided our schedules
follow sanely and soberly in each topic the current conventional
usage of specialists in that topic, cross-division will produce far
less confusion than would arise from a ruthless and literal application of canon 4.[2] I will go so far as to assert that, in my opinion,
cross-division is *essential* to the purpose of any general classification." Cross-division forms a definite feature of the Bliss
classification of which Burgess is an informed advocate, and in
the chapter on that scheme later in this volume the reasons will
be explained. In the ordinary way, however, cross-division means
the use of two characteristics in the sub-division of a single subject
which is the confusion of order. It allows buildings to go under
building and under architecture, gardening to go under useful
arts and under fine arts, and astrology to go under the occult and
under astronomy. In practical work in ordinary classing these
alternatives mean unnecessary separations of like subject-matter,
whatever may be their justification in individual cases.

59. *Classification is Non-Critical.* There is a tendency in all
men to view things as they are beneficial or inimical, useful or
useless, right or wrong, in relation to themselves. This tendency

---

[1] "The Canons of Classification: a revaluation." *Library World*, v. 34, pp. 3-10,
1931-32.
[2] The canon referred to was "characteristics must be mutually exclusive."

must be resisted by the classifier both in his construction of his scheme and, where it may be more likely to be indulged, in his application of it. This can be illustrated by examples more easily than by much assertion. The position of Astrology in Science is settled summarily even to-day by many orthodox scientists; that was so also in 1876 when Dewey in his schedule made a class under Mind and Body in Philosophy for Delusions, Witchcraft and Magic and sub-divided that into Apparitions, Hallucinations, Divination, Witchcraft, Astrology, Palmistry, Humbugs and Spiritualism. One can imagine the reactions of the convinced student of Astrology as well, it may be added, as the members of the Society for Psychical Research! The modern revisions have removed these indignities by renaming the heading Transcendentalism and Occultism in Dewey, and both Dewey and Bliss admit Astrology admirably under Astronomy, although Bliss prefers it to be placed in Folk Lore. Perhaps the cardinal example of criticism comes from Dewey, too, in the 800, Literature, class: he arranges the nine writers he considers to be representative under each period of literature and lumps all the others together as "Minor Writers." That too has been revised in subsequent editions. But the fault of criticism in classification (and in classing, as we shall see) is much more subtle in other ways. An author may represent views that are anathema to the classifier, for example, write a book like Brandes's *Jesus Christ a Myth*, or on some political question from a violent political bias. As classifiers our views and likings have no place in our work; Brandes's book is a life of Christ, however distasteful to the Christian; the political book is on its subject and must go there even if we think it ought to go under treason or in some other limbo for the unspeakable. I have known Brandes's book to be classed under atheism. Other books will occur to every student. The result of such placing not only confuses thought, it puts a subject in several places according to different points of view and may mean much cross-division and shelf-confusion too.

60. *Classification should be Exhaustive.* We may complete with one more principle our survey of the mechanics of knowledge classification. It is this: *In the construction of our schedules the enumeration of parts must be exhaustive.* On the face of it this means that the schedule must name every subject that exists or can exist. It must exhaust every subject. But it will be said at once, and quite rightly, that this is an impossibility. To begin with, no living man knows everything about everything. Bacon took the whole of knowledge for his province, he said: he did not; he took what he thought to be the whole of knowledge. No man can have more than an external acquaintance with the sciences as a whole

or can know even one of them, or even a part of one of them—say chemistry—in all its branches. No man, it has been asserted, can construct an entirely satisfactory general classification; a corps of philosophers and scientists might produce a satisfactory one. Even they, however, can only classify the known things of the universe. They cannot give names to things which have not yet been discovered. All this may be granted, and yet our rule will stand if we read it thus: *A classification must enumerate the whole of known things, and permit the insertion of additions to them.* It is in the words I have stressed that the vital implication of the rule lies. A classification must be elastic, expansible and hospitable in the highest degree. That is to say, it must be so constructed that any new subject may be inserted into it without dislocating its sequence. If a classification has not this quality it will become obsolete in a very short time. We shall see the all-importance of this principle when we come, as we shall now shortly come, to focus all we have learned so far upon the art of bibliographical classification.

A well-constructed classification may become obsolete in its terminology. That of Bacon is almost completely so; but it will still have its value if it be expansible. It may be that the discoveries of man may discredit evolution as we know it, or any other theory of knowledge, but so long as classification can take in the new discoveries, and give them a logical place in the hierarchy, so long it may be a practical working scheme.

CHAPTER V

BIBLIOGRAPHICAL CLASSIFICATION

61. *Can Books be Classified?*   We have now to consider the bearing of all we have studied up to the present upon library classification. Again and again we have emphasized the fact that the material of classification is the whole of knowledge—that is, the material of *knowledge* classification. We may now say that a classification of books is as artificial as the ordinary classification of knowledge, but, while the methods of the librarian may vary in important ways from those of scientist and philosopher, they deal with the same unlimited field. In addition to the abstract untrammelled ideas and objects which can be isolated and compounded in thought with which they work, he has to order subjects as they are recorded in books and the physical form of books introduces complications which are the special concern of the librarian. Knowledge classification groups, divides and registers thoughts, things, ideas, in an unlimited manner; but— on the other hand—a book is not an idea. In a sense it may be the expression of ideas, but it is infinitely more complex than any idea. For example, in a classification of geological elements the word water conveys a clearly defined simple idea; but a book on water may deal not only with water in the abstract, it may treat of its forms, of glaciers, snow and ice; its chemistry; its movements and mechanics; its relations to astronomy; the fauna and flora of water; its bibliography; it is a very complex thing. It is impossible, say the philosophers, to classify such a compendium as a book. Of such critics the most potent is Jevons, whose *Principles of Science* is so important a text-book in our study.

62. He writes: "Classification [of books] by subjects would be an exceedingly useful method if it were practicable, but experience shows it to be a logical absurdity. It is a very difficult matter to classify the sciences, so complicated are the relations between them. But with books the complication is vastly greater, since the same book may treat of different sciences, or may discuss a problem involving many branches of knowledge. A good account of the steam-engine will be antiquarian, so far as it traces out the earliest efforts at discovery; purely scientific, as regards the principles of thermodynamics involved; technical, as regards the mechanical means of applying those principles; economical, as regards the lives of the inventors. . . . In regard to literary works,

rigorous classification is still less possible. The same work may partake of the nature of poetry, biography, history, philosophy, or if we form a comprehensive class of belles-lettres, nobody can say exactly what does or does not come under the term."

63. We have apparently undertaken a fearsome and impossible thing in presuming to classify our books; we ought, we suppose, to leave them in unordered arrangement (if that be not a contradiction of terms), with only an author index; and, therefore, to leave them in such manner that they are accessible only to the man who knows every author in the subject in which he is interested, and, when his memory or knowledge fails on this point, inaccessible to him as well! Says L. S. Jast: "This statement of Jevons reminds me of the keeper who went up to the trespassing angler with the remark, 'My man, you can't fish here,' and who received the reply, 'But I *am* fishing.' " Librarians, in their wisdom or unwisdom, have trespassed on Jevons's precious waters and have shown that they can classify. But, coming as the statement does from so excellent an authority, we must examine it, and clarify our minds in regard to it. From the librarian's standpoint, the hypothetical book may deal, indeed, with all the subjects that Jevons enumerates but it is, after all, a "book on the steam-engine." Remembering the rule that convenience governs all classifications, he asks himself to whom the book will be most useful; for whom, primarily, it is meant; and according to his answer he will place the book—in this case—in engineering. Again, in pure literature, or belles-lettres, it does not matter much if we do or do not know the qualities of the books included— all the subjects of which they treat—because their importance does not lie in their subject-matter, interesting as that often is and must be in works of enduring character, but in their pattern as form or mode of expression; and in classifying them we adopt this characteristic and ignore altogether their subject-matter. We shall come to this question more fully in a moment. We ought to examine Jevons's statement in relation to the time at which it was made, and to the lack of knowledge of libraries which it unfortunately shows. In 1874 there were few reasonably good library schemes; hardly any of the libraries of England were classified, and those that were could not boast of anything wonderful in their arrangement. Moreover, Jevons seems not to have known of the schemes and methods laid down in Edwards's *Memoirs of Libraries*, published sixteen years earlier than his own book—which is not remarkable as the readers of books on librarianship are select indeed; had he known them he might have modified his statement.

64. One hesitates to accuse so logical and orderly a mind as

Jevons of confusion; but he *has* confused the functions of classification with those of cataloguing. Perhaps this is hardly a fair way of putting it, since his criticism is aimed at the classified catalogue—the actual classifying of books on shelves was a performance of which he had probably never heard. But even here his objection seems to rest upon the belief that only one entry of a book is made in a classified catalogue. A classification of books does not attempt to arrange them by all their subjects, but only by the predominating, or most convenient, subject in each. A book treats of a topic from forty sides; very well, if we had the means, and the lack of imagination, we could buy forty copies of the book and place one under each of the forty places on our classified shelves; but I need hardly say that the number of librarians who will achieve such a feat will not be great. On the other hand, our book is a concrete, indivisible thing; which will go into one place only on the shelves; and that place, as I have just affirmed, must be the one must useful to the user of the book. In the catalogue the book can be entered directly, or by reference, under every subject in it in which is of enough importance to justify such entries. There we are handling not the book but written entries—ideas—of it, and these we can multiply as fully as reason and convenience dictate. Jevons's hypothetical book would have to be a remarkably encyclopædic view of the steam-engine to justify an entry under each of the topics he names. We shall have much to say about the classified catalogue later on.

65. So, to summarize, experience aiding us, we get back to the position that books can and should be classified; that the order of knowledge and of the sciences is the basis of book classification; the primary difference being that while the knowledge classification arranges knowledge itself and its substances tangible and intangible, a book classification arranges the expression of knowledge in written or other form—the book, print, manuscript or what not. In general it may be said that at least half of the books in the world will fit logically and readily into a knowledge classification if viewed from the standpoint we are now examining; but a good many will not do so, owing to their miscellaneous subject-matter, or to the form in which they are presented. This brings us to the outward and visible difference between the knowledge and the book classification.

66. *Book Classification Requirements*. The study of knowledge classification is essential to the book-classifier who is to understand the making and working of his scheme. We have admitted, and again admit, that many schemes for book-arrangement seem to be the result of the mere scrutiny of books themselves and to be fortuitous in the worst cases and systematic, to some degree, in

others; but it never can be admitted that there is no relation between knowledge and its arrangements and books and their arrangement. It may be, in some cases, that the influence of such systems as Bacon, Gesner, and Comte is merely reflected indirectly, but arrangement itself must be logical; all classification must be to make sense. Even if main classes appear in different orders, as widely divergent as are Dewey and Bliss, in the working out of individual classes they tend to approximate at least on broad lines. In short, a classification of books must be a classification of knowledge. Let us, however, recall the point so often made that the Scientists (and Educationists may be added) make the schemes for their individual subjects, and then comes the generalizing Bacon or other philosopher who integrates these various schemes into one system in whatever order seems to him best. His system when completed is therefore a co-ordination of many schemes, each with its individual approach, If this is fully understood the principle that "characteristics must be consistent; no two headings must overlap" will not be interpreted as a skilful writer has done to mean that a single characteristic must be pursued undeviatingly and without change from the Universe to every individual thought or thing classified, which would be manifestly absurd. Book-classification uses many approaches to individual classes, many characteristics to arrange individual sub-classes and sections. The whole point is that every single act of classifying—every subject, array or series—must itself be divided consistently. Nor will it be thought that in speaking of the natural characteristic we are insisting that every subject is, or can be except by stretching of meaning, divided by the principles of homology.

67. Whether this assumption is accepted or not, there are requirements of bibliographical classification which rise from the subject, *books themselves*. Books are written representations of thought in general or in particular; they may cover, rarely, the whole of knowledge as a universal encyclopædia is expected to do; they may deal with several subjects; they may take certain literary patterns, as dictionaries, essays, journals, or as poetry or drama; they may be of a certain age or about that age; be of various physical sizes, shapes and in significant printing types, have illustrations or not which matter. The likenesses and differences may be multiplied and add to the complexity of the book-classification so greatly that the tendency of some librarians, overwhelmed with the magnitude of the task of classifying a library or not convinced that the resulting advantages would compensate for the immense labour, have solved the problem by not classifying, or doing it only in the broadest manner.

68. While all these considerations are vital ones, we practical

librarians know that at least sixty out of every hundred books in non-fiction that pass through our hands are in their bulk about subjects and most of them about one subject that can be recognized although it is not always apparent at a glance. We know, too, that the average serious reader thinks of them as subject representations however many aberrations from this general rule may be known to us. The choice, then, of a scheme ought always to depend upon its quality as an arrangement of subjects.

69. Having reached that conclusion, we go on to choose according to the practical virtues of schemes: their accessibility, hospitality, and the means they possess of differentiating the various sorts of books and their sizes, forms and modes of treatment. Although it is an accident, cross-dividing all books, *size* is the first and principal factor in book arrangement. Mere economy of space—the most valuable commodity in the modern library—makes it obvious that books of elephant folio size cannot stand with octavos and certainly not with duodecimos on shelves: every scheme of arrangement is therefore a series of parallels governed in the first place by the size of the books. This difficulty may be recognized at once. The value of classifying books may indeed be reduced but is by no means destroyed by such considerations.

70. Whatever the manner in which the book-classifier has made his scheme, be it by the direct approach without conscious reference to science schemes, or like that of Bacon or Bliss the result of long study of them, it must have, as necessary to its working for library use, a series of so-called classes as well as mechanical contrivances to distinguish format, form and miscellanea in books. It is sometimes said that these contrivances are apparatus "added to a knowledge classification to make it work" and that description is convenient enough because all classification-construction seems naturally to begin with an arrangement of subjects but, as has just been suggested, a classificationer may make what he considers to be a mechanico-practical arrangement of his subjects without reference to the recognized relations of knowledge and so may devise his "added" things first. The "index" classifier whose ideal is an alphabetical order of subjects—that shown in section 82 for example—could do this, I suppose. These contrivances may be summarized as

1. Generalia classes—for works covering all or many branches of knowledge.
2. Form classes—to accommodate books in which the main interest is the pattern in which the matter is written, as in poetry, drama and fiction.
3. Common subdivisions—to discriminate methods of treatment, or the outer form or pattern of presentation of subjects.

To apply the scheme, to economize space and to fix its order, a scheme must have

4. A Notation—or short symbol for each subject and to economize time by enabling the finding of the place of any class in the tables of the scheme without reading them through.
5. An Index.

Then there are auxiliary *signs and symbols* which are used to indicate such things as library collections, departments and individual libraries in a system of libraries and *their* departments, to show the dates of books or of subject-matters, or their geographical bearings, their sizes, shapes, distinctive physical character as broadsides, prints, pamphlets and so on. These, in the main, are developments of notation. The number of "form" possibilities has been dealt with in a useful discussion, which was initiated by A. J. Philip[1] in which three other experts participated, A. J. Hawkes, James Ormerod and H. E. Bliss, the last-named showing the remarkable variety of book nuances now subsumed under the name "form," which may be or ought to be provided for in a scheme. Bliss prefers less familiar but, as he submits reasonably, more distinctive names for "forms" (which term he avoids entirely), as "recurrent" and "ancillary" for "common" and "auxiliary."

71. *The Generalia Class.* We may consider first the Generalia class which every book classification possesses. In Dewey and Cutter this is called General Works; in Brown, Generalia; in the Quinn-Brown and various older classifications it is called Miscellaneous Works, Miscellany, or Ana. It is often called in the slang of librarians the waste-paper basket of the classification; from which we may not infer that it is a merely chaotic class. It is certainly not that; it is rather a class for containing works which are so varied in their content that they will not fit into any class of the scheme that deals with a subject, but overlap all or many departments of knowledge. Sometimes Generalia is called a "form class," the form of the works fitting into it being their formlessness; but this is a mere juggling with language. The content of Generalia has form; it includes general encyclopædias, general periodicals, transactions of general societies, and collected works; works, then, which within one cover range over the whole field of knowledge, or over several parts. Emphasis must be laid upon the *general* nature of all the parts of generalia; otherwise in practical work error will be frequent. It is clear that *The Times*, *The Encyclopædia Britannica*, *The Spectator* and *The Quarterly Review* are entirely general in their scope; there is no subject in the universe of things or thought which may not properly come within

[1] *The Librarian*, v. 26, pp. 31–4, 128–30, 1936–7.

their purview. To class any one of them as Sociology, Science, History or in any other specific class would be to ignore all the other subjects; it must inevitably, then, go in the Generalia class.

72. This leads us to the GENERALIA DIVISION, which is entirely distinct, because it is part of a *subject* class. In this connexion the word "division" does not mean a sub-division of a generalia class, but a sub-division of a subject class. In regard to periodicals we can easily illustrate this: *The Times* covers all knowledge; but the periodical *Nature* is a scientific periodical. But *Nature* in its turn covers all science, mathematical, natural and physical. Thus in relation to all knowledge *Nature* is a special periodical devoted to one subject; while in relation to science it is quite general. We may carry this still further. The *Journal of the Chemical Society* covers every phase of chemistry, is general in regard to that subject; but it is special in relation to Science, in relation to *Nature*. Only in a loose classification of scientific periodicals could it stand beside *Nature* on the shelves. Other examples will occur to you of periodicals which deal with special subjects in a general way. These have all to be provided for in a book-classification, and it is fair to assume that Jevons did not contemplate any such provision when he inveighed against the classification of books.

73. To return for a moment to the Generalia *class*. Brown has given a much more comprehensive—and controversial—connotation to his Generalia. He includes in it all subjects which are general, and adds to them all such subjects as are *pervasive* of other classes; that is, subjects which are necessary to the study of every subject in greater or less degree, and without which the arts, etc., cannot be. That is his contention, and his Generalia includes such subjects as Education, Logic, Mathematics, the Graphic and Plastic Arts, and General Science. All these things, by his theory, are involved in the study of other subjects, and, in the modern developments of knowledge some of the sciences which seemed once distinct have been so interwoven that the former clear-cut distinctions have become more formal than real, but Brown's "pervasive" classes in several cases really belong elsewhere. When we come to study the Subject Classification in detail we shall have some criticisms to make of this theory and its application; but it is useful for us to realize this revolutionary experiment in classification at this point. There are also interesting variations in the Bliss scheme which can be discussed more conveniently when we come to consider that scheme.

74. *Catalogue versus Classification.* It will be recognized in regard to Generalia classes and divisions that the catalogue possesses

enormous superiority over classification on the shelves as an exhaustive method of treating books. The periodical, encyclopædia, or set of transactions can be shelved in one place only in our library. Thus its use is limited; we know nothing about it except its outer form; any view of the subjects it contains is impossible, except by the examining of the individual volume; a time-wasting process which would deter any but the most enthusiastic worker; and even he, after hours of avoidable labour, is never quite certain that he has not missed something. It is a very important problem for librarians, seeing that knowledge as presented in periodicals is said to be on the average at least four years in advance of books.[1] The perfectly catalogued library may be made to bring all these articles to light if the periodicals are analysed and entries of the articles are made under their appropriate class headings in the catalogue. This has been done on a co-operative basis by such invaluable works as the Library Association *Index to Periodicals*, in which some scores of periodicals, general and special, are analysed under appropriate subject-headings. Few libraries, unfortunately, are able to do this work for themselves; the cost in time and money would be too great. Or, perhaps it would be better to say that such analysis is necessary but is usually beyond the powers of the average library and ought to be done by such co-operative effort as that which produces the Library Association Index, and the indexes published by the H. W. Wilson Company of New York.

75. *Form Classes.* Generalia, then, is roughly a form class; but the form classes proper are those which cover what Jevons, Brunet, and the earlier classifiers call *Belles-Lettres* and what we have called the fine art of writing. This class is called Literature in most classifications, and is named Literary Forms in the Subject Classification. It ignores the subjects of the books and arranges them into broad groups which show their form; thus we get the divisions Poetry, Drama, Fiction, Essays, Oratory, Letters, and so forth. Now these have very diverse subject-matter; for example, Dante's *Divina Commedia* is one of the revelations of mediæval theology, Shakespeare's *Hamlet* is a great contribution to human psychology, Browning's *Strafford* is the great political drama of the seventeenth century, while Tennyson's *Becket* and Eliot's *Murder in the Cathedral* are varied versions of the life of the great Saint-Archbishop and his times. Again, Addison's Sir Roger de Coverley essays reveal the social history of the Queen Anne period more vividly than a hundred formal histories; and I need not add examples of how novels present and illuminate actual

[1] This was an estimate made by the late Henry V. Hopwood; it must of course be only an estimate.

things, places, periods and persons. They form, incidentally, material for the student of history, manners, topography and what not, but they are not specially intended for the student of literature. Their subjects are but subsidiary when one considers the purpose of these works, and the people who want to read them. The form and not the subject is the important consideration. So we construct our schedules for Belles-Lettres arbitrarily by the outward form in which the works are cast; metrical form makes poetry for us; drama is simply literary matter written in acts and scenes in poetry or prose—of its relation to life and the dramatic unities we take no cognizance; and similarly throughout. But it may not be superfluous to say in regard to the divisions Essays, Oratory and Letters that we must be sure that only books which are interesting for their form merely or are general in character are placed here; and not essays, letters or speeches on specific subjects. We can place in the form division Augustine Birrell's *Obiter Dicta* and E. V. Lucas's *Domesticities*, because they deal with no particular subject; but not Butcher's *Essays on Greek Drama*, or that at one time very famous book, *Essays and Reviews*, which dealt with the theological position in its day. These latter books are on special subjects and are interesting from the points of view of Drama and Theology. Letters, as a general rule, would be much better if they were considered to be "the man's life in the letters of the man" as they are the best illuminants of Biography and should be classed there. The placing of them in literary forms is a Dewey expedient and it has its justification only when the letters have a very strong literary interest and not always then. The famous letters of Gray, Cowper, Horace Walpole and Lady Mary Wortley Montague come into the latter category, but those of the Brownings and of most other folk ought not to do so. In any case neither class takes such works as the Marquis of Dufferin's *Letters from High Latitudes*, which recounts travel experiences in Spitsbergen, and Cobbett's *Letters on French Grammar* both specific treatments of specific subjects, travel book and grammar in the accidental form of letters; they must be classed with the subjects. Thus too, with speeches and other divisions of this class.

76. The master rule of the classifier is: *classify first by subject and then by form, except in the form classes, in which form is paramount.* It must be said, too, that some classifiers have made interesting attempts to classify pure literature by subject. Wordsworth, it will be remembered, classified his poems as poems of imagination, sentiment, reflection, narrative, and so on; but few are satisfied with the arrangement, as it is full of cross-divisions and much of the placing is purely arbitrary. The most common form of experiment is that which attempts to classify fiction by subject: all

historical novels by the period they present; all topographical at the country or county; and such novels as Reade's *It is Never too Late to Mend*, and Marcus Clarke's *For the Term of His Natural Life*, at penology; Dickens's *Nicholas Nickleby* at schools; and so on without limit. This arrangement has an immense interest, and is in many ways a useful one; but as the principal arrangement of the books it is thoroughly bad. For one who is interested in penology, a thousand are interested in the stories which Reade and Marcus Clarke tell; and again the law of convenience must prevail.

77. To sum up: when Jevons says that if we form a comprehensive class Belles-Lettres nobody can say exactly what does or does not come into the class, our answer is simple. We are not, as classifiers, concerned with the subjects that come into it; we are concerned with the form in which they appear, and that is clear and tangible to all of us.

78. *Outer and Inner Form.* It will have been remarked that the term "outer form" has been used, and I think from the examples I have given that its meaning has been clearly understood. It is a valuable distinction in classification, as there is also an "inner form" which is almost of equal importance, and the understanding of which alone makes the right application of the rule, "classify by topic" and then by "form," possible. We can see this quite easily by setting side by side Dewey's Generalia class and his general divisions (but any other scheme will show us very much the same features):

Generalia Class.		*Generalia Divisions of*	
General Works.		Science.	
010	Bibliography.	501	Philosophy, Theories.
020	Library Economy.	502	Compends, Outlines.
030	General Cyclopædias.	503	Dictionaries, Cyclopædias.
040	General Collected Essays.	504	Essays, Lectures, Letters.
050	General Periodicals.	505	Periodicals.
060	General Societies.	506	Societies, Associations.
070	General Newspapers (Journalism).	507	Education, Study, Teaching.
080	Special Libraries.	508	Polygraphy, Collections.
090	Book Rarities.	509	History.

If we examine these closely we shall at once see that they are almost alike; the main difference being that the first column represents form divisions of the whole classification—they cover all the tables of the scheme; while those in the second cover only the schedules of the class Science. A careful consideration will show that in the form divisions (the second column) two kinds of form are employed. The *outer* as represented by Compends,

Dictionaries, Essays, Periodicals and Polygraphy—and perhaps to a lesser extent by Education; the *inner* as represented by Philosophy and History. A dictionary, encyclopædia, periodical or newspaper is clearly a thing having a definite outer form which in a sufficient degree is known to us. Poetry, drama, etc., have also a definite form—poetry is words according to a pattern—or, if we prefer it, has a metrical shape. In all of these works the form is visible, objective. But it is not so with works which come into our inner form group. History, for example, may be a subject, or it may be a form. In such books as Harrison's *A Meaning of History*, Croce's *Theory and History of Historiography* and Burckhardt's *Reflections on History* it is a subject. But Macaulay's *History of England* is a record of England in a certain length of time treated historically (by a form) and, clearly, a history of the steam-engine is definitely upon the steam-engine, but in the manner of a history. This gives us the clue that we want. Outer form is physical, as it were, the literary shape in which things are presented; inner form is subjective, the method by which the thing is presented. Thus we may have a book, in fact we may have many books, bearing some such title as *The Theory of Science*, or *The Philosophy of Art*, or *The Theory of Politics*. Each of these is distinctly upon a subject; upon Science, Art, and Politics respectively; but each is viewed in a special manner, from a special standpoint; in short, is in a special form. So with the history of a science, art, or thing in which the science, art or thing is the dominant idea of the book, and the history merely the method; in all these history is form. You will now see the bearing of the rule *classify by topic and then by form*. In all subject-classes we seek first a place for our book at the most specific heading that will contain it, and afterwards sub-arrange by form. The forms we have discussed are usually set out in separate tables in modern schemes and where they, the forms, have a *constant* meaning they have also numbers which are constant and by that name Bliss calls them. The tables he calls *systematic schedules*, which of course is what they are.

79. This brings us back to a position which was insisted upon earlier. Our book must modulate into the main heading under which we place it. If we read the form divisions without clearly understanding them, we are prone to place a work on philosophy as a subject under philosophy as a form—a quite disastrous error; and equally we are liable to make the reverse error. But a clear perception that these divisions are modes of treatment of material and not the material itself will save us from any such mistake.

80 *Form Classes are Adjustments*. A book classification, it may

be repeated at the risk of being wearisome, is a classification of knowledge; that is to say, a schedule of the subjects in the universe of literature arranged by definite characteristics, and showing in the arrangement the rules of order and of sub-division which we have discussed at considerable length in our preceding chapters. Generalia and form classes are necessary practical, and in the main accidental and artificial, auxiliaries of that classification called for in the form of books. We stress this again because when new-comers to classification make experiment they quite often do so upon the theory actually expounded to me in these words: "Books as a whole do not fit into a knowledge classification; therefore a book classification must be something entirely different. Let us discard all those supposed relationships of knowledge, and shuffle the subjects in our classification in the way that best helps us to find books on the shelves and aids our memory in so doing. Thus, we are obeying the law of convenience; the essential characteristic of their arrangement being not the subjects of the books themselves, but something exterior, some accidental fact about those subjects." As a result of such reasoning we get the theory—quite seriously enunciated and quite attractive; moreover, partly true: *It does not matter where we classify a book so long as it is properly indexed.* That is to say, in approaching the finding of a book on our shelves we ought first to consult the index-catalogue. (The index-catalogue, you will observe, being thus a necessary tool in the library.) If the subject is indexed, the reference there given will serve every practical purpose.

81. *The Index versus Classification.* This is very specious reasoning and, as I have admitted, it is partly true because a purpose of classification is to make the finding of particular books an easy process. There the advantage, or merit, of a system which places books indifferently and relies upon the index, ends. It is only a small part of the work of classification to make the finding of particular books easy, although admittedly a most convenient and practical part. The accepted definition of classification not only implies this, it implies a cardinal purpose which this ignores—the arrangement of books so that the law of union of properties is made visible; that is to say, so that the likeness in subject-matter between them is revealed. Thus a classification cannot justly be called a good one which does not show the sequence of subjects; show on the left of a particular book, or group of books, the books that lead up to it, and on the right the books which lead away from it. This is quite elementary; but the assertion that the index will do the work of classification proper has often been made, and it is most desirable that we should be convinced that classification is primarily arrangement with a definite revealing purpose and

not a mere filing of books, irrespective of order, in separate pigeon-holes to which a mere index is a key.

82. *An Index Arrangement, not a classification.* It was this confusion of ideas—this belief in the functions of classification as a mere indexing expedient—which led an American enthusiast, Robinson Smith, into an interesting experiment in classification-construction which was published in *The Library World* for July, 1919 (v.21, p.4), which he calls an Alphabetical Mnemonic Classification, but which is, strictly speaking, not a classification at all. In these he takes the broad classes of literature, and arranges them alphabetically by the names of the groups. Here is his outline:

A	Art.	N	National, Industrial and Social Problems.
B	Biography.	O	Oriental Languages.
C	Christianity and Judaism.	P	Philosophy.
D	Dictionaries.	Q	Quartos.
E	English Language and Literature.	R	Roman Antiquities, Languages and Literatures.
F	Fiction.	S	Science.
G	Greek Antiquities.	T	Technology.
H	History.	U	Unclassified.
I	Industries.	V	Voyages and Travels.
J	Juveniles.	W	Weeklies and Monthlies.
K	Knowledge	Y	Year Books.
L	Law.	Z	Newspapers.
M	Modern Languages and Literatures.		

Each of these is subject to alphabetical sub-division as an example will show:

L	Law.	LF	Feudal.
LA	Administration.	LG	Greek.
LB	Banking, Bankruptcy.	LH	History.
LC	Criminal.	LJ	Jurisprudence.
LE	Ecclesiology.		

and so on, with alphabetical re-divisions of each.

Every student of classification will see at once that this is not classification at all; it is arrangement for quick-reference; and is an indescribable jumbling of topics, the only relation between them being the alphabetical letters of the class names. It has several cross-divisions, mixes characteristics, jumbles topic and form, and has every theoretical fault we can name. It even has defects as a mnemonic arrangement; we search our minds in vain for the possible place in this scheme of many subjects. In short, it is the best example known to me of a so-called classification in which the compiler has ignored or is not cognizant of the main purpose of classification, and has bent all his efforts to the producing of a scheme in which, as he avers, things are easy to find. His principal argument in its favour is that the notation is definitely related to the name of the subject it represents; and thence we gather that he laboured under the delusion that notation was more important than classification itself. This we can best answer by a consideration of the purpose of classification.

CHAPTER VI
NOTATION

83. *What Notation Is.* It has already been said that when our classification was equipped with Generalia and Form Classes and Divisions it required two accessories to make its application to books practicable. These were a notation and an index. The more important of these is the notation, and we must now give very careful consideration to this subject.

A notation is defined by Richardson as a shorthand sign,[1] and that definition is a convenient one. Almost every art and science has a series of symbols which stand in the place of terms. We meet it very early in our school days; the arabic numbers 1, 2, 3 and so on, stand in our minds for quantities or measures expressed by the words, one, two, three; in all branches of mathematics figures and symbols stand in the same manner for terms, quantities, measures, ratios, etc. Even punctuation, in ordinary composition, is a notation of a kind; a comma is a symbol indicating that here you take breath; a semi-colon tells us that here we pause to introduce a balancing phrase; a full-stop is a sign indicating that the expression of an idea ends here; and, so on, throughout such literary symbols, each is a shorthand sign. In every activity where terms occur repeatedly and with an invariable meaning such notation is general; the most convenient example for our purpose being the notation used by chemists to indicate the chemical elements, compounds and other parts of chemistry.

84. In book classification a similar notation is especially necessary, as we cannot write at full length the classification names of each subject upon every book, or against every entry in our catalogues. Librarians have therefore borrowed hints from the chemist and other similar workers, and have attempted to express all classification terms in symbols. A book-notation, then, is a series of signs or symbols standing for the names of terms, and forming a convenient means of reference to the arrangement of our classification. If, then, it is merely a symbol for terms, it cannot be more important than the terms themselves; it is a piece of apparatus added to the classification. That seems trite enough;

---

[1] Bliss says it is not, on the ground I suppose that it does not actually translate the term it stands for into another shape. He prefers "short" sign. He is precisely right but "shorthand" conveys what is usually meant by a symbol which stands in the briefest manner for something else. This is the sense in which W. W. Sawyer in his capital little "Pelican" book, *Mathematician's Delight*, 1943, calls algebra "the shorthand of mathematics."

but, if you consulted the files of the professional library magazines, you might be forgiven for concluding that the only thing that mattered in a classification was its notation; because nearly every discussion of classification has been a wrangle about the merits of the notations of rival classification schemes. Indeed, in past years, some librarians have chosen their schemes exclusively by their preference for this or that form of notation, and have quite ignored the fact that the primary virtues of a classification are scientific order, consistent sub-division, mutual exclusiveness of terms, and generalness of application. Were all these things present in equal degree in any two schemes of classification, then, indeed, the choice between them might be based upon the notation; but the choice should never be made by notation in the first place. This necessary disparagement of the subject is made at this point, because we are dealing with our study in a systematic manner, and it is desirable that every part of the subject should be seen in its true perspective. Nevertheless, as notation is essential to the practicability of a classification of books, it is by no means a negligible subject. It is quite an important one, governed by rules which we must understand.

85. *The Criteria of Notation.* The rules of a good notation most commonly accepted may be summarized in this manner. It must be *brief, simple and flexible.* These we must develop with examples.

86. (1) *Pure and Mixed Notation.* A classification may be made up of figures, Arabic or Roman; of letters; or of arbitrary signs; or of a mixture of several or all of these. A notation which consists of one consistent kind of symbol is a *pure* notation; one consisting of more than one kind is a *mixed* one. There are those who hold that the best notation yet achieved is that which makes decimal use of Arabic figures as in Dewey, whose scheme is the outstanding one with pure notation. They have therefore inferred as a rule that the ideal notation is a pure one. But it can be seen now that such an ideal imposes vertical limitations on a notation; it moves in tens and multiples or series of tens in ten main classes, ten divisions of each, ten sub-divisions of the divisions, and so on to infinite sub-divisions. Ten main classes are too few for all modern methods and so the ideal proves not to be ideal. The Expansive system is, in the main, also pure, as its classes divisions and sub-divisions are marked by ordinary capital and lower-case letters, a method giving a longer base than the Decimal notation; but the purity of the Expansive system is "sullied"—perhaps "varied" is a better word—by the numerical tables of common sub-divisions and the Local List which are indispensable parts of the schemes. Although other pure alphabetical notations exist and pure decimal systems (that of Richardson's Princeton Scheme

for example) modern methods usually employ the alphabet to one or two places and sub-divide further by numbers and usually decimal ones. They are therefore *mixed*. Our later discussion of individual schemes in the second part of this Manual will show the many and interesting methods used in symbolizing classes. A few may be instanced here.

87. The scheme of William T. Harris, 1870, the first *real* "inverted" Baconian scheme, has a notation with initial alphabetical symbols for the main classes, with figures for divisions, and italic letters for sub-divisions. This can be demonstrated from the Peoria Form of this classification in which the class Art is marked thus:

> B   Art.
> B12   Fine Arts, General.
> B13   Fine Arts, History.
> B13*a*   Architecture.
> B13*b*   Sculpture.
> B13*c*   Drawing.

and so on. The British Museum Scheme has a mixture of the form and not the kind of symbol, marking main classes with Roman figures and the divisions with Arabic; thus:

> VI   History.   VI3 History of Asia.
> VI2 Universal History.   VII Chronology.

and there are many schemes, including that of Horne and the Royal Institution, which are similarly marked. Usually, however, the earlier schemes have an alphabetical marking of main classes, and these are divided by Arabic figures *used consecutively*. But the cardinal example of a mixed notation, using not only letters and figures, but arbitrary signs as well, is that of Lloyd P. Smith, 1882. This scheme is quite a good one in many ways; but its curious notation has prevented its wide adoption. The main classes are marked A—Y, the principal divisions a—z, the sub-divisions 1 to any number used consecutively, and the sections receive such marks as + △ □ IV; thus in marking Ecclesiastical History we get this result:

> A Religion.
> Ao   Ecclesiastical history.
> Ao2   Latin churches.
> Ao2+   Jansenists.
> Ao2 △   Gallican Church.
> Ao2 □   Spanish Church.
> Ao2IV   Roman Catholic Church in U.S. and
>   Canada.

88. The notation of the Subject Scheme of Brown is mixed, in that the main classes are marked with letters, and divisions and sub-divisions throughout with numbers used consecutively, but capable of being used decimally.

89. Apart from the Decimal, the only other classification named after a feature of its notation is Ranganathan's interesting Colon Scheme. It consists of a number of systematic schedules representing subjects, methods, points of view, values and other features which may be combined in various ways by means of the colon : . It is the most original recent notation.

90 (2) *Brevity*.—The second requirement of a notation is brevity, or, as Mr. Jast expressed it, "denotative economy." This is determined by the number of main classes in a scheme, as will have been gathered from our remarks on Dewey. The value of brevity in notation is clear to us all; if we can make two symbols stand for a subject instead of three or four, it is evident that they will be more easily written and carried in our minds. That is simple enough; it may not be so clear that the number of main classes conditions the matter, but a little thought will show us that this is so. If we have twenty-four main classes, we can mark each distinctively with *one* letter of the alphabet. If we compress these twenty-four into twelve, the subjects which appear in the twenty-four must find places in the twelve, and to mark them we have to get the same number of symbols into a smaller vertical space, with a corresponding horizontal expansion. The Decimal notation must, of necessity, be longer than the Expansive notation, seeing that it has only ten main classes, while the Expansive has twenty-four.

91. (3) *Simplicity*.—The brevity of a notation has something to do with its simplicity, but not necessarily everything. In the first place, rather, simplicity depends upon the kind of symbol used. We have looked at a mark from Smith's scheme—Ao2IV, to represent a single subject, the Roman Catholic Churches of the U.S. and Canada. Now Dewey marks this in the Decimal Classification by a longer symbol, 283·71; but few would be prepared to say that the longer was the less simple notation. As a matter of fact, the Decimal notation is infinitely the simpler, merely because 283·71 can be expressed in sound, in the words "Two-eight-three-point-seven-one," while reduced to the same result we should have to say for Smith, "Ay-nought-two-four-in-roman-figures," which is not only longer in the saying, but the symbols have no particular pictorial (ideographic) value and therefore cannot easily be carried in the mind. In the Expansive Classification RCZ stands for the Extractive and Productive Arts, which in Dewey are marked 670, and it is a very moot point which

of these two notations, which are of equal length, is the simpler. But admittedly it is difficult to say that the "mixed" notation of the Subject scheme is necessarily more difficult; for example, Brown's mark for Asia is P29, while that of Dewey is 950; perhaps they are equally simple; certainly neither is difficult. It will be seen, therefore, that while theoretically a "pure" notation is simpler than a "mixed" one, it is not invariably so; and this brings me to an important point. It is not desirable to sacrifice any very considerable *classification* advantage for the sake of purity or brevity or simplicity. If these qualities can be gained in a notation without such sacrifice so much the better.

92. (4) *Flexibility.*—But while the axioms of purity, brevity, and simplicity are merely useful guides to what is to be sought in a notation, there is, on the other hand, one quality without which a notation is almost valueless for modern library purposes. This quality is variously named flexibility, expansibility or adjustability; and it is in the possession of this quality that modern notations surpass those of all the earlier schemes. Expansibility for our purpose may be defined thus: *a notation which is so constructed that by the addition of a symbol or symbols any new subject may be inserted into any place in the classification without dislocating the sequence of either the notation or the classification itself.* All that has been said before can be brought out and illustrated in considering this vital feature of notation.

93. The classification-constructor, having mapped out his main classes, next determines upon the character of his symbol. This must have been the process as it worked in Cutter's mind; he chose the alphabetical notation; he had marks for twenty-six main classes; which he proceeded to mark as in the example: Dewey decided upon the decimal notation and limited himself to ten such classes:

Expansive.		Decimal.	
A	General Works.	0	General Works.
B	Philosophy.	1	Philosophy.
BR	Religion.	2	Religion.
E	Christianity.	3	Sociology.
F	Biography.	4	Philology.
G	Geography.	5	Science.
H	Social Sciences.	6	Useful Arts.
L	Sciences, Natural.	7	Fine Arts.
M	Natural History.	8	Literature.
N	Botany.	9	History, Biography and
O	Zoology.		Geography.
P	Anthropology.		
Q	Medicine.		

Expansive.

R	Useful Arts.
S	Constructive Arts.
T	Fabricative Arts.
U	Art of War.
V	Athletic and Recreative Arts.
W	Fine Arts.
X	Language.
Y	Literature.
Z	Book Arts.

On the face of it, Cutter's is a much more extensive scheme than Dewey's; but it is not so; all the subjects in Cutter's twenty-six classes are contained in Dewey's ten. Cutter's classes are merely broken up for notation purposes, while Dewey's are compressed. It is often alleged that Dewey devised his notation before he arranged his ten main classes, but as these classes are a replica of the classes in W. T. Harris's Peoria scheme this does not seem proven. Each, as you will recall, uses a pure notation; so Cutter will make his first divisions by adding a letter; Dewey by adding a figure. Thus Cutter obtains 26×26 places $= 676$, while Dewey obtains only $10 \times 10 = 100$; for Cutter can divide every main class into 26 divisions; Dewey into 10 only; and sub-division proceeds in the ratio of 26 to 10. So that while in three places Dewey gets $10 \times 10 \times 10$ places, Cutter gets $26 \times 26 \times 26$ places; proving to us quite clearly that the length of the notation depends upon the number of main classes, if, as is to be premised, a logical method of notation division is employed.

94. A logical notation is one in which *each* symbol may be re-divided by itself, so that any number may be increased to an unlimited extent merely by adding symbol after symbol to the notation. This is so, of course, when decimal division is employed. If 2 is the class number, 22, 222, 2222, 242, 282, 296 are all divisions of that 2; they are read decimally; they arrange before 3 and *its* decimally-read divisions. Similarly when logical alphabetical division is used, A is the main class, and AA, AB, AG, AAM, AXZLQ, or whatever combination you will which is preceded by the initial A, are parts of A and come before B in the arrangement. This simple, and it may be superfluous, explanation leads up to an essential in a good notation. *A notation should convey a representation not merely of the division, but also of the sequence, and not only of the artificial sequence, but of the logical sequence, so far as it can be expressed.* That is Richardson's requirement, which for our purpose may be reduced to: "a notation must indicate the sequence of the classification."

95. This can perhaps best be illustrated by an effort to equip

the Baconian classification with a notation. There are three main classes in that scheme:

> History.
> Poetry.
> Science.

We can, if we follow our rule consistently, have only three main symbols in our notation. Let us choose a decimal notation, and mark these 1, 2, 3, and then set out our table in the proper order, adding a second figure for our first divisions; thus:

> 1 History.
> 11 Natural.
> 12 Civil.

and proceeding to redivide these decimally until the whole of the parts enumerated have been exhausted. The result will appear thus:

1	History.	*3*	Science.
11	Natural History.	31	Philosophy.
111	Generations.	311	Natural Theology.
1111	Astronomy.	312	Natural Philosophy.
1112	Physiography, etc.	3121	Speculative.
112	Pretergenerations.	3122	Operative.
1121	Monsters.	32	Human Philosophy.
113	Arts.	321	Philosophy of Humanity.
12	Civil History.	3211	Body of Man.
121	Ecclesiastical.	32111	Physiology, etc.
1211	Church.	3212	Soul of Man.
1212	Prophecies, etc.	32121	Psychology, etc.
2	Poesy.	322	Civil Philosophy.
21	Narrative.	3221	Law.
22	Dramatic.	3222	Government.
23	Parabolical.	3223	Society.
		323	Theology.

96. Thus we prove that the notation must be a relatively long one, but you will have noticed that the sequence of the notation has been made to correspond with that of the classification; so that, if we are aware that 3 stands for Science, we know that 322 must be some phase of Science. All classifiers do not obey this rule. In Cutter, who uses V for Recreative Arts and Vv for Fine Arts, we have one of a very few aberrations from the rule. It seems that the length of the notation, and the desire to employ all the symbols that the chosen medium allows, have led such classifiers to sacrifice the sequence-subordination to the practical advantages of brevity.

97. It will be seen that this notation also illustrates the principle of flexibility which is the main subject of my present remarks. Any one of these subjects may be sub-divided at the appropriate place, by the addition of the appropriate decimal symbol. Thus, if we desire to divide Speculative Philosophy—as Bacon does—into Physics and Metaphysics, we merely insert them so that the division reads:

312	Natural Philosophy.
3121	Speculative.
31211	Physics.
31212	Metaphysics.

and the classification "closes up," as it were, and is as workable as ever.

98. The search after all-comprehensive and at the same time completely individualizing hospitality, which not only allows the insertion of new subjects but makes the notation an exact translation into symbols of every feature of a book, has brought about the Colon Classification tables, devices and symbols (*see* Chapter XIX). These endeavour at the same time to show the scientific relations of classes in the symbolic language and do so with much skill. The numbers resulting appear to me to confirm the impression that too much is expected of notation, which, through it, becomes too long, complex and unmanageable for ordinary library use. A notation itself can never wholly do the work of catalogue and index; and, so far as libraries are concerned, must always be an economical means of fixing the place of a book in the library.

CHAPTER VII

NOTATION—*Continued*

99. In addition to the qualities of brevity, simplicity, and flexibility, and the power of showing in its own sequence the sequence of the classification, there is a very general quality in modern classification notations which is ingenious, and, within limits, of great value to the clasifier. This is its mnemonic quality; its power of assisting the memory and of reducing the work of reference to tables and indexes to the minimum.

100. *Mnemonic Notations in General.* By mnemonic notation we mean that wherever a subject or form appears it has always the same notation throughout the classification. The simplest example of it is the marking of the form divisions, or, as they are more generally called, the *Common Sub-divisions*, in the Decimal Classification. In those the sequence is approximately

·1 Philosophy or theory.	·6 Societies, transactions, etc.
·2 Compends, outlines, systems.	·7 Education, study.
·3 Dictionaries and cyclopædias.	·8 Polygraphy, collections.
·4 Essays.	·9 History.
·5 Periodicals.	

The notation used here, ·1—·9, has this power in many parts of the classification. Thus, in the Religion class, these figures form the termination of the general heads 201—09, and they serve, with minor variations, at every succeeding general class-heading throughout the scheme. You can check this by turning to the classes marked 300, 400, 500, 600, etc., throughout Dewey. But the notation applies not only to these headings but to many of the divisions and even sections. Thus at 320, Political Science, we get the same form divisions with the same notation; so, at the section International Law, 341, we get ·01 Philosophy, ·02 Compends, etc., in precisely similar manner. The "o" here is necessary in order that the power of the number 341 may be increased and ·1—·8 be used for subject divisions of International Law. In most subjects we can go on using these form divisions according to this mnemonic method. Thus 341·7 is Diplomacy, and 341·701 may be theory of diplomacy, 341·703 dictionaries of diplomacy, 341·709 the history of diplomacy. It will readily be recognized what an addition this is to any scheme; it permits very exact arrangement of even comparatively minor subjects. You will see how close this may be by studying heading 349·37,

Roman Law, where the addition of these numbers makes it possible
to arrange a collection of Roman Law with great, and as I think
it will be agreed, valuable definiteness. The point is that we have
only to learn the meaning of these form symbols once, and to
know that their application is invariable throughout a large part
of the system; and that is a time-saving device which need not be
despised.

101. Every approved classification notation has similar devices.
In Cutter, for example, the compiler uses this form notation:

D	Dictionaries.	P	Periodicals.
E	Encyclopædias.	Q	Quotations.
I	Indexes.	R	Reference Books.
M	Museums.	S	Societies.

Here the notation is not only mnemonic in that it may be applied,
as in Dewey, to any required class heading; it is also mnemonic
in that the initial letter of the name of the form to be indicated
is used as its notation. The Library of Congress Scheme has a very
similar arrangement of form divisions, but has not exactly this
mnemonic power in its notation.

102. The Subject Classification has the most elaborate apparatus of this kind, worked out most minutely. Brown removes
forms and standpoints from the tables and sets them out separately
in a large table of what he calls "categorical numbers," which
forms an integral part of the scheme. Dewey, as we have already
observed, has nine such form numbers which are of general
application; Cutter has eight; but Brown appears to have no less
than 975. It would seem that Brown has brought into his table
many things which in the other systems are provided for in the
main tables; and this is so to a large extent; but the Subject
System has undoubtedly a valuable, and unlimited, dividing
material in these Categorical Tables. A few examples from the
tables will help us to show their application.

.0	Generalia.	.50	Epitaphs.
.00	Catalogues, Lists.	.51	Portraits.
.01	Monarchs, Rulers.	.52	Directories.
.1	Bibliography.	.53	Concordances.
.2	Encyclopædias.	.54	Miscellanies.
.3	Text-books, Systematic.	.55	Annuals.
.4	Text-books, Popular.	.56	Exhibitions, Shows.
.6	Societies.	.57	Museums.
.7	Periodicals.	.58	Specimens.
.8	Collections, Series.	.59	Prints, Pictures.
.9	Individual Authors.	.60	Programmes.
.10	History, etc.		

These numbers are added to mark form and standpoint, *to any heading to which they can reasonably be applied*, in the system. Note that the point (.) is not a decimal point, but merely an arbitrarily chosen and convenient separating device. If we are marking books on, say, Woman Suffrage, the specific number from the main classification is L274; the history of the subject is L274.10, a bibliography of it L274.1, an annual of woman suffrage, called *The Woman Voter's Year Book*, L274.55, and so on. But it is clear that all the categorical numbers cannot be applied to this subject. Monarchs of woman suffrage, or epitaphs, are examples of numbers that can only be made to apply in a ludicrous sense. Many of the numbers *will* apply to any heading, will divide any subject, but by far the greater number of them will not. For example 1835.956 means the Ink of Whisky, and 1925.200 the marine engineering of Jams and Jellies, and a hundred similarly peculiar effects can be reached with these tables. As a matter of fact, marine engineering and jam are not *views, standpoints* or *aspects* of subjects, but are specific *subjects*, and any table merely of "common sub-divisions" or "form-divisions" cannot contain them. The Categorical Table is not merely that. In it are the recurring as well as the constant sub-divisions of the scheme. That is to say, when a subject or a method or form or aspect can be found in several classes in the main tables, it is removed from them and relegated to the table. An example might be the organs of the body which would be the same or similar under Anatomy, Physiology, Pathology, Surgery, Materia Medica and under Veterinary. One set of terms for them, having one number for each, could be placed in the Categorical Table and thus one printing serves all uses and the table has a mnemonic value. Nevertheless, it should therefore not be inferred that this table of categorical numbers is an unnecessary numbering refinement, although it may present traps to inexpert classifiers. It is a valuable device; and as we have said, from the point of view of our present study it is a purely mnemonic device: .10 is always history, .38 travels, .1 bibliography, and .3 treatises, and so on, wherever they occur; and once these numbers become familiar— as in practice they very soon do—their application to books, and the recognition of any number and its meaning when applied, become easy enough, and much time is economized thereby. In connexion with the categorical numbers and their use, let me again call attention to the rule: classify by topic and then by form; that is, place your book first by the specific number in the main tables and then *add* the categorical number. I have known students to produce such combinations as .9361835 and .10U65, which are inversions of the rule, and, as such, classification absurdities.

103. Brief mention may be made of the complex and elaborate series of form marks employed in the International Decimal Classification, in the hope of returning to them at much greater length later when we shall deal with the subject of the Universal Decimal Classification (Chapter XIV). The Institute International de Bibliographie, the predecessor of the Fédération International de Documentation, for the purpose of making a classification by which the whole bibliography of the world might be arranged in the minutest manner, took the Dewey system, expanded it to many times its original size, and thus produced the largest and most detailed system that now exists.[1] It is a revelation of the fact that a fairly complete system, in which the enumeration of the parts is meant to be exhaustive, runs to thousands of pages, and must be extended continually. This extension—it is popularly known as the Brussels expansion of Dewey—retains and employs all the form divisions—01 Philosophy, 02 Compends, etc., of the original scheme, but has, in addition, a series of arbitrary form marks which are common to the system, and are, as Brown expresses it, "an elaborate and ingenious attempt to graft the features of analytical cataloguing on to classification with a particular view to the sorting and arrangement of documents of all kinds as well as books." The marks are to show:

1. *Form* (01–09); form sub-divisions as in Dewey written here in curves.
2. *Place* (2–9); here Dewey's divisions of 900 are used, with the substitution of the curves for the original 9.
3. *Time* "   "; here the date is simply enclosed in commas.
4. *Language* = 2–9; here Dewey's numbers for Philology are used after the mark of equality.
5. *Relation to other subjects:* ; here a colon: is used to separate two related subjects.
6. *Relation to detail of same subject* —; here a dash — separates the detail from the subject.
7. *Proper names, A–Z;* this is the use of the alphabetical initial for arranging works, such as biography, etc., or the form classes, in alphabetical order.

104. These are the principal marks employed, and there are others; for instance 00 and 01, which are used in conjunction with special separate tables in the system; and a plus mark +, which shows a work treats of two subjects. The use of these marks is much more simple than may appear at first sight, and they permit of the most minute arrangement of books and other material. Thus a

---

[1] This is probably true, although the classification of the Library of Congress must approach it nearly in size.

periodical of a certain date in a certain language dealing with it
in relation to a certain place may serve as an example—*Le Journal
des Chemins de Fer de Rouen en 1919* would be marked first with the
substantive Dewey number 656; to which would be added (05)
to indicate its periodical character; then 44·25, from 944·25, the
number for Rouen (the historical 9 being omitted); then "1919"
in inverted commas to indicate the date; and finally with = 4,
from Dewey's 440 French philology to indicate the language.
Thus the complete mark for our periodical—a most extreme thing
as you will see—is

$$656(06) \ (44·25) = 4 \text{ "1919"}$$

Similarly, an English work, say Sach's *History of Botany*, 1915,
would be marked

$$580·9 = 2 \text{ "1915"}$$

or the Dewey *Decimal Classification*, 1916 edition itself,

$$025·4 = 2 \text{ "1916"}$$

(the American and English language marks being the same,
naturally). So three journals on Chemistry of the same date in
English, French and German respectively, would be marked

$$540(05) = 2 \text{ "1916" (English).}$$
$$540(05) = 3 \text{ "1916" (German).}$$
$$540(05) = 4 \text{ "1916" (French).}$$

The relation mark is simple enough. Thus the book *Geology in
Relation to Military Topography*, if I have understood aright that
it is a work primarily for the military engineer, 355 +550, or, if
it is decided that it has a primary appeal to the geologist, these
numbers may be reversed, 550 +355, and a further plus and 10
from 910 may be added if it is necessary to connect the book with
topography; thus the work is classified to all its relative subjects
in the symbol 550 +355 +910. This is clearly a cataloguing expedient, as the book can only be in one place on the shelves, but
in the catalogue may (and probably should) appear under all
the headings represented by these numbers. We shall deal more
fully with this when we study the classified catalogue.

105. Before leaving this side of the subject of mnemonic
notation a warning is worth while so far as Dewey is concerned.
While these form divisions and relations have a consistent number
the number does not always consistently indicate these divisions
and relations. The form philosophy is always ·1 or ·01, and
periodicals are always ·5 or ·05, but ·1 is not always philosophy or
·5 periodicals. Dewey is precise about this, as you will see in his
Introduction, page 19 (1942 ed.), where he says, "While Italian
is always 5, 5 is by no means always Italian. Grammar is 5,

Periodicals are 5, Asia is 5, Oratory is 5, etc. Even if it were possible, to limit 5 to Italian would waste numbering material, and results would not justify cost. The purpose is to give practical aid, not to follow a fanciful theory. A cataloguer marking a German grammar remembers that all Philology begins with 4, and, as German is always 3 and grammar 5, he knows the number must be 435. Italian 5, poetry 1, is as plainly 851 with no danger of being mistaken for 'poetry of grammar' or 'theory of Asia,' because the numbers also have that meaning." Only familiarity with the systems of classification in detail will show the limits that must be imposed upon this mnemonic feature of notation; but, with all its limitations, it is an admirable and helpful feature.

106. *Notation Manipulations: Geographical Numbers.* The quotation just given has anticipated somewhat our next point. One of the most valuable of mnemonic features of notation is seen in the application of geographical and linguistic divisions to other parts of the classification, an application which would be impossible without notation. One of the commonest forms of book with which a librarian has to deal is a book on a specific subject with a geographical bearing. Such titles as

"The Folk-Lore of France."
"The Zoology of Borneo."
"The Geology of London."

come before the classifier every day, and there are many such books say, as the one on London. Now even on the shelves it is desirable to separate these in geographical order from the more general books, and from one another; and all the modern classification systems have methods by which this may be done. In Dewey the note frequently occurs: "divided like 940-999"; it merely means that the appropriate number is taken from the *place* (history) class, and is added to the subject number.

398·0944 Folk-Lore of France.
591·9911 Zoology of Borneo [i.e. 9 = Geographical distribution of animals, 911 the place numbers from 991·1].
554·21   Geology of London. [From the table where the numbers 554–559 represent in the 4-9 of this combination the Geology of Europe, Asia, etc., to Oceania, and each of these is divided as in 940-999; hence from 942·41, London is represented by 421, but the 4 is already provided in the number and is not repeated.]

The value of the method is clear enough, I hope.

107. It is obtained in the Expansive classification somewhat similarly by applying the Local List to every subject-heading that may require this division. The Local List in the expansive

classification is an exception to the rule of pure notation in that scheme. The historical and geographical classes, G and H, however, are given a numerical notation in their divisions; that is, a distinctive and invariable number is given to every country— a device which proves to be most convenient in practice. In this table 45 is England and 39 France, and these numbers when written against any heading indicate either the country or language of England, or the country or language of France; thus

> F is History, F45 is English History, F39 French History.
> HC is Economics, HC45 is English Economics, HC39 French Economics.
> X is Language, X45 is English, X39 French.

and so on in the most unlimited manner; thus, SGb is Building Laws, and SGb45 is English building laws.

108. In the Subject classification, the Local List are the geographical and historical classes O—W and their divisions and minor parts. These are lifted bodily, and usually exactly as they stand, from their own class, and the numbers added to the numbers of the specific subject which it is desired to divide geographically. Thus our three books, *The Folk-Lore of France*, *The Zoology of Borneo*, and the *Geology of London* are marked first with the class numbers for Folk-Lore, Zoology, and Geology and then with the class-numbers of the places involved:

> J521Roo.
> FooP220.
> D300U900.

Any part of the system can be qualified in this way.

Bliss has an admirable table for geographical sub-division which is number 2 of his systematic auxiliary schedules. It uses a lower case letter notation, and the full extent of its sub-divisional power may be judged from this example:

> F   Botany.
> FB   Experimental Botany.
> FBJ   Experiment Stations.
> FBJe   British.
> FBJeh   South Coast.
> FBJehm   Isle of Wight.

109. *Linguistic Numbers.* As subjects have geographical bearings so subjects may have language ones, as when we divide Literature. In the Expansive classification, the Local List may represent a language or a country. In the Dewey classification this is true only to a certain extent; i.e., the following table

2 English.	6 Spanish.
3 German.	7 Latin.
4 French.	8 Greek.
5 Italian.	

is systematic in regard to the sub-division of the European languages and, occasionally, for books in those languages. The numbers except 7 and 8 are the same as those used in the geographical number combinations of Dewey and the differences can be seen in the following numbers

944 History of France where the final 4 = France.
440 = French Language, where the medial 4 = French.

The languages are always marked by these numbers in whatever combinations they may occur. It will be noted, however, that 947 is not Latin; indeed, as we have already seen, while the languages always bear these numbers, the numbers do not always indicate the languages.

Bliss's Schedule 3 has a table "for Sub-division by Languages or by Nationalities," which groups the main families of languages, as all such special tables ought to do. It consists of a capital letter introduced by a comma; thus, to give samples only:

, A	Ancient.	, K	German.
, B	Greek.	, L	Dutch.
, C	Latin.	, M	English.
, D	Celtic.	, N	Scandinavian.
, E	Roman.	, P	Polish.
, F	French.	, Q	Czech.
, G	Spanish.		etc.
, H	Portuguese.		
, I	Italian.		

110. *Other Numbers.* At the end of the book of *Decimal Classification* Dewey give five tables, showing in detail all the mnemonic geographical, form, language, philological and literature divisions which he recommends should be used with his system.

CHAPTER VIII

THE INDEX

111. The final equipment of a bibliographical classification is the index. There is not a great deal to say about this subject. An index, however, is the method of approach which the layman uses to consult his library and it fixes and unifies the work of the classifier. It is therefore not unimportant.

112. There are two kinds of indexes, inspired by opposed ideals in classification; neither of them perfect in actual result, it must be admitted. The first of them attempts give one entry to each subject and one only and is called a one-place or, somewhat loosely, a *specific* index; the second is the *relative* index, which is more generally in favour, which gives the one entry, but adds to it all the views, standpoints, and relationships, as well as synonymous words, and, in fact, everything that may form a sub-section of the subject indexed. Both indexes are specific in that they specify the whereabouts of classes in the tables but the terms in italics are now in common use to distinguish them.

113. A simple statement of the meaning of the index may be given. In a general way we all know what an index to a book is; but it is always a sound mental exercise to construct a definition even of very simple things. An index, in our definition, is

A list of all the subjects mentioned in a book, or literary piece, arranged in alphabetical order with such reference signs as will guide the user readily to the place where the subjects are treated.

This is somewhat cumbersome, but is comprehensive and useful. The index to a classification obeys this definition in that it is an alphabetical list of all the topics named in the schedules with the notation of each. Here, then, is a sample of such an index in its simplest form, from the Subject Classification:

Aden	Q294	Adirondacks	W241
Adhesion	B012	Adjectives	M026
Adhesives	D952	Adjutants	B836

The index is specific, in that it gives the detailed subjects from the schedules, but gives one entry only to each. The theory of this *specific* form of index is that as every subject has one and one place only in the classification, so it can have one place only in the index; and you will remember that the ideal book classification was one which placed a book at one place only on the shelves. Moreover, strong in this theory, Brown invites us actually to

75

classify by his index; says he, "Anyone who wishes to simplify the process of classifying books has only to use the Index numbers, qualified by those from the Categorical Tables, and follow the easy rules for determining the choice of subjects, and he will be saved from many of the difficulties and doubts which at present surround book classification." Apart from the fact that this recommendation is self-contradictory—because one cannot follow the rules for determining choice of subject if one confines oneself to the Index—it is a dangerous recommendation. It proposes a practice which would reduce classification from an intellectual exercise to a mere mechanical process of reference. That, however, may justly be thought to be a sentimental objection, of no practical value; but there is the more solid objection that Brown's whole position is untenable. His classification is not a one-place classification; nor is his index; and classification by the index, while it might answer in ninety cases out of a hundred, in the remaining ten would lead to confusion unutterable.

114. The second form of index—the Relative Index—is a far more logical and complete instrument, although it may not be so easy to use. So far as book classification is concerned, Melvil Dewey was the inventor of this form of index and his description of its plan and purpose is as follows:

"An index in which all the heads of the tables are arranged in one simple alphabet, with the class number of each referring to the exact place in the preceding tables. This index includes, also, as far as they have been found, all the synonyms or alternative names for the heads, and many other entries that seemed likely to help a reader to find readily the subject sought. Though the user knows just where to turn to his subject in the tables, by first consulting the index he may be sent to other allied subjects, where he will find valuable matter which he would otherwise overlook." The relative index, then, has alphabetical simplicity. It enumerates in that order all the headings in the classification, but it also shows synonyms, and to a large extent the relation of each subject to other subjects. But the immediate relativity of the index is shown in the form of the index entries, in which each entry is placed in relation to the higher heading of which it is a part, and to all other subjects in the schemes to which it is applied. This may be shown by the entries from the relative index for some of the subjects already given from Brown's specific index:

Adhesion, physics		539.2
Adirondacks, history		974.753
Adjective forms.		
etymology, English lang.		422.66
inflexion,	,, ,,	425.16
syntax,	,, ,,	425.6

In each of these you will observe that the index is self-explanatory, while that of Brown is in no way so, and must be taken on faith. We want to stress this form of index as a very practical thing for the reader himself to construct; he will, no doubt, at some later stage be called upon to make indexes of subjects as represented in books. The way that experience approves as the best is the relative way, where the subject is shown in all the ways in which it enters into the classification scheme. Thus these entries illustrate what is to be desired:

Aerial erosion, geology	551.37
,, ,, navigation	533.6
Aerolites, astronomy	523.51
,, geology	552.6
Affinity, chemical	541.3
,, family law	347.6

Here the second term always shows in what connexion the first term is used. Take the word "Adhesion" in Brown's index; unless we are physicists and always think of physical adhesion in the scientific sense when we come across the term, we might be forgiven for putting a book on the *Adhesion of Political Parties* under the heading—that is, if we followed the absurd injunction to classify by the index—although now we see how bad the placing would be from other points of view than that we are discussing. But what is meant by relative index in general is the setting out of the varying ways in which a subject must necessarily appear in a classification. For example, on the next page are the Subject and Dewey index entries respectively for Africa.

All the places shown in Dewey must necessarily appear in the Brown classification; and a brief examination of main schedules and the Categorical Table will show that this is the case. For example, the geology of Africa must find a place in a geological collection arranged by Brown; and a reference to the numbers under geology will show us that there is a place for local geology qualified by the place number (if we follow "the simple rules of classifying"). In Dewey the index informs us of the fact; in Brown we learn it from other sources, in part from the Categorical Tables which is part of Brown's method of indexing as it is of his main scheme. Index and Categorical Table will in many cases produce in a rough and ready way the required class-mark. It is not a commendable method as we have asserted. The point is that there can be only one place in either classification for the book on African geology, and Dewey shows that place, while Brown does not; and it is probable that the index which gives the greater information—the relative—is to be preferred. We ought rarely or never to classify by the index. It is a key to a classification,

Subject.	Dewey.
Africa, Central	Africa
East	antiquities 913·6
General	botany 581·96
North	geology 556
South	history 960
West	statistics 316
	travels 916
African languages	North history
Literature (English)	travels
	Central history
	Propria, ancient „
	South „
	Central „
African Episcopal	African,
Zion Church.	colonization, sociology
African Methodist Epis.	discovery of America
Church.	geese
	languages
	Ethiopic
	Hamitic
	Methodist church
	mortality, public health
	sheep
	slave trade
	swine

and is a most valuable check upon it; but the fuller the index, the more liable to confusion is the user who *classifies* from it; he may easily mistake a standpoint or aspect of a subject for the concrete subject, and may make his work ridiculous by so doing. There is only one sound method of classifying, I repeat:

115. *First*, class the book in your mind; *second*, place it by the main tables, reading up from the chosen heading to the name of the main class in order to see that the book modulates into that; and *third and finally* look at the index, as a mere check.

After all, the index is a rapid means of finding specific subjects in a classified library or catalogue, and is not primarily, if it is wisely regarded, a *means* of classing.

116. *Additions to a Printed Classification Scheme.* A classification scheme is usually provided with an introduction which explains the origin and method of applying it. Some of these introductions are quite elaborate and contain the best account of the classification although naturally they always have a bias towards the scheme. Synopses of the main divisions, with more extended outlines usually follow or form part of this introduction, which must never be neglected by the student.

CHAPTER IX

CANONS OF CLASSIFICATON

117. To conclude our study of the purely theoretical aspects of our subject there will be interest in gathering together those condensed precepts of classification which various writers have enunciated. To my early version of these I gave the name Canons, with no greater authority than my own, thirty years ago, and although I was aware and am still that a canon may be an *ex cathedra* pronouncement of the Church, its original Greek meaning was all that I meant by it, which is a rule, regulation, standard test or criterion. It is a word that is useful in its own way and I retain it.

THE AUTHOR'S CANONS

118. *As to Definitions:*

1. The word *classification* has four accepted meanings. It is
   (a) The intellectual process by which our mental concepts or pictures of things are recognized to have likeness or unity and by this likeness or unity are set *in relation* to one another. This is the logical and real meaning.
   (b) The act of arranging actual things, such as geological specimens, plants or books, so that they represent the abstract arrangement in (a). This is practical *classifying*.
   (c) The written or printed schedule of terms which represent a system of classification. This is called a classification *scheme*.
   (d) The act of placing things or books in their appropriate places in the classification scheme. This is *classing*.

2. All *Being* may be a subject for classification; that is to say, everything in the mental universe and in the universe of things that has existed, exists, or may exist.

3. A *General* classification covers the whole of Being; a *Special* classification some part of it, as a Science, Art or special subject or group of subjects.

4. A *Class* is a group of concepts or of things assembled by some likeness which unifies them. This likeness is called the characteristic of classification.

5. A scheme of classification is an assembly of *classes* in a systematic order.

6. The order is based upon a theory of knowledge which the author of the scheme believes to be that most useful to those who are to use it. There are as many possible orders as there are likenesses in subject-matter, or in possible approaches to knowledge. A general scheme should therefore be based on characteristics which are generally recognized as useful.

119. *As to Division:*

7. Classes assemble things according to their degrees of likeness and separate them according to their degrees of unlikeness. The chosen likeness (characteristic) may be (a) natural or (b) artificial.

(a) A *natural* characteristic is a quality or complex of qualities in the things classified, inherent and inseparable from the things, and without which they could not be the things they are; i.e., mammalian character, upright gait and reason are a complex of qualities which is the characteristic of man.

(b) An *artificial* characteristic is a quality which is possessed by a group of things in common, but is not a necessity of their being; e.g., colour in man, or maleness, or height, weight or health, which things are not confined to man and are an inadequate description of man.

Natural and artificial characteristics may be used at different stages in a classification scheme.

8. The chosen characteristic, which is that most useful for the purpose of the scheme, is called the *essential* characteristic.

9. A classification proceeds by the assembly of the groups of sciences or of the principal fields of knowledge into main classes (or divisions) which are co-ordinate with the theory of knowledge adopted. Such classes have great extension and small intension. The process is continued by the addition of *differentiating qualities* in each main class, and thus sub-classes or divisions are made, the differentiating qualities being the likeness which groups the things in each division. Each division in turn is divided by further differentiating qualities to produce the sub-divisions, and by others successively to make the sections and sub-sections, until further sub-division is impossible.

10. It follows that every sub-division of a class is subordinate to the class heading and the sum of these sub-divisions is the whole meaning of the class term, but each single set of sub-divisions may consist of classes of equal rank. These must be co-ordinated by likeness or collocated.

11. The dividing process must be gradual, the smallest amount of difference possible in the class being used at each stage. This is "separating things according to degrees of likeness," and its result is to keep things nearly related as near together as the material permits.

12. The use of characteristics must be consistent at each stage of division, one principle of division being exhausted before another is introduced.

120. *As to Terms:*

13. A classification is expressed in class-names or terms.

14. Terms may be any word or phrase which expresses adequately the connotation of the class it names.

15. Terms should be unambiguous. They may be technical or popular, but with a tendency towards the technical as likely to be more permanent.

16. Terms should be used with a consistent meaning in every act of classification.

121. *As to Book Classification:*

17. A *Book Classification*, or classification scheme, is one devised for or adapted to the arrangement of books or other library material, by subject or form or both, or by any recognizable logical order.

18. It must be general, inclusive of all matters that are, have been, or may be the matter of books.

19. It must be capable of expansion in order that without dislocation it may admit new subjects or new sub-divisions or new aspects of old ones.

20. It must be equipped with
   (a) Generalia Class to accommodate books too general for inclusion in any single class; for example, general encyclopædias and journals.
   (b) Where the general characteristic of the scheme is arrangement by subject, it must have form classes for the arrangement of books which are more usefully placed under the forms in which they are written; for example, fiction, poetry, drama and orations.
   (c) Systematic schedules for the discrimination of the forms in which subjects are presented; for example, the *theory*, or *history*, or *bibliography* of a subject (e.g., History of Botany).
   (d) A notation which shall provide a symbol for every class-term (or group of class-terms where a heading consists of several terms).
   (e) An index which shall provide a means of rapid reference to the place of any term in the schedules of the scheme.

21. It must be uncritical in its terms for subjects, and in classing a book any placing that implies criticism of it is inadmissible.

122. *As to Notation:*

22. The notation of a scheme is a systematic and logically ordered series of short signs representing the class-names in the classification.

23. The notation may consist of any symbols that are capable of marking all parts of the scheme. It should, however,
   (a) be brief, (b) simple, (c) flexible, and (d) mnemonic.

24. A notation is said to be *pure* when it consists of one type of symbol, as decimal figures, or letters of the alphabet. The tendency is to employ alphabetical symbols for main classes or main divisions (or both) and to sub-divide by numbers used decimally.

25. Flexibility in a notation is variously called adjustability and expansibility, and means that as classification must permit the insertion of any new class or part of a class, so also the notation symbols must be capable of expansion to mark that insertion without dislocating the rest of the notation. This is the cardinal requirement of notation.

26. A mnemonic notation is one that marks any series of subjects or forms or aspects of subjects which recur in the scheme. These

may be relegated to a table (or systematic schedule), and each subject, form or aspect is always indicated by the same number, which therefore may be easily memorized.

123. *As to Book Classification Schemes:*

27. A classification scheme is printed in columnar schedules in the order of the precedence of subjects, as far as that is possible, so that the hierarchy of the subjects, again as far as possible, is exhibited.

28. The printed tables should be prefaced by an introduction explaining the methods and use of the scheme, with tables showing outlines of the Main Classes and the Main Divisions so that the order and compass of the scheme are easily seen, and tables of the systematic schedules.

29. A classification scheme needs continuous study and revision so that it is maintained in currency with knowledge. Schemes in general use are likely to be kept so because they come under the scrutiny of regular application.

124. A valuable comparative study may be made of these in connexion with the "criteria" of E. C. Richardson, the "Principles" of H. E. Bliss, and the "Canons" of S. R. Ranganathan. All of these writers had this advantage over their fellows that they all wrote them as a preliminary to, or in the case of Ranganathan to rationalize, a classification scheme of their own. I have not undertaken such an enterprise, for such wherever it has been undertaken has proved to be the core of a life-work.

RICHARDSON'S CRITERIA

125. These, given in his *Classification* are:

1. It should follow as nearly as possible the order of things. A properly classified library is perhaps the nearest thing that there is to a microcosm. A human mind which knew all things might be more perfect in this regard, but in reality no one can or does keep the whole of things in mind as a library does. It must therefore follow the order of complexity or of history, or, if you please, of evolution.

2. It should be carried out in minute detail.

3. It should be provided with a notation which will allow for indefinite subdivision, using mixed symbols, but with a predominant decimal base.

4. It should be provided with a detailed and specific index.

5. The value of such a system is increased in direct ratio to the generalness of its use.

BLISS'S PRINCIPLES

126. The "principles" are thirty-two in number and form the summary of his *Organization of Knowledge in Libraries*, where they must be read. The reader who has followed me so far will find

them to be somewhat severe but will appreciate their comprehensiveness and precision. Nearly every one of them adds some new facet to previous canons, because the author has not found it "easy to discover passages [in Richardson, Berwick Sayers, or elsewhere] explicit or implicit, that approach to clear or adequate statement of these principles, and for some of them none has been found." The student who goes to the original for these will be well repaid. Their cardinal points are given in a Summary which Bliss appends to his book. I have endeavoured to condense it here:

1. A bibliographical classification system should be logical in its construction. Such a classification is a series of classes so arranged as to show the relations that exist between the classes. For every class the mind has a corresponding idea, or picture, which we may call our concept of the class; and the class must agree with that class concept. It must also agree with the name we give it, and of course when we make a definition of the class there must be agreement of class-concept, definition, and term with the class itself.

2. A class may consist of real objects, which we may handle or see, and of natural objects—which are surely also real—of artificial things made by man or animals, or merely may be of mental things like thoughts, beliefs, dreams, etc. There are natural relations between natural things, and real things have real relations—i.e., there is nothing unique and unattached or part of nothing else; and for every thing there is a corresponding mental idea of it—its conceptual correlative. The objective realities—things we can see and touch—are found side by side with mind-pictures and conceptions of them, which are the cause and outcome of studies, sciences and arts. The real and natural things, in the order in which we discover them, are as it were *more* permanently arranged (as Nature is the original arranger, or, in real things, there is the physical work of arrangement involved) than are our concepts or mental things—because ideas and concepts may change under various conditions, as new views and aspects of things pass through the mind. In the end all classifications should agree in their order with the order the mind sees in and allows them, and thus we may say that so far as any class has a conceptual correlate—and all of them have according to the theory above given—so far is the class and the classification made of such classes conceptual. Systems made of natural classes are called natural classifications. Such natural systems are more permanent—as they change only as nature changes and not with the changes of man's mind or fancy—than classifications based on some special interest which makes a special artificial arrangement of things ignoring natural order. The latter sort of scheme is called an *arbitrary* classification; and some of these arbitrary schemes are philosophical [mental exercises] rather than scientific [arrangements of facts].

3. A class consists of all the things defined by its definition and

named by its name or terms. That is to say, if all the things which can be expressed by a name are added together they form the class to which we give the name. The name we know as the *class-term*. Terms should be used consistently, as far as possible with one meaning and one only, at least in the class we are making or defining. The classification should be self-consistent as well as consistent with its purpose.

4. Temporary arrangements of things for a special purpose we call a group. These are often made in libraries by taking books from all parts of the library and arranging them to serve some local or passing interest. Thus they come from various classes and are selective, accidental, local and, as we have noted, temporary. They are not permanent totalities. They differ thus from classes which are permanent. But classes may be grouped and regrouped as may subject-matters, studies and sciences, and so may books, documents, maps. Arbitrary or artificial book classifications differ little from mere groupings of books. Such groups frequently need to be regrouped to serve new needs. If a logical classification exists these temporary groupings are easily made whenever and however required.

5. A class is divisible into sub-classes by a specified characteristic, and these may be sub-divided again and again more specifically. Each stage therefrom produces a number of parallel sub-classes which have common likeness, each stage is also obviously subordinate to the class out of which it has been divided. Each stage in turn becomes the genus from which the next stage (or species) is sub-divided. If the division followed a single term from stage to stage a scalar series would result. But a whole classification produces at each stage a series of parallel classes. These co-ordinates should be collocated or assembled by degree of likeness and separated by degrees of difference.

6. A bibliographical classification becomes most efficient or reaches *maximal efficiency* if being in proper order—of subordination, graduation by speciality, co-ordination and collocation—and is consistent with the special classifications in the various departments of knowledge and with the organization of knowledge established in the consensus of scientists and educationists.

7. Logical, natural and scientific classifications are more efficient and lasting than philosophic or arbitrary ones, because they are more adaptable to changing knowledge. Their stability rests upon *the constancy of the order of nature*.

8. The adaptation of this classification to bibliographical classification should be systematic; the logical subordination and co-ordination of classes resulting in a *schedule*. The schedules should so be printed that the subordination of main division to class, sub-class and section is shown in the tables by appropriate indentions. The schedule should be preceded by a condensed table of the classification or a synopsis showing the logical and scientific relations. Each main class should also have a synopsis. "Complex branching classifications, sub-classifications and cross-classifications may likewise be reduced to schedules."

9. *Alternative locations* should be provided for the more important aspects of subjects not too inconsistent with the system. The schedule should be expansible to admit new topics, and details in the schedule should at need be alterable. It should provide for re-classification and be adaptable to the plan of the library building (or, alternatively, these should be adapted to the classification).

10. *Notation* is correlative to and subsidiary to classification. It should be *readjustable*, and should be simple, short, have sufficient capacity; its base should equal or exceed the number of main classes, and be expansible; should not exceed four or five factors for *classmarks* and an equal number for *internal notation*; and mnemonics if used should not distort the classification.

11. *Auxiliary schedules* for recurrent or common sub-divisions may give system to the schedules and be an economy in making and using them. Where more than one of these combine in minute classifications the schedules should show the order in which they are to be used. For these schedules the notation may be *mnemonic*. It should, however, be simple and avoid unfamiliar and confusing devices which are too indefinite for books although they may be serviceable to documentation.

12. An alphabetic index should give all terms and their synonyms and their notation so as to reveal their place in the scheme. It should have a relative character.

127. In endeavouring thus to summarize what itself is so condensed, I have probably not succeeded. The reader is advised to go to the original. Bliss himself condenses his own summary as follows:

A systematic bibliographic classification consistent with the logical principles of correlation, subordination, and co-ordination, and with the synthetic principles, of comprehension and collocation under general classes, may be consistent moreover with the comprehensive organization of knowledge maintained in the consensus of scientists and educators, and self-consistent in its terms and notations, and in the development of its schedules. In alternative locations and methods and in expansion of schedules and readjustment of notations it may become adaptively available for various applications and uses, especially for collections of books and documents and for their subject-catalogs, for bibliographies and for documentation. In *systematic schedules* it should economize *recurrent* specifications or *common subdivisions* and it may provide *systematically* for *composite relations* that can not economically be detailed in schedules. Such a system will prove not only functionally more efficient but structurally more stable and permanent than arbitrary and inadaptive classifications or groupings. Such a system should be co-operatively compiled, revised, and standardized by a representative international institution or association.

For special interests, institutions, sciences, technologies, industries, etc., special classifications, or expansions, should be co-operatively compiled and institutionally standardized. They should be consistent with the comprehensive standard, availing of alternative locations and methods, omitting irrelevant parts, readjusting or reapportioning the notations, or even adapting a different notation. For the different national requirements there should be similar adaptations, especially for histories and for literatures; and they should be institutionally developed and standardized also. Thus a plurality of classifications, special and national, may be consistent with and coherent and unitary in a comprehensive, standardized, international classification and system of standardization.

RANGANATHAN'S CANONS

128. Ranganathan's book is a statement of the principles of classification as he arrived at them after some years of work on his *Colon* scheme. They were energized, as it were, by a record reading—in twelve hours, he tells us—of the two books of Bliss and were expounded in his *Prologomena of Classification*, an entirely systematic, enthusiastic, well-documented treatise on theory with excellent examples and many comparisons and indications, mainly relevant to the use of the Colon scheme but most useful to us all. It consists of a statement in formal mathematical shape of the process and a discourse on terms; this is followed by a long section expounding over thirty canons, some of which are my own or extensions of them, but there are new ones, and the whole is made more systematic. Ranganathan had some novel terms, the most used of which are *array*, to indicate a sequence of classes arranged amongst themselves according to their ranks, which I interpret to mean a class and its ordered sub-classes; and *chain*, a sequence of classes made up of a given class at first, second and other removes (or a class and its sub-divisions). To each canon he gave a name which is an aid to memory and sometimes to meaning.

129. *As to Characteristics:*

Canons 1-7

Each characteristic should

be an attribute that differentiates at least two classes [Differentiation].
be exclusive, no two characteristics being concomitant [Concomitance].
be relevant to the purpose of the classification [Relevance].
be definitely ascertainable [Ascertainability].
be definable and unchangeable so long as the purpose is unchanged [Permanence].
be relevant in sequence to the purpose [Relevant Sequence].
be fixed and adhered to consistently [Consistency].

130. *As to Arrays:*

Canons 8-11

Classes in arrays should

be totally exhaustive of their immediate universe [Exhaustiveness].

be mutually exclusive [Exclusiveness].

be in their order according to some convenient and not arbitrary principle where this does not violate more important requirements [Helpful order].

and wherever the same or similar classes occur in different arrays be the same or similar in all, unless this violates more important requirements [Consistent order].

131. *As to Chains of Classes:*

Canons 12-13

The intension of classes should increase as their extension decreases progressively down a chain of classes [Intension].

A chain should comprise one class of each and every order that lies between the orders of the first and last link [Modulation].

132. *As to Terminology:*

Canons 14-17

Terms in a scheme should be those in current use amongst those who specialize in the subjects of which they are the name [Currency].

be non-critical [Reticence].

The meaning (denotation) of each term should be decided by a summing-up of the values of all the terms in the chain [Enumeration].

The denotation of each term in a scheme should be decided in the light of the different classes of lower order in the chain denoted by the term [Context].

133. *As to Notation:*

Canons 18-21

Notation should be pure [Purity]. (But Ranganathan approves the statement that every practical system sooner or later makes use of both letters and figures.)

be, in length of numbers, proportional to the order or intension of the class it marks [Relativity].

Class-numbers belonging to an array should be so constructed that new numbers for new subjects can be inserted, or added at the end of a chain without disturbance of existing class-numbers [Hospitality in array].

The figure or figures of a class-number which stand for an entity should be the same in every part of the scheme where that entity is represented and thus be mnemonic, unless more important requirements are to be served [Hospitality in chain].

134. *Other Canons special to Library Classification:*

Canons 22-28

In every array there should be a set of classes of the same order which comprehend the classes of the array only partially to accommodate books which deal only partially with the subjects in the array itself [Partial comprehension].

The schedules should provide for national variations due to local or other interests [Local variation].

There should be some device for differentiating books from different points of view or adapted to special interests [Viewpoint].

There should be a device for bringing editions of classics together and next to them their commentaries [Classics]. (This is claimed to be special to the Colon scheme, but it is a general rule that all editions of books should come together and their commentaries be placed next to them.)

There should be a schedule of common subdivisions to differentiate the forms of exposition in books belonging to the same class [Common subdivisions].

The notation of these common subdivisions should be clearly distinguishable from the notation used for marking subject classes, and it should satisfy the general rules of notation [Distinctiveness].

A scheme should be provided with a scheme of book-numbers to individualize all books [Individualization].

135. *Conclusion.* It will be seen that there is a range of precepts which, in their main features, harmonize. They have been criticized, especially my own in their first form, as "vague and theoretical", but is it not in the nature of theory to be theoretical? And are not all canons vague, as are all proverbs, axioms and other postulates of knowledge, until they are explained? That explanation I have endeavoured to give in the foregoing pages. But, when all is said, there are few rules which cannot be challenged. As I have said in my *Introduction to Classification* (Ed. 6, Preface, p. xix) the only "Canons" that *seem* to me to be impregnable are: "What we expect in a classification is that it will *work*. This it will do so long as it is

1. Comprehensive;
2. In a consistent and recognizable order;
3. Is as minute a statement of things as is humanly possible;
4. Is flexible enough to keep abreast of the changes in thought and in literature which is its reflection;
5. Has a simple notation which is also flexible; and
6. A full index."

DIVISION TWO
THE HISTORY OF CLASSIFICATION

CHAPTER X
PRELIMINARY CONSIDERATIONS

136. The history of classification, effectively written, would almost necessarily be a history of the attempts to organize human thought. Since man began his long endeavours to distinguish and understand the parts of his universe, he has consciously or unconsciously formed some system in which those parts were related to one another. We need not follow here his unconscious exercise of this power of classification construction because that has been described by many logicians and psychologists. Our concern is rather with the systems which have been written down in schedules by their makers or can be inferred from their writings. Of these there are now hundreds. The most compact and convenient account of them is the "Essay towards a Bibliographical History of the Systems of Classification" which forms the valuable appendix to Ernest Cushing Richardson's *Classification: Theoretical and Practical*. In this are registered, with useful bibliographical material, no less than 161 such systems, beginning with the system somewhat uncertainly abstracted from Plato's *Republic* (428-347 B.C.) and concluding with that of E. Barthel (1910). All these are pure-thought compilations to aid the mental plotting out of the universe of thought and things; in no case were they intended for practical library use. Many of them have been considered critically by Robert Flint, in *A History of the Classifications of the Sciences* (1904), a work of clarity and much learning, but somewhat difficult for the student who has not a large library at hand, because it does not set out even in outline many of the systems which it appraises. The later work, *The Organization of Knowledge and the System of the Sciences*, by H. E. Bliss (1929) has equal erudition, wider scope, more detail, and purposes to show the bearing of the systems upon a valid library system; it is therefore both parallel with and complementary to Flint, and, because of its library focus, is of great interest in our study. It embodies at least thirty years of work and is without rival in its field.

137. Of the value of the study of philosophical systems of

classification there can be no doubt. Modern systems reflect earlier ones, modern terminologies are in the main inherited, although their meanings may be extended or narrowed; almost every system it may be said in some way helps the interpretation of every other. On the other hand, the average student of librarianship cannot afford the protracted study which this side of his subject undoubtedly demands. Our consideration, therefore, will be limited to such systems as appear to have had a bearing upon the construction of library schemes, but it should be realized that the study which is here passed over can be a fruitful and even a practical one; and those who can pursue it have in Flint, Richardson and Bliss an admirable trinity of guides.

138. Edward Edwards makes a distinction in the types of library classification which is helpful and brings us back to these philosophical schemes. There are, he tells us, library classification systems which have a metaphysical basis, and there are those which are merely practical and convenient arrangements, made without reference to any ideal order of knowledge. A system with a metaphysical origin is clearly one based upon a mental order of the things it covers existing in the mind of its compiler or, as was more often the case, borrowed or adapted from another mind: it is therefore one in which its maker had laid out some ideal order for his classes before he began to put books or other material into them.

139. Naturally there is a close affinity between many library classifications and philosophical classifications; in fact, as we have repeatedly suggested, the most-received book systems are merely adaptations of philosophical systems; the adaptations being in the nature of form classes, common sub-divisions and various tables designed to accommodate certain forms of books. Such systems, it may be said somewhat loosely, passed through stages of university studies, as exemplified in the mediæval (and earlier) orders of the Trivium and Quadrivium, with which we shall deal later, and were crystallized at a somewhat later stage in the scheme of Konrad von Gesner (1548), which formed the key to his *Bibliothéque Universelle*, and has been called "the first bibliographical system"; by the influential "Chart of Learning," which forms the synopsis of the Second Book of Bacon's *Advancement of Learning* (1605), and which, with inversion, much modification and re-interpretation, forms the basis of Melvil Dewey's *Decimal Classification*. It may be affirmed, too, that the systems of Charles Ammi Cutter and James Duff Brown are partly based upon metaphysical considerations. In short, the principal schemes in use to-day have a similar origin.

140. The second category of classifications observed by

Edwards, "Schemes directed, more or less specifically, to the practical arrangement of books," begins, we may say, in 1498 with that of Aldus Manutius, and is merely an arrangement on a single leaflet, entitled *Libri graeci impressi*, of fourteen entries divided into five classes—1, Grammar; 2, Poetry; 3, Logic; 4, Philosophy; 5, Holy Scripture—and proceeds through the systems of Naudé, Garnier and others to that of Ismael Bouilliau[1] (1605-1698), which is generally considered to be the foundation of what is called the French System, or, alternatively, the System of the Paris Booksellers. This system, worked out in great detail and with excellent scholarship by Jacques-Charles Brunet (1780-1867), became the most influential and widely used of all bibliographical schemes, especially on the continent of Europe; and, indeed, appears to be the basis of the system of the British Museum.

141. In his useful chapter on "Catalogues et Classification," in volume 4 of his *Le Livre* (Paris, 1907), Albert Cim quotes Albert Maire to the effect that no less than 150 systems of classification have been directed to the actual arrangement of books and bibliographies. It will be seen, therefore, how expansive is the field before us. I have, however, already indicated the limits which may usefully be set to this part of our work. I shall therefore proceed to deal briefly with schemes which have a philosophical basis as far as the Baconian Chart; then with non-philosophical schemes as far as those of Brunet and his adaptors; and finally review at greater length separately the six schemes which exercise most influence upon modern libraries, and which to a greater or less extent combine the characteristics of both types; namely, The Decimal System, The Expansive System, The Library of Congress System, The Subject System, the Bliss Bibliographic System, and the Colon System.

142. *An Interlude on Order.* Before we get down to the more individual studies we may remind the reader that throughout our study we have insisted on the canons which assert that a scheme of classification is an assembly of classes in order and that the order is based upon *a theory of knowledge* (section 118 (5–6). This, we have also stressed, is the crucial question in the present-day study of the subject and the search for a satisfactory and agreed order has been going on for centuries. It is asserted that such an order has been found. In a library bulletin, read with appreciation,[2] is the statement that two Americans, Professor W. M. Malisoff and Henry E. Bliss have at last solved the problem. "This is the order of nature," remarks the writer; "libraries and

---

[1] "On ecrit aussi, mais moins exactement, Bouillaud."—*A Cim.*
[2] Derby Public Libraries Book List and Bulletin, No. 41, p. 5, 1943.

museums should be organized on these lines and teaching in schools and universities should follow the same pattern." The result of such reasoning, if it is applied to the details of a scheme, must be obvious. It asserts a finality which is at variance with the educational and scientific consensus. Nor, I think, does the writer mean exactly what his words seem to convey—that a final, unchallengeable, unalterable order of the sciences has been fixed, canonized and in consequence petrified; for this might be the result of the acceptance of all the implications of such a doctrine. Yet there is a certain truth in it and further examination is necessary. As we show, in the folding tables and in the studies that follow, man, from the time when he realized that he could not control his own relation to his world unless he knew its extent and divisions, has sought to map out that world. By nature a religious creature, he quite justifiably began with his relations with deity and most of the earlier schemes did begin with the theological point of view. Later, more abstract speculation prevailed; later still, he came to experimental study of his universe and finally to the study of man in all his relations. This is a rough approximation only to what took place but it results in an order which is a crude form of the more sophisticated and systematized order proclaimed by Auguste Comte. Many of the schemes, as we shall see, were conditioned by the order of teaching in the universities and these certain influences persisted, that of the Trivium and Quadrivium (see section 155) being the most effective and influencing almost every classification, even that of Bacon and certainly that of Gesner. The composite influence of Bacon, Comte, Spencer, and Karl Pearson has led to the quite modern sequence of studies. All these vary in detail, sometimes even in their method of approach, but the present position is expressed in a general way in the words of Bertrand Russell:

> "We may divide the sciences into three groups: physical, biological and anthropological. In the physical group I include chemistry, and broadly speaking, any science concerned with the properties of matter apart from life. In the anthropological group I include all studies concerned with man: human physiology and psychology (between which no sharp line can be drawn), anthropology, history, sociology and economics. All the studies can be illuminated by considerations drawn from biology; etc."[1]

The theory of Comte determined that such sciences as were simple, self-contained and complete preceded and influenced those which were more complex, derivative and dependent; thus astronomy, mathematics and the physical sciences went before the biological and sociological and led finally to his terminus

[1] *Icarus: or the Future of Science*, pp. 8–9, 1926.

science, morals. Spencer declared Comte's order to be impossible and proceeded, however, to construct an order which resembles it closely. He divided sciences into those which are abstract—mathematics and logic—as preceding sciences which are descriptions of facts, and lying between them are sciences which are partly abstract and partly description; thus, his order becomes: *Abstract Sciences*—Logic and Mathematics; *Abstract-Concrete Sciences*—Mechanics, Physics, Chemistry; *Concrete Sciences*—Astronomy, Geology, Biology, Psychology, Sociology. Other variations of these orders may be found in Flint and Bliss, and Malisoff's order of physical, biological and human sciences represents what may be called the present most general order of main classes. Bliss, whose many progressions to his final order are set out fully in his first *Organization* and are summarized briefly in section 268, hereafter, affords us the following outline which may be useful anticipation of our necessary study of his system:

1. The Physical Sciences [Mathematics, Physics, Chemistry, Astronomy, Geology].
2. The Biological Sciences [Biology, Botany, Zoology].
3. The Anthropological Sciences [Physical Anthropology, Psychology].

This is the merest outline and obviously class 3 has been developed to cover the whole of man's mental and physical activities, his religion, art, craft, literature, etc. The order is not original, but in its working out, as we show later, Bliss has shown an individuality and a thoroughness that give remarkable precision and, as I think, validity to his scheme. It is derived in its details, which are of course only hinted at here, from the findings of scientists and educationists and represents as nearly as possible their present position, so far as there is any general agreement amongst them. The question we have to face is: what permanence is there in any such scheme that will justify our adopting it to the exclusion of other existing or possible orders?

On the critical side the considerations are probably these. If any order could be fixed and would never shift we should be fully justified in abandoning gradually all other schemes than that of Bliss. One does not aver that such a course would be a real library economy; and at present it is obviously a Utopian suggestion. The evils that this order seeks to remove, which we are assured burden the academic librarian, arise mainly because the prevailing schemes are still traditional and do not coincide in their main classes with the various departmental divisions of the modern university. Dr. R. Offor remarks that "though it is unnecessary to follow exactly the divisions of the academic curriculum, it is inconvenient to cross them too much." Out of that have arisen many home-made schemes,[1] and methods such as the system in University College, London, where the library stock is distributed amongst a general library and a number of special departmental libraries in separate apartments and in different buildings such as the English, the Classical, the Medical Sciences, the Librarianship and several other libraries. In a way, it is most convenient in its working; in another, there are the difficulties that professors claim many books as belonging to them, which have got into the departmental collections of other professors; and the effectiveness of the general library is greatly reduced by the various separations. Frankly, no system yet devised or suggested has been able to satisfy this criticism and it will remain even under a system which possesses the power to alter and expand. Thus, although we may accept the order of Bliss as the best now available, that it will remain so is problematical; it can never be asserted dogmatically that it will. The one principle that experience proves and contemporary criticism is prone to miss is that the general scope of many class terms has been remarkably consistent for centuries. That, first; secondly, that the order of the main classes, by which I mean their relation to one another, is not of prime *practical* importance. It is in the ultimate divisions, sub-divisions and sections of the main classes that changes are frequent and inevitable. And these are easily dealt with by means of the flexibility which we presume to be a necessary feature of all acceptable schemes. Main classes should be reasonably co-ordinated and be comprehensive, well-planned and expansive. A simple example will bring us down to the "brass-tacks" of the situation. The popular schemes of to-day were formulated when there were no radio, airplanes, Einstein theory, electric telephones, automobiles or electric trains—inventions which have changed the face of earth and sky. Was any well-constructed schemes made obsolete by their appearance? Certainly not; there were always such classes as Communication, Physical Theory, Engineering, which embrace them all; there was always, or has been at least for eighty years, a flexible notation available; the subjects could therefore be inserted without any serious, and certainly without fatal, dislocation of the scheme. Thus, while we seek to improve schemes and to create new and better ones, we must not exaggerate the defects that they are designed to remove. The changes in the ultimate sub-divisions to which we have referred can be made without the gargantuan job envisaged by Dr. Arundel Esdaile ten years ago when he

---

[1] Dr. Offor, indeed, prefers a home-made scheme. *See* Woledge, G., and Page, B. S., *A Manual of University and College Library Practice*, pp. 63–66.

in a paper on "Library Economy at the end of the Seventeenth Century," says it was usual "to divide the books into a certain number of general classes and then to place them in fixed location according to size, in the shelves set apart for each class. . . . The books were sometimes put under the classes in alphabetical order of the authors' names. Century and nationality were also used as the basis of division." He tells us, further, of the system favoured by the Jesuits: on entering the library, if you turned to the left, you beheld the resplendently bound collection of choice and exquisite authors; if you looked to the left, you beheld "the unhappy books of the heretics placed in mourning and dirt, and indeed bound in black skins or black parchment, and all coloured on top with black colouring." The "fixed location" here mentioned, an impracticable method in any growing library, is a form of the at-one-time common collegiate press-marking system which is dealt with Chapter XX (see section 309).

145. France has always been essentially the home of bibliographers, and, indeed, it may be said that until quite recently the best works on that subject were French. The sixteenth century saw catalogues which have points of interest, amongst which may be mentioned those of Gabriel Naudé, 1643, whose *Advis pour dresser une bibliothèque* was translated by John Evelyn, and is a work of such liberality of ideas that it would do honour to the most modern librarian. It has twelve main classes, which, because of the eminence of the compiler, deserve transcription:

Theology.   Military Art.
Medicine.   Jurisprudence.
Bibliography.   Council and Canon Law.
Chronology.   Philosophy.
Geography.   Politics.
History.   Literature.

146. Almost contemporary with Naudé's system was the birth of the famous French system, or System of the Paris Booksellers, which is our principal consideration in this chapter. "The honour of originating it has been claimed, sometimes for the learned Jesuit, Jean Garnier, and sometimes for Gabriel Martin, for so long a period the most eminent of the Paris booksellers; but the claim which is best authenticated seems to be that of Ismael Bouillaud, the compiler of the sale-catalogue of the famous Library of De Thou."[1] Édouard Rouveyre, on the authority of Gustave Brunet, claims that this outline was originated by Gabriel Martin, a bibliographer who between 1705 and 1761 had compiled 147 library catalogues. The point does not seem to be

[1] Edwards's *Memoirs*, v. 2, p. 773.

important, as various contemporary bibliographers use an almost
identical outline, amongst them being Prosper Marchand,
Guillaume Francis de Bure, his cousin Guillaume de Bure, Née
de la Rochelle, and others, who all introduced variant sub-
divisions. It was, however, modified and extended enormously
by Jacques-Charles Brunet, who made it the basis of the classified
part (volume 5) of the most influential of general bibliographies,
his *Manuel du Libraire et de l'Amateur de Livres*, which first appeared
in 1809, and has been revised and extended many times since.

The scheme has five main classes only:

  1. Theology.
  2. Jurisprudence.
  3. History.
  4. Philosophy.
  5. Literature.

147. In the hands of Brunet the scheme had for its object the
arrangement of a great general bibliography, in which the books
are classified by their predominating characteristics. French
bibliographers are almost lyrical in their praise of the system, as
is natural, seeing that nearly all their bibliographies are classified
in accordance with it, and it is the scheme with which they are
most familiar. "It has been reproached," remarks Gustave
Brunet, "for not being philosophical enough or rigidly scientific.
On the other hand it is clear, simple, easy, and as Charles Nodier
says with reason, 'It embraces, without too great an effort, all
the innumerable and capricious sub-divisions which human
ingenuity has been pleased to introduce into the literary form of
books, and it is sanctioned by excellent catalogues which have
become classics of their kind.' " Rouveyre compares it with
Dewey, greatly to the disadvantage of the American scheme, of
which he contends, "en Europe, en France particulierement, son
emploi serait desastreux." These bibliographers have naturally
endeavoured to proved the logical and philosophical value of their
favourite system, and Gustave Mouravit has written what Cim
calls a very beautiful chapter devoted to an analysis of and apology
for Brunet, from which the following may usefully be quoted:
"This method is at the same time synthetic and analytic: synthetic
in that it presents in its principal divisions the great spheres into
which the activities of human thought are deployed; analytic, in
that it offers in their minutest details, the products of those
activities, and follows all the ramifications on which those activities
are exercised.

A. At the summit of things, man first beholds God, his Author
    and End. THEOLOGICAL SUBJECTS therefore group into a
    FIRST DIVISION.

E. After God, directly man returns to the world, he meets men, his familiars. Then are revealed to him the great notions of Law and Duty, of Justice and Injustice. JURISPRUDENCE, which examines these, their formula and rules of application, form a SECOND DIVISION.

I. Then man returns upon himself. He wishes to know himself and the external world, and the connexions more or less intimate which bind him to that world, the modifications which he experiences, and which in his turn he makes himself. These are properly the domain of the SCIENCES AND ARTS, embraced in a THIRD DIVISION.

U. But the human mind has its own life. While it seeks to extend the field of knowledge, it endeavours to translate it, and it uses the form of language to show its own manifestations, often of a type that it has dreamed and that realizes more or less the essence of the beautiful. Studies of language and of the rules which should govern the creations of the mind, works which have birth from the vision of some ideal—all this group of knowledge and literary production ranges under the name of BELLES-LETTRES in a FOURTH DIVISION.

Then after God, justice, the external world, and the manifestations of thought, man desires to know the destinies and environment of the humanity of which he is part; he desires to know the various evolutions which have brought about so many of the objects of his speculations. The HISTORICAL SCIENCES, appropriate to this end, combine in a FIFTH DIVISION.

As an appendix BIBLIOGRAPHY which bears its investigating torch into all parts of Science, has its place—SIXTH DIVISION.

And for the sake of order, and also to reserve a great edifice of apartments for the accommodation of subjects which cannot conveniently be placed elsewhere, POLYGRAPHY and COLLECTION forms the SEVENTH and last DIVISION."

148. It will be noted in passing that M. Mouravit has exalted to the dignity of sixth and seventh classes subjects which occupy the subordinate position of appendices to History in the scheme itself. As to the theory above enunciated, it is clearly fanciful. Certainly tradition has consecrated the view that man first beholds God, but that he immediately turns from God to the contemplation of ideas of Justice and Law is extremely debatable. These considerations were probably not present in the mind of the deviser of the system, and appear to be an ingenious after-apologia.

149. The full tables of the Brunet Classification occupy 18 closely printed double-columned pages of large octavo size in the fifth volume of his *Manuel;* and as a reasonably detailed outline of this famous system is not available, apparently, in English,

I have thought well to translate as much of it as will give a comprehensive idea of its character. I have drawn this version, which is an abridgement of the full tables, from Rouveyre,[1] but have had recourse throughout to the full tables. The notation used is that of the Bibliothèque Nationale. (See folding table.)

150. The scheme has great vogue in France, especially for the arrangement of bibliographies and for booksellers' stocks and private collections. So far as it is classified, the Bibliothèque Nationale bases its arrangement upon Brunet. The great and well-adminstered public library of Sainte-Geneviève in Paris is also arranged by it, the scheme having been expanded considerably to meet the needs of modern literature, and I am assured that it is successful. As I have already noted from Edwards, the scheme Thomas Hartwell Horne proposed to the Trustees for the classifications of the British Museum in 1825 is a modification of the French scheme.[2] The scheme actually in use in the British Museum also bears a rather remote resemblance to it, but sufficient to suggest that it was an influence.

151. Criticism of the scheme is easy from the standpoint of to-day, and yet difficult because I have not had that experience in its use without which criticism is likely to be academic merely. The obvious remark is that the scheme is already old-fashioned and is conditioned, as one might expect, by the state of knowledge in its day. Moreover, the tables are far too brief, even in the most fully expanded version I have examined, for immediate application to a modern library. Such ugly terms as Prolegomena and Parilopomena do not clarify or render the scheme more attractive, although one need not press this small particular too far. A more serious fault is that subjects which have in modern schemes the rank of full classes are often relegated to the various appendices. For example, Australia, New Zealand and Polynesia are merely an appendix to the History of Asia. The literary history of all countries is pushed away as a subject division of Historical Parilopomena, and there are other cases equally objectionable.

152. Finally—not to continue this criticism beyond what is reasonable or desirable—the notation of the scheme is mixed. cumbrous, and obsolete. In his *Manuel*[3] the main classes have no symbol, the divisions are marked with Roman figures, the subdivisions with Arabic figures, sections with Roman capital letters, sub-sections with small italic letters, and individual works receive

[1] *Connaissances Nécessaires à un Bibliophile*, v. 9, pp. 21-37. N.D., Paris.
[2] *Outlines for the Classification of a Library.* Printed by G. Woodfall, Skinner Street, London, 1825.
[3] My edition is that of 1865.

a running Arabic number. Thus a Turkish version of the Holy Bible might be marked

Theology IlAm82

In the table I have printed the vowels a, e, i, o, u, are used to mark the respective main classes as in the version used by the Bibliothèque Nationale, and with this notation our book would be marked

AIlAm82

Such a notation offers no attractions to the modern librarian. I do not advance this point as vital because any reader who has followed this book to this point would be able to reconstruct the notation on a decimal or alphabetic base sufficiently for most practical purposes. The scheme, however, lacks an index, and, in short, its main interest for us nowadays is not the possibility or desirability of applying it to library shelves, but in its value as a clue to the labyrinths of many Continental bibliographies.

153. It has not appeared to me to be necessary to enter upon the fertile and interesting field of German bibliographical classifications, as their vogue, so far as I have been able to trace it, has not been great outside the country of their origin. In what is a standard manual of library economy in that country,[1] Dr. Arnim Graesel has given a satisfactory amount of space to the brief description of library classifications current in 1902. From this it would appear that the classification of Otto Hartwig, 1888, which is applied in the University at Halle is that which is most favourably regarded, but the learned author also selects the system of Schutz and Hufeland, 1785-1800, as one of the best and one which has been recommended as a model to librarians. Neither of these schemes, however, appears to me to be important in comparison with the schemes selected for special consideration here, but I have to admit that this judgment is founded upon a study of the mere outline that Dr. Graesel provides. Nor do I think it necessary to draw attention to Italian schemes, especially that of G. Bonazzi entitled *Schema di Catalogo Sistematico per le Biblioteche*, Parma, 1890, in which Signor G. Bonazzi has attempted to combine the system of Hartwig with that of Dewey.[2] This much restraint is necessary in order that the student may focus his attention, at least at this early stage of his study, only upon schemes which have a wide acceptance.

[1] Graesel, Dr. Arnim. *Handbuck der Bibliothekslehre.* Leipzig: Weber, 1902, pp. 508-38.
   There is a translation in French of an earlier edition entitled *Manuel de Biblioth-économie*, translated by Jules Laude, Paris: H. Welter, 1897.
[2] See R. Bliss's *Bonazzi's Scheme for a Classed Catalogue Library Journal*, 16, pp. 5-8. 1891.

154. James Duff Brown's little but good *Manual of Library Classification*, 1898, his later *Library Classification and Cataloguing*, 1812, Edwards's *Memoirs of Libraries*, 1859, Richardson's *Classification*, 1891, and Bliss's *Organization of Knowledge and the System of the Sciences*, 1929, as well as the authors quoted in this and other chapters, furnish ample material for those who would follow the comparative study of classification. Writers in all the periodicals for librarians are a cloud of witnesses to the perennial fascination of the study for certain types of librarian.

CHAPTER XII

CLASSIFICATION WITH A PHILOSOPHICAL BASIS: GESNER TO BACON

155. *The Trivium and Quadrivium.* Systems which appear to have a philosophical basis would seem to deserve treatment first in a work of this kind, but in chronological order schemes which do not possess this basis are found first. When we come to consider philosophical schemes we are enabled to skip several centuries with a quiet mind, because nothing that can be so described occurs until the middle of the sixteenth century. But we shall find a clue if we consider the nature and order of studies which were evolved by the universities. It found early reflection in Duke Humfrey's Library, the early part of the University Library at Oxford, in about 1431, when the statutes ordained that books for the study of "the Seven Liberal Arts and the Three Philosophies were kept apart in a chest, and might be borrowed by Masters of Arts lecturing in those subjects."[1] To-day if we enter the Bodleian Quadrangle we notice that the doors are inscribed with the names of the studies embraced in the *Trivium* and the *Quadrivium*.[2] These name studies derive originally by inference from what is known as the Greek Triad, an arrangement of Philosophy into Physics, Ethics, and Logic (or Dialectics to use its long-recognized name); and especially from Aristotle's indicated order, Logic, Metaphysics, Mathematics, Physics, Ethics, Politics, Economics and Arts. This is an order of studies, not of course a realized classification of the sciences,[3] and when the enduring and almost pervasive influence of Aristotle in the mediæval universities is remembered, it will be expected that this order will also be visible. Indeed it became systematized in the seven groups, or classes, of the liberal arts which were known as the *Trivium* and the *Quadrivium*, the seven preparatory studies or disciplines which were regarded as preliminary to the highest human studies and ultimately Theology. In the terminology of Cassiodorus in the sixth century these seven preparatory studies were further specified as *Sermocinales* or sciences of *words*, or *Reales* or sciences of *things*. These studies are:

Trivium: Artes or Scientiae Sermocinales
> Grammar
> Dialectics
> Rhetoric

---

[1] Strickland Gibson. *Some Oxford Libraries*, p. 15.   [2] *Ibid.*, p. 34.
[3] See Bliss. *Organization of Knowledge and the System of the Sciences*, pp. 309–11.

Quadrivium: Scientiae Reales

> Geometry
> Arithmetic
> Astronomy
> Music

which are preparatory to

> Theology
> Metaphysics
> Ethics

and later was added

> History

156. *Gesner's Scheme.* The Trivium and Quadrivium appears in varying form in every scholastic and philosophical classification and most strikingly in the work which is called by some "the first bibliographical scheme", which is that of the German-Swiss scholar, naturalist, and author, Konrad von Gesner (1516-65). Gesner's life is one of the romances of the history of learning. Son of a poor furrier in Zurich who died when his famous son was fourteen, Gesner at that age started out in the world in the hope of relieving the dire poverty of his mother and many brothers and sisters by the use of his pen! Coming to Strasbourg, he entered the service of Wulfgang Fabricius Capito, with whom he studied Hebrew; whence, returning to Switzerland, he was granted a small travelling scholarship which enabled him to continue his studies in France; and, later, he became a schoolmaster in his native city. A course in medicine at Basle followed, and in 1537 he received the appointment of professor of Greek at Lausanne; but this he relinquished to continue medicine at Montpellier, to graduate at Basle, and to return to Zurich in order to commence practice. The University of Zurich made him professor of physics and natural history in 1541, and this office he dignified until his death occurred, prematurely as a result of devotion to his medical duties, in a plague which swept the city in 1565. In a life of little more than forty-eight years, his industry and fertility were enormous. His learning, we are told, in its width and comprehensiveness has rarely been surpassed. Cuvier called him "the German Pliny." He published no less than seventy-two works on grammar, botany, pharmacy, medicine, natural philosophy and history, and was working on eighteen others at his death. His claim to remembrance, however, rests mainly upon his *Bibliotheca Universalis* (folio, Zurich, 1545), which is a catalogue of Latin, Greek and Hebrew books with critical notes and extracts from the more important ones, and its supplement, *Pandectarum sive partitionum universalium Conradi Gesneri Ligurini libri XXI* (1548), of which, however, only nineteen of the twenty-one books indicated in the title were published, the books on medicine and theology not having satisfied the compiler. In the *Pandectarium* Gesner classified the entries according to subjects and in such manner as to make the system employed an immense advance upon its predecessors. The scheme is a classification of knowledge according to definite principles, and this will be seen best if we quote the synopsis which Gesner placed at the head of his section, "Partitiones theologicae."[1]

PHILOSOPHIA comprehendit Artes et Scientias.

Præparantes

Necessaria

Sermocinales
- 1. Grammatica et Philologica.
- 2. Dialectica.
- 3. Rhetorica.
- 4. Poetica.

Mathematicas
- 5. Arithmetica.
- 6. Geometria, Optica, etc.
- 7. Musica.
- 8. Astronomia.
- 9. Astrologia.

Ornantes
- 10. De divinatione et magia.
- 11. Geographia.
- 12. Historia.
- 13. De diversibus artibus illiteratis, mechanicis, et.

Substantiales
- 14. De naturali philosophia.
- 15. De prima philosophia, seu metaphysica et Theologia Gentilium
- 16. De morali philosophia.
- 17. De philosophia economica.
- 18. De re politica id et civili ac militari.
- 19. De jurisprudentia.
- [20. De re medica.]
- 21. De Theologia Christiana.

157. While many writers on classification have commented on the originality of Gesner's scheme, none of them has explained it. So far as I understand it, apart from its scholastic order origin,

[1] This outline is quoted from Edwards's *Memoirs of Libraries*, v. 2, p. 763.

Gesner obviously had the progressive order of studies in his mind. Philosophy stands for the whole sum of knowledge which is to be approached through the arts and the sciences. Of the arts and sciences there are two kinds: (1) those which are primary or preparatory, and (2) those which are fundamental. Of the preparatory sciences he finds some to be (a) necessary and others to be (b) embellishments or enrichments. His necessary arts are (aa) those of discourse, and (bb) mathematical sciences and arts. What he terms (b) *ornantes* (a word for which an exact English equivalent is difficult to discover, simple as the problem seems to be) form a curious class, but are clearly a progression of studies through divination and magic, geography and history to the illiterate or mechanical arts. From these the prepared mind may proceed to his great class (2) *substantiales*, which holds the higher forms of knowledge, and connotes all forms of philosophy, metaphysical, natural, moral, civil, economic, political, legal, medical and theological. The result is a hierarchy of knowledge of an ideal kind, in no way dependent upon the fortuitous appearance of books on this or that subject. Brunet remarks that the system sufficed in its time for the arrangement of a library *bien composée*, and that Gesner, being a man of good sense, had avoided those arbitrary combinations of different sciences into one class which have seduced so many savants. In any case it is the great mediæval attempt to relate the arrangement of books to the educational and scientific consensus of the day.

158. It does not seem to be necessary to do more than to refer to the scheme of Florian Trefler, the Bavarian (1560). Nor need we dwell on that of Christofle de Savigny (1587), for, although Brunet remarks[1] that it was anterior to Bacon by nearly twenty years and may have been the model for the latter, Edwards quite justly says,[2] "it bears scarcely any resemblance" to Bacon's system, and "it would have been much more to the purpose to have pointed out the very obvious similarity which exists between the classification of Savigny and that of Gesner, which had preceded it by forty years."

159. *Bacon's Chart.* Of much more importance in this history is the famous classification, or as it is frequently called, chart of human learning, which formed the frame-work of Bacon's treatise on *The Advancement of Human Learning*,[3] published in 1605. There have been many schemes of classification, many of them unique

---

[1] *Manuel*, v. 6. VI.   [2] *Memoirs of Libraries*, v. 2, p. 765.
[3] The edition of W. A. Wright (Oxford Clarendon Press, 1873) contains a chart of the scheme. The quotation on p. 107, giving the basis of the chart, is from Spedding's translation. (See Spedding's *Works of Bacon*, v. 4, pp. 292-3, 1864). The best criticism from the philosophical standpoint is in Flint's *History of Classification of the Sciences*, pp. 104-113.

in the sense that they have not been used by anyone besides their authors; but it is not too daring to say that almost every scheme from the seventeenth century until the present has been affected in a greater or less degree by the scheme of Bacon. It is therefore necessary to give rather special attention to it.

160. The origin of the scheme may be outlined briefly. Bacon, in laying the foundations of his philosophical system, commences with a review of what has been accomplished in the field of learning, and of the documents in which that accomplishment has been recorded. The ambitious character of his project will be observed; he is the prototype and in all ways the greatest British example of those remarkable men of whom the world has produced about a dozen who take the whole field of knowledge as their province; his mind was encyclopædic. *The Advancement of Learning* is therefore a history of the record of thought as it was at the date of its appearance in 1605; but it is rather a discussion of the state of knowledge than of the books or records themselves. Bacon rarely, and only then by allusive methods, mentions the names of books. The treatise is one that none of us dares to neglect, and for some years I have been commending its study to young librarians, not only as an example of the classifying mind in the exercise of its highest powers, but because of the unfolding clarity of its logic, and the beauty of its prose. I cannot refrain from quoting his beautiful reference to libraries as

"The shrines where all the relics of the ancient saints, full of true virtue, and that without delusion or imposture, are reposed."

not because any librarian of this workaday world regards it as a statement of the purpose of his library, but because there is a nobility in the utterance which strikes something responsive in all of us.

161. Bacon's method is subjective; and he proceeds upon a definite principle of division that we can recognize and appreciate. In fact, as applied to books he is the first of all the classifiers who is quite consistent in the characteristics upon which he bases his outline. He says: "The sense, which is the door of the intellect, is affected by individual objects only. The images of these individuals—that is, the impressions received by the sense are fixed in the memory, and pass into it, in the first instance, entire, as it were, just as they occur. These the human mind proceeds to review and ruminate on; and, thereupon, either simply

rehearses them,
or
makes fanciful imitations of them,
or
analyses and classifies them.

Therefore from these three fountains—Memory, Imagination, and Reason—flow these three emanations—History, Poesy, and Philosophy; and there can be no others."

162. The characteristic at the basis of the arrangement is "the faculties of the rational soul"; or the mental treatment we give to the perceptions of our senses. We observe "man and nature and human life," Bacon tells us in effect, and we rehearse what we see, that is we write the history of things; or using our imagination we construct fictitious history which resembles in all its chief characteristics the things we have observed; thus we produce what he denominates Poesy, but what we in modern times call fiction in all its forms whether in verse or prose; and, finally, we may reason over and arrange our observations, and the art (or if you like science) which does this was then called philosophy, and is now called in part by that name and in part is natural science.

163. A brief description may help us: Memory, then, produces history, and history is of two kinds, one recording the works of Nature (Natural History), the other (Civil History) the works of Man. Natural history has sub-divisions which show Nature working in her ordinary course without hindrance (Generations), or obstructed in that course and thus producing monstrosities (Prætergenerations). Then we get the Arts, Literary and other; then Civil History itself, first in its ecclesiastical form, and then in the records in annals, memorials, commentaries, registers, and so forth. [Note that the history of literature comes here (inevitably according to the basis of the scheme) and not as poesy as we, in our modern manner, might be led to suppose.]

164. The second class, as we have indicated, simply shows the imagination working on the materials provided by our senses, "combining, magnifying and idealizing them at pleasure,"[1] from which we get poetry, or feigned history—verse, according to Bacon being only a form of style, an accident as we should call it, not affecting his classification. *Narrative* poetry is fiction in all its forms; *dramatic* poetry is simply feigned "history made visible, for it represents actions as if they were present, whereas [real] history represents them as past," and *parabolical* poetry is the representation of ideas as though they were visible objects (the moods, etc., which make up lyrical poetry, and fables, allegories, etc.).

165. Philosophy is, like all the other branches of the classification, a human science; it springs from the mind of man, not from the Divine Mind. Hence there is no place for Theology, as we understand it, in this class. Bacon says that Theology consists either of Sacred History or of Parables, or Doctrines and

---

[1] Flint's *History of Classification of the Sciences*, p. 107.

Precepts—part of which may indeed belong to Divine Philosophy as shown in this class, but it mainly goes (in this scheme) under Ecclesiastical History. *Natural Theology*, however, *does* lead off the class; that is to say, the inferring of God from his works—the discovery of God through the mind as distinct from revelation. But Bacon does not give us any sub-divisions of Natural Theology. The class Philosophy covers all those now distinctive sciences which make up that part of knowledge which we call Physical Science, as well as Philosophy proper, Sociology and Economics. The doctrine of Nature is divided into speculative and practical; then the speculative sub-divides into Physics, the investigation of efficient causes and matter, and into Metaphysics, the investigation of final causes. Practical he sub-divides into Mechanics and what he calls Magic, which in some degree is the counterpart of our modern experimental science. To these classes, Speculative and Practical, he adds as an appendix Mathematics pure and applied. The doctrine of man has two divisions called Human and Civil Philosophy. Human consists of a doctrine of things common to both. Four sciences are comprised in the doctrine of the Body—Medicine, aiming at health, Cosmetic, at beauty, Athletic, at strength, and Voluptuary, at pleasure. The *Soul* is used by Bacon in the scriptural sense of the phrase "man became a living soul," and deals not only with the breath of life in man but with his mental and moral faculties (psychology and ethics); the understanding, will, affections. Civil philosophy divides into the Art of conversation, the Art of negotiation, and the Art of State Policy.

Although the Trivium and Quadrivium influenced Bacon, that influence is not very apparent. The introduction of the faculties of the mind as the fundamental characteristics by Bacon has led to much criticism, which psychology confirms, such as that which urges that the faculties do not work in compartments as he gives them; that science can be applied to history, and that imagination enters into nearly every subject; in short, that the faculties of memory, imagination and reason work simultaneously in man. That is true, but need only be stated. What we as classifiers are more concerned with are the practical difficulties of the scheme; its inevitable separations when applied to literature. Thus Natural History is away from such laws of nature as are expressed in applied mathematics, natural theology is away from revelation, literary history away from poesy, and several other such separations may be detected. However that may be, the influence of the system has been profound. It formed the basis of the great French Encyclopædia of Diderot and D'Alembert in the eighteenth century. "If," wrote Diderot, "we emerge from this vast operation, we shall owe it mainly to the chancellor Bacon, who sketched the plan of an universal dictionary of sciences and arts at a time when there were not, so to speak, either arts or sciences. This extraordinary genius, when it was impossible to write a history of what men already knew, wrote of that which they had to learn." It influenced, I am told, the early classification of the Bodleian Library; it was the outline of the first classification applied in the Library of Congress; in 1870 it formed the plan of the famous inverted Baconian classification of Dr. W. T. Harris; and the scheme of Harris is the one upon which the Dewey Decimal Classification is based. No philosophical or other classification has had such important results.

166. The study of schemes which are philosophical in origin may be pursued further with profit and interest in the schemes which in outline are set out in the folding tables which accompany this chapter, but the limits I have set myself do not admit of further discussion here. The schemes of Prosper Marchand, 1704, Samuel Taylor Coleridge (in his remarkable *Essay on Method* which is the introduction to the *Encyclopædia Metropolitana*, 1826), Merlin, 1847, and those of Herbert Spencer (*Essays, Scientific, Political and Speculative*, v. 3, pp. 9–56, 1875), and Karl Pearson (*Grammar of Science*, p. 513-32, Ed. 2, 1900), will occur to any student of the subject, but these, valuable and suggestive as they may be, have not exercised any direct influence on library classification as a whole, although they have played their part on the path to the order of knowledge at which Bliss and his supporters have arrived, and only a general reference to these and to many schemes I have not named can be made here.

CHAPTER XIII

DECIMAL CLASSIFICATION. THE DEWEY CLASSIFICATION

167. A classification scheme which is used in all five continents, has been translated, at least in part, into nine European languages and into Chinese, and has reached a fifteenth edition in English, must take priority of place in our discussion of modern library systems. That, briefly, is the record of the Decimal Classification of Melvil Dewey. Its cardinal virtues are universality and hospitality, a simple expansible notation which is now almost an international classification vocabulary, excellent mnemonic features and an admirable index. It has many defects, but nevertheless has such adaptive qualities that it has survived much cogent and seemingly unanswerable criticism and has progressed in spite of it; indeed, for some years to meet a real demand the Library of Congress has printed the D.C. numbers as well as its own on its printed catalogue cards. Even more significant is the fact that its main classes and divisions and the essential parts of its notation form the basis of the Universal Decimal Classification (the so-called International Classification) with which we shall deal in our next chapter. The British Standards Institution has adopted the Universal D.C. as an official standard, has published an abridged English edition, and is in process of publishing an edition in English of the entire scheme.

168. Decimal arrangement, as applied to book-shelves, did not begin with Melvil Dewey, nor does he claim such priority. Cim[1] tells us that in 1583 the learned Lacroix du Maine presented to Henry III a curious and singular project for the arranging of a library "perfect in all ways". This library was to consist of 10,000 volumes accommodated in 100 book-cases (or cupboards), each of which was to contain 100 volumes. The first order of these cases, numbers 1–17, was devoted to Religion; the second, numbers 18–41, to Arts and Sciences; the third, numbers 42–62, to the Description of the Universe; the fourth, numbers 63–72, to the Human Race; and so on. It will be seen that this is a vague decimal system applied not to subjects but to book-cases or shelves. All decimal systems before that of Dewey that I have examined have this peculiarity—they number the shelves and relegate subjects to shelves so numbered; they do not number the subjects themselves decimally. The modern arrangement of a library

[1] *Le Livre*, v. 4, p. 309.

ignores the shelf and numbers the book or, to be precise, the subject of the book. This makes books capable of movement backwards or forwards on shelves. Another primitive, although much later, scheme is that described in a small manual of library economy by Nathaniel B. Shurtleff, *A Decimal System for the Arrangement and Administration of Libraries*, Boston, U.S.A., 1856, which very closely resembles that of du Maine. Alcoves with ten bays, each of ten shelves, were to be employed, and both bays and shelves were numbered from 1 to 10. The notation was of a non-expansive kind not essentially related to the shelves. It bears no relation to that of Dewey.

169. Melville Louis Kossuth Dewey—a name which in his passion for time-saving shorthand he reduced in due time to Melvil Dewey—was born in Adams Centre, New York, on December 10th, 1851, the descendant, it is supposed, of Welsh pioneers. Son of a small storekeeper, he came to librarianship through a Spartan process of self-education, a few years of teaching, followed by higher studies at Oneida Seminary, Alfred University, and finally at Amherst College, where he graduated in 1874 and became Assistant College Librarian. During his tenure of office he did many things for librarianship, not the least of which was his fervent participation in the founding of the American Library Association. Later, he became librarian of the New York State Library at Albany and there founded and directed the first "library school". As an organizer, writer, pamphleteer and speaker in the advocacy of our craft he was the most energetic and fertilizing personality of his long lifetime. His *Library School Rules* still have value, and he founded and for some years edited the *Library Journal*. However, just as Charles Ammi Cutter will be remembered by his *Rules for a Dictionary Catalogue*, so is the name of Dewey likely to survive in connexion with his Decimal Classification.

170. A glance at the classifications in vogue in libraries in 1874, the date at which Dewey became librarian of Amherst, showed very little to the advantage of the then librarians. In England the British Museum was classified by the free adaptation of Brunet, which still survives; at the Bodleian Library were a series of partial classifications which appear never to have been resolved into a coherent whole; the Bibliothèque Nationale had been arranged partly by Brunet, but was to a large degree unclassified; the Library of Congress possessed a variant of the system of Bacon. Dewey almost immediately realized the need of some more competent classification than appeared to be available. He therefore made a comprehensive study of existing schemes, and devised

---

[1] *Manual of Library Classification*, 1898. London: Library Supply Co., 1898.

his own. He tells us in his Introduction that he was most indebted to Natale Battezzati's *Nuova Sistema di Catalogo Bibliografico Generale* (Milan, 1871), and to the systems of Jacob Schwartz, 1879,[1] and W. T. Harris,[2] the last of which was devised for the public school library of St. Louis in 1870. It is not clear, however, to what extent Battezzati and Schwartz influenced his work. Its relation to that of Harris is more obvious.

171. Harris's system was the first of the "inverted Baconian" schemes, of which there have been several. It will be recollected that Bacon, from his three human faculties of Memory, Imagination and Reason, produced his three main classes: 1, History; 2, Poesy; and 3, Philosophy. With modern connotations of the terms, Harris took this outline and inverted it. In its details this system was expanded in the Peoria Public Library version, which is later than the original scheme, but the outline—Science, Art and History—remains the same. A comparison of the outlines of Bacon, Harris and Dewey indicates sufficiently the origin of the last system:

	Bacon.	*Harris.*	
Original.	*Inverted.*	*Science.*	*Dewey.*
History.	Philosophy.	Philosophy.	General Works.
		Religion.	Philosophy.
		Social and Political Science.	Religion.
			Sociology.
		Natural Sciences and Useful Arts.	*Philology.*
			Science.
			Useful Arts.
		Art.	
Poesy.	Poesy.	Fine Arts.	Fine Arts.
		Poetry.	Literature.
		Pure Fiction.	
		Literary Miscellany.	
		History.	
Philosophy.	History.	Geography and Travel.	History.
		Civil History.	Biography.
		Biography.	Geography and Travel.
		Appendix.	
		Miscellany.	

Such a comparison has its purposes in our study. It is true that Richardson remarks: "the system itself is supposed to be in some way an adaptation of Bacon, but the relation is hardly to

---

[1] *Library Journal*, 1879, v. 4.
[2] *Library Association Transactions*, 1882, p. 181; *Library*, 1900, p. 295.

be discovered and it really should be counted as independent." On the other hand, certain points in the order are susceptible to criticism from the modern standpoint, and can only be explained by a reference to its pedigree. For example, the separation of Sociology by five great classes from History to which it is more nearly related than it is to any other subject, can be understood only in this way. Again, in the Peoria classification, Philology is a sub-division of the Social and Political Sciences and ranks immediately before Natural Science, exactly as it does in Dewey; and is therefore separated in the latter system by three classes from its natural partner Literature. The Dewey outline does not seem to be explicable on any other ground, although efforts have been made by various students of classification, including the present writer, to give it a philosophical basis of its own. Dewey selected the ten dominant terms in the Harris classification; numbered them successively o to 9; and proceeded to divide and re-divide these decimally. The folding chart shows the outline and the first one hundred divisions of the classification.

172. Briefly, the classification regards knowledge as unity, which is to be divided into nine classes, and works which are too general for inclusion in any of these form a tenth class, o·o. These are properly written thus:

o·o General works.	o·5 Natural Science.
o·1 Philosophy.	o·6 Useful Arts.
o·2 Religion.	o·7 Fine Arts.
o·3 Sociology.	o·8 Literature.
o·4 Philology.	o·9 History.

The ten units of decimal division are thus reached. In practice, however, the initial o and point are assumed and the classes are written merely: o General works, 1 Philosophy, 2 Religion, etc. An extract from the introductory Explanation to the abridgment of the classification will give the salient features of the scheme in the words of its author:[1] "The classification divides the field of knowledge into 9 main classes, numbered 1 to 9. Cyclopædias, periodicals, etc., so general as to belong to no one of these classes, are marked o (nought) and form a tenth class. Each class is similarly separated into 9 divisions, general works belonging to no division having o in place of the division number. Divisions are similarly divided into 9 sections and, it may be interpolated, sections, sub-sections and sub-sub-sections, without limit other than that imposed by the material to be classified, may be simi-

---

[1] See page 6 of 10th ed. of *Decimal Classification* (1919) which is almost identical with the passage quoted, which is from *Abridged Decimal Classification and Relative Index*, by Melvil Dewey, M.A., LL.D., Ed. 3 revised. Forest Press, Lake Placid Club, N.Y., 1921.

larly divided. Thus 512 means class 5 Natural Science, division 1
Mathematics, section 2 Algebra, and every algebra is numbered
512. Its class number, giving class, division and section, is applied
to every book and pamphlet in the library.

"Where o occurs in a class number, it has its usual numerical
value. Thus a book numbered 510 is class 5, division 1, but no
section; i.e., the book treats of division 51 (Mathematics) in
general, and is limited to no one section, while geometry, which
is so limited is marked 513; 500 indicates a treatise on science
in general, limited to *no* division or section. A number beginning
with o means 'not limited to a class'; e.g., a general cyclopædia
treating of all 9 classes.

"Books are arranged on the shelves in a simple numerical
order. Since each number means a definite subject, all books on
any subject must stand together. These tables show the order
of the subjects. Thus 512 Algebra precedes 513 Geometry, and
follows 511 Arithmetic."

173. The first edition under the title of *Decimal Classification
and Relativ Index*, appeared in 1876, and consisted of 12 pages of
prefatory matter, 12 of tables and 18 of Index, a total of 42 pages;
and of this modest work 1,000 copies were printed. It is curious
to know that it was immediately challenged by librarians as
being too minute in its sub-divisions for the arrangement of any
but very large libraries. The fourteenth edition, 1942, however,
consists of 1,927 pages, including index, a growth which suggests
the enormous number of sub-divisions that are possible, because
literature exists, or may exist upon them, and are necessary when
minute classing is undertaken; and the flexibility of a scheme
which has permitted such expansion.

174. Although the tiny tables of 1876 were too complex for
their earliest critics, who had not yet applied them, the development which followed their use, especially by larger libraries,
brought out the most enduring criticism to be made of them. They
confined knowledge to "the procrustean bed of the decimal tens",
or tried to do so. A great disproportion in the size of the various
classes developed because, by the laws of the notation, every class
number consisted of the digit for the main class, and all the digits
for its divisions, sub-divisions and sections, and therefore was
relatively brief in such main classes as Philosophy and Language
and very long in Applied (or Useful) Arts and in History. The
scheme was of course linked to its notation, was named after it,
and from the first although that notation as we have said was a
class digit, divided by successive digits, Dewey established a conventional base of three figures or more precisely a number divided
decimally to the third place; thus, Philosophy was denoted not by

1 but by 100, Language by 400; when a fourth division continued this, a point (·) was introduced, as at 425·2, to aid the eye in reading. In course of time the development of subjects, and the introduction of what appear to be quite new ones, which had somehow to be accommodated within this decimal notation, caused it to expand in places to lengths which are not conveniently usable in ordinary libraries. Thus, while such a subject as English grammar may be marked by 425, a subject on which the ordinary library has relatively few books to mark, the great subject of Mechanical Engineering on which books are legion begins with 621 and reaches in "Radio principles" 621·3841 which in itself may require many sub-divisions. Such contrasts are common in the subject classes and are all due to the limited initial base of the scheme. An attempt has been made to give better proportions to the scheme in the fifteenth edition, as will be seen later.

175. It has been shown that decimal classification is older than Dewey. He tells us that he is not interested in the priority of its invention, but continues, "extended investigation by others fails to show this most important feature of the system—the Relativ Index, on which all else hinges—had ever been used as here to index by a single reference most diverse material". It is certainly a valuable contribution, and original in the form in which he uses it, but, apart from the facts that no classification can hinge merely upon an index, and no relative index can show all the possible relations of subjects, the most significant contribution he made to classification was, in the first stages, the process of decimal division itself, by which the symbols 0–9 are divided by 0–9 and again by the same method indefinitely; that had not been done before and all notations since have used the method, even when the symbols are A–Z divided by A–Z indefinitely: the method is "decimal" to that extent.

176. Remarkable in their priority were the further methods which emerged in process of time in the D.C. for the precise placing of subjects and their combination and analysis. These were woven into the notation in memory-aiding figures (*mnemonic* symbols) in connexion with the general works class, language, literature, history and geography and most obviously in the common sub-divisions. It is clearly useful if an idea can always be expressed by the same number. Mnemonics have been described in Chapter VII of this book, but a few features may perhaps be recalled and developed somewhat here. There are those that pervade the scheme. At 016, Bibliography of special subjects, we meet with the direction "divide like the classification" which means that the subject number of any class may be added

here after a point (·) in order to collect all subject bibliographies, thus:

016	Bibliography	of Special Subjects.
016·1	„	of Philosophy.
016·17	„	of Ethics.
016·22	„	of the Bible.
016·54	„	of Chemistry.

and, again, at 375, Education, Curriculum:

375	Education—Curriculum.	
375·4	„	Language.
375·42	„	English.
375·5	„	Science.
375·57	„	Biology.

and so for every subject.

176.1. In section 100 the common sub-divisions of the scheme are set out. They were the first, most pervasive, of all the D.C. mnemonic devices. They probably had their origin in the *Generalia class* (000 General Works) of the scheme. That class, as we know, is apportioned for books or collections of them which deal with subjects which either pervade the classification; that is to say, affect many or all subjects, or have in them too many subjects to be confined to any subject class. It also contains such subjects as have a "museum" interest. The outline is:

000 General Works and Universal Knowledge.	050 General Periodicals.
	060 General Societies.
010 Bibliography.	070 Journalism.
020 Library Science.	080 Collected Works.
030 General Encyclopaedias.	090 Book Rarities.
040 General Collected Essays.	

176.2. These usual common sub-divisions have been given a widened validity in later editions, as is shown in Table 2 which appears after the Index to the fourteenth edition. In the main tables ·01 is the common sub-division for the philosophy or theory of a subject; in Table 2 it expands thus:

01	Philosophy. Theory.
011	General conception.
012	Classification.
014	Language.

and so on. The method is carried further in two additions to the table, the first of Viewpoints, the second of Miscellaneous Signs of Relation, thus:

001 Speculative point of view of a subject. Conception.
Purpose.
002 Point of view of realization. Construction.
Materials, etc.
003 Economic point of view. Production. Cost. Selling.
004 Point of view of service and use.

and so on. Three zeros are used for the "Miscellaneous" table, which appears to be in more common use than the "Viewpoints" table. Thus:

0001 Relation (divided like the classification).
0002 Sources.
0003 Administration.
00031 Statistics.
00032 Quantities.
00033 Contracts.

and so on. A single example may suffice to show their use:

Contract for a public park in Surrey

712·50942100032	
712·55	Public and semi-public parks.
712·50*9*	Common sub-division sign intro-ducing place concerned.
712·5094*211*	Added place numbers, Surrey.
712·5094211*000*	With relation symbol.
712·50942110003	With sign for administration.
712·509421100032	Contract.

Such lengthy numbers are more useful, however, for minute entries in indexes and bibliographies than for books.

176.3. Mnemonic tables of first-rate importance are those in Class 9 at 930–999 which are used not only for the sub-division of Geography and History, but can be used throughout the classification wherever geographical sub-division is desired. 914–919 and 940–999 deal with the same countries, but the 91 signifies geography or description of them and (without the 1) their history; thus, in the sense in which in section 78 we define history as a form class, geography is also one. One of the values of this table is that every place has a consistent number; for example, England is always 2, Germany 3, France 4, and so on; and in numbering continents Europe is always 4, Asia 5, Africa 6, North America 7, South America 8, and Australasia and Oceana 9. It will, however, be observed that while places have constant numbers, numbers do not invariably mean places; for example, 5 is used in Science, Asia, Italy, and in many other numbers.

This is one of the most-used tables in the scheme as very many subjects have reference to a place; for example:

England,	history	942
England,	geography	914·2
Geology,	England	554·2
Law,	English	342·42
Railways,	English	385·220942
Birds,	English	598·20942

The required sub-division is obtained by adding to the subject number the place number after 9 in 940–999. Where this can be done is indicated in the main tables and a check list of such places is given in Table 1 after the D.C. index. It should not be done elsewhere (as there is the possibility of confusing numbers for subject sub-divisions with these geographical sub-divisions), except by first adding to the subject number the common sub-division 09 which means that a "place treatment" follows. These two uses are shown in the examples just given.

176.4. *Literary Form Classes.* The outline repeated in section 172, and shown more fully in Table IV, shows that most of the main classes 1–3 and 5–7 are subject classes. On the other hand, 0, 4, 8 and 9 are subject in part and, as we have shown above in considering geography and history, in a greater or less degree Form *Classes*; or classes which may be arranged by the manner in which they are written—often their literary pattern—rather than by their subject. The principal form class is 8, Literature, in which, however, the group 800–809 provides for books which deal with the art, theory, aesthetics and other matters in which literature is a *subject* and because of their general character provides for collections, anthologies and histories of literature, which, although their interest is mainly literary, are too general to go in the language sub-divisions, 810–890. In the groups 810–890 the arrangement is by the language in which the literature is written although, by a quite natural anomaly seeing the origin of the classification, the whole of 810–819 is given to American (English) literature; thus 820 is English, 830 German, 840 French, 850 Italian, and so on.

These are sub-divided by the literary forms: 1 Poetry, 2 Drama, 3 Fiction, 4 Essays, 5 Oratory, 6 Letters, 7 Satire and humour, 8 Miscellany. The complete marking is obtained by the addition of numbers for the principal authors according to their periods, for example:

8	Literature.
82	English.
822	Drama.

822·3   Elizabethan Literature.
822·33   Shakespeare.

The chronological arrangement of authors in this manner is not much favoured in British libraries, the usual practice being to divide by language, then by form and, under that, to arrange works by and about authors by their names alphabetically.

176.5. Literature, 8, derives its language numbers from class 4, Language (Linguistics in the fifteenth edition). Here again Language is a subject as in 810–819, Comparative Linguistics, where etymology, lexicography, phonology, morphology, grammar, syntax, etc., irrespective of particular languages, are placed. The remaining classes 420–490 are devoted to individual languages where again the now familiar mnemonic numbers occur, 2 English, 3 German, 4 French, as already shown; and these are divisible by linguistic forms, 1 Writing, 2 Derivation, 3 Dictionaries, 4 Synonyms, homonyms, antonyms, 5 Grammar, 6 Prosody (removed in the fifteenth edition to 808·1 General literature), 7 Patois, slang, dialects 8 texts for learning the language. These subdivisions with variations are used to divide any language. Classes 420–489 are occupied by the modern and classical languages of the western world; but at 490–499 are crowded all the Indo-European, Asiatic, Semitic, Hamitic, Mongolian, African and the primitive languages. These are developed with some minuteness in a table which is made to serve for both Language and Literature; by the substitution of an initial 8 for 4 any linguistic number becomes a literature number; thus:

499·4   Polynesian.
899·4   Polynesian literature.

and to these literature numbers the literary form numbers may be added; thus Polynesian poetry is marked 899·41, drama 899·42, and thus for all literary forms.

177. The eighteen pages of the first *Relative Index* had expanded when the fourteenth edition was reached to 738, and it had become a vast alphabet of about eighty thousand terms, arranged so that as many relations of the subjects indexed are shown as are useful. The more important terms are differentiated by heavy type and further relations than those printed are suggested by superior figure references to the tables of relationship and combinations which follow the Index, as described above. It is a work of considerable suggestive value to the trained classer but may lead the inexperienced one into errors, but the former rarely uses any index in classing except as a final check. All later indexes in other schemes have to some extent followed the model of this one.

·178. These appear to be the main features of the system. From the physical point of view it may be desirable to describe a little further in detail. Although the order of the outline was derived from the inverted Baconian system, and therefore does not show any modern order of studies or represent the modern consensus or the order in which scholars arrange the main studies and sciences, in the *working out* of each main class Dewey has, at least in part, drawn upon the special classifications which each philosophy and science has approved. The schedules under Science, for example, were, I believe, drawn up for him in the first place by the faculties of his own University. They resemble the order Comte advocated, but only in part; but the result is a series of separate special classifications co-ordinated into one convenient outline.

179. Dewey left actual library work some years before his death in 1931, but he kept the management of the scheme, although other editors supervised the various editions. A feature of the work, at least from the sixth edition, was the use of a phonetic simplified spelling which increased in unlikeness to that of ordinary folk with each successive edition. This did much, I am assured, to interfere with its acceptance by some would-be users. The Lake Placid Club Educational Foundation, which was another enterprise of Dewey's, has cared for the classification during this century, and for some years after Dewey's death, until ill-health prevented, his policies and practices were continued by his chosen editor and loyal fellow-worker, Dorkas Fellows, who produced the thirteenth memorial edition in 1932. This was a considerable expansion of the twelfth in some parts. The revisions, however, were never radical and balanced; its editors made expansions to meet the obvious needs of knowledge, but side by side with some of the most modern schedules, as, for example, the alternative tables for Psychology in the 1932 edition, such obsolete schedules survived as that for Photography. The death of Miss Fellows in 1938 was the end of what may be called the direct author tradition. Fortunately the sales of the Classification have produced enough income to justify the formidable expense of continuous revision; and, confident that the scheme was "an instrument of service to libraries and to all persons interested in the organization and use of knowledge," the Foundation established a committee to be in charge of the scheme in 1937, of which Milton J. Ferguson was chairman and Constantin J. Mazney, formerly of the University of Michigan Library, was editor. This committee had the co-operation of many librarians, and especially of the staff of the Library of Congress. The ultimate aim of the committee was to produce at some future date

a Library Standard Edition. The fourteenth edition appeared in 1942, and in about thirty important subjects considerable expansion was effected, as well as other changes of importance; for example, Social psychology had a new brief schedule at 301·15; the Statistics table 312 was enlarged and better defined; Economics 330–339 was enlarged from 14 to 38 pages; but the most marked expansion and improvement was in 700–770 Fine Arts, where 13 pages were increased to 147; and American History naturally received much added elbow-room. Some sections "which seemed needlessly elaborate" were reduced; the alternative schedule for Psychology at 159·9 in the last edition being absorbed, as far as necessary, in 150. Ordinary spelling was restored in the Relative Index.

180. These appear to be the main features of the system as it was before the publication in 1951 of what is called the "Standard (15th) edition". After Dewey's withdrawal from library practice he kept the management of the scheme and other editors supervised various editions. A feature of the work, at least from the sixth edition, was the phonetic simplified spelling used in it which with each further edition became less like ordinary spelling. The profits of the publication, which were substantial, were employed to further its expansion and revision. From the second edition its users were assured that the main terms and numbers of the scheme would be expanded but would not be changed otherwise, so that virtual uniformity of classing would be possible to all users. The Lake Placid Club Educational Foundation, another enterprise of Dewey, has cared for the classification during this century and has recently had its office most conveniently in the Library of Congress and, from January 1954, that Library has assumed responsibility for developing the next, sixteenth, edition. The last normal edition, if that word may be used, the fourteenth, was produced by a committee of which the chairman was Milton J. Ferguson and the editor Constantin J. Mazney. A new committee with the same chairman and with Mrs. Esther Potter as director of a new staff was appointed in 1944 and was given "the difficult undertaking of modernizing the D.C.". The chairman became editor in 1949. The result of their work, the Standard edition, was undertaken after consultation with the American Library Association, the Special Libraries Association and, "in 1945 the pattern of the new revision was furnished by instructors in library schools and by librarians in a variety of libraries in North and South America and Great Britain".

180.1. The principles that have controlled the revision seem to have been these. To provide only those features of the earlier editions on which general agreement exists; to allow places for those books on which literature exists and to omit any terms on which there is no book in the Library of Congress with the necessary elimination of many terms in tables and index; to modernize existing terms, omitting those which no longer represent modern concepts or practice; to eliminate all but elementary methods of synthesis, rejecting such directions as "may be divided like" and also the extended form divisions, viewpoints and other supplementary tables; and to reduce the notation to a maximum length of five, or at most six, digits. These principles are realized in various ways. The main class terms for 400 and 600 become Linguistics and Applied Science and 700 Arts and Recreation. Class by class such tidying up proceeds. In General Works 010 Bibliography becomes Bibliographical science and technique, 020 Library economy changes to Library science; in Philosophy many of the classes are telescoped, numbers 102-108, 114-119, 125-129, 165-169 and 172-176 have disappeared; the whole of 140 has been transferred to 180-190 and the latter change from Ancient and modern philosophers to Oriental and ancient philosophy and Modern philosophy. Many of the remaining terms have been redefined and some of those rejected have in fact been re-allocated to what has seemed to be more appropriate parts of the scheme. A class by class study of the scheme would exceed the space at my disposal, but in summary there are over 1,000 re-locations of subjects, and in many of these cases the old numbers have been allowed to fall out of use.

180.2. Examples of re-locations that appear to be desirable are the transference of 656 Transportation in its entirety to 385-388, and of Flower gardening from 716 to 635·96, and there are many others that can be justified by modern practice.

180.3. It is in the omissions, however, that the edition challenges criticism. The whole of 914-919 Geography is without place sub-divisions beyond the names of the continents; and the whole of the History of England in 942 has only eight period sub-divisions and three further sub-divisions for Twentieth-Century England, the First and Second World Wars and Post-War England, and then this set of divisions:

942·1	London.
·34	Channel Islands.
·89	Isle of Man.
·9	Wales.

as the whole provision for the British Empire, Great Britain, England and Wales. The rest of the British Isles are given thus:

941	Scotland: Gaelic period to the present.
·5	Irish Republic, Eire.
·6	Northern Ireland. Early history to the present.

These are remarkable in a scheme which is known by its compilers to be used in this and in every country of the world. Perhaps the ingenuous belief of the compilers "that the user does not need to be told how to arrange his collection" is a reason. There is also the declared attachment to Fremont Rider's words, in his *Melvil Dewey*,[1] "many would-be experts in classification . . . have not realized that because a certain amount of classification is a good thing, an indefinitely larger amount of it is not necessarily better. It should have been obvious that the more detailed a classification is made, the more quickly it tends to become obsolete; that the more complex it is made, the more its original easily grasped simplicity becomes lost".

180.4.   The Index, which seemed satisfactory in narrow limits, was not so in practice. A Standard Edition, Revised appeared in 1952 and the index was revised. It seems unnecessary here to pursue comment, as the Committee to produce the sixteenth edition makes good progress and that edition will soon restore many of the features which the fifteenth has removed and, like it, modernize those in older editions. It should be said, however, that the work has been skilfully done. Every placing in it can be justified. It can be used with confidence by a small library or any new library where rapid and large growth is not probable, but, seeing that Dewey's promise made in the second edition in 1885 that the notation then used would not be changed radically in future editions has now been broken in many divisions, its users will to some extent be out of step with those who use, and I think will continue to use, the fourteenth edition. It will lead to many more individual expansions in spite of the fact that the editors warn of their inadvisability. But already a few libraries have adopted the revision and some few others in America use both old and new in some way or other. Although the characteristic Introduction from which most of us learned the art of classing has gone, it has been replaced by a lucid introduction most useful for beginners and pleasant to read for those who are not.

181.   The literature on the Standard edition is various. The official account of the changes made is given in *Decimal Classification, Fourteenth and Fifteenth Editions, Annotations on their concurrent use by the Decimal Classification Section*, published by the Library of Congress. The A.L.A. *Journal of Cataloguing and Classification*, v. x, pp. 3–16, 1954, also publishes a critical account; this and an excellent and very complete study by W. R. Aitken in the *Library World*, v. liii, pp. 299–304, 1951, deserve a word of thanks.

182.   *Criticism and Appreciation*. Criticisms of the scheme have been mentioned in passing in this chapter. A few should be

---

[1] Chicago, A.L.A., 1944.

discussed. That the Bacon–Harris schemes do not coincide with the modern order of studies is admitted, but any scheme of the so-called "enumerative" type cannot move its classes with every shift of knowledge. Tested by the canons in this book and those in Ranganathan's *Prolegomena*, the classes do not modulate into one another and many other faults of order are notorious. Again, the limits of the Decimal base are continuously proclaimed. Its American bias and use of American terms rather than English in main tables and index some unreasonably find irritating, as irritating as no doubt an English classification with its own bias and idiom would be to an American. The most formidable study is that of Bliss, in his *Organization of Knowledge in Libraries*, Chapter X, which attacks the index illusion, the basis of which is the notion that it does not much matter where in a scheme a subject is placed so long as that place is efficiently indexed, a well-known precept of Dewey; describes the inverted Baconian order as unphilosophic and unpractical; the important main sciences as separated and mangled; the notation as ill-proportioned and uneconomical; and shows many other faults as causing confusion which expansions have only increased.

183. No one now rushes to defend the D.C. on the grounds of the modernity of its order or the brevity of its notation. The curious fact remains that more and more libraries throughout the world continue to use it, many of them modifying it; somehow it works. We should fail in our appreciation of services rendered if we did not say that a scheme which has survived for eighty years in ever-growing currency in spite of merited criticism must have virtues which in practice outweigh our theoretical objections. These are its accessibility and the ease with which it may be applied in whole or in part to collections of books and other material of any size, and expanded as these collections grow. Even if the order of the main classes and of some divisions is unacceptable to many minds, there is in ordinary general library practice no obvious necessity for an optimum order, although such an order is in some way necessary to the ideal scheme, which should be one of logical classes in logical relations. Unfortunately all order is conditioned when applied to books, by the size of the books, the physical shape and division of a library into departments and branches, which make it impossible to run all books in one sequence of class-numbers whatever they may be.

184. After a lifelong use of the Decimal scheme, in which I have read and listened to thousands of comments, I am convinced that the oldest and most persistent one comes from the expert who wants all material together on his subject, whatever its verifiable place; it is the most understandable one and the least reason-

able. The notation was and remains the most obvious reason for the world-wide use it enjoys; that is, an international "language" understood by all nations. Some day the Decimal scheme may disappear, as do all human efforts, but now we look forward to the necessary sixteenth edition.

CHAPTER XIV

THE UNIVERSAL DECIMAL CLASSIFICATION

185. *History*. Thirty-six years ago the late Henry V. Hopwood read before the Library Association a paper entitled "Dewey Expanded," in which, with blackboard illustrations, he represented publicly for the first time to organized British librarians the remarkable experiment being made in Brussels. That paper, if somewhat limited, is still readable.[1] Three years later I led a party of librarians to the Musée des Beaux Arts in Brussels so that we might examine in action the work he had described. There we met the two originators of the Institut International de Bibliographie and the Office International de Bibliographie, Senator Henri La Fontaine, in whose house we had tea and a memorable talk with him and Madame La Fontaine; and Paul Otlet, by profession an advocate, who for four mornings discoursed to us with a fluent enthusiasm and clarity which were equally memorable on the organization of the Institut.

186. The Institut International de Bibliographie, colloquially to us the Brussels Institute, was the outcome of an international conference of bibliographers held in Brussels in 1895, the purpose of which appeared to be the search for the universal catalogue which immemorially has been the dream of librarians; a catalogue, that is, which should include every book in existence and every article of worth in periodical literature. It seemed quixotic enough as an enterprise and not less so when Otlet told us—this was in 1923—that the number of books published was 150,000 yearly, and there were at least 72,000 periodicals and, as for the past, the number of bibliographical units, his phrase for books and the principal articles in periodicals, which had appeared from the discovery of printing to the year 1900, was a mere 25 millions! Nevertheless, the conference entered upon the project; the Belgian Government, no doubt through the high influence of La Fontaine, provided funds and so became the first Government to sustain bibliography; the I.I.B. and the Bibliography Office were given premises in the Musée des Beaux Arts, and La Fontaine and Otlet became the secretaries. Later the collections, which became extensive, were moved to larger premises in the Palais Mondial, where they remained with an interregnum of exile in Paris during the German occupation of Belgium, 1914–19, until the Belgian Government were seduced from bibliography

---

[1] *Library Association Record*, v. IX, pp. 307–22, 1907.

by the British promoters of a Rubber Exhibition in 1923, who were allowed to turn out the Institut in order to use the Palais. No doubt in any but an ideal state caoutchouc will oust learning.[1] The work came to a standstill for a while; then the League of Nations proposed to base its intellectual activities on the work of the Institut, so that what two nations failed to appreciate had a chance of being appreciated by the nations in concert. Meanwhile the Institut had changed its name to express more comprehensively its purpose to the Institut International de Documentation; and in 1937 another World Congress, of Universal Documentation, was held in Paris which determined that the Institut should be the world authority on documentation, its classification scheme the standard one; and in order to express the world-range of the organization its name was changed again, this time, and I hope finally, to the Fédération Internationale de Documentation. Therefore if the student meets with the combination I.I.B., I.I.D. and F.I.D., he will know hereafter they are all the same organization at different stages. In later years the seat of the Institut was removed to The Hague, where Heer F. Donker Duyvis, who is also secretary of the International Commission for the Decimal Classification, shoulders the main work of the Secretariat. As I write during the Second World War I am without immediate direct information as to the actual position of the Institut. Such an organization would naturally have national filial societies, and these exist in Germany, Belgium, France and Holland; and in England we have the interesting, active British Society for International Bibliography which describes itself as the British National Section of the F.I.D.

187. *The Project.* To return to the purpose of the organization. The plan of operations was set out in the *Manuel du Répertoire Bibliographique Universel*, the great record of the organization, methods and classification employed, in which is given a synoptic view of the questions the catalogue envisaged was destined to answer; and these deserve translation.

I.—Researches Concerning a Single Book

The information desired might concern:

(*a*) A particular edition (Ex. The 9th edition of Ganot's *Treatise on Physics*).

(*b*) The last edition (Ex. The last edition of the works of André Vèsale).

(*c*) The first edition, or *l'édition princeps*. (Ex. The first edition of J. Mariana, *Liber de ponderibus et mensuris*).

---

[1] So small was the interest in the fate of this patiently built-up enterprise that *The Times* refused to accept a short letter of protest.

(*d*) A particular translation (Ex. The French translation of the works of Aristotle by Barthélemy Saint-Hilaire).

(*e*) All translations of the same work (Ex. All French or Dutch translations of Goethe's *Faust*).

(*f*) All editions and translations of the same work (Ex. All editions and translations of Aristotle's *De Anima*).

(*g*) The library or other place where any work may be found.

II.—*Researches Concerning Several Books*

The information required might concern:

A. *Books because of their connexion with a certain subject:*—

   (*a*) With a science or art (Ex. Treatises on physics).

   (*b*) With a part of this science or art (Ex. Treatises on electricity, works on the reflection of light, on the treatment of tuberculosis, etc.).

   (*c*) With a selection of the principal works on this science or part or on any part of it (Ex. Principal works on political economy, hygiene, history, etc.).

B. *Works because of the author-connexion between them:*—

   (*a*) Works of a single author (Ex. Renan's *Works*).

   (*b*) A certain class of his writings (Ex. The literary works of Taine).

   (*c*) Works in relation to the birthplaces or homes of their authors (Ex. Works of Manchester authors).

C. *Works because of their connexion with a certain epoch:*—

   (*a*) The century as a whole (Ex. Fiteenth-century works).

   (*b*) The century in connexion with a certain country, region or place (Ex. Works published in France in the sixteenth century, or at Tours from 1789 to 1815, or works published by Didot, 1870–75).

D. *Works in connexion with the place where they were printed:*—

   (*a*) Works printed in a given country or province (Ex. Works printed at Toulon, works published in Ceylon, or in Canada).

   (*b*) Works from a given publisher or printer (Ex. Works issued by a particular printer of Laon).

E. *Works in a given language* (Ex. Works written in Latin since the eighteenth century, works in Arabic, Sanscrit, etc.).

F. *Works, because of special features in editions* (Ex. A copy of Buffon's works with coloured plates).

188. A card catalogue (or index) was first determined upon and the international standard card, 12·5 cm. by 7·5 cm. (approximately 5 in. wide by 3 in. deep), was adopted. In order to make a foundation, the entries in the British Museum Catalogue of Printed Books were cut out and mounted upon these cards, as were those of many other catalogues, amongst them, I believe,

that of the Bibliothèque Nationale; and the cards of such institutions as the Concilium Bibliographicum of Zurich. Booksellers' catalogues were not ignored.

189. *Dewey Adopted and Adapted.* The arrangement of the cards obviously required a more detailed type of cataloguing than was commonly in use, wherein analysis could be carried to an almost extreme fineness. Moreover, to accomplish arrangement by subject a minute classification of infinite expansibility was a primary necessity. Such a classification, in order to show such *nuances* as the relation of books to subjects, places, languages, epochs, etc., would demand a series of common sub-divisions much more comprehensive than those in any then existing system. The Decimal Classification of Melvil Dewey was adopted as the parent of the envisaged scheme, and this, in its adapted form, was reaffirmed in 1937 to be the standard classification by the World Congress referred to above.

190. The result may be summarized briefly before we give consideration to the important differences in the "Expanded Dewey," as it is called, and its original.[1] In spite of the interruption of the war years, 1914–19, the great index contained in 1921 over twelve millions of cards. The I.I.B.'s second activity was to create a great vertical file of newspaper cuttings, pamphlets and other fugitive documents, also arranged in minute classified order, and forming a mobile international encyclopædia of gargantuan proportions. Its third was to collect the bibliographies of all countries. There were many other activities, designed to promote standards in method and thereby to increase international co-operation in various directions; but these matters, important as they are, do not concern our subject in an immediate manner.

191. The choice of the Decimal Classification was a notable one in view of the antipathy to the system in French-speaking countries and the ascendency of the system of Brunet. The notation must have been very evident, as of course was the universality of the significance of decimal numbers. The instrument was there to hand, although in its existing shape it might be inadequate. The classification as a whole was taken and examined critically by a large number of specialists, "who completed, amended, rehandled, according to the necessities of their specialities," while preserving the general order and character of the Dewey original. This eventuated in the publication of the *Manuel*, above referred to, which contained the full scheme. The second edition (four volumes in two) appeared in 1927–33, and

---

[1] Its best-known name was the *Classification Internationale Décimale* (the International Decimal Classification), but now it is referred to as the U.D.C. (Universal Decimal Classification) more popularly. In England we formerly spoke of it as the Brussels Expansion of Dewey.

bears the title, which is a good statement of the field it covers, *Classification Décimale Universelle: tables de classification pour les bibliographies, bibliothèques, archives, administrations, publications, brevets, musées et ensembles d'objets pour toutes les espèces de documentation en général et pour les collections de tout nature. Institut International de Bibliographie, Palais Mondial, Bruxelles.* After some divergence the current ordinary Dewey and the Universal Decimal Classification have been brought into harmony so far as the first three figures. As a result the latter is now an invaluable interpretation of the more important features of Dewey; its re-division, additional subjects, and its generous explanatory annotations, the want of which was sometimes felt in the original although the thirteenth and fourteenth editions have good notes, make it a first-class tool for the librarian who uses that system.

192. While the general order and nomenclature have been preserved, the possibilities of the notation have been explored effectively. Two kinds of numbers were employed: (1) the simple decimal numbers with which we are familiar in Dewey, which form the notation of the main tables; and (2) compound numbers consisting of the main table numbers combined with other main table numbers and, where desirable, with signs from the auxiliary tables. The auxiliary tables are not used if the specific classing can be accomplished by means of the numbers in the main tables. In the main tables the "three figure minimum" method of writing numbers which is invariable in Dewey is abandoned for the logical contracted form. Thus class 5 (Science) and 54 (Chemistry) are so written, and not 500 and 540, as in the original. This sets free the cyphers for use in the special system of common sub-divisions which is the peculiarity of the Brussels expansion.

193. There were other peculiarities in the treatment of the main tables which differentiated them almost entirely from Dewey. Thus, for example, in class 900, Dewey's 930–999 disappeared from the main tables, and the numbers omitted—i.e., the figures after the initial 9—are relegated to a separate geographical table in which the numbers after the 9 are written in curves (3–9). Class 9 in the two schemes appears thus:

	Dewey.		Brussels.
900	History, General.	9	History.
910	Geography and Travel.	91	Geography and Travel.
913	Archæology.	913	Archæology
914–919	Local Geography and Travel.	92	Biography.
		929	Genealogy and Heraldry.
920	Biography.		
929	Genealogy and History.		
940–999	Modern History.		

In the treatment of the class, all History is arranged in one sequence under 9 and all Geography and Travel under 91, the local number being given in brackets. Thus we got this perfectly parallel arrangement:

9 (42) History of England.	91 (42) Description of England.
9 (73) History of United States.	91 (73) Description of United States.

And so on for all countries. Later, however, the desirability of using 913–919 for geographical marking of topography, description, and geography itself, was recognized, and these numbers were restored. The geographical special table (3–9) is now used for the sub-division of other subjects.

194. How far and in what manner sub-division goes can be seen from a section of a science subject, External Geodynamics:

551·3	External Geodynamics.
551·31	Terrestrial Formations and Phenomena.
551·311	Sub-aerial and continental erosion.
551·311·1	Facies, phenomena and erosion due to the action of temperature.
551·311·11	Phenomena due to action of cold.
551·311·12	Glaciers.
551·311·121	Nature and origin of glaciers.
etc.	

This example also illustrates the special uses of the point, which is placed after every three figures and is merely to help the eye to read the notation. Such minute division helps users of the orthodox Dewey to define some of the headings in that scheme.

195. The second kind of number is for the minute registration of forms, points of view and relationships in books, and is obtained by means of a series of common sub-divisions, which may be regarded as a development of the notions contained in Dewey's ·01–·09, the form divisions (or common sub-divisions), which lead off every one of his main classes and are applied to many others. These common sub-divisions are reinforced by a series of signs of combination and of abbreviation. The whole table of them is as follows:

Symbol.	Called.	Significance.
+	plus	includes two classes.
/	to	extension over several consecutive sections.
0/9	plain U.D.C. number	numbers in Main Tables
:	colon	in relation to.
=	equals	language sub-division.
(0)	brackets o	form sub-division.

Symbol.	Called.	Significance.
()	brackets	place sub-division.
-	hyphen	special analytical sub-division.
·oo	point double o	common auxiliary division of point of view.
·o	point o	special analytical sub-division.
.	point	used to separate the numbers into sets of three to make them easier to read.
..	dots	replaces figures omitted.

It may be pointed out that as the main tables of the classification are in much detail, many ordinary things, including books, can be sufficiently differentiated by the unqualified use of the numbers in them. Common sub-divisions are usually necessary, however, *but* the signs of combination, +, /, :, ·oo, ·o, etc., should not be used unless very minute classing, unobtainable without them, is desired. The editors point out that unnecessary detail may hide rather than reveal.

196. Each of these signs deserves some further explanation.

+ Co-ordination ("Plus"), / Extension ("To")

196·1. The first, or plus, sign is used when a work joins subject matter of about equal interest from two classes; for example, 622 +669 is the combination for Mining and Metallurgy. Its use is in the catalogue, for of course in shelving books the work can go only under the first of these numbers.

The second / "to" is a connective symbol which is used to mark the fact that such a sequence as 592 /599 covers the same subject, Systematic Zoology. It is an expedient to save writing 592 +593 + 594, etc., to 599. It is of doubtful value in my own view.

: Relation ("Colon")

196·2. Relationships between subjects are innumerable, and this "Colon" represents simply another way of doing what is done in the ordinary D.C. by +, but while the + shows a subject and an added subject, the : restricts the subject to the service of another subject. For example, 31 is statistics, Agriculture 63; the statistics of agriculture are 31 : 63 in the library where statistics is the main interest, but, where it is agriculture, the figures may be reversed, 63 : 31. This is clearly less than the whole subject, Agriculture. Insurance Bookkeeping is 368 : 567·5. The combination 341·63(44 : 45) *Treaty on boundaries between France and Italy* shows the number for International Arbitration, the two countries involved being the numbers in the brackets brought by the colon into relation.

= *Language ("Equals")*

196·3. The equals sign merely replaces the 4, Language, of the Main Tables, e.g., =2 Works in English, =3 in German. Two or more languages are written =00; modern languages 083; artificial languages 089; and the other languages are as in Class 4. There is a special table showing the sub-divisions of language. Examples of use are: Primer of library classification in English 025·4(021)=2; History of Botany in German 58(09)=3; Polyglot Bible 22=00; Dictionary of Astronomy in Esperanto 52(03)=089; The original language and the language of translations are given thus: Aristotle's Politics, in German 321·01=75=3.

(0) *Form ("Brackets 0")*

196·4. These correspond with the ·05–·09 common sub-divisions of Dewey; thus 53(03) is a Dictionary of Physics, 53(09) a History of Physics. They are usually used only in this sort of combination with figures from the main tables, but, we are told, a catalogue "can be made in which all the documents of the same form are listed together"; for example, (05)53 periodicals on physics, etc. In addition to the usual (01–09) of this series, there is provision for other forms, shown as (0 : . . .), for example, 335(0 : 823) marks a novel dealing with socialism

(1/9). (=) *Place, Race and Nationality ("Brackets")*

196·5. These are the place numbers from 930 to 999 of Dewey, with extensions; thus (3) is instead of 93 and signifies places in the Ancient World, while (4) to (9) are the usual geographical numbers; for example, 385(4) European railways, 385(5) Asiatic railways, 385(42) English villages, 385(4221) Surrey villages, etc.

There are special uses of the figures (1), (100), (2), and the two symbols (−) and (=); thus (1) is an indication of situation in general.

196·62. 55(1) is regional geography, 92(1) biographical collections arranged geographically, and the (1) is merely an indication that these subjects are so divided.

196·63. (100) means that the treatment is universal as to places; examples, 9(100) is universal history and, if a work is on several countries or is concerned with them, it is marked as, for example, (44+100), which means France and several other countries treated in one work, but if it deals with only two countries the + is used, thus (45+44) Italy and France.

196·64. (−) indicates smaller geographical units of a country, for example, (44) France, (44−2) French towns, (44−201) Brest.

196·65. (−) is used also to mark boundaries of various kinds; for example, (43−04) Boundaries of Germany, (4−015) the Mediterranean Region.

196·66. (2) is used to discriminate physical features which cannot be marked satisfactorily with geographical divisions (4) to (9); and the numbers themselves are drawn from section 551·4, Physical Geography, when the ordinary use of numbers in that section is not more appropriate; thus, (21) Continents, (210) Areas of the earth, (210·3) Headlands, etc.

196·67. (=) marks a place in reference to ethnological (race) relationships; thus, (494=4) is French Switzerland, (437=3) German Sudetenland, (71=4) French Canada. The caution is given that nearly all these signs, except these special signs, are impracticable for shelf-work and are for indexing and bibliography arrangement only.

" " Time ("Inverted Commas")

196·7. The inverted commas, or "time" signs, are used to enclose figures marking the date (*a*) with which a work deals and, or, (*b*) at which it appeared; e.g., 942"1066" History of England at the date of the Norman Conquest. Dates B.C. have the minus sign prefixed; e.g., (−55) the year B.C. 55. The distinction between (*a*) and (*b*) is made by the order in which the time sign is written; the date of the subject, not of publication, is the classing figure, but sometimes the publication date is necessary. Examples of use are 62"18"(05) a periodical on nineteenth-century engineering, 62(05)"18" a periodical on mining published in the nineteenth century. Years, months and days can all be shown in the logical sequence of year, month and date, and must always consist of eight figures, in this way, "1905·04·03," "1906·12·25" are respectively the third of April 1905 and the twenty-fifth of December 1906. Centuries are indicated by the use of two and three figures, as "03" the fourth century A.D.; "19" the twentieth century; and "194" the decade 1941–1950. Periods other than decades are connected by the /, "to", sign; "1945/64" is the time from 1945 to 1964. Time in general has a dot between the commas, ".": Ancient times, B.C., a dash, "-"; and a plus, "+" the Christian era; and, to complete the series, "04/14" is the Middle Ages and "15/19" modern times. There are, however, many other sub-divisions of time, as seasons, months, days, hours, and even minutes, while we can get down to such numbers as "414·21" which indicates "sunrise," and "5−2," "twice a week."

A–Z Alphabetic Division

196·8. This division simply indicates the use of a letter in the notation to allow an alphabetic arrangement of subjects already specifically classed, or for making alphabetic sub-classes in such cases as games, stars, chemical elements, plants, where it is thought to be convenient.

·0 ("*Point* 0"), - ("*Dash*") *Special Auxiliary Numbers*

196·9. These are, to beginners, the most puzzling numbers in the scheme, but they are quite simple in practice. There are two distinct kinds of sub-divisions indicated by .0 and -. The first must not be confused with the form numbers in (01) to (09). The purpose of the point nought numbers is to narrow the scope of a subject to a particular phase; thus, 53 is Physics, 53·05 Observation and recording of physical phenomena, 537·05 Observation, etc., of physical phenomena. The numbers are limited in use to the particular section in which they occur.

196·91. The hyphen sub-divisions have a wider significance, and where they are to be used, as indeed is the case with point 0, is shown in the main tables of the scheme. If the method of sub-dividing a class is the same as that used in another, or several, succeeding classes, the hyphen indicates this; thus at 621 we get a series of analytical sub-divisions applicable not only to 621 itself, but 621/629; thus 621–1, general character of machines, 621–2 elements of motors, 621–3 machines moved by fluids, etc. Such sub-divisions, where appropriate, are applicable throughout engineering, i.e., to 629.

·00 *Point of View* ("*Point, double* 00")

196·92. This, the other unfamiliar symbol, is used to express a subject when looked at from a particular standpoint, e.g., ·001 theoretical, ·002 executive, ·003 economic, ·007 staff, ·009 moral, point of view understood in each case. The example given in the English edition is the papers of a large British engineering firm which can be arranged from the points of view of accountancy, premises and staff, thus:

62:061·2(42)·003·3 Book-keeping and Accountancy. Here 62 is Engineering: in relation to 061

62:061·2(42) Point of view of premises and situation

62:061·2(42)·007 Point of view of staff

and the British engineering firm's papers which deal with the telephone staff are marked 62:061·2(42)·007:651·374·4.

197. The order of use of the symbols is as they are given in the table above; i.e., +, /, number from main tables, :, =, (0), (1/9), " ", A/Z, —, ·00, ·0, 1/9.

198. The appearance of a drawer of the resultant card catalogue can be judged from the arrangement of the guide cards shown on p. 132.

199. At first view these remarkable symbols give a sense of bewilderment, but their apparent complexity dissolves to some

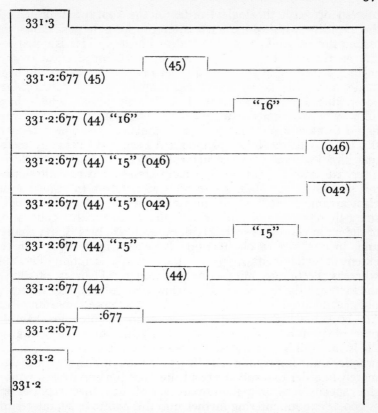

extent when we remember the simple rule that they are never used unless the matter to be discriminated cannot be marked suitably from the main tables, which are themselves adequate, with the addition of the simple + and (0–9) sub-divisions, for marking nearly all books and most other documents. Users of the scheme acquire a remarkable dexterity in their use, and they have that logical intricacy which makes them a joy to certain types of scientific mind. It must always be remembered that libraries, as such, were only incidentally in the mind of its designers; minute indexing on an illimitable and infinitely expansible scale was sought, and has been achieved. The scheme has had its criticism, because most of the arguments as to order which apply to Dewey obviously apply to its extension. It is therefore unnecessary to repeat them. The editors of the English edition, in their general introduction, counter with the assertion that, although many classifications have been evolved to satisfy the ideal criterion that the order of the sequence of the classes should correspond with the logical order of the concepts represented, the rapidity with which such attempts have lapsed shows the assumption to be false and the ideal illusory. This is going too far, as there is no evidence that any scheme accurately and entirely based upon the logical order of concepts has really been made and, this being so, it can hardly have lapsed. More acceptable is the statement that "classifications which have initially been designed to meet a specific purpose are nearly always found to have a reasonably logical sequence. . . . The success of the D.C. in its original and modified form is a testimony to the qualities inherent in its structural order. It is easy to devise alternate arrangements for the main classes, but any alternative yet devised is equally open to adverse criticism in regard to its class arrangement if a suitable standpoint be selected." Undue stress therefore is not laid on any theory of relative collocation of the main classes, as such theories usually are biased and change and, in any case, a classification is necessarily restricted in the extent to which it can represent closeness of association of groups, whereas the human mind is not so limited. There is, of course, the fact, as Bliss has shown, that what were subordinate classes in old classification order may in time become more important than the classes to which originally they were subordinated; for example, psychology in relation to philosophy; but, the introduction argues, "it is impossible to legislate for posterity in this respect", and in practice quite impossible to redistribute the symbols at a later date merely in order to satisfy the condition that the brevity of a symbol shall specify accurately the importance of the subject represented.

200. Without entering further into this controversy, interesting as it is, we may say that the ultimate value of the Universal Decimal Classification, as compared with orthodox Dewey, is its fineness of specification. It is qualified as few schemes are to assemble, sort and identify the most minute material, to show subjects in all forms, physical and intrinsic, in all languages, of all times, and in all aspects. The expedients enumerated go beyond what is economically usable for shelf classification, although since the scheme is merely, as far as three places, Dewey untouched, to that extent it may be applied to the shelving of books. The notation as a whole is too long and complex for such application. This has been the reason, no doubt, why some of its advocates go so far as to say that only the broadest shelf-arrangement is advisable, which certainly does not square with general library experience. The U.D.C. is a magnificent analytic and synthetic filing and indexing apparatus for bibliographies, business correspondence and the more detailed documents, notes and ana of business and the learned world.

201. Its use is widespread and increases. In a list of *Users of the U.D.C.*, published by the British Society for International Bibliography, 1936, it was shown that the specialist publications of 28 British, 12 German, 4 Czech, 4 Polish, 1 Hungarian, 14 French, 2 Italian, 2 Spanish, 3 Russian, 1 Finnish, 1 Latvian, 1 Lithuanian, 1 Norwegian, 2 Danish, 8 Dutch, 12 Belgian, 6 Swiss, 1 Indian, 1 American and 2 Argentine learned institutions applied the notation to their articles, so that these could be indexed systematically, as has been done with many of them in the Science Library Subject-Matter Index. Twenty-one British institutions, among them the British Thomson Houston Co., Imperial Chemical Industries, the Imperial College of Science and Technology, the Pharmaceutical Society and the Science Library, apply it. It was the constant occupation of the British Society for International Bibliography, now part of Aslib, in bibliographical studies in meetings and conferences, as it were, against a background of the U.D.C., which has been its main advocate in England. To such of its members as Professor A. F. C. Pollard, Dr. S. C. Bradford, Mr. E. Lancaster-Jones and Miss M. Gosset, its former Honorary Secretary, all associated with the Science Library or the Imperial College at Kensington, amongst others, we owe much research and missionary work on its behalf. Their writings can be found in the publications of the Association of Special Libraries and Information Bureaux (Aslib) and elsewhere; a few of them are indicated in the Bibliography, but I may call special attention to the brief but most satisfactory account of the classification which Dr. Bradford contributed to my *Introduction to Library Classification* (Chapter XIII). This society, with the assistance of Aslib and the co-operation of the Lake Placid Club Educational Foundation, is sponsoring the English translation which is the fourth edition of the U.D.C., and the first part, consisting of an invaluable General Introduction and Fascicules 1–2 of Volume I, which are the Auxiliary Tables and the Generalities (after all, the most distinctive parts of the scheme) appeared in 1936. The work is voluntary and must wait on the ordinary avocations of the many specialists who assist, and the war has interrupted it to some extent. But it has not disrupted it, and now the British Standards Institution[1] has appropriately taken over its publication it is expected that the project will be brought to a sound conclusion—if a working scheme of classification can be said ever to be concluded. For the B.S.I., Dr. Bradford made and published in 1948 an abridged U.D.C. of great value with all its necessary introductions; and in the same

[1] See Bibliography, p. 332.

year his *Documentation*, which is the best account of the scheme. A new edition, with an introduction by J. H. Shera, appeared in 1953.

Progress continues. In 1948, I learn from a review in the *Library Association Record* by Anthony Thompson (August, 1958, p. 265), the full edition has now appeared, in whole or in part, in five languages, and the abridged edition in twelve. In the same year appeared the *U.D.C.: Trilingual (abridged) Edition*, the works of the Deutscher Normenausschuss (German Standards Commission) and the British Standards Institution, the Association Belge de Documentation and the Union Français de Documentation assisting, the two French-speaking bodies producing the most modern abridged edition in French. The notation, generally short enough to go on book-spines, is set out on each page in the left column and there are side by side columns for the German, English and French terms. There are separate alphabetical indexes for each language.

CHAPTER XV

THE EXPANSIVE CLASSIFICATION OF CHARLES AMMI CUTTER

202. *Its Author and Origin.* Amongst American librarians whose work has been of seminal value is Charles Ammi Cutter (1837–1903). He was, by about fourteen years, Dewey's senior, was a divinity graduate of Harvard College who, after a few sermons, was engaged to catalogue a collection of theological books under the guidance of the cataloguer of his college. The success of this experience led to his becoming assistant to the cataloguer, and eight years later, in 1868, to the librarianship of the Boston Athenaeum, the aristocrat amongst American proprietary libraries, a place which recalls the names of its distinguished members, Emerson, Hawthorne, Longfellow, Quincy and Webster. His life-story, which has been told pleasantly but only too briefly by his nephew, William Parker Cutter,[1] was as undramatic as that of most librarians, and it does not seem that any but fading impressions of a cultured, kindly and thorough personality survive to-day. It may be that much of his work will survive only through its undoubted influence on others, but he was one of the small band who made librarianship as we know it and pioneered the American Library Association. His early recognition came from his almost monumental dictionary catalogue of the Boston Athenaeum Library, 1876–1882, which was the progenitor of the form of catalogue which prevails to-day. It led to his participation in the important first meeting of librarians at the exhibition of educational work arranged at Philadelphia in 1876, to celebrate the centenary of independence, and in connexion with this the Bureau of Education published the *Report on Public Libraries*, a massive octavo of 1,300 pages, to which the prominent librarians of the day contributed. Part II of the book contained the first published edition of Cutter's *Rules for a Dictionary Catalogue*, a work recognized immediately as the treatise on cataloguing, which has been revised and reprinted four times and remains classic.[2] The 1876 *Report* showed that until that time classification was not a common study in America. In general, some account of various experiments is given with a few brief outlines, the only one printed fully, with one exception,

[1] A.L.A., Chicago, 1931.
[2] Now out of print in America. An English off-set reprint of the last edition was published in England by the Library Association in 1935.

being W. T. Harris's St. Louis public schools scheme. The exception is the new Dewey Decimal scheme, of which its author gave a full account, with arguments for subject arrangement indicating that little had been done towards it previously. The Decimal Classification, as we know, was at first received with some doubt as being too detailed and complex, but later occupied nearly the whole field. There were, however, some librarians who, for reasons contrary to those that delayed Dewey, agreed with Cutter when he said: "Its notation would not afford that minuteness of classification which experience had taught me to be needed in our library. I did not like (and I do not like) Mr. Dewey's classification." It would seem at first sight that the arraignment was of the decimal notation only, which was indeed for years the commonest objection taken to Dewey by critics, but Cutter had also his own ideas of order. However that may be, his own early experiments were with a scheme alphabetical in notation, employing the 26 letters, and, on Dewey's suggestion we are told, ten additional numerical classes. Of this he was convinced that it "worked well in the Athenaeum; but no other library was likely to adopt it." He devised a new notation and tried it in the smaller library of Lexington, Mass. A further modification was soon required to make the scheme generally available, and this need produced in due course a slender volume entitled *Expansive Classification | Part I: | The First Six Classifications | Boston | C. A. Cutter | 1891–93.*

203. To complete the brief account of Cutter's life. In 1893 he became librarian of the fine new Forbes Public Library at Northampton, where he built up the library, from the beginning with adequate funds, and at Northampton, after much strenuous service, he died in it at the age of sixty-five in 1903.

204. *The Scheme and Its Parts.* The volume described above is out of print and not easily available to some who may read this book; it will therefore be of some advantage if I quote freely from its introduction the incidental commentaries, as no one has described the scheme or advocated it more cogently than its author. His aim was ambitious: "I have been led to prepare a scheme applicable to collections of every size, from the village library in its earliest stages to the national library with a million volumes." The method adopted was not new; indeed, the Dewey Classification already exhibited it in that it develops the scheme in four progressive stages: (1) Main Classes, (2) the First 100 Divisions, (3) the First 1,000 Divisions, and (4) the fully expanded tables; but these were intended it seems as a progressive way to the understanding and use of the Main Tables from the first application. Cutter carried the method as far as six stages

in his 1891–93 volume, and later to an uncompleted seventh stage.

205. The following passage describes his first classification:

"Divide your books into the following eight sections:

A   Works of reference and general works which include several of the following sections, and so could not go into any one.
B   Philosophy and Religion.
E   Biography.
F   History and Geography and Travels.
H   Social Sciences.
L   Natural Sciences and Arts.
Y   Language and Literature.
Yf   Fiction.

"When," he goes on, "you have got your books sorted into the eight sections, arrange them within each class alphabetically by the authors' names, except in Biography, which is to be arranged by the subjects, that is, by the names of those whose lives are told."

206. This rudimentary scheme is clearly intended for a library of a hundred books or so; but when the books are more than one bay will hold, it is clear that a more detailed method is necessary. Cutter gives examples of how books would stand on the shelves under it, and we find side by side, because they are history and his alphabetical order demands it, Carlyle's *Frederick II of Prussia*, Dickens's *Child's History of England*, Dickson's *Japan*, Dole's *Russia*, and Duruy's *History of Rome*. That is to say, if we want all the books on Rome, we must read through the whole of the shelves, and reassemble the books upon it; in short, we make sub-divisions of the class every time we consult it.

207. Cutter, we have shown, realized this. "The very small library grows," he tells us, and "as a library increases and books accumulate under each section, it becomes worth while to divide some of the classes." In suggesting his first elementary arrangement he gives the hint that quite early class F History and Geography and Travels would need to be sub-divided; as

E   Biography.
F   History.
G   Geography and Travels.

In that brief expansion we have the key to the name and character of the classification. It is not to be supposed that Cutter had merely made an elementary outline for amateur users; from the first he visualized the possibilities of the instrument he was using; and he has shown his regard for them in the notation he applies to this first classification. His seven classes (and one sub-division,

Fiction) traverse the alphabet from A to Y, with significant omissions of letters; letters which he has left for expansion.

208. The name of the classification, "expansive," is worth some repetition. It means, of course, adjustability, the power of expanding to accommodate new and increasing literature, the importance of which it is no longer necessary to emphasize. To Cutter it has an additional rather special meaning, although it is part of the general meaning of the term. In simple statement, the Expansive system consists of seven separate classifications; the first one extremely broad, as we have seen; the second less broad; the third less still, and so on in progressive stages of minuteness. Cutter's recommendation is that when a library is small and likely to progress slowly, one of the earlier classifications should be applied, and as the library develops, another and another of the classifications should be developed from it as required. Thus, according to the compiler, we get a scheme of classification in seven versions, from the very simple to the very complex; the first classification is elementary and fit for 100 volumes, while the seventh may be applied to a library of 10 million volumes—a library, of course, which does not at present exist, but undoubtedly will come. Each classification develops from the one before, and in turn picks up the letters which have been omitted from the notation of the preceding schemes.

209. Cutter's view that we can begin with classification number one, and progress gradually to number seven needs modification. As he shows in the note before the index, one cannot have simplicity of classing in a small library without altering the marks of many of the books as it becomes larger. "But it will be noticed that all the most comprehensive books need no alteration; thus a general work on the Useful Arts which is marked R in the second classification remains R in the Seventh. The general sub-divisions need little change. . . . Only the works on the more limited subjects, and not all of them, need change at every advance of the classification. Still there is a lesson to be drawn from the long lines of marks in the Index. Such a reference as L, 2R, 3S, 4ST (for Arts of Communication) is a warning against the inexpediency of selecting a too simple classification for a fast-growing library. Always classify ahead of your stock of books. I am tempted to say the farther ahead the better." He further hints at this when he advises librarians in classifying to "be minute, be minute, be not too minute."

210. It is in the Fifth Classification that we see the whole of the initial notation A–Z in application; we have, therefore, in that classification all the main classes set out; and this affords us the means to study the order of the system. Cutter has claimed

that it is evolutionary in method. It has been called a subjective evolutionary scheme, but I do not want to lay stress upon such terminology as this; or on the assertion, made, I think, by James Duff Brown, that it is an inverted Baconian scheme, for if it is it has progressed so far from its original as to be unrecognizable as its offspring. Attempts have been made, as already has been done in this book concerning the Brunet Classification, to rationalize the outline, as thus: allowing A, General Works, to stand for chaos, that which contains the materials of the universe, but without form and void; we first presume that man exists. When he becomes *conscious* of existence he may be said to have developed mind, which is covered by B (Philosophy); then the first question man asks himself is that which we all asked our parents at the beginning of things: "Where do I come from?" and man finds his answer in the existence of God, which is covered by Br–C (Religion). Simultaneously, or as an early development, man is conscious of and interested in his life as an individual (Biography); then his life as a member of a race (History); then, naturally, of the place in which he lives (Geography). Within that place his relations with his fellows come before everything (H–K, Social Sciences). After that he turns his attention to the forces which govern existence (Science); then to the Arts that sustain life (R–U, Useful Arts); then, having discovered his origin, and provided for his physical existence, he develops his higher life, through the Fine Arts in all their forms, and he reaches the highest form of his mental life when he records his inner and outer life in Literature in all its forms. Cutter does not claim this sort of thing for his scheme, any more than do Brunet or Dewey with the similar rationalizing of theirs. Such accounts are interesting speculations only.

211. In the sub-divisions of the classification, however, an evolutionary order is claimed: "The expansive classification follows the evolutionary idea throughout, in natural history putting the parts of each subject in the order which that theory assigns to their appearance in creation. Its science proceeds from the molecular to the molar, from number and space, through matter and force, to matter and life; its botany going up from crypto-grams to phanerogams; its zoology from the protozoa to the primates, ending with anthropology. The book arts follow the history of the book from its production (by authorship, writing, printing and binding), through its distribution (by publishing and bookselling), to its storage and use in libraries, public and private, ending with its description, that is, bibliography, suitably divided into general, national, subject and selective. Economics, too, have a natural order—population, production, distribution

of the things produced, distribution of the returns, property, consumption. Fine arts are grouped into the arts of solid—the landscape gardening, architecture, sculptors, casting; and the arts of the plane—painting, engraving, etc.; and the mixed arts, being the smaller decorative and semi-industrial arts.

"Similar examples of logical, or, if you please, natural arrangement, are: putting Bible between Judaism—to which the first part, the Old Testament, belongs—and Christianity, whose sacred book forms the second part; putting Church history between Christian theology and history; putting statistics between geography and economics, since it might have gone in either; putting music between the recreative arts and the fine arts. There are many such transitions, part of them at least, novel in classification. They are not merely ingenuities pleasing only to their contriver; they have a certain practical value, since they bring books together which one may wish to use at the same time."[1]

212. The scheme produced the pioneer logical alphabetical notation, for which Cutter claimed, with some show of reason, that it gave more minute headings than a decimal notation could with fewer symbols. Each of the main classes is marked with a letter, the whole alphabet being employed. Thus, he has 26 main classes, but this claim of more main classes than Dewey is on examination *merely* a notation fact, because a comparative study of the first six classifications shows that there are really only about eight main classes; the remaining eighteen being merely sub-divisions—albeit extremely important ones—of these eight; and, as we know already that the brevity or length of a notation is dependent upon the number of main classes and that a classification with many main classes has a shorter notation than one with few, the Cutter notation must be shorter than that of Dewey. It is evident that in the division and re-division of the alphabet by the alphabet we have in mathematical expression a power of 26^2 as against 10^2 in Dewey for the notation (although its full power is quite unlikely to be needed in either); thus by adding one digit to each of Dewey's 1–10 we get 100 places, by adding a letter to Cutter's initial letter we get 676 places. Of course, brevity in itself will not win our choice unless we are convinced that the briefer notation is the simpler and easier to carry in mind. And it is a moot point whether the mark Vz which Cutter gives to vocal music is easier to remember than 784, which Dewey gives to the same subject. The reader must form his own conclusions. Bliss says that "the supposed simplicity of

[1] Cutter, C. A., "The Expansive Classification", in the "Transactions and Proceedings of the Second International Library Conference", held in London, July 13–16, 1897, pp. 84–8, London, 1898.

numerical notation has rested on unjustified prejudice, and the objection to notation by letters, or by letters and figures combined, have been magnified."[1]

213. The Cutter notation has been quoted as an example of a pure notation, as being composed entirely of letters; but only to a degree is this the case; his Local List—a most important, and indeed an integral, part of his system—is numerical. The Local List which is used for his division of geography itself and of subjects which admit of geographical sub-division may be described briefly. It consists of a series of numbers (11–99) with an invariable meaning, one of which is given to every geographical place; thus

30 Europe.
39 France.
45 England, Great Britain.
47 Germany.
60 Asia.
70 Africa.
80 America.
83 United States.

F is the class number of History; therefore the history of England is F45; G is Geography, G45 the Geography of England; and the numbers may be applied anywhere in this way; the List is in consequence mnemonic.

Examples are

IU SCHOOLS
IU45 English schools.
IU47 German schools.

and

K LEGISLATION.
K45 English law.
K47 German law.

and so on as required. As is the case in Dewey, Cutter usually indicates where a geographical division by this list is necessary or may be used with advantage.

214. The common sub-divisions were formerly provided with a letter notation, but it was thought that a letter did not distinguish clearly that it marked forms rather than subjects, and so the numbers as shown below were substituted. Incidentally, it will be noted that they cannot be confused with the numbers of the Local List, which are not decimal, and begin *after* these form division numbers—

[1] See his interesting advocacy of alphabetical notation in his *Bibliographic Classification*, v. 1, 1940, p. 26 *et seq.*

1 Theory.	6 Handbooks.
2 Bibliography.	7 Periodicals.
3 Biography.	8 Societies.
4 History.	9 Collections.
5 Dictionaries.	

Thus, to give one example, Zq is Libraries and Zq.7 is the Library Journal. It will be observed that a point is used to mark off these form divisions from the subject number.

215. Cutter's summary of the features of the notation of his *First* expansion remains essentially true of all the classification, and is worth a place:

A LETTER, which may be followed by one or more letters — when the class is a SUBJECT (as History, Philosophy, Science, the Arts) or a KIND of Literature (as Fiction, Drama, Poetry);

A SINGLE FIGURE — to distinguish books written in a certain form (as Dictionaries, Encyclopædias, Periodicals, etc.) from other works of the same class;

TWO FIGURES — to distinguish books relating to a place (as America, Africa, Egypt, Massachusetts, Boston, White Mountains, Lake George, the Mississippi) from other works in the same class.

We have seen that as in other schemes there are mnemonic features, as there must necessarily be in common tables such as the Local List, and the common sub-divisions, where he is able to do so without strain Cutter uses the initial letter of a subject as part of the class mark; thus from the Sixth classification

RT	Electric Arts.
RTD	Dynamos, Batteries.
G	Galvanoplasty.
L	Lightning rods.
U	Telegraph.
V	Telephone.
W	Lightning.
X	Power, Motors.

but obviously it is not an essential part of the scheme, is rarely if ever completely carried through, as the example shows, and is merely an additional aid where it occurs to the memory of the classifier.

216. The famous Cutter Author Mark, which has far wider vogue than his classification, was in some sense regarded as a

part of his scheme. It is described sufficiently for our purpose in the chapter on Book and Work Numbers (XXI).

217. *The Index.* Cutter writes in his volume of the Six Classifications: "An index will be given with each section of the Seventh Classification and a full index to all, possibly annotated, will end the work. But as it must be some time before these get through the press, a temporary index is placed here to the subjects named in the first six classifications. About as many more names have been added of subjects, which, though not named, are of such importance and frequent occurrence that classifiers ought to be provided with a guide in their cases." A sample from this will suffice to show by means of a superior figure the place of the subject indexed in each of the schemes and also reinforce the fact that progression from one expansion to another involves uneconomical changes in notation.

Plants	L	^{2}M	^{3}N	
Plastic arts	L	^{2}W	^{5}WD	
Playing cards	L	^{2}V	^{5}VM	^{6}VN
Pleading (law)	H	^{3}K	^{5}KL	^{6}KW

To a certain extent it is relative. It is a matter for regret that the great cumulative index of the Seventh never eventuated.

218. *Appreciation and Criticism.* Any account of the merits and faults of the classification is conditioned by its final incompleteness. The Seventh expansion, which was published serially with separate indexes, in much the same way as the parts of the Congress scheme, was the work of experts, and although some parts saw the light, Cutter died before several important classes had been prepared. Moreover, one of those he did publish was the work of others and Cutter's connexion with it is confined almost wholly to the notation; and, as his nephew says, consisted of the parts devoted to Natural History and were "of a distinctly lower level of usefulness." This fact helped to mar the reputation of the scheme rather undeservedly. In any case, after Cutter's death, in spite of the efforts of William Parker Cutter, the great World War of 1914 combined with other circumstances to prevent its completion. That, however, does not alter the fact that the Sixth classification exists and in 1931 this was in use in about one hundred libraries in the United States. "I know of only one instance where it was abandoned after being adopted."[1] The Sixth has therefore some advocates even to-day.

219. The modest volume containing the First Six classifications is a model of the simple statement to which I wish we could all attain in writing of classification. It proceeds in the manner

[1] Cutter, W. P., *Charles Ammi Cutter*, p. 44.

of an essay from table to table with introductory explanations, clear indications of the compass of terms where this seems useful, and examples of the application of class-marks. If my suggestion that to lay two schemes side by side and to study them comparatively will clarify our understanding of both is correct, the assertion I made many years ago, that the scheme has all the virtues we have premised in a good classification of elucidation and suggestion in relation to other schemes, will not seem altogether vague. I asserted further that "it answers the soundest canons of construction in a remarkable degree." This H. E. Bliss denies, while admitting as "probably true," when it was written in 1901, E. C. Richardson's much more definite eulogy: "It is distinguished as being the most logical and modern in its nomenclature of the recent systems. . . . The painstaking intelligence of sub-division are of the highest order, both of scholarship and method. The author's unsparing industry and unwearied enthusiasm for his scientific aim and the welfare of libraries have produced a really scientific (though, of course, not perfect or final) work of high value." The denial by Bliss prefaces the severest indictment I know of the scheme, and although it would be attractive to tilt at some of his strictures, it would be futile to do so. After all, much of them is the result of Bliss's own more profound studies of scheme-order, which showed that the once accepted division of science from philosophy, which is at least older than Francis Bacon, is no longer tenable, as well as many other things. New scheme-makers will probably prefer Bliss's findings; and there does not seem to be any profit in defending Cutter to-day, as it is improbable that the scheme will be completed or revised and its future is problematical. As we shall soon see, its real significance is that it provided a plan on which the Library of Congress Classification was built. However, to those few who study classification schemes for their own sake, I commend as one of the best of our studies Cutter's own writings on his scheme, both in the book of the First Six Classifications, and in the *Library Journal* and elsewhere.

CHAPTER XVI

THE LIBRARY OF CONGRESS CLASSIFICATION

220. *The Library and its Classification.* For ninety-seven years after its foundation in 1800, the Library of Congress was housed in the Capitol at Washington; and at the end of this period, as may be readily supposed, its collections exceeded by far the space there available. It came into its new and magnificent home in 1897, a separate building of ample and handsome proportions having the orthodox huge-domed reading-room, something resembling that of Panizzi at the British Museum, and ample space for marshalling the various divisions and correlating their contents, which consisted of about one and a half million volumes and pieces, with annual accessions approximating to over one hundred thousand. The first four years in the new building were years of organizing work of the first order. They saw, to quote the *deus ex machina,* Dr. Herbert Putnam, "the collections, formerly indiscriminate, divided into certain main groups and in large part arranged and digested; most of these groups conveniently located; and the physical equipment and personal service appropriate to each determined, and in part provided. They have seen determined also, and initiated into each group, a system of classification which not merely recognizes present contents but provides elastically for future development; and catalogues which, also elastic, when brought to date will exhibit adequately the collections as they stand and be capable of expansion without revision."[1] They saw, too, the establishment of the Library of Congress printed catalogue card, a standard card which could be obtained by all other libraries, and which made the Library the greatest bureau for the distribution of catalogue entries in the world; and, by combination of architecture, cataloguing, classification and an ingenious and effective book-carrier system, the most rapid book service in any national or other large library came into being at Washington. We are concerned with only one factor in this remarkable result, the book classification which came into existence during these four years.

221. The earliest classification as exhibited in the earliest catalogue put forth by the first Librarian of Congress, John Beckley, in April 1802, was *by size,* as might have been expected from a librarian who held also the office of Clerk to the House of Representatives. At that date the United States, as a nation,

[1] Report of the Librarian of Congress for the Fiscal Year ending June 30, 1901, p. 5.

possessed in all only 964 volumes and 9 maps; and the order of the catalogue ran: folios, quartos, octavos, duodecimos, maps. This system remained in vogue until 1812, by which year the Library had increased to 3,076 volumes and 53 maps, charts and plans. In this year the second Librarian, Patrick Macgruder, ventured on a catalogue, the fourth issued, of much more ambitious design, in which the works were classified under eighteen headings which reflect those of a few well-known scholastic systems, and sub-arranged in each by size.

222. On August 24th, 1814, occurred one of those war tragedies which occasionally scar the history of libraries. That day the British soldiery under General Robert Ross—who appears to have been unaware of the existence of the Library—burned the Capitol, and the greater part of the Library with it. At this juncture ex-President Thomas Jefferson offered Congress his private library of nearly 7,000 volumes, a collection which was, according to a later Librarian, Mr. A. R. Spofford, "an admirable selection of the best ancient and modern literature up to the beginning of the present [nineteenth] century." After a Congressional wrangle in which little of the modern American library spirit, but much of the average stepmotherly English attitude to books, was shown, the library was acquired. This collection was catalogued and classified by Jefferson himself, and his *Catalogue of the Library of the United States*, published in 1815, was based upon a modification of Francis Bacon's divisions of knowledge; forty-four divisions were employed and the arrangement of the titles under each was alphabetical.

223. It is interesting to know that this Baconian classification was maintained in the form given in both the books and catalogues of the Library until 1864. Indeed, with further modifications, it was in use until the end of the nineteenth century. The modifications were made by the Librarians, John Silva Meehan, in 1861, and A. R. Spofford at a later period, but their contributions were revisions of detail, involving indeed the transposition of certain classes and the expansion or curtailment of others, and the addition of form classes, geographical sub-divisions, and alphabetical sub-divisions; but essentially the classification of the Library of Congress for the first century of its existence was that of Francis Bacon.

224. When, with the approach to the twentieth century, the Library had reached its high position, in number of volumes as in character, amongst the national libraries of the world, the Librarian determined upon the formidable task of providing his great collections with an entirely new minute classification. Older libraries have made efforts and experiments, but no national

library of long history has yet accomplished the gigantic task of classifying its books according to any modern system of knowledge, or to any plan that the science of to-day would accept. The task is incredibly great, and could only be accomplished by such a fine organization as that of the Library of Congress, where there is a large force of workers who are primarily cataloguers and classifiers, and who have been chosen because of their technical qualifications; and where there are adequate, if not excessive, financial appropriations for the work. Even in these happy circumstances the work has been long and arduous. It is now nearly half a century since the scheme was inaugurated, yet it is still in the making; indeed it can never be wholly complete or static; special committees, each specialist in kind, have it under constant supervision. Classes are revised wherever this is necessary. The former Librarian, Mr. Luther Evans, tells me that the policy is that no class shall be allowed to remain out of print. At the end of 1950 the state of the classification was as shown in our Bibliography at the end of this book.

225. Before we go on to describe the system it may be well to note the progress the Library of Congress Classification has made in gaining acceptance by librarians. The system was designed, of course, for the Library of Congress only—with no thought of its use elsewhere—and the special needs of the Library account for some of its structural features. Nevertheless, when a sufficient number of the schedules had been printed to give a good conspectus of its general character, quite a number of librarians in the United States became enamoured of its qualities, and in a short time the librarians of some of the Federal state departments, of the state libraries, the universities, and similar institutional libraries, began to introduce the system into their own libraries. The movement grew and from the 1941 *Report of the Librarian of Congress*[1] we learn that 221 were classified by the system, in whole or in part. Naturally, most of these libraries are in the United States, but outside that country 2 are in Australia, 11 in Canada, 5 in China, 3 on the Continent, 1 in Hawaii, 4 in New Zealand, 2 in South Africa, 2 in South America, 3 in the Philippines, and 28 in Great Britain. It was first introduced into Great Britain in 1912 in the National Library of Wales.[2] Various academic libraries followed the Aberystwyth example and now 28 British libraries are using the system.

---

[1] *Annual Report of the Librarian of Congress* for 1942, p. 18.
[2] Mr. Hawkes had just been appointed an Assistant Librarian in the National Library of Wales and it was on his advocacy, based on several years of study, that Sir John Ballinger (as he was later) adopted it, although his earlier inclination had been towards Dewey.—W. C. B. S.

226. *A Brief Description of the System*. At the time the resolution was taken to classify the Library of Congress there were in existence *The Decimal Classification* of Melvil Dewey, which long use in not inconsiderable libraries had approved, and the first six expansions of *The Expansive Classification* of Charles A. Cutter, while the seventh and final expansion of the latter was in progress. Both were detailed and equipped with flexible notations, and embodied the best professional experience of that time. Theoretical objections could be offered to the order of the first, but the only obvious objection to the second was its unfinished state. It might have been expected that the Library of Congress would have adopted one of these systems for its re-classification, and no doubt the suggestion was carefully considered. However, the circumstances of the Library were thought to require special treatment and an independent scheme was determined upon. The design was to be governed by the actual content of the Library. This last statement is important, because no other system had been based upon the actual review and individual examination of such a large and representative collection of books. The comment of one writer that "Classification has preceded notation" means much more than the words seem to imply. All schemes have taken their rise from a collection of books—large or small—augmented by the author's knowledge of other books. These were classified first and the schedules made afterwards. But owing to the *comparative* smallness of the basic collection of books it is fair to say, in these other cases, that their structural plans bear the impress of that limitation, and their notations were constructed before the systems were applied to the great mass of books to be found in the larger libraries. In the case of the Library of Congress *all* the books had their places in the scheme before the notation was constructed. The comment quoted does not mean that the staff started the great task of classifying the Library of Congress without having first made a general plan; but it does mean that the plan was sufficiently fluid to permit of reconstruction when experience gained in the preliminary stages of arrangement demanded a reconsideration of the original design.

The *Outline of the Library of Congress Classification* was not published until 1904, which is to say that it had been maturing for at least five years. If the student will compare the original edition of the *Outline* with the latest edition (1942), or even the 1920 edition, it will be seen that even the printed version was not sacrosanct. A good deal of change is apparent in several classes, whilst one —Religion—has been completely remodelled; some sub-divisions have been transferred to other classes and important adjustments made in others. In the *Report of the Librarian* for 1901 Dr. Putnam explained that "The system of classification thus far applied is one devised from a comparison of existing schemes (including the 'decimal' and the 'expansive') and a consideration of the particular conditions of this Library, the character of its present and probable collections, and its probable use. It is assumed that the departments of history, political and social science, and certain others, will be unusually large. It is assumed that investigators will be more freely admitted to the shelves." It is clear from a comparison of the schemes that the books of the Library were first arranged in class groups corresponding to the Expansive system and, as will be shown presently, this structural basis has been largely maintained in the final scheme. Hints as to the general procedure followed by the classifiers are given in the prefaces to several published schedules. In the volume for the Fine Arts, first published in 1910 (3rd edition, 1923) it is noted that "The schemes were produced originally in the Classification Section in the intervals of other work, and have been subsequently developed to their present form by the actual classification of the collection of books in the Library." A still more revealing passage is to be found in the volume for Technology, also published in 1910 (3rd edition, 1937): "In 1903 the original schedules for T to TT inclusive were prepared by the undersigned (C. W. Perley). . . . In 1904 . . . Technology was in charge of Mr. S. C. Stuntz, who constructed the scheme for TX. In 1905 Mr. H. H. B. Meyer took charge of Technology and reorganized the system into the groups 'Engineering and Building,' 'Mechanical,' 'Chemical,' and 'Composite.' Mr. Meyer also revised the schedules for TA to TN with the exception of TH and TK. In 1907 Mr. A. L. Voge . . . constructed the schemes now known as TH and TK and developed certain features of the scheme for TA. . . . Since 1907 the classification of Technology has been in charge of the original classifier, who has revised the whole scheme, . . . under the general supervision of the Chief Classifier, Mr. Charles Martel." Thus it is seen that the Classification as originally founded has not only been expanded to accommodate newer subjects, but has been recast in the light of ten years' experience and always with the actual books in hand. It has been made and overhauled; remade and overhauled again. It is doubtful if any other book classification has been subjected to such rigorous criticism and such careful review. That is what is meant when it is stated that the "Classification has preceded notation."

227. How closely the Library of Congress scheme in its class

arrangement follows the Expansive may be seen by a direct comparison:

EXPANSIVE.		LIBRARY OF CONGRESS.	
A	General Works.	A	General Works. Polygraphy.
B	Philosophy.	B	Philosophy.
Br	Religion.	BL+	Religion.
C	Christianity.	C	History—Auxiliary Sciences.
D	Historical Sciences.	D	History and Topography (other than America).
E	Biography.	E	America General and U.S. general.
F	History.	F	U.S.A. (local) and America outside U.S.
G	Geography and Travel.	G	Geography, Anthropology, Sports.
H	Social Sciences.	H	Social Sciences.
I	Demotics. Sociology.	HM	Sociology.
J	Civics.	J	Political Science.
K	Legislation.	K	Law.
L	Sciences and Arts.	L	Education.
M	Natural History.	M	Music.
N	Botany.	N	Fine Arts.
O	Zoology.	P	Language and Literature.
Q	Medicine.	Q	Science (all branches).
R	Useful Arts. Technology.	R	Medicine.
S	Constructive Arts.	S	Agriculture.
T	Fabricative Arts.	T	Technology.
U	Art of War.	U	Military Science.
V	Recreative Arts.	V	Naval Science.
Vv	Music.		
W	Fine Arts.		
X	Language.		
Y	Literature.		
Z	Book Arts.	Z	Bibliography.

It needs but a cursory glance at these tables to decide that the later scheme is a modified copy of the earlier. The changes are due to the pressure of contingent literature and the need in a library for Parliament of raising certain groups to the status of main classes—Education; and Agriculture; for instance. The adjustments, however occasioned, destroy Cutter's "ideal order," but the resultant outline is not so arbitrary as some criticism would have us believe. If we regard *books* as the deciding factor in our major groupings we have to admit that the association of the classes Music, Fine Arts, and Literature meets that condition. Many books dealing objectively with æsthetic criticism traverse all these expressions. Similarly with the group combining Geography, Anthropology, and Sports and Pastimes; or making Medicine and Agriculture links between the Biological Sciences and Technology, rather than subordinating them under the latter head, where they would have to follow the multitude of general works on Technology. Very few indeed of these general technological books touch upon either Medicine or Agriculture, and inserted among technological subjects medicine and agriculture merely disperse the books that are related to 'general technology.' There is much to be said for the Congress order from the bibliographical point of view. Nevertheless, those responsible for the Congress scheme do not pretend to a strict logical sequence. Dr. Putnam has stated: "The system devised has not sought to follow strictly the scientific order of subjects. It has sought rather convenient sequences of the various groups, considering them as *groups of books*, not as groups of mere subjects." The words I have italicized are important since the *book* aspect should be regarded as primary in a bibliographical classification.

228. The outline of the Congress scheme has been developed with great minuteness; and the method of that development cannot be exhibited by mere description. A complete chart is therefore given of the main classes and principal sub-divisions (facing page 145), to which the reader must refer in considering the special features of the system. Classes A and B present little deviation from earlier schemes in their content, but one novelty in each is worth mentioning. AZ is General History of Knowledge and Learning, and this scheme is the first to provide a place for such general works on the history of scholarship, difficult to place in earlier systems. Later editions of the "Decimal" provide for them at 001. In B the finely conceived Psychology and "Metapsychology" section (BF) deserves close attention from the student; the final subsection (BJ) Ethics concludes with "Manners; Social Customs; Etiquette," which follows Practical and Applied Ethics; this is not only a logical sequence, it is nicely elaborated and enables one to find a certain place for the etiquette of public meetings—"How to conduct a meeting." Class C resembles the Historical Parilipomena of Brunet and is notable only in including Numismatics on the just assumption that coins are historical documents rather than art-work, or material on the history of exchange. D, E and F are the historical classes proper. D is novel in treatment, though not in content. The preliminary sections covering general works and the ancient, mediæval, and modern periods are confined to general works; all other works, whatever the period of which they deal, are allocated to the locality to which they relate, so that under Egypt, for instance,

there is a complete continuity from the earliest times to the present day. In other words, chronology is subordinated to locality, on the quite reasonable ground that there is, logically, no more reason for separating the countries of the ancient world from the modern, than for making a separate section of the mediæval period. Another novelty is that the arrangement of countries is primarily alphabetical under each continent. As an exception Great Britain heads the European series; countries which are constantly associated together in literature and possess a recognized group-name (e.g., Scandinavia, the Balkans) are kept together under the group-name. This, of course, is merely making the classification fit the books. Italy conveniently follows Greece in the alphabetic sequence so that it was easy to place the general works on Classical Antiquity before Greece, to precede both, although it has the slightly odd effect of coming after Germany. As is natural, America is treated with great fullness and absorbs the full notational capacity of E and F, the general works relating both to America and the United States going in E and the books on the parts of United States and the other American countries going in F. Class G comprises Geography, Anthropology, Folklore, Manners and Customs (general), and Sports and Amusements. This grouping, which at first sight may seem curious, is in accordance with modern studies, as exemplified in what is styled "Human Geography." It may be said to cover the whole world, its exploration, scientific measurement and plotting; its inhabitants, their kind, distribution, folklore, culture, customs and amusements. The inclusion of recreative arts is unusual and noteworthy, as is also the inclusion of Prehistoric Archæology, which must not be confused with descriptive antiquities. This class is really the "generalia" of D–F but, as placing it between C and D would destroy the close association between those classes, it is made a link, by way of culture and customs, between the historical and social sciences. H to L comprise the Social and Political Sciences; they differ only in order, and in the omission of the Art of War, from the well-known content of the Decimal class 300–380; the Congress treatment and order, however, are very different and we shall deal with this aspect in a subsequent paragraph. Classes M, Music, and N, Fine Art, call for no comment except that Landscape Gardening is omitted from the latter and appears at SB as a division of Agriculture. The tentative section NF, Photography (as art), has been cancelled, all books on Photography finding place in TR. P, Language and Literature, is a noteworthy example of the Congress scheme's insistence on practical convenience in arrangement—meeting the needs of users. Only the literature of the major or more familiar

languages are grouped separately in a division headed "Literature." The literatures of the less familiar languages are grouped
with the language. Some alteration has been made in the original
design so that the Greek and Latin Classics also go with the
languages, forming a Classical section. This leaves only the
literature and literary history of the Romance and Teutonic
languages forming a separate group as "Literature." Such an
inconsistent procedure is, of course, anathema to believers in
"ideal order," but if it better serves the *purpose* of book classification the adjustment is justifiable. Judgment in these matters of
detail will differ, but experience may confirm the Congress
practice. Class Q, Science, follows the arrangement of the
Decimal class 500, but with the already quoted exclusion of
Anthropology, and with the inclusion of Human Anatomy and
Physiology, which sections lead up to the next class R, Medicine.
Class S, Agriculture, Plant and Animal Industry, corresponds to
the Decimal 630, but includes Landscape Gardening, Horse-
racing, Angling, and Hunting. The great class T, Technology,
is divided logically into four groups: the Engineering and Building, Mechanical, Chemical, and Composite, respectively; Photography, TR, is now wholly included in this class in the "Chemical"
group, though actual collections of photographs to illustrate a
particular subject go with the subject. Quite properly the
comprehensive classes U, Military Science, and V, Naval Science,
which rightly includes Seamanship, Shipbuilding, and (more
doubtfully) Marine Engineering, are auxiliary to Technology.
W, X and Y are unused so far, but it would be a logical development, in view of the comprehensiveness of V as noted, to use W
for Aviation in all its aspects, a subject which is now split up into
small sections in the various cognate classes. The Classification
is rounded off by class Z, Bibliography and Library Science. This
class might as well go first as last; it is comprehensive in character,
serving particularly the interests of the librarian to the detriment
of the student; it is not well developed and the original notation
was so closely numbered that with the latter-day expansion of
library science considerable recourse to "points" for sub-division
has been resorted to.

229. This brief conspectus intends no more than to exhibit the
main features of the system; its detailed working out, in which
some divisions bulk as largely as main classes, can only be appreciated by an examination of the completed tables. Each class
receives specialized treatment; that is to say, the nature of the
material, and its utilization in normal studies, dictate the kind
of development each receives. The classifiers have refused to be
fettered by any overriding doctrine demanding a consistent

method of treatment to each class; consequently the description of the arrangement of any one class will only approximately exhibit that of any other, and in some cases will be of no help whatever. It is necessary, however, that a few examples should be given in order that the student may gain some idea of the general method of development, the variety of treatment, and the magnitude and minuteness of the schedules. We may first consider class J, Political Science, since here we have exhibited the most revolutionary notion introduced into the scheme. It is no less than the application of the "national" method of grouping (familiar in the treatment of literature), conjoined with a chronological development, in complete contrast to the "topical" method so familiar to users of the Decimal scheme. The class occupies 434 quarto pages (Synopsis 19 pages, Main schedules with intervening auxiliary tables 355 pages, Relative Index 60 pages); the main pages being printed in single column with an average of 40 terms to a page, providing about 10,000 places; these are greatly augmented by the application of the auxiliary tables, and the frequent use of alphabetical arrangement of minor end-topics. For instance, the application of the auxiliary tables to English City Government would quadruple the "places" allotted in the printed schedules. The actual number of "places" allowed for by the notation is 45,000. The outline of the class is as follows:

J	Official Documents.
JA	General Works.
JC	Political Theory.
JF	Constitutional History and Administration, General and Comparative.
JK	United States.
JL	British America. Latin America.
JN	Europe.
JQ	Africa. Asia. Australia, etc.
JS	Local Government.
JV	Colonies and Colonization, Emigration and Immigration.
JX	International Law.

Each section of this outline is sub-divided by numbers, and a section taken without thought is as follows:

JC	Political Theory. Theory of the State.
20–45	The Primitive State.
47–50	The Oriental State.
51–95	The Ancient State.
101–126	The Mediæval State.
131–299	The Modern State.
301	Origin of the State.

311–323	Nation and Territory.
325–347	Nature, Entity, Concept of the State.
348–499	Forms of the State.
501–628	Special Relations of the State.
541–561	The State and Social Groups.
571–628	The State and the Individual.

The full tables for one of these sub-divisions is:

The Ancient State

JC 51	General Works.
53	Special Topics, A–Z, e.g., Plebiscite.
61	Assyro-Babylonian Empire (Code of Hammurabi).
66	Egypt.
67	Hebrew.
71	Greece. Contemporary treatises, e.g., Aristotle.
	·A4–6 Texts.
	·A7–Z Criticism, etc.
72	General works: Early works.
73	Modern general works.
75	Special, by subject, A–Z, e.g., Citizenship, Ephors, Federal Government, Suffrage, etc., etc.
79	Local, A–Z.
81	Rome. Contemporary treatises.
	Cicero: ·C4–6 Texts.
	·C7–Z Criticism, etc.
	Plinius Caecilius Secundus:
	·P4–6 Texts.
	·P7–Z Criticism, etc.
83	General Works.
85	Special, by subject, A–Z, e.g., Citizenship, Democracy, Judiciary, Magistracy, Provincial Administration, Senate, etc.
88	Special, by period. The Republic.
89	The Empire.

Finally the compass of a group under modern Constitutional History and Administration may be illustrated by the outline for England:

JN	Constitutional History—Great Britain.
111–125	General works.
128–237	By period.
251–297	Special Constitutional Questions.
	Government. Administration.
301–327	General works.
331–389	The Crown.

401–421	The Cabinet.
425–453	Departments.
500–608	Parliament.
617–653	House of Lords.
671–695	House of Commons.
750–841	Judiciary.
851–869	Government Property, etc.
901–925	Citizenship.
931–944	Naturalization.
945–1097	Suffrage, Franchise, Elections.
1111–1129	Political Parties.

It will be seen that all these topics are part and parcel of the study of the Constitutional History of the country. They are all assembled together under one head and are repeated with more or less elaboration (as required) for every other country; so that the student of the constitutional history of any given country has all his material, general, special, and ancillary, grouped together. This is the "national" method. Under the "topical" method so remarkably exemplified by the Decimal scheme all the books relating to a particular *topic* are assembled together. There may be a heading Parliaments and all the books relating to Parliaments in every country are brought together; all the books relating to Suffrage in every country are assembled at another point; and all the books relating to Political Parties in every country are grouped together in another place. Since the great majority of students study one country at a time in all its constitutional ramifications, their studies are thwarted by the "topical" method of classification, but greatly assisted by the "national" method; only the very small number of readers who are making a comparative study of, say, Parliaments, receive benefit by the topical method. The topical method may be right in Technology; it is wrong in Political Science. The Library of Congress classifiers are the first to recognize the necessity of variations of treatment as between the different classes, and it is this feature of the scheme which has found so much favour in academic libraries. In class H, Social Sciences, the method is more mixed. In the topics where international comparison is the great importance—currency, for instance—the compass is limited, but where the study of the individual country is predominant—Public Finance and Taxation, for instance—the country schedule is elaborate and comprehensive. In such classes as Science and Technology the usual topical method prevails. The order is usually from theory to application and in some cases the more advanced works in pure science preliminary to the study of the technical subject are brought into the technological compass; for example, Hydraulic

Engineering proceeds from the history of the subject, through the theoretical treatises on Hydrostatics, the preliminary engineering operations, and thence to harbour, river, and canal works. This, however, is not a general principle of the system as in the Subject Classification where all sciences, arts, and industries are traced from their bases to their application. It is selectively applied and is the exception rather than the rule. The selection is not fortuitous; it is based upon the recognition that owing to the actively developing condition of the originating science some technicians must be constantly referring to the latest developments. Judgment in such matters may err, of course, but that is not sufficient ground for impugning the general practice. One other example of novel or individual method may be mentioned —the treatment of Literature. The usual method of arranging the substance of literature, so excellently displayed in the Decimal scheme, is first by the original language of the text, then by form, and finally by period. The Congress method is first by the original language, then by period, and finally by authors irrespective of form. There is one exception. In English Literature Elizabethan Drama is separately grouped in its period. The exception is a recognition that Elizabethan Drama is special study.

230. The method of treatment described in the foregoing paragraph (229) necessitates considerable repetition. The schedules have to be set out separately for each country and each subject, since not only would a schedule for the constitutional history of Russia be quite inappropriate to Portugal, the schedule for history of Banking could not by any chance be made to suit the history of Insurance. This has caused enlargement of the schedules as compared with other bibliographical schemes, and has been made the occasion of much uninformed criticism. The practice of repeating the terms for the preliminary form divisions whenever they are required has been particularly condemned. There is some justification for this criticism, though not so much as is supposed. The trouble is the difficulty of devising a set of common sub-divisions which would be comprehensive enough to cover all circumstances. The examples on p. 158 are frequently cited.

Whilst it must be admitted that this repetition could in some measure be reduced by a schedule of common sub-divisions, the frequency with which the schedule would have to be modified to meet special circumstances hardly makes its adoption worth while. It will be seen in the first example that the compass of numbers allotted to the items varies considerably: 1 to 39, 1 to 195, and 101 to 1130; indeed, if the schedules are analysed instead of being merely glanced at there is little correspondence between

EXAMPLE 1.

HA Statistics.	HB Economic Theory.	HD Economic History.
		Production.
1 Periodicals.	1–9 Periodicals.	22 General works.
9–11 Congresses.	21–29 Congresses.	31–37 General treatises.
13–15 Collections.	31–55 Collections.	41–61 Special treatises.
16 Comprehensive	61 Encyclopædias.	67 Exhibitions.
works.	71–74 Method. Utility.	82–91 Economic Policy.
17 Essays.	75–125 History.	*Land and Agriculture.*
19 History.	151–195 Theory: General	101 Periodicals.
23 Biography.	works.	103 Associations.
29–39 Theory. Method.		105 Congresses.
		109 Law and Legislation.
		111 General works.
		113–156 History, General.
		166–279 United States.
		301–1130 Other countries,
		Table VII.

EXAMPLE 2.

H Social Sciences.	H Social Sciences.	H Social Sciences.
Periodicals.	Societies.	Congresses and Exhibitions.
	10 International.	21 International.
1 American and	11 American and	22 American and English.
English.	English.	
3 French.	13 French.	23 French.
5 German.	15 German.	25 German.
7 Italian.	17 Italian.	27 Italian.
8 Other.	19 Other.	29 Other.

them. The treatment is special to the subject; the dissimilarity is much greater between classes; there is no comparison between the theory of economics and the theory of the fine arts. Under HB, Economic Theory, the books on "theory" demand the following schedule:

> Economic Theory
> Treatises, "Systems," Compends
> Before Adam Smith (to 1776/89).
> Classical period (1776/89–1843/76).
> Recent works (1843/1876–   ).
> General special.

all of which divisions are again sub-divided. It is a schedule that could not be applied to any other group. On the other hand, "Theory" under HF, Commerce, requires only one number. The repetition of the language divisions in the second example cannot be defended, especially as in other cases a set of such sub-divisions is given as a preliminary, the numbers only being given in the schedules, as "1–9 Periodicals." This defect has been magnified; it is really a minor matter and merely results in a slightly excessive use of paper; on the other hand, it saves the classifier's time by avoiding frequent reference to auxiliary tables.

231. It is not possible to devise a common table of sub-divisions under territorial headings suitable for all occasions; even where such tables have been constructed they are applicable to not more than half the instances requiring sub-division by country, owing to the diversity of the matter dealt with under the various country headings. Where such a device is possible it has usually been resorted to, but the result is a most complicated system of auxiliary tables. A section of the series of tables at the end of class H will give some idea of what they are like and how they are applied:

I	II	III	IV		V	VI	VII	VIII	IX	X
(100)	(200)	(300)	(400)		(130)	(200)	(830)	(840)	(420)	(1000)
(1)	(2)	(3)	(4)		(1:4)	(2:5)	(5:10)	(10:20)	(5:10)	(5:10)
42	81	122	161	Europe	44	52	281	251	136	421
43	83	125	165	Great Brit.	45–48	54	291	271	141	431
47	91	136	181	Austria-H.	49–52	66	331	301	151	471
48	93	139	185	France	53–56	70	341	321	161	481
49	95	142	189	Germany	57–60	75	351	341	171	491

The top line is the number of the table.

The second line indicates the *total* of numbers allowed by the table.

The third line indicates the number of divisions allowed to each country.

In the text will be found such a direction as this:

HV Social Pathology.
1571–2220   Blind.
              By country.
1783–1796   United States.
1800–2220   Other countries, Table IX.
              Under each

(10 numbers)	(5 numbers)	
(1)	(1)	Documents.
(3)		State or Province.
(4)	(2)	City.
(5)	(3),	Associations.
(6)		History.
(7)		
(8)		Biography.
(9)	(4)	Policy.
(10)	(5)	By State or Province, A–Z.
		By City, A–Z.

To classify a book on the History of the Blind in France the classifier refers to Table IX and finds France is allotted 10 numbers beginning with 161 (Germany is next, commencing at 171). The 161 is added to 1800, making 1961, which is the first of the ten numbers allotted to France. History, as shown by the table in the text, is (5), so that the precise number required is HV 1965. The smaller countries have only five places allotted to them in Table IX, Bulgaria, for instance, is 261–265, so that the History of the Blind in Bulgaria becomes 1800 + 263 = HV 2063. Even this elaborate system of interweaving tables cannot provide for some of the extensions under country headings and special tables, applied in the same way, are given in the text. This occurs almost throughout HF, Public Finance. Similar auxiliary tables are appended to nearly all the classes. In class J they are usually at the end of the section instead of the end of the class schedule. It will be seen that the charge of needless repetition has little foundation in fact, and may arise from an impatient examination of the schedules rather than a study of them. It is clear that a great effort has been made by the Congress classifiers to economize schedule space by the use of tables applicable to a large number of cases, and when it has not been done it is because it is not feasible in view of the special nature of the matter to be classified. It must always be remembered in criticizing the Library of Congress Classification that the classifiers are dealing with millions of books—over four millions have already been classified— whereas no British library classified by the Decimal scheme contains as many as one million volumes.

232. A subsidiary, but not unimportant, feature of the system is the arrangement of Biography. For Biography which does not illustrate a particular subject, whether collective or individual, a general place is provided in CT, where it is regarded as an auxiliary to the study of History, as is usual in other systems. Biography which illustrates a subject, however, is classified with the subject, provision being made for it in all the schedules. In other systems this distribution by subject is usually permissive; here it is the rule.

233. The notation of the Library of Congress Classification is of the "mixed" variety and uses a combination of letters and figures—usually two letters, and figures up to four units. Main classes are marked with a single letter, as

A General Works,	C History,
B Philosophy,	and so on.

Principal divisions are denoted by an added letter, as

BC	Logic.	BH	Esthetics.
BD	Metaphysics.	BJ	Ethics,
BF	Psychology.		

and this is the limit in the use of letters in the marking of classes and divisions. It will be remarked, on reference to the chart, that the second capitals are added arbitrarily, gaps being left for possible intercalations of new topics. It has been said that the distribution of the letters in the main classes in no way shows the subordination of subjects, but this is a needless comment. The classes themselves are not subordinate, they are parallel except in the case of D, E and F. Political Science, J, is not subordinate to the Social Sciences, H, it is a parallel class of cognate affinity; similarly Law, K, and Education, L. The same is to be said of the divisions within the main classes. Whilst TH, Building Construction, is subordinate to the class T, Technology, it is not subordinate to any of the other divisions of T; all the divisions of Technology denoted by letters are parallel subordinates to the class T. The combination of two letters makes for an excellent and directive symbol for all the great sections of knowledge. It is very useful to be able to direct inquirers to such groups by clear labels. "You will find books on Painting at ND"; "Domestic Science you will find marked TX"; "Socialism—in HX"; and so on. It is noteworthy that the first completed schedule to be published, Z—Bibliography, is numbered right through without sub-letter divisions and proves highly inconvenient for direction.

234. Further sub-division is secured by the use of Arabic numerals read arithmetically, beginning at 1 in each of the main divisions. A few examples will illustrate:

TA	Engineering		TC	Hydraulic Engineering.
	Periodicals and Societies.		353	Sea Locks.
1	American and English.		355	Docks.
2	French.		357	Piers, etc.
3	German.		361	Dry-Docks.
4	Other.		363	Floating docks.
5	Congresses.		365	Other special docks.
		TH	Building.	
		7561	Steam heating, general works.	
		7562	Pocket-books.	
		7563	Specifications, etc.	
		7565	Theory.	

Two letters and four figures are the common *limit* of the length of the notation, though this is sometimes expanded by alphabetic or other sub-division, but the majority of the places in the schedules fall between one and three figures. The numbering is rarely continuous; even where there is little anticipation of further intercalation one or two places are usually left for future use. Where developments may reasonably be expected the numbering is wide open, and usually there are substantial gaps between the sections.

235. The notation does not end here, however, as one of the features of the Congress scheme is the frequent use of alphabetizing for the end-topics of a group. Turning back to the third illustration in section 229, the reader will find a number of typical

instances of this usage. It is a device used with great effect throughout the scheme. Excellent examples will be found in Q and T; here are a few instances:

QD	Chemistry.	QK	Botany.
	Metals.	881	Metabolism.
171	General works.	882	Photosynthesis.
172	By groups, A–Z.	887	Formation of new organic matter.
181	Special topics, A–Z.	891	Respiration.
		896	Fermentation.
		898	Special Plant Products, A–Z.

TL	Aeronautics.	TS	Manufactures.
	Airships.		Leather.
650	General works.	1045	Imitation Leathers.
654	Special projects to 1900, A–Z.	1047	Special, A–Z.
658	Special makes, A–Z.		
659	Individual ships, A–Z.		

An example from N, Fine Arts:

ND Painting,
Illuminating, etc.

3375	Missals.
3380	Other service books.
3385	Other religious books.
3390	Cartularies.
3395	Classical authors, A–Z.
3399	Other similar works, A–Z.

The method has been used with enterprise and discretion and combines great expansibility with ease in "finding." It is a method that might be adopted with advantage in other systems. Where the numbering has been unwisely close and an alphabetical arrangement is unsuitable, further sub-division is gained by the use of the point, thus:

QL Zoology.
Fishes.

638	Teleostei.
.1	Cyclomstomi.
.2	Dipnoi.
.3	Ganoidei.
etc.	

In addition to the tables described in section 232, there are also special geographical tables alphabetically arranged. These are notably to be found in G, H, T, U and V. We give a simple form:

Abyssinia	A2	Argentine	
Afghanistan	A3	Republic	A7
Algeria	A4	etc.	

They are used after a point for dividing subjects according to the direction in the schedules: "local, A—Z" or "by country, A—Z." The symbols have not a constant meaning; thus in three separate alphabeting tables A8 may mean Australia or Arkansas, A2 may mean Abyssinia or Alabama. There is frequently a double system of alphabeting in which the use is equally arbitrary, although there is no difficulty since the list is usually set out where it is required. Other instances of the arbitrary use of letter sub-division occur throughout the scheme, either to bring general or official works at the head of the series, or to bring important aspects into prominence; thus at HJ Customs and Tariffs, 6015 is German Tariff Acts, which is sub-divided:

	Serial Collections.
.A1–2	Imperial.
.A21–4	States, by date.
.A41–59	Non-Official, by editor.

	Other Collections.
.A6	Imperial, by date.
.A62–79	States, by date.
.A8–Z	Non-Official, by editor.

At HJ 6082 we have "Texts in foreign languages issued by foreign governments" which is divided as

.A2	British.	.A5	Spanish.
.A3	French.	.A6–Z	Other, A–Z.
.A4	German.		

Nothing is gained by quoting further instances, since these arbitrary symbols are only applied to very exclusive documentary material and although the method seems to loom large in the schedules it is infrequent in practice.

236. The indexing of the system leaves little to be desired. Each class, as far as published, is equipped with its separate index. This is of the relative variety, and when, as it is hoped will be the case, these indexes are cumulated finally, the result will be an instrument of great value. A sample of its method must be given:

Automobiles	TL 1–290
Alcohol	TL 217
Auto-trucks	TL 230
Automobile trains	TL 235
Biography	TL 139–40
Catalogues	TL 160, 200–29
Collections	TL 8
Compressed Air	TL 225
Congresses	TL 6

Design, construction	TL 9
Electric	TL 220
Endurance tests	TL 290
Essays, etc.	TL 155
Exhibitions	TL 7
Gasoline	TL 205–15
History	TL 15–125
Law	HE 5619–5720
Patents	TL 280
Periodicals	TL 1–4
Steam	TL 200
Tables	TL 151
Pocket Books	
Tyres	TL 270
Treatises	TL 144–5
Year Books	TL 5

It is scarcely possible to imagine an index carried to greater fulness.

237. *Criticism and Appreciation.* The theorist, with a determined set of canons for the guiding of the judgment, in considering the Library of Congress Classification, is confronted at the outset by the declared intentions of the designers. These have been modestly stated, far too modestly for the colossal nature of the task undertaken and the resultant achievement. We have already quoted from these pronouncements in sections 226 and 227, from which it must be clear to the student that the scheme is fundamentally pragmatic and is not open to assessment along the usual lines. Scientific theory requires that a classification shall be a microcosm of all knowledge, an atlas of the field of learning in which all the territories are clearly defined and their relations affirmed; but when the theory is applied to book classification it is immediately conditioned by two further considerations—the manner in which knowledge is related in books and the facility with which that knowledge is made available to the users of books. It is the user's point of view that has primarily to be kept in mind, for it is for his benefit that the books are classified. It is for this reason that the searching criticism of the Congress scheme, based on theories of the relationship of the several parts of knowledge, which Mr. Bliss has given it in his treatise on *The Organization of Knowledge in Libraries* (pp. 248–50) seems to fail. It is said that the main classes as a whole do not modulate into one another. They certainly have not the same complete consistency displayed by the sequence of the Expansive, yet it can be said that some of the changes made by the Congress classifiers in adapting the basis of the Expansive actually improve the sequence. This is noted in section 227. But the criticism is of

small value. Since the total number of books classified (or to be classified) approaches five million volumes, each of the eighteen classes contains more books than the majority of great libraries. The modulation of the classes is, therefore, of no great moment. Even Mr. Bliss is constrained to admit that the "six classes Q to V are well grouped and are, for the most part, well sub-divided." We are inclined to make the same comment of the æsthetic group, M to P. To admit, however, that the scheme in reality is a series of large special classifications is not a disparagement in view of its immense size and compass. One man designed the general outline and supervised the working out of the schedules, but that working out was accomplished by specialists in the various classes, and in the result they have produced a remarkably cohesive whole.

238. Without withdrawing any one of the requirements laid down in our canons, we have to admit the very practical answer of the compilers, an answer not urged in words, but in the little less than glorious fact that this classification is no unimportant factor in the wonderfully rapid service of the Library of Congress, which is equalled by no other library of a similar size in the world. Any criticism of the scheme from the academic standpoint is corrected by its accomplishment. A feature which has been much criticized is the alleged inflation of the tables by repetition. This we have shown is largely imaginary. It arises out of the extreme minuteness to which the classification is carried, which entails a good deal of repetition in order to introduce the frequent variation which minute detail involves. This minuteness must not be regarded as a fault, since it is the everyday experience of classifiers that the most minute tables yet produced are not sufficiently minute for every purpose to which bibliographical classification may be put. One would suppose, for instance, that the Congress class, R, Medicine, would be detailed enough for medical libraries; yet this does not seem to be the experience. Mary Louise Marshall and Irene Jones, writing on classification in medical libraries,[1] referring to the Congress scheme, state that: "Medical libraries using this system report need for expansion in sections of pharmacology, psychiatry, therapeutics, biological chemistry, and industrial medicine." Some idea of the minuteness of this system may be gained from a consideration of the fact that thirty-one places are provided for editions of a single work of Thomas Paine, *The Rights of Man*, which form part of a special table of Paine at JC 177. As it stands the system is unlikely to be adopted by many libraries of less proportions than those of

---

[1] (American) Medical Library Association: a Handbook of Medical Library Practice, 1943, p. 153, Chicago, A.L.A.

our great cities. Yet minuteness of schedule need be no deterrent. Nothing is lost because your library would only use a tenth (or less) of the registered places. Smaller libraries, for instance, would reduce the Paine numbers to the ordinary proportions. It so happens that the Congress Library possesses the greatest Paine collection in the world—an exhaustive collection; other libraries using the scheme would just ignore the schedule. On the other hand, it provides a useful model for the special author collections to be found in other large libraries.

239. The notation has received a fair share of criticism, and not without reason. Its greatest weakness lies in the inability of the notation to demonstrate the descent of the hierarchy. No "arithmetical" notation can do this; yet it is certainly simple and, on the whole, brief. It is not fair to exhibit a few extreme examples which show great length or complexity, for such are rare, although inevitable, in a scheme providing for such minutiæ as the Library of Congress does. Imagine any town "local collection" expanded to national proportions—a nation comprising about fifty separate states—and one gains some idea of the minutiæ embraced by the Congress Library. We can say, then, that the notation as a whole is brief, and in the opinion of those who have used it for years it is apt and handy.

240. A feature of the system, and one which makes for great usefulness even to those who will never use the scheme as a working classification, is the excellence of the terms chosen for the headings, and the fullness with which they are set out. In some parts of the system, too, as, for example, freely in the America schedules, definitions are given of the sense in which the headings are used. A practical classifier, who has felt the want of what may be called annotations of the terms in the Decimal and other classifications, can only express gratitude. These America definitions run to pages of letterpress in places. Owing to the detail included, caption and hierarchy indentation are not always as clear as one could desire, but this again is a minor matter, and criticism of the scheme on this account is—shall we say?—"captious!"

241. We have already expressed our opinion that the system is not likely to be adopted except by libraries of large size, yet it is clear that it is growing in popularity. It has a distinct vogue in America with federal, state, departmental, and university libraries. A complete list of the libraries using it is given in the 1937 *Report of the Librarian of Congress*, supplemented by an additional list in the 1941 *Report*. It would be very natural for it to be used in part by American libraries, since the tables on America, for example, with the admirable definitions to which reference

has already been made, form in many ways the fullest, as in some ways they are the ideal, classification of the country. Again, the fact that the schedules on America, as well as most of the others, have already reached a third edition, and one or two even a fourth, shows that an extensive use has been made of them. In the United Kingdom the system is now fairly well known, though it is still regarded by some librarians as a gargantuan scheme far too complex for general application. It has evoked much interest since, as mentioned in section 225, Sir John Ballinger decided to adopt it for the new National Library of Wales; Mr. A. J. Hawkes introduced it into the Wigan Reference Library in 1920, and later Mr. Ernest A. Savage adopted it for the Edinburgh Public Libraries and Mr. B. M. Headicar used it in a modified form at the British Library of Political Science; since then it has been widely adopted, and at the moment of writing twenty-eight or thirty British libraries are making use of the scheme. The general verdict is that it is easy to apply and effective in use.

241.1. Whatever may be the future of the system in Great Britain, it is really a remarkable achievement. It is not the first time that an attempt has been made to apply minute systematic classification to a very great library; the late E. A. Nicholson attempted it for additions at the Bodleian. It is the first time, however, that such a scheme has been gradually built up and published as it advanced. To experiment, and to publish the results, is a daring and an invaluable work; and, if the results fail in places to meet some critical tests the achievement is undoubted. The scheme has now been applied to over four million works, and every day is adding to it new parts and new usefulness. The completion of the tables is not far distant; and with that may come a further study and understanding of the greatness of the work. Meanwhile some conception of its aim and its difficulties may be gained from the words of the former Chief Classifier, Mr. Charles Martel, which in the nature of an apologia justify the experiment, but are sufficient to warn librarians with smaller resources from attempts at imitation.

"It has been the endeavour from the beginning to incorporate in the classification scheme the results of the experience gained both in the first application of the schedules in reclassification and in later continued use in classifying new books. A certain ideal was kept in view, but it was a practical one. The ambition was to make the best of an unrivalled opportunity and to produce a classification in which the theory and history of the subjects as represented in a great collection of books should constitute the principal basis for the construction of the Scheme, compared and combined of course with their presentations as derived from other classifications and treatises. It was recognized beforehand and confirmed over and over again in the course of the undertaking that no amount of preliminary study, consultation, and taking pains in the preparation of the provisional draft could produce other than a largely theoretical scheme, more or less inadequate and unsatisfactory until modified in application. A clearer and wider view of many a problem provisionally disposed of would often present itself as class after class was conscientiously worked over, discovering new aspects and relations of certain subjects or the same relations in a different light and making it desirable and sometimes necessary to revise an earlier and adopt a better solution. It may be admitted that with all the effort spent in improving the schemes in the light of further experience, an approach to the ideal in mind has been realized if at all only in a slight and imperfect degree. On the other hand, that degree might have been advanced materially if printing could have been postponed until all the schedules were completed. Many omissions, imperfections, and inconsistencies might have been eliminated if there had been more time. The responsibility for some of these may be laid in part at least upon the hindrances incidental to the conditions under which the work had to be carried out that the other service of the Library might not be unduly interfered with. Whether the principle adopted and the manner and extent of its application were in the line of progress remains perhaps for the future to demonstrate. That the attempt has succeeded in some measure is indicated, I think, by several communications which have reached us from the outside with regard to the classification, in which that element is commended and recognized as more or less distinctive of the Library of Congress System."[1]

[1] Report of the Librarian of Congress for the Fiscal Year ending June 30, 1911, pp. 61–62.

CHAPTER XVII

THE SUBJECT CLASSIFICATION OF JAMES DUFF BROWN

242. *The Subject Classification* of James Duff Brown is a British classification designed for British libraries in response to the frequent, not very reasonable, complaint which in the 'nineties had some currency that the Dewey scheme gave too great prominence to American matters. Its author was one of the leading figures in librarianship of his own or any age. I have prefaced the third edition of his *Manual of Library Economy* with a brief memoir of this interesting, fertile, and industrious personality. Here it is enough to say that James Duff Brown (1862–1914) occupied a place in British librarianship equivalent to that held by Dewey in American. He was trained in the Glasgow Public Libraries; showed very early that he possessed originality, daring, and industry; educated himself; published a musical dictionary and edited a history of Scotland when he was barely out of his 'teens, and in various ways displayed unusual talents, if not, on the whole, very dramatic ones. He became Librarian of the Clerkenwell Public Library in 1888, and made a reputation when he introduced there the open-access system, with safeguarded methods. Some of us are old enough to remember the controversy to which this innovation led. It seemed that if one allowed readers in to the shelves to choose their books one was in some way immoral and dishonest and actively injurious to the State. The matter seems laughable now; it was real enough then.

243. A library can be worked in a crudely imperfect manner without classification as we understand it in shelves or catalogues so long as readers are not admitted to the shelves. On the other hand, it is essential in open-shelf libraries that the books be classified. Naturally, then, Brown turned his attention to the study of classification. At this time, the early 'nineties, close classification, to quote Brown, has "not often been adopted in Britain save in the case of a few reference libraries, and where the decimal system of Mr. Dewey has been applied." Little was known of the Dewey scheme in any case; certainly for lending departments none of the larger libraries had adopted it; in fact, their librarians were either afraid or contemptuous; it was, as before noted, too American, and certainly too complex. This view may or may not have been shared by Brown. I know he was no lover of the classification in later years, although he admitted that it had its merits; but I also know that he was a

man who would take a line of his own rather than follow others; a dangerous attitude for most men, but in his case having its uses.

244. He made the first scheme that bears his name in collaboration with John Henry Quinn, then the Librarian of Chelsea, and he laid it before the Belfast Meeting of the Library Association in 1894.[1] The Quinn-Brown Classification, as it was called, was that used in the library in which I was trained, and I can say that it is useful enough in a small library, but inadequate for one of even moderate size. It had the following classes: A Religion and Philosophy, B History, Travel and Typography, C Biography, D Social Science, E Science, F Fine and Recreative Arts, G Useful Arts, H Language and Literature, J Poetry and Drama, K Fiction, L General Works. This notation had divisions numbered 1, 2, 3, etc., with a few alphabetical sub-divisions in some of the classes. In fact, it soon proved to be inadequate, and in 1897 Brown published a second scheme which departed considerably from the first scheme, named the *Adjustable Classification*. This had a proper notation, and was indexed. The main classes resembled those in the Quinn-Brown system, but were in slightly different sequence, and the numerical notation was a simple arithmetical one with numbers left vacant to permit of insertions. This classification was adopted for the time being by many libraries, Hornsey, Croydon, and of course Finsbury, amongst them. But any classification, the notation of which provides for new subjects merely by leaving vacant numbers, is certain to break down sooner or later, if only on that ground; and this proved to be so here. Meanwhile, the Dewey system was gaining a gradual but firm hold upon British libraries, and provoked by the American bias, inequalities and other now admitted faults of that scheme, and perhaps even more by his ambition to produce an obvious British system, Brown set about the compilation of an entirely new scheme, the *Subject Classification*,[2] which he gave to the world in its first edition in 1906. A second edition was published in 1914, the alterations in which are useful but of no radical importance; and a third after twenty-six years of experiment and application appeared in 1940, with many useful additions, but still retaining every feature that Brown devised or adopted.

245. This third edition showed the vitality of the scheme, and that it had a certain vogue in this country. Although it has not been applied in a great library, such substantial municipal

[1] Classification of Books for Libraries in which Readers are allowed Access to the Shelves. *The Library*, v. 7, pp. 75–82, 1895.
[2] Ed. 1, the Library Supply Co.; Eds. 2 and 3, Grafton and Co.

libraries as those of its birthplace, Islington, and Hornsey, Bethnal Green, Rochdale, and Bournemouth, which have an average stock of 100,000 volumes, testify that it meets their needs. The scheme, therefore, must be described and considered. Brown produced it almost single-handed, although he had much help from his nephew and fellow-librarian, James Douglas Stewart, who has now edited the third edition; and it was thought in 1914 that it would in all probability be the last of the important classifications to be made by one man. Modern knowledge seemed to be too wide and complex for a really satisfactory classification to be so made; even the Dewey classification was in its schedules the work of a university college faculty, and its revisions were carried out by committees rather than by Dewey himself. To-day this view is challenged by Ranganathan and Bliss, who have both produced what appear to be individualistic schemes. It is not to be assumed that any of them, however, has neglected to avail himself of the critical suggestions of experts. Of Brown this is to be said: it is based on a personal theory; one that is attractive, and, as the sequel has proved, one that other librarians have felt able to adopt and to develop.

246. The compiler was modest enough in his claims. He wrote that he had attempted to provide "a simple, fairly logical, and practical method" for British libraries. Its attractions are that it is well-proportioned, simple, and, up to a point, effective. It can be grasped without protracted study, and it is prefaced with an introduction, written with sterling common sense, and embodying useful classification hints and decisions.

247. On the surface it fulfils all the requirements of a practical classification. It has a generalia class, form classes and divisions, a clear, brief, and simple notation, and an index. Of each of these I shall have something to say, but it is the logical basis of the scheme that ought first to compel the attention of students of classification.

It begins with the postulate that every science and art springs from some definite source, and in the basic outline a serial development of being is assumed. In the order of things there were first the factors of Matter and Force, which gave rise to Life, and Life in time produced Mind, which in turn reached at length the making of its Record. Allowing, as all schemes must, a Generalia class—somewhat different here from that in other systems—we thus get the base with the divisions of which it is formed:

> *Generalia.*
> *Matter and Force.*
> Physical Sciences.

Life.

Biological Science.
Ethnological and Medical Sciences.
Economic Biology.

Mind.

Philosophy and Religion.
Social and Political Science.

Record.

Language and Literature.
Literary Forms.
History, Geography, and Biography.

248. In the sense that the outline is developmental it may be called evolutionary, so long as the word is applied in its simple dictionary sense of a progression from simple to complex things. Bliss says it crudely resembles in part the order of the sciences. That it is a true record of the history of the development of things, or one widely accepted, was not claimed by Brown; but that it is an attractive plotting out of a possible order will not be denied.

249. The theory that every science or art springs from a definite source is applied to its extreme logical conclusion in many subjects with a consistency which becomes embarrassing. The root science is shown and then in one sequence is followed to all its possible applications. He writes: "The divisions seen in most classifications in vogue—Fine Arts, Useful Arts, and Science— are examples of the arbitrary separation of closely related subjects"; and goes on to declare that "as the systematization of science and teaching improves, the separation between physical basis and practical application, hitherto maintained, will no longer be insisted upon." An order of "scientific progression" is therefore used, applications which are derived from a science or other base being placed as so derived. "Composite applications of theory have been placed with the nearest related group, and, as a general rule, all through the classification the endeavour has been to maintain a scheme of one subject, one place." We have thus, to quote examples only, in B, C, D, Physical Sciences:

Cooo   Electricity and Magnetism.
  001   Electricity alone.
  002   Electro-dynamics, etc.
  030   Magnetism.
  050   Electrical Engineering.
  051   Dynamos.
  070   Wiring and Switches.

and

C100	Optics (light).
101	Wave theory.
120	Colour.
140	Illumination—Artificial Lighting.
141	Lamps.
152	Telescopes.
170	Microscopy.
173	Microscopes.

and

C200	Heat.
201	Combustion.
206	Ovens.
210	Boilers.
215	Chimneys.
216	Chimney stacks.
217	Steeple jacks.
218	Fireplaces.
225	Fire producers.
230	Fire extinction.
231	Fire engines.
260	Thermodynamics.
270	Steam engines.
280	Stationary engines.
281	Locomotives.

and

C300	Acoustics (Sound).
C400	Music.
C500	Vocal Forms.
C510	Choir Training.

and this remarkable placing of Music is immediately followed by Astronomy. Somewhat similarly, Physiography leads through Physiography proper to Meteorology, then to Storms, thence to Pneumatic engines, Aerial engineering, Aeroplanes, Time, Clocks, and Watch-making. Again, Chemistry leads through the science itself to Chemical technology, Explosives, Gas manufacture, Oils, Colours, Pottery and Glass. This bringing of sciences in their pure state into proximity with the trades which are closely or remotely based upon them is quite logical in principle, but really tends to separate things which are thought of, or studied, or used together. Thus the trades are themselves separated by the masses of written material on the pure sciences, and this, having regard to the probable users of the material to be classed, would appear to ignore convenience. The *Subject Classification*, however, does not in every case pursue subjects from the root science to the final application; for example, Botany does not lead up, as one would expect, to Agriculture, which is, after all, an ultimate application of botanical knowledge; and, of course, the study of Mineralogy as in granites, etc., does not lead up, as might be expected on the theory, to Architecture and Building. Bliss has pronounced that the principles here adopted are good if not carried to extremes, but agrees, and indeed asserts with more examples and emphatically, that many of the groupings that result from them are neither practical nor scientific.[1]

250. Another striking difference between the *Subject* and other classifications is the make-up of the Generalia class of the scheme. This is as follows:

A000	Encyclopædias.
	Collections.
A100	Education.
A300	Logic.
A400	Mathematics.
A600	Graphic and Plastic Arts.
A750	Photography.
A790	Sculpture.
A900	General Science.
A950	Science, Travel and Surveys.

The recognized principle of the Generalia class is that it accommodates subjects of too general a character to go into any other class. Brown extends the notion; he says: "The divisions of this main class comprise most of the rules, methods and factors which are of general application, and which qualify or pervade every branch of science, industry or human study. They are universal and pervasive, and cannot be logically assigned to any other single main class as peculiar or germane to it." This is a very controversial position. Logic is surely a mental science, although logical method applies to most subjects. Mathematics are the formal statement of natural laws; while the Graphic and Plastic Arts are, *on Brown's logical basis*, one form of Record. Again, Education is either a part of Psychology or a Social Science. Bliss asks, also, why General Science is separated from Philosophy and Logic.

251. We have seen repeatedly that nearly all practical modern classifications have what we have called generalia divisions, or, as they are frequently called, "common sub-divisions"; and I need hardly repeat that these are those headings which appear at the beginning of every main class of Dewey 01–09, and they take works which are general to the class at the head of which they appear, but differentiate (mark off) the "form" in which the subject is treated, or the method or viewpoint adopted in relation to it. When, however, we turn to the main tables of Brown's *Subject Classification*, we are immediately struck with the

[1] *Organization of Knowledge in Libraries*, p. 280.

absence from them of these common sub-divisions. For example, in the class Physical Science (B–D) we get

Booo   Physical Science, General.
Booi   Physics.
Boo2   Molecular and Molar.

where the progress is made from the unqualified general head Physical Science to the major class of physical science in Physics —the standpoints of the books which are to be gathered here on General Physical Science are not shown; nor is Physics itself shown in any of its relations. On the face of it we might assume that there was no provision for them. But this is not so. The absence of such common sub-divisions from the main tables is one of the features peculiar to this scheme. Such sub-divisions are provided separately and most liberally in a table which for want of a better name Brown called Categorical Tables. He had a reason, good or bad, for this separation. His endeavour was to construct a "one place" classification; that is to say, a classification in which every book whatsoever on a subject should arrange at one place. That indeed is an ideal for all classifiers to work to; one I have already emphasized sufficiently. The question is, on the other hand, Is a one-place system possible? ⍟The Decimal System is by no means a one-place scheme. For example, money will be found in about three places in the scheme, as a factor in currency under 332·4 "Coins and Coinage," as a part of the Taxation system at 336, and again as the product of the art of sculpture at 737 "Numismatics." The assumption is that the person who is interested in money as currency is rarely, if ever, interested in coins as works of art or *vertu*—is not, in short, a coin collector. Brown works on the logical, and in general perfectly accurate, rule of classifying, that the history of a subject should go with the subject; and the coin collector is, strictly speaking, a person who deals with the history of money tokens. There are numerous such separations in Dewey, all of which can be defended by another fundamental rule of classification: that of the essential place—"a work must go where it is most useful"—and defenders of Dewey would argue that Brown is wrong. The reader may decide the matter for himself. But Brown would probably argue thus: "There are in Dewey only nine common sub-divisions; that is, nine standpoints from which any subject may be treated or regarded. As a matter of actual fact there are many more such standpoints, and Dewey is reduced to one or two expedients in regard to them. (1) He must ignore them altogether, or (2) he must find separate, specific places for them in his scheme, and thus bring about the separations which are admittedly a defect of his scheme. On the other hand, in the *Subject Classification* I have provided no less than 980 standpoints, and rather than expand my tables beyond all practical proportions by printing them under every head that will take them, I have relegated them to a separate table at the beginning of my classification."

252. The matter is perhaps a little simpler, and more fundamental to the Subject Classification, than this. The categorical tables are a grouping together of those terms which are used for the division of all *or many* subjects. Common sub-divisions, properly called, are applicable to *every* subject, and of these there are necessarily few, although Bliss has shown that there are more than is commonly supposed.[1] But there are nevertheless many classes which have similar formal sub-divisions, and if we print these sub-divisions under each of them we get inflated tables, as in the case of the Library of Congress scheme. This repetition can be defended on the ground that a different shade of meaning is conveyed by the sub-division term in most classes; but the differences are often such as are recognizable and do not cause any confusion. The theory, then, that wherever a term appears in a number of classes it can be taken out of the main tables and included in the categorical table and be given an invariable number, is carried out by Brown more fully than by any other scheme-maker.

253. Turning back to Dewey's common sub-divisions, we have:

  501 Philosophy.
   02 Compends, Outlines.
   03 Dictionaries, Cyclopædias.
   04 Essays, Lectures, Addresses.
   05 Periodicals.
   06 Societies, Transactions.
   07 Education, Methods of Study and Teaching.
   08 Polygraphy. Collected works.
   09 History.

All these headings can be provided with equivalent numbers from the Categorical Tables. Thus:

B000	Physical Sciences.	B000	Physical Sciences (continued)
B000.5	Philosophy.	B000.2	Dictionaries.
B000.3	Compendiums.	B000.3	Compends.
B000.2	Dictionaries.	B000.5	Philosophy.
B000.954	Essays.	B000.6	Societies.
B000.7	Periodicals.	B000.7	Periodicals.
B000.6	Societies.	B000.8	Polygraphy.
B000.65	Education.	B000.10	History.
B000.8	Polygraphy.	B000.65	Education.
B000.10	History.	B000.954	Essays.

[1] See the elaborate Systematic Auxiliary Schedules in his *Bibliographic Classification*, Table IV, etc.

These in use would rearrange in the order shown on the right as the numbers are always used as an orthodox method in simple arithmetical order. These numbers, then, qualify the general class-heading exactly in the way in which Dewey's sub-divisions 01–09 do. Moreover, as there are 980 such sub-divisions, there is a dividing power of great value although, as our previous and following remarks demonstrate, they cannot all divide such a subject as Physical Science or anything else. The numbers fall into a position exactly similar to those of Dewey; they all come before B 001 Physics; but, in its turn, Physics can, if need be, be divided by such of the 980 as may be applicable; and so may every division, sub-division, and section throughout the scheme. The point which introduces the categorical number is not a decimal point, and care must be taken not to regard it as such or to read the numbers decimally as we do in Dewey or similar schemes. It is a separating device merely, and when we meet with a book or catalogue entry which is marked with any number of which the point is a part, we know immediately that some "form" or "standpoint" of a subject is treated in the book.

254. That the categorical tables are not "common sub-divisions" or form divisions in the usual sense is easily demonstrable; we find in them, to quote at random,

Sermons	.693	Sleep	.716
Sewage	.180	Splints	.552
Sheriffs	.815	Synagogues	.716

It is quite clear that these cannot be regarded as standpoints or forms at all—except perhaps "Sermons," and even that is a form that is definitely limited to one class, "Religion." For we cannot imagine books that will bear such titles as

B000.815 Sheriffs of Science in general.
   .552 Splints „   „   „   „
   .716 Synagogues „   „   „   „

255. Passing from this unique feature of the system to another which may be said to depend upon it; we find that in class O–W, History and Geography, one substantive number only is used for each country, while its history and geography are standpoints from which the country is regarded. This logical and useful arrangement has much to commend it; I have always thought that the absolute separation of geography and history in Dewey is a defect of the scheme. There are few students, for example, who desire to read works on Italian travel who do not also desire to read works on the history of Italy; but these works, if arranged by Dewey, are often hundreds of shelves apart. In Brown that

separation occurs, but to a much more limited extent. Let us take S600 Germany as an example. All *general* histories (that is to say, histories which cover the whole of German history, and are not limited to any period), are collected at S600 and the categorical number for history is added, the number reading S600.10. Similarly, all general geographical and travel books on Germany are marked S600 with the categorical number for Travel, and the resultant notation is S600.33. In this case the .33 is unnecessary. If travel in Germany is simply marked S600 all other standpoints are clearly shown by the categorical numbers and are so divided from Travel. Reading down the schedules we get the period divisions, similar in result to those of Dewey's 943·01–943·09, which receive their own separate numbers. Thus, S706 is the history of Germany under Frederick the Great. If by any chance we have a book of travel in Germany during Frederick's reign, we can mark it S706, and add the categorical number .33 for travels. After the period divisions come the local history and description divisions, which again can be differentiated by the use of the categorical numbers. Thus, the number for Berlin is S725, and the history and travel of Berlin are S725.10 and S725.33 respectively. In this manner the books on the shelves are fairly closely related, to the advantage of readers.

256. Geographical division—to proceed to another part of our subject—is a necessity in all modern schemes; and we all know now how to divide any subject in Dewey by the geographical numbers under 940–999. Brown secures a similar result by adding the number from the History and Geography class to the number which it is desired to divide. Thus, if we desire to classify the Botany of Berlin—which, of course, is not a work on Berlin really, but a work on Botany and should go at Botany, and not at Berlin —we take the number E100 Botany, or, in this case, E172 Local Floras, and add to it the number for Berlin, making a resultant notation E172S725; and to this number, if the circumstances require it, the categorical number can be added; thus the history of the flora of Berlin is E 172S725.10. The corresponding notation in Dewey would be 581·9431509, which, however, only takes us down to the history of the botany of Brandenburg, and does not specify Berlin. The notation of Brown is definite and not unduly long. Similarly, to quote Brown's own examples, D398V222 is the Geology of Arran, L185So is Freemasonry in Russia, J851Ro is the Cathedrals of France. In the last two examples it is seen that the geographical number is contracted; Sooo is the full number for Russia; but the second and third noughts add nothing to the significance of the number and are omitted when it is

used for the geographical division of other subjects. As every country has a similar number composed of a letter and three noughts such a symbol as Ro, Wo, etc., tells us immediately that the work deals with the whole of a country.

257. A further interesting innovation in the classification is the treatment it gives to Literature. Brown abandons the linguistic and chronological arrangements of Dewey and other classifiers, and simply provides four great divisions, Fiction, Poetry, Drama, and Essays. Under each of these he has headings for collections in the various forms, but following these come all individual authors in one alphabetical sequence. Thus, in Poetry, Beddoes, Browning, and Byron follow one another without relation to period, and Dante, Darley, and Davidson, without relation to the language in which they wrote. The same principle of alphabetic arrangement applies in Fiction, Drama and Essays. It is a practical method, and one of some "finding value" in a popular library. It ignores, however, the superior claims of the student, who presumably wants to study a period of literature, or the literature of a specified country, more often than the works of any one author.

258. In the great class, Individual Biography, Brown arranges all lives in alphabetical order of the names of the persons written about, and not as in Dewey where they are grouped according to the subjects with which they were most concerned in life.

259. The notation has been dealt with to some extent in an earlier chapter, and only a brief word is necessary here. The main classes are marked with a single capital letter, and the remainder of the notation is in general a consistent three figures one, running from 000 to 999, with occasional gaps for insertions. This is not, on the surface, a flexible notation, as the numbers are not decimals; and this is a grave fault. Brown himself recognized this, and proposed that the numbers should, if necessary, be treated as decimals. If they were so treated, the expansibility of the notation would, of course, become unlimited.

260. Finally, Brown's index is a specific or one-place index, and not relative as is Dewey's. Dewey's index not only shows a subject; it shows also as many aspects of the subject as may be found in the tables; although, as Brown himself pointed out, even the Dewey index is not exhaustively relative: no index can show every possible relation of every subject. Brown's gives one entry in the index for a subject, and leaves the reader to infer that at the place indicated every aspect of the subject will be found. This hardly proves to be the case, however, as will easily be seen at Trees, a subject which receives only one entry in the index, but which really appears in the tables at Botany, Forestry,

Topiary, and other places. In my view the index is the most defective part of the system.

261. The Third Edition does not depart from any of the principles of the system as Brown devised them. It is "extensively revised and enlarged," as may be expected after an interval of thirty years, and this has been done by many librarian collaborators who have applied the scheme. It introduces the newer subjects, of course, and does this without disturbing the numbering of existing subjects more than is absolutely necessary; indeed, very few subjects have changed numbers, except in the historical and topographical classes. In these latter classes it is at present impossible to assign a class order which has any likelihood of permanence. The plan is still a straight series of general history headings for each country, followed by a series of local headings, and these are qualified as shown in paragraphs 255–56 above, and the European order prevails as it appeared in March 1939. The index has been much enlarged and its value much enhanced. This conservative revision will commend itself to most librarians.

262. A scheme of this importance—the most considerable from a British classification-maker—has naturally attracted much discussion. Bliss has considered it with a scrupulous fairness, affected only to a very slight degree by his predilection for the order of his own classification; his chapter is thoroughly worth while.[1] Ranganathan[2] on many pages contrasts it with other schemes, especially with reference to his own Colon System. It has many defects, but it has survived thirty-five years of use and is still regarded as an acceptable working tool by very competent librarians; so much so that, as its Editor tells me, a Fourth Edition is in preparation (1954).

[1] *Organization of Knowledge in Libraries*, pp. 279–89.   [2] *Prolegomena.*

CHAPTER XVIII

THE BIBLIOGRAPHIC CLASSIFICATION OF HENRY EVELYN BLISS

263. Woven into the texture of this book are many yarns from the loom of the most scholarly of American classifiers. Henry Evelyn Bliss published his now well-known *Organization of Knowledge in Libraries* eighteen years after the first edition of this book was written, and in it he pays me very generous, and as I think too kind, tributes to the teaching of this book. At the same time, it must be remembered that he has devoted quite thirty years of his life to a more or less intensive study of the classification arts; indeed, I doubt if any man in any country has so consistently specialized in our subject. He therefore brings to his books an equipment which has not been surpassed, I think, in the whole history of the study. His earliest articles were published in *The Library Journal* and in other American periodicals, and all pointed to a new scheme of classification that he must always have had in mind, which would be based upon a theory of knowledge deduced from long and precise studies of all the methods of organization, so far as they were available to him, that man has used in the ordering of his activities and mental processes. Bliss was born in New York on January 29, 1870, and completed his education in the College of the City of New York, in which he became a librarian in 1891. He served there until his retirement in 1940, and during the latter part of the time had been allowed facilities by the College authorities to pursue the studies which have had so important an influence upon librarians of late. The record of the life of such a man cannot be dramatic, but it is interesting to note that his pursuits have been of a quiet, literary character, which, if taken by themselves, would not seem to indicate a purely scientific mind—that is to say, a prosaic one. In his sixties he surprised his friends by publishing a volume of poems entitled quite appropriately *Better Late than Never*[1] which showed that he possesses a real gift for song, a poetic imagination and a lyrical quality, as well as deep philosophic insight. Apart from the articles which he has contributed to library journals, his first considerable book resulting from his long studies was his *Organization of Knowledge and the System of the Sciences.*[2] He describes it himself as furnishing the scientific, philosophical, and logical grounds for the study of

[1] N.Y.: Putnam's Sons, 1937.   [2] N.Y.: Henry Holt & Co., 1929.

bibliographical classification, and the educational foreground. That statement is rather modest. In this book, which was immediately recognized as being of unusual depth and quality, Bliss set out, as I have already indicated, on a study of all methods of organization—in nature, in society, in intellectual occupations —and he deduced from this arduous course the principle which lies at the back of all his classifying, which is, as we already know, to the effect that arrangements in classification, in subject catalogues, and in other bibliothecal services, should be organized in consistency with the scientific and educational consensus which is relatively stable and tends to become more so. It seems a circuitous route by which to reach the conclusion, which I think may be simplified in interpretation as a classification should be arranged in accordance with the methods of the workers in educational and scientific occupations. But no one can dispute the value of the process through which he went and the assurance it has given him of his own conclusions. The book is not easy reading: it requires consideration and careful thinking for every page. The purpose was, as I say, to lay down a foundation for a relatively stable, scientifically acceptable, and consistent scheme of classification. But before constructing his intended scheme he went on more specifically to describe the theory of classification in another admirable volume, *Organization of Knowledge in Libraries and the Subject Approach to Books*.[1] As a general statement of its subject I think the book occupies quite the first rank. There are few positions that it holds that I do not also hold, and this must have been evident to the readers of this book; indeed, I have revised many of my own earlier views in the light of the teaching of Bliss, as well as of Ranganathan and many of my younger colleagues. I admit this quite freely and, I think, wisely. Both books, as I have said, lead up to the promised system of classification which was awaited very eagerly by those who had read these two volumes.

264. The system of bibliographic classification was issued in outline in the *Organization of Knowledge in Libraries*. A two-place expansion of the scheme was, however, published separately under the title of *A System of Bibliographic Classification*.[2] This was presented in typescript by means of the offset process, which, while perhaps slightly more difficult to read than normal printing type, has many outstanding advantages to the compiler of schedules—as will be appreciated by any reader who has had occasion to edit or revise a piece of intricate printing, involving variations of type-face, spacing, and registration. In

---

[1] N.Y.: H. W. Wilson Company, 1933; edition 2, 1939.
[2] N.Y.: H. W. Wilson Company, 1935.

this instance, the tables are reproduced directly from the author's own most careful and accurate typescript, with a reassuring authority; and the same method has been followed in reproducing all tabular matter in the full schedules described below. A second edition of the *System* was published in 1936 and incorporated some small but very important items of revision.

265. Volume I of the fully expanded tables appeared in 1940, the second volume in 1947 and the concluding volumes III and IV in 1953. The full description is as follows:

A Bibliographic Classification | extended by | systematic auxiliary schedules | for | composite specification and notation | by Henry Evelyn Bliss. | In four volumes. | Vol. I | Introduction | Anterior Tables and | Systematic Schedules | and | Classes A–G. N.Y.: H. W. Wilson Company, 1940.

> Vol. II. Classes H–K. The Human Sciences. With introduction and index. 1947.
> Vol. III. Classes L–Z. The Special Human Sciences. History of Peoples and Nations, Religion, Ethics and Special Social Studies, Languages and Literatures, Bibliography and Libraries. 1953.
> Vol. IV. General Index, containing vols. I, II, III. 1953.

The General Index thus replaces the indexes in vols. I and II and so the remaining pages in these volumes were so reduced as to enable them to be published as one volume in the 1953 issue; hence the work now appears as "4 v. in 3". For purchasers of the original volumes a pamphlet was provided, showing 323 emendations made between the two issues. The whole work resembles in size of page the *System* volume of 1933; the main tables are again in reproduced typescript, but the massive introductions and the index are in printing type. Altogether, the scheme, which as the *System* occupied 352 pages, now runs to approximately 2,000 pages.

266. Whilst admitting that this is not the place to discuss Bliss's teachings on classification in general, I think that nevertheless it may perhaps assist in the understanding of his schedules if we briefly summarize the main principles upon which his practice is based. In order to clarify the issue, I have adopted a summary form of statement in my own words of the major principles of classification according to Bliss. These are:

(1) That the order of things can be established.
(2) That the order of things is the basis of the classification of knowledge.
(3) That that order is determined by its use by, and usefulness to, the thinkers and workers in the various branches of knowledge.

(4) That these branches may be integrated into a coherent whole, and this whole is a general system of classification.

(5) That the system thus created is the essential basis of a book classification.

To put it in another way, and making use of Bliss's own words: "Knowledge should be organized in consistency with the scientific and educational consensus, which is relatively stable and tends to become more so as theory and system become more definitely established in general and increasingly in detail."

267. Other basic principles illustrated by the schedules may be tabulated briefly as:

Gradation by speciality, proceeding from the more general to the more specific.

Serial dependence, of threefold complexity—logical, developmental, and pedagogical.

Maximal efficiency by reason of the collocation of the greatest number of most closely related subjects of study and thought.

These points of theory are not original inventions by Bliss; but he has contributed more to their elucidation than any other individual writer. The discerning reader will already have noted the peculiarity of Bliss's vocabulary, in that he uses words like a scientist, as instruments of precision. The meaning of the statements given above emerges from a few moments' clear thinking. For the rest, we must refer the interested reader to the earlier sections of this *Manual* and to Bliss's own writings. For present purposes we are concerned only to note how these principles are illustrated in the author's own schedules.

268. If we examine the five propositions given above, we shall observe that they constitute in themselves an example of "serial dependence" in that each later statement emerges from, and is dependent upon, all its predecessors. To realize propositions (4) or (5), therefore, we must study the various usages of the "scientific and educational consensus" implied in proposition (3). In the *Organization of Knowledge* Bliss sets out (on pages 232-5) five tables, *each* of which attempts the ordering of *all* knowledge on a distinctive principle. These tables are:

I. *The order of nature:* i.e., of occurrence of phenomena, not of studies.

II. *The developmental order of knowledge:* i.e., the historical order of the development of studies.

III. *The pedagogic order:* i.e., the order in which the individual acquires training in the various studies.

IV. *The logical order of knowledge:* i.e., an extension to all knowledge of the "natural order of the sciences" which normally is strictly confined to the pure sciences.

V. *The order of speciality:* reproduced herewith: an ordering of actual studies influenced by consideration of all the other tables.

269. Despite the basic divergence of points of view, these tables all approximate, in the final analysis, to a single order—that of Table V above. It would, however, be unfair to Bliss and evidence of superficial thinking to assume that any mere "one-dimensioned" table represents adequately the inter-relations of the various branches of knowledge. For this reason we have reproduced in a folded chart herewith Bliss's own synopsis of all knowledge, alongside the table mentioned as Number V above—of the "order of speciality"—and, in addition, for purposes of comparison, the outline of the schedules of the Bibliographic classification. The first of these tables has the advantage of being in two dimensions, so that inter-relationships of topics may be worked out horizontally as well as vertically; whereas the other two tables represent successive degrees of compromise, that inevitably lose some degree of accuracy in gaining a higher measure of practicability. It will be observed that in the third table the proportion of the parts has been adjusted to conform with extrinsic factors, such as the numbers of books available in each class of knowledge. I consider this chart capable of affording to the intelligent student first-class material for studying the processes which Bliss designates "schedulization."

270. For example, let us examine in more detail the first of our tables—the synoptic chart. Students will immediately note the existence of four columnar sequences, each in serial dependence. Each of these columns (Philosophy, Science, History, Technologies and Arts) represents here not a closed "subject," but rather a basic discipline or expository mode, pervasive of all knowledge (and incidentally giving rise to those phenomena, so puzzling to the young classifier, of "internal form," such as "history of . . .," "philosophy of . . .," "special applications of . . .," etc., in seemingly unrelated topics). Bliss's subjective approach by discipline is in sharp contrast to Brown's attempt to classify objectively, and is, indeed, strikingly reminiscent of Bacon's method, which is thus seen to be far sounder in essence than the methods of most of his critics.

271. It will be apparent by now that Bliss's two-dimensioned plan is itself only an approximation to the intricate inter-relationships of topics and disciplines: an accurate representation might require not merely a third dimension but possibly a fourth or fifth! But when we pass on to consider the second of our tables, that of the "order by speciality," we soon appreciate how much subtlety has necessarily to be jettisoned to attain a manageable

sequence. We should be unjust to our author, however, if we failed to observe how much of the accurate cartography of the original scheme has been retained. The "scientific and educational consensus" now emerges clearly, and few of us would venture—or desire—to quarrel with either its hierarchy or its sequential order as we normally quarrel fiercely with those of certain other well-known schemes of book-classification. Indeed, we shall find as we proceed that even those dissentients who prefer to collocate Religion next to Philosophy or Sociology next to Education rather than where Bliss here places them, are actually catered for by the provision of alternative schedules—a handsome concession to other legitimate schools of thought embraced within the folds of the "scientific and educational consensus."

272. The third table "fixes" the outline by adding a notation. What is more, the classes are apportioned to fit the practical consideration of the "spread over" of books over the classes. Note, for example how the "knowledge classes" of Astronomy, Geology and Geography have been telescoped together in "bibliographic class" D, while "knowledge class" Biology has been expanded to cover "bibliographic classes" E Biology, F Botany and G Zoology. Even more striking is the case of History and Human Geography, logically sub-classes (a term which Bliss prefers to Dewey's "main divisions"), which emerge in the schedules as classes L–O, a considerable proportion of the whole table. No one who has ever worked in a public library will dispute that this represents a fairer approximation to the actual proportions of stock; neither will he do less than acknowledge at once the practical utility and the sensitive scholarship which characterize all Bliss's work in this operation of "schedulizing"—or converting a knowledge scheme into workable schedules.

273. The notation of the scheme is equally practical. It utilizes the alphabet (in its full English form of twenty-six letters) as the base for all classification by knowledge, reserving the Arabic numerals for considerations of form. Full advantage has been taken of the area of the base (26^n—or $(26+9)^n$), in conjunction with sound planning of the classes and their sub-division in relation to book-content, to keep down to modest dimensions the average length of symbol. The use of letters suggests potential adoption of the "literal mnemonic" device; and, in point of fact, this device is freely used, though never at the expense of logical order. A table of the chief mnemonics is published with the schedules, and it includes such items as:

AL   Logic.
CT   Chemical technology (Chemistry being C).
IC   Consciousness.
NA   North America (America being N).

274. One of the most distinctive features of the scheme—and one sufficiently important for mention on the title-page—is the use of Systematic Auxiliary Tables. In this, there is involved no novel principle; for the idea is common to all modern systems, except that of the Library of Congress; they fulfil and go beyond the functions of the common sub-divisions of Dewey, the form sub-divisions and local list of the Expansive Scheme, the categorical tables of the Subject Scheme, and the more detailed series of tables used in connexion with the Classification Décimale and are outstanding examples of the synthetic method applied systematically and mnemonically; and in recent years the Colon Scheme has illustrated how this method can ensure great minuteness whilst actually reducing the length of the printed schedules.

275. In the Bibliographic Scheme twenty-two principal Systematic Schedules are listed, but many of them have subschedules appended for more detailed expansion, making in all forty-six in the revised list in Table IV in volume III. As in the use of similar tables incorporated into other schemes, a symbol drawn from the main (or topic) schedule indicating the subjectmatter of the book. The added symbol gives precision to the original placing by introducing some such consideration as external forms or locality. It can be added without confusion at any stage of sub-division by topic. Actually, only the first three Schedules are of general application; and even these are not equally applicable throughout the main schedules: the remainder are applicable to groups of classes, to single classes, or to subclasses; but all are mnemonic and consistent throughout their field of use.

276. Schedule 1 is for numeral sub-division (1–9) of considerations of form and in normal cases closely resembles the group of nine Anterior Numeral Classes which we have listed in the outline of the Scheme. Here is a condensed outline of Schedule 1:

1. *Reference books* including dictionaries, glossaries, encyclopædias, indexes, handbooks, pocket-books, atlases, concordances, etc.
2. *Bibliography*, historical, evaluative selective. Abstracts.
3. *History*, scope and relation. Books about the subject; its study, profession, organization, etc.
4. *Biography* relevant to subject.
5. *Documents* and ancillary matter. Institutional and government publications, reports, bulletins, annuals, catalogues, maps, etc.
6. *Periodicals.*
7. *Miscellanies.* Collected or selected writings of several authors, essays, addresses, lectures, readings, symposia, etc.
8. *Study* of the subject, books about it.
9. *Antiquated or superseded books or other materials* or those under a superseded classification.

277. Of the above sub-divisions, Nos. 1, 2 and 6 are constant mnemonics; but the scheme allows for the remainder to be interchanged, if desired, in several possible ways. This may appear a trifle strange to many readers, but we shall soon discover that one of the most characteristic features of this scheme is its tolerance of modes of thought divergent from that of the author. If a user of the scheme prefers the items in Schedule 1 in a different order, he is allowed to adopt an alternative. (He will naturally record his decision and apply it consistently.) Apart from this, when Schedule 1 is used in conjunction with various particular classes, certain numerals take on a special significance for that class. Thus in classes L–O, 3 signifies Geography and Description of a country or district, etc., while in class X the same symbol 3 signifies the study of a language and its literature together. These special meanings are all clearly indicated in the appropriate context, alongside the knowledge classes affected.

278. Sub-division by Schedule 1 may be made freely at any point of sub-division. To illustrate at random: we discover from the main schedules that BOR stands for radio telegraphy, BOV stands for broadcasting, and BOY for television. Applying Schedule 1, we observe:

BOR 1   Dictionary of Wireless Terms.
BOR 6   "Wireless World."
BOV 3   The History of the B.B.C.
BOV 6   "Radio Times."
BOV 8   The Art of Broadcasting.
BOY 4   The Life of J. L. Baird.

In passing, compare the length of symbol with that employed in other schemes to designate a similar topic.

279. Auxiliary Schedule 2 is for geographical sub-division, and will be described in more detail when we come to deal with History and Topography in this scheme. Here it will suffice to say that a table using a notation of lower-case letters is employed to sub-divide by locality. The table is mnemonic and consistent; but it is *not* identical with the main schedule expansion used for the subjects of History and Topography. The symbol DHI i stands for the subject, "The volcanoes of Italy", where i comes from Schedule 2 and is, characteristically enough, a literal mnemonic.

280. Schedule 3 for sub-division by language was originally devised to be used for translations on classes W–Y, but it may be used in many other places, often as an alternative to Schedule 2, which it resembles in some particulars (e.g., its symbol, I stands for Italian). The notation is alphabetical (capitals) differentiated by an initial comma, and is *not* derived from classes W–Y. Thus

a book on modern Russian philosophy may be classified at **AD,R** as an alternative to ADn (using Schedule 2).

281. Schedule 4 is for sub-division under historic periods, and is only applicable to classes L–O. It has two sub-schedules for its more detailed expansion; but we shall deal with all of these in some detail in considering Bliss's treatment of History and Topography. Similarly, with Schedule 5 for the sub-division of the philology of any language and its sub-schedules 5a, 5b and 5c; all clearly restricted in application to classes W–Y, in conjunction with which they will be dealt with in detail. Schedule 6, which we will deal with at the same time, allows for detailed expansion under a particular author, and a similar Schedule, No. 7, allows a like facility in dealing with any personage.

282. Schedules 8 to 20 are all limited in scope to single classes or, in most instances, to sub-classes. Their general character and utility are illustrated by the case of Schedule 16, by which any religious system or sect (in class P) may be mnemonically sub-divided by such considerations as: sacred books, ritual, holy places, priesthood, heresies, etc. All schedules of limited application are printed with the schedule of the class to which they apply: for this reason the detailed and revised versions of many of them are not yet available. In most cases the alphabetical notation is used with the comma as separating device. This obviates any risk of confusion with the ordinary expansion by topic. Perhaps this is as good a place as any to speak of one highly distinctive feature of this scheme—which has already been mentioned in passing,—that of alternative locations. Consistently with the principle of the "scientific and educational consensus," Bliss recognizes the existence among scholars of alternative points of view; and he does so in a practical way by reserving places in his scheme for alternative usages sanctioned by scholarly authority but differing from his own recommendations. Clearly a library would need to choose one practice and adhere to it to the exclusion of the alternative; so that the rejected place would be left blank in the schedules as far as that library was concerned. (Readers may recall the parallel from the thirteenth edition of Dewey's scheme of the alternative placings of the subject Psychology.) To illustrate the Bibliographic Scheme, Religion is preferred by the author at P, where its associations with History and Ethics are stressed by contiguity. Another legitimate mode of thought stresses rather the associations with Metaphysics; so AJ is reserved as an alternative place, where Religion may be expanded, if so desired, like class P, as given in the schedules. Alternatively again, only a part of the subject Religion may be placed at AJ, where a special table is provided for sub-division, the remainder,

including studies of the religious systems of the world, remaining at class P. Again, it is permissible to interchange classes P and K (Social Sciences) if so desired. It may prove an interesting exercise for the student to work out the associations stressed by the two schools of thought thus provided for. Similarly, Psychology, while preferred at class I (where we should note its associations with Anthropology and Education), has an alternative place provided at AI, where the emphasis is upon its relationships with Metaphysics (from which study it originally emerged) and with Logic.

283. Many of the alternatives given solve dilemmas that face all classifiers, whatever scheme they adopt. Thus, many books have a twofold significance—as contributions to knowledge and as bibliographical specimens calling for special location as such. In Bliss, the pull is between the topic classes A–Z on the one hand and the Anterior Numerical classes 1–9 (where arrangement is primarily by form) on the other. Thus, Bliss allows the obvious alternatives for government publications, pamphlets, periodicals, antiquated books, and bibliography. The alternative sequence for collected bibliographies is at ZJ, and, by a similar line of reasoning, books on the law of a subject may be either placed with the subject or arranged together at SL to SS in class S, Law. Biography is preferred by Bliss as distributed by subject of life-work or interest (differentiated with the mnemonic symbol 4 (or 9)); but biographies may be arranged in one sequence at L9 (note here that 9 is a recognized alternative to 4 for Biography in modifying schedule 1). Throughout there are many provisions for alternative locations. In practical use, it would only be necessary to record decisions; for guiding is so carefully done throughout the schedules that there would be little danger of confusion.

284. Another important group of alternatives is concerned with Applied Science and Technology. Bliss gives a preferred arrangement by which the more specialized technologies are subsumed under their parent sciences while the more general are grouped together in class U. However, alternative places are provided for all major technologies, whichever point of view is adopted.

285. There are two major topics, or groups of topics, which call for more detailed treatment, notwithstanding the fact that both groups incorporate interesting examples of alternative location. We shall deal with some of these examples when we come to them, but our main concern now is to explain Bliss's treatment of History and the allied studies and of Languages and Literature, covering between them no less than seven main classes—rather more than a quarter of the whole scheme.

286. We have noted in passing that classes L to O are devoted

to History, Travel and Topography, Biography and other ancillary studies (i.e., approximately the same as Dewey's class 900); but it is evident at a glance that the ordering of these classes has more in common with Brown's Subject Scheme than with the more familiar arrangement of Dewey: quite clearly locality is here of paramount importance as an arranging factor, taking precedence over the "study factor"—e.g., you arrange *first* under England or France or China and *then* separate travel from history or archæology: Dewey, on the other hand, separates first into History or Travel, etc., and then sub-divides by locality. The student should think out for himself the relative advantages or disadvantages of the two methods.

287. Class L covers all the general topics and, in addition, Ancient History, Mediæval History and Modern History, in their world-wide aspects. The remaining three classes are allocated to Europe (M), the Americas (N), and Asia, Australasia, the Polar Regions, etc. (O). These classes are further sub-divided among the countries, according to the probable extent of the literature. These sub-divisions are further sub-divided consistently by locality down to the smallest unit. By means of a series of Systematic Auxiliary Schedules, which can be applied at any stage of sub-division by locality, it is possible to differentiate between history, topography, archæology and a great range of other special topics. I repeat, this can be done, not just for large countries, but at every stage of sub-division down to towns and villages. I can best illustrate how it is done by examples; but unfortunately the full schedules are not yet available, so in at least one instance, a little guess-work has been required—as we shall indicate in its proper place.

288. Let us first consider the case of sub-class MN, which embraces *all* books on Russia, whether of travel, history, economic or social or administrative history (unless preferred under the obvious alternatives, in accordance with Bliss's usual practice). Sub-division of MN is by Systematic Schedule No. 4a, which has 35 places (9 numerals constituting a modified version of Schedule 1, together with 26 places of alphabetical sub-division). Now MN can be sub-divided by Schedule 4a into 35 headings, of which the following are typical:

MN 3   Topography of Russia.
MN 9   Collected biography of Russia.
MNA   Comprehensive histories of Russia.
MND   Diplomatic history of Russia.
MNE   Economic history of Russia.
MNM   Military history of Russia.
MNN   Naval history of Russia.
MNV   History of contemporary Russia.

(Note in passing the handy alphabetical mnemonics incorporated in some of the examples given above.) Schedule 4a can be applied to every stage of sub-division, exactly as we have applied it to Russia as a whole.

289. Passing now to a country with a larger literature (in English or American libraries, of course), let us consider the case of France, which has no less than three sub-classes assigned to it:

> MR   France: general considerations.
> MS   France: history by periods.
> MT   France: sub-divided by localities.

Of the above, MR can be sub-divided by Schedule 4a, exactly as in the case of Russia. There are, however, some places—those for historical periods and for local sub-division—which will now be redundant, as we have MS and MT available for more detailed expansion. MS is sub-divided by Schedule 4b, which is really a detailed expansion over 26 places of that part of Schedule 4a dealing with periods in only 7 places. Thus MSM is France in the early eighteenth century, while MSO stands for France in the Napoleonic era. Schedule 4b is of course mnemonic and consistent for all countries and sub-divisions. The sub-division of MT cannot be mnemonic, for obvious reasons. But at any stage of sub-division by locality, Schedule 4a may be applied, exactly as in the case of Russia.

290. It is not surprising that special provision is made for the enormous literature about our own country. Here are the sub-classes:

> MU Great Britain. The British Empire. England. (Subdivided by Schedule 4.)
> MV Great Britain: England. (Subdivided by Schedule 4b, i.e., by periods.)
> MW England and Wales: countries, districts, towns, etc.
> MX Scotland. (Probably treated like MN in earlier example; i.e., MXA for Scotland in general, subdivided by Schedule 4, with MXB–MXZ for local subdivision.)
> MY Ireland. (Presumably treated like Scotland above.)

It is evident that this scheme is more comprehensive and accommodating than any other published scheme whatsoever.

291. I mentioned earlier on the existence of Systematic Schedule 2 for local sub-division of topics. This is, of course, the "local list" for dividing by locality any other topic than history or travel: e.g., "Religions of India," "French cookery receipts," etc. A few moments' reflection will show us that the mnemonic

use of symbols drawn from classes L–O is impracticable—at any rate, if we intend to use our notation economically. Consequently, Bliss's Schedule 2, though mnemonic and consistently used, has a different notation from classes L–O, thus reducing the average length of symbol. The notation here is of lower-case letters. Thus the symbol for England is not mw but e. Scotland es and Ireland ev. A flora of the Riviera is FH fr. The use of lateral mnemonics is well illustrated by these examples.

292. We have now to consider the very important topic of Language and Literature, treated together and covering classes W, X and Y, as follows:

W Philology: Linguistics and Languages other than Indo-European (including Literatures).
X Indo-European Philology, Languages and Literatures.
Y English (or other) Language and Literature; and Literature in general, Rhetoric, Oratory, Dramatics, etc.

293. Let us consider these three classes in turn. First, class W is sub-divided so as to allocate WA–WG to General and Comparative Philology and Linguistics; WH and WI are reserved for universal and artificial languages, while WJ–WY are devoted to languages other than Indo-European: languages likely to be of minor importance in Western libraries. Under each language, books on language and literature and specimens of literary forms are arranged by the use of Schedule 5, allowing an expansion of 35 places. Thus WS stands for Japanese language and literature; whence:

WS 1 Japanese lexicons.
WSA History of the Japanese language.
WSC Etymology of the Japanese language.
WSG Japanese grammar.
WSK History of Japanese literature: early period.
WSL Later Japanese writers.
WSO Individual Japanese authors.
WSP Japanese poets.
WSQ Japanese drama.

Schedule 5 is, of course, mnemonic and constant for all non-Indo-European languages.

294. Passing on to the Indo-European languages, we find that the leading languages each have three places assigned to them (very much in the same way in which we found three places assigned to the leading countries in classes M, N and O). We discover, too, that in expanding these places we shall use Auxiliary Schedules 5a, 5b and 5c. These three schedules are, in reality, only Schedule 5 spread in greater detail over three places instead of one, giving 87 places (9 + 26 + 26 + 26) instead of 35. Schedule

5a is confined to Language and Linguistics; Schedule 5b is limited to Literary History and Criticism; while Schedule 5c is concerned with the actual literature itself.

294.1. To illustrate the use of these schedules, we propose to confine our attention to one language only, in this case Spanish. The sub-classes affected are:

> XO   Spanish language, its history and linguistics.
> XP   History of Spanish literature and criticism.
> XQ   Spanish literature.

Of these the case of XO is straightforward and allows of no variation: sub-division is clearly by Schedule 5a. But when we come to XP and XQ we are confronted with one of Bliss's most important provisions for alternative schools of thought. The treatment of literary history and criticism and literature itself allows of no less than four methods of approach, and all four are recognized in this scheme: our allocation of sub-classes XP and XQ depends upon which method our library adopts. (It follows, of course, that a method is used consistently throughout classes X and Y—not just for Spanish.)

294.2. Here in summary are the four methods, as illustrated by sub-classes XP and XQ:

Method I. The literature, arranged in one alphabet of authors (in this case at XQ and clearly not further sub-divided except by author's name) is separated from the history, biography, criticism and collections (here at XP) which may be classified historically, by "form" or otherwise (all by Schedule 5b).

Method II. Historical classification throughout, for literature, histories, biographies, criticism and collections. (In this case we should use XP only, expanded by Schedule 5b, using another Schedule—No. 6—for expansion under individual authors where required.)

Method III. Method I for modern literature and Method II for earlier periods. (Presumably the early literature would be subsumed in our example under XP—by Schedule 5b—while in the modern period XQ would be expanded—by Schedule 5c —for literary form.)

Method IV. Classification by forms and by contents for the literature, individual writings and collections; the history, biography and criticism being classified historically. (In our example, therefore, XP would contain the history, biography and criticism, expanded by Schedule 5b, and XQ would contain the literature grouped by form.)

We may best illustrate the differences between the methods by classifying the same three books by the four methods in turn. Here they are:

	Method I	Method II	Method III	Method IV
Cervantes Saavedra, M. de:				
Don Quijote	XQ.CER	XPO.CER	XPO.CER	XQG.CER
Blasco-Ibaniez, V.:				
Sangre y arena	XQ.BLA	XPR.BLA	XQ.BLA	XQG.BLA
Roscoe, T.: Spanish				
novelists	XPF	XPF	XPF	XPF

295. We now pass on to class Y devoted to English Language and Literature: it could equally well accommodate any other "home" language and literature. We discover that this class comprises English Philology, English Literary History and Literature, together with Literature *in general* and Rhetoric, Dramatics, etc.—all general topics. Their collocation with English literature at the end of the language sequence is startling in its unorthodoxy; but further consideration reveals the practical utility of the arrangement. (We have only to think of the books on our own shelves on English literature and on literature in general.) Most of the schedule is devoted to periods and writers: thus, YE Elizabethan literature, YF Shakespeare, YG Seventeenth and Eighteenth centuries, etc. YJ is reserved for English local literature, and YK for Scottish literature in English. With a most refreshing modesty, American literature is accommodated at YL. The rest of the schedule is sub-divided by forms. Throughout class Y, the four alternative methods are applicable. The special Schedule 6—for special consideration of individual authors— has been referred to already. We may illustrate its practical utility by examples relating to Shakespeare:

YFE   Shakespeare's sources.
YFK   Criticisms of Shakespeare's chief works.
YFP   Authenticity of Shakespeare's authorship.
YFU   Paraphrases and parodies of Shakespeare.
YFV   Illustrated editions of Shakespeare.

Notice in passing the extreme brevity of the notation in these and other illustrations—not specially selected for this purpose.

296. Class Z, which was left unused in the *System* on the expressed ground that in writing the letter confusion with S was possible, is now occupied with Bibliology, Bibliography and Librarianship and provides an original class for these subjects which is simple and, so far as I have tested it, adequate. It replaces, or is alternative to, Anterior Numeral Class Z.

297. The General Index is, as most modern classification indexes now are, of the relative variety. Its fullness may be inferred from the fact that Banks and Banking has 53 references; and not only the names of subjects, general and special, are included; it contains also personal and place names, names of lakes, mountains, rivers, artists, writers, and so on; and altogether there are

45,000 items or subjects indexed. As is the case with the Brown Subject Classification index, which can be extended greatly by the Categorical Tables, the Bliss index can be so enlarged by the feasible use of the Supplementary Auxiliary Schedules that something like a million placings—specifications as Bliss prefers to call them—may be made.

298. The first reactions of librarians when this great work appeared were that it has come late in the career of libraries and there was little prospect of its displacing schemes that had served libraries so long if only on the grounds of the great cost of reclassification. The other prospect was that in a new world of peace that might be nearer than international indications seemed, and still seem, to promise, there should be much development, many more libraries with new buildings and new ways of regarding their organization; and in such conditions librarians would have at hand in the B.C. a scheme unequalled in completeness, catholicity and scholarship; in the adequacy of the alternatives it provides; the brevity of the notation; the expository value of the introductions and of the notes throughout the schedules and the conscientious and lucid index. An Englishman cannot but recognize the acknowledgement made to his own countrymen for their assistance in the making and enlarging of some of the classes.

298.1. The scheme is in use in the College of the City of New York Library where Bliss first applied it, but it has not yet been adopted very generally in America; nor do I know of a public municipal or county library that uses it as its basic scheme there or here in Great Britain. That may be a matter of time, for it is already applied in whole or in part in about fifty university, college, school and other non-municipal libraries in the ordinary sense. A list of these, to January 1954, by Dr. D. J. Campbell and C. B. Freeman, appeared in the *Library Association Record*, v. 55, p. 198, and v. 56, p. 26. These two compilers remind us of the important fact that every scheme needs the oversight of a continuing society or institution, as exists for the Decimal and Library of Congress schemes, to ensure that it is kept current with the advance of knowledge and man's activities, and there is now a British Committee for the Bliss Classification,[1] of users who will exchange information—a scheme which Bliss himself assisted, and his publishers, the H. W. Wilson Company, commenced in August, 1954, the issue of the *Bliss Classification Bulletin*, which will appear occasionally to concentrate revisions and comments.

---

[1] Dr. D. J. Campbell, of *ASLIB* is hon. secretary.

298.2. Librarians who have themselves applied the scheme write appreciatively of it. Articles well worth study have been written by J. Mills, the librarian of the City of London College, "Classifying by Bliss",[1] which describes his experience in applying it at the College, his comparative study, "The Bliss and Colon Classification",[2] and a review of the complete scheme.[3] C. B. Freeman, who has applied it in the University of Hull Education Library,[4] finds not only that its framework is sound; the shape assumed by the literature of a subject emerges rather than its abstract pattern. Various other accounts are worth mention. In the *Guide for School Librarians*, published as long ago as 1937 by the Oxford University Press for the Incorporated Association of Assistant Masters in Secondary Schools, is a useful, favourable account by C. A. Stott. The chapter on the scheme in Phillips's *Primer* is, I understand, by Lawrence A. Burgess, who has also written a useful paper on it which appears in *Aslib Proceedings*.[5] The completed scheme has been reviewed discerningly by W. B. Paton,[6] and a good critical examination worth mention is that by K. C. Harrison.[7] All agree that the scheme survives present tests with remarkable success and the veteran philosopher, thinker and master-classificationist has made what is undoubtedly a great gift to library organization and economy.

His work completed, Bliss died on August 9th, 1955.

[1] L.A.R., v. 52, pp. 370-2   [3] *Ibid.*, v. 53, pp. 146-53.
[2] *Ibid.*, v. 55, pp. 298-300.   [4] *Ibid.*, v. 52, pp. 436-67.
[5] Feb. 1950, II, 1, pp. 7-13.   [6] *Library Rev.*, Winter, 1953, pp. 237-8.
[7] *Librarian*, v. 42, pp. 97-9.

CHAPTER XIX

THE COLON CLASSIFICATION

299. Each country in turn seems to produce a distinctive librarian who is the prototype of his profession. Edward Edwards and James Duff Brown in Great Britain, Dewey in America, Graesel in Germany, de Lisle in France, Paul Otlet in Belgium, are examples which come to mind without any thought of slighting their compatriot librarians. India would probably choose Shiyali Ramarita Ranganathan, born 1892, and now professor of library science in the University of Delhi. After graduation he lectured in mathematics in the Government College, Madras, 1917–20, and from then, 1920–3, was assistant professor of mathematics in the Presidency College, Madras. Without prior library experience he was then appointed Librarian of Madras University Library and was sent to England to study methods at the British Museum. There the Director suggested to him the advantages of the University of London School of Librarianship. At the school at that time he found the only subjects taught upon his own level to be library administration and classification, and, as I was then lecturer in the latter, we soon came into close association. Some of his problems he explained to me and, it being my own view that many of the subjects then in our course were not pertinent to him, I gave him the advice, which I confess I had forgotten but which he recalls in *Abgila*, 1953, March, page A 141, to read library economy, to work for a month in a public library and, with that experience, to visit different types of libraries. He proved to be one of the most alert, critical and inquiring students I had met, knowing exactly what he wanted and travelling England for it, as he has travelled much of the world since. He returned to Madras as one with a mission for the improvement and extension of libraries for his people in town and country. He was a founder of the Madras Library Association and in 1928 delivered a university extension course to nearly one thousand teachers on library science, which led to the founding in the following year of the first Madras Summer School of Library Science. Thereafter for twenty years he combined with his librarianship at the university his headship of the school. The next two years he spent as university librarian and professor of library science at Benares Hindu University; and from 1947 to 1955 he was professor of library science in the University of Delhi,

which university bestowed its doctorate upon him as "the father of librarianship in India". The teacher in him was accompanied by an enthusiastic urge to write of his experiences, experiments and speculations; so much so that he set out apparently to re-write the whole of librarianship, first in terms of Indian necessities and to instil the library idea into countrymen not well aware of them, and gradually to promulgate his theories on a world basis; he became in consequence the world's most prolific writer on these subjects.

300. *Colon Classification.* Early he told me he felt that a specially constructed classification was necessary for India. I pointed out to him the Herculean labour involved not only in the first lay-out of a general scheme, but in keeping pace with the continuously shift-ing ultimate sub-classes; moreover, those who had constructed classifications usually became immersed in them, often of course quite willingly, for the remainder of their lives. These arguments failed to deflect him; his Colon scheme was soon in being, was tried out in his own university library, and appeared in two slim volumes in 1933. His first substantial book, however, had been his *Five Laws of Library Science*, 1931, which students of Colon should read, as upon the "five" simple universal precepts, his subsequent work, modified though it may be, is based, and only his own exposition of them in that book is adequate. Between the first and second (1939) editions of Colon he read the two *Organization of Knowledge* volumes of Bliss, and forthwith enunciated his own theory in his *Prolegomena to Library Classifi-cation*, 1937, in which he expounded twenty-eight Canons of varying importance, but in the sum, a valuable statement of practical principles. In this emerged some of his individual classification terminology; i.e. *array* for the primary divisions of main classes or indeed of any classes in a determined order, *chain* for the tracing of an ultimate class step by step from its original genus, as in Physiology:

2	Digestive system.
21	Mouth.
212	Cavity of mouth.
2125	Palate.
21253	Soft palate.

and so on; *hospitality* for that flexibility which allows the insertion of any new class without dislocation of existing class order; these are samples of terms that must be assimilated by those who would understand his work. This, important as it was, was only the beginning of his vocabulary; for in his *Library Classification Funda-mentals and Procedure*, 1944, he produced, in what is the most extensive body of classificatory exercises that exist, a whole series of novel terms and first developed the statement that a notation is an *artificial classificatory language* into which the natural language of the classification terms is translated; and that classing proceeds by the translation of the right subject name by a process of recognizing and analysing the *phases* in literature, and the *facets* of subjects, and the *foci*, or stressed points on subjects in facets. Roughly, a phase is any aspect of one subject; a work on one defined subject is one-phased and one on two or more subjects, i.e. Mathematics for Engineers, Science and Divine Revelation, is two-phased, three-phased or poly-phased, as the case may be. Facets are the consistent subdivisions of a subject in a book; our author provides an example in *ultra-violet therapy for tuberculosis of the pylora* of which the facets are Medicine, Tuberculosis and Ultra-violet therapy; the names of the facets being Medicine [Organ facet, Pylora], Tuberculosis [Problem facet], Ultra-violet therapy [Handling facet]. There has been much development of facet-analysis since.

301. The Colon Classification is not a series of co-ordinate schedules setting out a graduated conspectus of the universe of thought and things in a continuous sequence with each subject developed to its *infima species* and with a notation for every term from the most general to the most minute; is not, in modern jargon, an enumerative scheme. As our preceding studies of notation have shown, nearly every scheme has not only its main tables worked out "enumeratively"; it has systematic, mnemonic schedules which develop and qualify all or some of the subjects in those tables. Ranganathan devised a set of independent tables for subjects, for relations, forms, and other classification factors, each of which could be used in combination with the other tables to sub-divide. These tables were, in Colon language, like the parts of a Meccano set which by the use of nuts and bolts can be used for many different constructions. The colon (:) represented the nuts and bolts and its importance is shown in that it gives its name to the scheme. By the use of the tables in the accurate combinations everything significant in a book can be expressed in the final individualizing number its receives.

302. The subject outline is of traditional canonical character and is as follows:

1 to 9 Generalia.	Δ Spiritual experience and mysticism.
Sciences.	*Humanities: Proper.*
A Science (General).	N Fine arts.

B	Mathematics.	O	Literature.
C	Physics.	P	Linguistics.
D	Engineering.	Q	Religion.
E	Chemistry.	R	Philosophy.
F	Technology.	S	Psychology.
G	Natural science (General) and Biology.	T	Education.

Humanities: Social Sciences.

H	Geology.	U	Geography.
I	Botany.	V	History
J	Agriculture.	W	Political science.
K	Zoology.	X	Economics.
L	Medicine.	Y	(Other) social sciences, including sociology.
M	(Other) applications of science, Useful arts.	Z	Law.

In *Prolegomena*[1], pages 204–5, can be found a rationalization of this outline in the manner in which Mouravit dealt with Brunet (see paragraph 147, *ante*), but seems not to stress it, as he adds, (page 210): "the order of the main classes in the lay-out of a scheme of classification is not of much moment so long as it is reasonably tolerable". In each class its first array or series of canonical divisions is set out and following this sub-divisions of them, as follows in B Mathematics; B1 Arithmetic.

B1	Arithmetic.
B11	Lower arithmetic.
B111	Numeration.
B112	Notation.
B113	Arithmetic operations.
B114	Approximations.
B12	Concept of numbers.
B13	Integers (theory of numbers).

Then follow directions for facet and foci sub-division thus:

$$B13 \ [N]: [P]: [M]$$

which signify number, problem and method, for each of which there is a table; samples are as follows:

Foci in N facet	*Foci in P facet*	*Foci in M facet*
1 Prime numbers.	1 Primality and divisibility.	1 Elementary.
2 Numbers defined by factor properties.	2 Distribution.	2 Algebraic methods.
21 Highly composite numbers.	3 Diophantine equations.	21 Elementary Algebraic methods.
5 Numbers defined by partitions properties.		

[1] 1937 edition.

Any of these may be added to B13 to qualify it, i.c. B131: N21: P2, if the book, or work, requires such sub-division.

The subject schedules are unusually short, the whole range from B to Z being carried in 106 double-column demy-octavo pages; not all of these filled. The facet and foci sub-divisions, as just illustrated, are printed in the class to which they intimately refer, but these "supplementaries", as we may call them, are in addition to the general "form divisions" which lie before the subject classes in the schedules. These are numbered 1–9 under the heading Generalia. Extracts from this table are

Common Sub-divisions (sample).

a Bibliography.
b Profession.
c Laboratories.
d Museums.
f Maps, Atlases.
h Institutions.
k Cyclopædias, Dictionaries.
l Societies.
v History.
y1 Scope.
y2 Syllabus, etc.
z Digests.
z4 Parody,
z61 in verse,
z62 in dramatic form, etc.

Geographic Sub-divisions (sample).

1 World.
10 Empires.
103 British Empire.
13 Pacific Countries.
15 Atlantic Countries.
19 Physiographic divisions.
2 Mother Country.
21 Madras.
3 Great Britain.
8 Australia,
   etc.

Mnemonic Digits

To be applied after a
Geographical number.
C Cities, towns, etc.
D Deserts.
L Lakes, tanks, etc.
M Mountains, hills, etc.
R Rivers, canals, etc.

Language divisions (sample).

1 Indo-European.
11 Teutonic.
111 English.
113 German.
12 Latin.
15 Sanskrit.
16 Iranian.
2 Semitic.
3 Dravidian.
41 Chinese, etc.

303. The main classes are sub-divided by Arabic numbers read decimally but without the decimal dot. A reduced example is

B *Mathematics.*
B11 Arithmetic.
B111 Numeration.
  112 Notation.
  113 Operations.

B21 *Algebra*, etc.
B3 *Analysis.*
B6 *Geometry.*
B7 Mechanics.

114 Approximations.	B9 Astronomy.
115 Fractions.	B9:1 Chronology.
1151 Vulgar.	B9:17 Calendars.
1152 Decimal.	

304. In classing any book the combination moves in the usual order, if I understand the scheme aright. The subject mark comes first, followed by the common sub-division number, and this, in turn, may be qualified after a colon by any appropriate sub-division table. Here are samples of class marks given us by the author himself:[1]

> D66:2 G 7 Cotton, H. Transmission and distribution of electrical energy.
> D66:2 is the *class number* where D=Engineering, D6 Mechanical engineering, D66 Electrical engineering and D66:2 Transmission; and G7 is a *book* number, where G=year 193– and G7=1937.
> O:2 J64:9 G52 Sprague, A. C. Shakespeare and the audience; a study in the technic of exposition.
> Here O is Literature, O: English literature, O:2 English drama, O:2 J64 Shakespeare; i.e. the English dramatist born in 1564 (J=15; J6=156– and J64=1564) and O:2 J64:9=Criticism of Shakespeare. G52 is the book number—G=193–, G5=1935; and G52=the third English book in the library on Shakespeare criticism published in 1935.

There are many other combinations and permutations of the notation which are, as a whole, peculiar to the scheme. Enough has been said, however, to show that the method is the using with the class number each schedule in turn that may be applicable, each change of schedule being marked by the inserted colon. In appearance the numbers are, like the classification, complex. One result of this method is that the very full tables which all other schemes possess are unnecessary. A series of relative short tables can be used to mark the widest range of subjects.

A theory, which pervades book arrangement by C. C., is that all division of subjects is conditioned by one or more of five concepts, called here fundamental concepts: Time, Space, Energy, Matter and Personality; and these affirm that a thought, act, process, indeed anything, occurs at a particular time, place, is the result possibly of definite operation, involving a material substance, and the totality of the thing in question, its identity, is its personality. All these concepts are subject to variant meanings which depend upon the context in which they occur. The most difficult is personality, which means just what has been said, but its familiar meaning is extended here in an unusual manner to

[1] Colon Classification, Part IV.

things which in fact have no personality in the traditional sense.

305. The second edition, in Part I, has a most exhaustive description of the Rules of Classification applied in order to produce the comprehensive call number for a book which is to consist of class number and book number in the usual sense. The first digit of a class number is the symbol representing the main class; then follow its subject divisions; then one or more of the eight *devices* comes into operation, the first being the colon which introduces a new characteristic as a rule; the second, the geographical device, which is represented in the sub-divisions that are printed above and is a familiar notation feature, as are the chronological device which follows it, the subject device, the alphabetic device. Two less familiar are the favoured category device used at places indicated in the schedules to individualize categories on which a large number of publications are possible and to place in order of their importance such subjects as crops in Agriculture; the classic device used to bring together in one class the editions of a classic, and its commentaries and sub-commentaries; and the bias device for arranging subjects which influence other subjects, as *Mathematics for Engineers*. All these are manipulations of notation and the effect of all this precise apparatus is to secure that a notation represents every useful factor in a book. The results in numbers vary from the very brief, such as A : P31k, the class number of a dictionary of scientific terms in Tamil, and J : E for C. H. Wright's "Agricultural analysis", and Δ : R for Hughes's "Philosophic basis of mysticism", to such lengthy and complete specifications as:

$$35 : 4261 : 63; \ J641 : 94183 : 6\cdot44\,N50$$

which stands for "The treatment of the after-effect of quinine treatment of malaria on the ear, in India in 1950", a number submitted by K. A. Isaac in *Depth Classification*, p. 86. But Ranganathan himself submits a tentative number for "Documentation service of pamphlets in steel industries in the British Parliament in the 1830's", as he expected to construct it from the Fourth edition of the scheme which is now in preparation:

$$248. \ W023. \ d\ 3. \ a\ M3: 75.\times9F183. \ mZ$$

(*Philosophy of Classification*, p. 72). It will be noted, however, that these numbers exhibit rather the remarkable capacity of the notation than its practicability for library purposes; in any case they are realistic only for denoting and describing what Ranganathan calls micro-units of thought as used in documentation indexing.

306. Each of the existing editions of the C.C. progresses,

although they are basically the same. The Second has, in Part IV, 286 pages of Call Numbers which are, in effect, a most complete series of examples of the scheme in class order, prefaced by analytical examples of their application. In the Third the work is greatly slimmed; the introduction has been reduced by about fifty pages; the examples (Part IV) have been omitted; the subject classes are reduced because the explanations given in former editions are now supplied by the *Fundamentals* and other works; and the terminology of Foci, Facets and Phases has been adopted. Further, in the earlier editions topics on Indology were scattered in the various main classes with ready-made notations; they are now brought together in a new Part IV. All parts are briefly but adequately indexed, the relative method being used where applicable. The Fourth edition, 1953, embodies many results of the research continuously pursued at Delhi. I have not yet studied it.

I am conscious that the method and complexity of the scheme, mainly because of the author's method of providing a new term for every new process, and thereafter assuming it to be adopted and familiar, has made it impossible for this writer at least to do the system justice or even to explain it to his satisfaction. The matter has increased in difficulty in that since 1939 Ranganathan has tended to regard classification as a method for documentation and the minute discrimination of micro-units of thought and the building up of these towards the main classes of which they are part. He has introduced ideas of value; one of them, the Octave device, adopted by the International Federation for Documentation in 1948 for use with the U.D.C., is probably important. The array in Dewey's classes is limited to ten terms, 0–9, but 0 is the "general" symbol for the contents combined of 1–9; when nine terms are used up, there is no easy way of providing further subjects in the array. The octave method uses 1–8 as now, but regards the present final 9 merely as a "repeater" which introduces another sequence of co-ordinate classes as 91, 92, 93, etc., to 98, when 991 becomes the beginning of another octave.

306.1. The scheme, and particularly the analytic and synthetic methods associated with it, have influenced recent classification study greatly, even to fascination. A detached onlooker may think that the methods are possibly greater than the scheme. It is, however, ingenuity itself, which results in standard mnemonic class tables and other divisions and operators leading to a notational expression for everything. As has been said, the aim is to produce method so condensed and so perfect in operation that every user will automatically give the same call-mark to a book without reference to the classificationist. Meanwhile, in Delhi and elsewhere groups are working on further developments. The results of these studies are seen best in *Depth Classification and Reference Service and Reference Material*, edited by Ranganathan and in part written by him, and consisting of papers many of which expound and develop Colon methods, discussed at the All-India Library Conference at Delhi in 1953. This work contains a useful glossary of current terminology by B. C. Vickery, who has given scholarly study to the methods of the scheme.[1] Since 1949, the study of optional facets has formed a serial subject in *Abgila*, the bulletin of the Indian Library Association, much of it by Ranganathan and his students.

Undoubtedly the best method of understanding Colon is to read its author's own books; there are at least ten of them which are directly upon classification (see Bibliography). They are not easy reading, especially if the later works are undertaken first. Read chronologically, each volume repeats much in its predecessors and adds to them so that familiarity with the terminology is gained. To this order I would except the *Elements of Classification*, a brief series of lectures to students on helpful order which could profitably be read first. The actual classing of books is dealt with at great length in *Fundamentals*, a valuable book for Dewey as well as Colon, but rather long for our use as it stands: a much reduced version would be a desirable class-book. If to these the student adds one of his most readable works, *Classification and Communication*, 1951, he will be in a position to esteem his author's general position and, if he wills, to go on to the more minute work that engages him in his later writings and to appreciate his most mature summary of his classificatory labours in his *Philosophy of Classification*. Among his advocates or interpreters in England are Bernard I. Palmer and A. J. Wells, whose lucid *Fundamentals of Library Classification* is on his methods with their application to other schemes. They have contributed simple practical accounts of the theory and working of the C.C. to my own *Introduction*. Other writers who deal with the C.C. are J. Mills, who writes with knowledge, and D. J. Foskett, who has also given us the results of his special application of the scheme to the subject of Packaging.

306.2. Bliss is an appreciative but severe critic. He questions the need, even in documentation, for such lengthy and formidable symbolizing as the C.C.'s complete specifications carry; they are certainly unlikely to be used in ordinary libraries. The importance of the C.C. lies, he thinks, in its exemplification of the valid principle of composite classification, systematic and synthetic, for

[1] As evidenced by his able revision of the Facet formula, and alternative schedule, for Chemistry. *Abgila*, March 1953, pp. 11–24.

specification of complex subjects and for recurrent sub-divisions. He feels, however, that "its systematic devices and its complicated pseudo-mnemonic notation are too much of a burden for any bibliographic classification. Nevertheless," he concludes, "the erudition, insight, and ingenuity of the author are truly admirable. The system is well worth study by those who contemplate constructive developments in bibliographic classification."[1]

307. *Farradane.* Already classification is moving further in synthetic methods which seem to show the influence of Ranganathan, although they evade Colon. Of these the most interesting is J. E. L. Farradane's *Scientific theory of classification and indexing.*[1] Like the later work of Ranganathan, its aim is the accurate definition and relating of subjects required in special indexing. If inspired by Ranganathan methods, there are interesting deviations which are probably regarded as radical. The model summary with which he introduces his accounts begins with the assertion that "a classification is a theory of the structure of knowledge. From a discussion of the nature of truth, it is held that scientific knowledge is the only knowledge which can be regarded as true. The method of induction from empirical data is therefore applied to the construction of a classification." The defect of existing classifications is that they depend upon headings derived deductively, which are not "accurately characterizable". The method proposed is to isolate subjects which have been "uniquely defined" by unique terms. Such terms, which must always be nouns, he therefore calls *isolates*; and between them and other isolates only four basic relations exist expressing appurtenance, equivalence, reaction and causation. These relating terms are *operators*. If the isolates are combined or qualified by the right operators—those which express the only possible relations between them—a linear symbol called an *analet* may be constructed. Alphabetical arrangements of such analets by their first factors will provide "a complete, logical subject index. . . . A classification can then be constructed by selection of deductive relations arranged in hierarchical form." Farradane claims boldly that his method results in the only true representation of the structure of knowledge and that his principles provide accurate and adequate indexing and classifying with complete flexibility.

The symbols by which analet and operator are conjoined are:

1 Appurtenance /(
2 Equivalence ≠
3 Reaction /-
4 Causation /:

[1] *Organization of Knowledge in Libraries*, p. 304.
[2] *Journal of Documentation*, v. 6, 1950, 2, pp. 83–9.

The combination appears thus:

A/(B, i.e. A contains B.
B)/A, i.e. B contains A.

The operator to mark the subject affected is placed on the side of the stroke nearest to it.

In subsequent issues of the *Journal of Documentation* Farradane has developed and considered the difficulties of the theory which is merely indicated here. It is obviously provisional and makes great claims; it is also clearly a long-range method which calls for an unusual skill in making and relating the uniquely defined isolates; certainly more than I possess. Experience only can discover its use in arranging books, for Farradane is an information officer rather than a librarian. I have, however, found his work remarkably stimulating and, as Ranganathan workers have already incorporated his terms into their writings, it may have influence on future classification.

Note. The third edition of Colon is that described in the foregoing chapter which should not be regarded as the current statement of its continuous progress although what is given is correct in fundamentals. The scheme has now reached a fifth edition, V.1, 1957, much revised in several particulars; for example, there are new schedules of the constituent States of India as re-formed in 1956, and otherwise the experience of recent years of Ranganathan in his work has been incorporated. V.2, which is promised, will deal with Depth Classification such as is deemed necessary in the minute arrangement used in documentation.—1958.

CHAPTER XX

THE STORY OF CLASSIFICATION IN ENGLAND

308. Few things would be more instructive, and perhaps salutary, than a candid record of the experiments in classification in England and America; the motives that led to them, their history, and their abandonment in some cases and the reasons for it. Such a history cannot be written at present, partly because librarians have a natural, if not quite reasonable, objection to the making public of their failures, and partly because the data we have is unreliable. It is admittedly some time since a systematic inquiry was made in which the question "by what system is your library classified?" was asked. A large number of answers gave "Subject Classification," and were indexed on this information under the Subject system of Brown—a scheme to which, it is safe to say, not all of them used. Others were described as classified libraries which had such Goliath classes as 1, Science, Art and Literature, 2, Religion, Philosophy and Economics, and so on; in truth, were libraries which were not classified at all. There are now more trained librarians, and all of these necessarily use classification.

309. Cataloguing, annotation and classification in a form more or less erudite have been practised in England for more than a thousand years; but I do not propose to repeat in detail the accounts of those earlier arrangements which are to be found in the writings of M. R. James, particularly in his *The Ancient Libraries of Canterbury and Dover*; J. W. Clark, in his *The Care of Books*; and E. A. Savage in his *Old English Libraries*—writings which are most deservedly precious to all librarians. All that need be said is that the library of Christchurch, Canterbury, was classified in the twelfth century, and succeeding monastic and, afterwards, cathedral libraries, had simple, effective schemes of arrangement. The norm of all such schemes is what is sometimes called the collegiate press-marking system, which is worth brief description. The books are arranged in broad classes:

    A Grammar and Classics.
    B Medicine and Astrology.
    C Philosophy.
    D Commentaries on the Sentences.

and so on. A tier of shelves is given to each class; each shelf is given a second letter; and each book receives a running number.

The diagram on page 205 shows the two variants of the system that were (and are, it may be said) most common.

310. It will be seen that in the first example the broad class may be divided so that a shelf is given to each division, as

AA Greek.
AB Latin.
AC Mediæval Latin.

and so on. The books are marked with these letters, plus an accession number; thus a copy of the *Iliad*, occupying the fifth place on its shelf, would be marked AA5. The method is convenient both for shelving purposes and for catalogue indications in a library which has finished its growth, since as each shelf is filled the scheme as a class order is overflowed and collapses. This, and the companion scheme, which is curious in that the shelves are read from right to left and then from left to right alternately from the bottom shelf upwards, are classifications for dead libraries.

311. In a most interesting paper, written in 1911, entitled *The Development of Notation in Classification*,[1] H. Rutherford Purnell has demonstrated that in the successive classifications in use at the Bodleian Library may be seen the growth of various forms of classification from the press-marking plan down to a curious decimal classification introduced as late as the eighteen-eighties. It was with the coming of the municipal public library that the question of library classification became a really practical one. Edward Edwards saw this need at the very beginning, and proposed a scheme of classification, which had some influence in its day, but is now nowhere in use so far as I am able to discover. It was a curious scheme when it is viewed in the light of modern knowledge; there is no place in it for books on non-Christian religions, and its other omissions are serious; but it is nevertheless more interesting for its virtues than for its defects. It is to Edwards that we owe the beginning in England of the serious study of the subject. But it was only a beginning. Edwards towered above all his contemporaries both in his knowledge of book classification and in his recognition of its potentialities. He had few followers for nearly forty years. A few broad groups represented the average library arrangement of books in the public libraries. Then one or two calamities fell upon libraries. The most popular logician of his day, W. S. Jevons, declared roundly that the classification of books by subject was a logical absurdity, and proved his argument in a manner quite conclusive to many

[1] In *The Library Assistant*, v. 8, pp. 25–33, 44–50, 1911. Reprinted as No. 3 of the Library Assistant's Association Series, 1911.

librarians. That his argument was founded upon a misunderstanding of library classification was not pointed out until twenty-four years later.[1] How potential his dictum was may be seen in a paper on *The Art of Cataloguing*, by the late Dr. W. E. A. Axon,[2] written in 1877, in which he says, "There is a prejudice in favour of a classified arrangement [in catalogues]. It has a scientific appearance, and it is only when the mazy intricacies of the classes have to be threaded that the fallacy of these appearances become evident. The arrangement in proximity to each other of works on the same subject is, of course, desirable, but it should be at once confessed that this is only possible as an aid to memory and not as a genealogical chart of human knowledge. Supposing such a logical classification were devised, the existence of so many books treating of more than one subject would invalidate its perfection." Such a pronouncement in the day of the untrained librarian must have been a great consolation to him, as it seemed to absolve him from learning what, in the then absence of good guides, seemed to be a formidable subject.

312. The second calamity was the invention of the ingenious and seductive "indicator," a contrivance by means of which readers were able to tell what books were or were not available. As it is now extinct, it may be described briefly. It was for use in libraries where the public were not admitted to the shelves. It consisted of columns of numbers in a glazed frame standing on the library counter. These numbers were on a blue ground if the books were available, and on a red ground if they were not. The would-be reader found the number of the book he required in the catalogue, and consulted the indicator before calling for the book by that number. The number was really written on the turned-up ends of a small metal slide which fitted into a little shelf in the column of the indicator, and one end of the slide was red and the other blue. This slide held the charge when a book had been borrowed. The whole machine was thus a remarkable help to the librarian; it threw the finer work of librarianship upon the reader himself, and saved brain wear effectively. As it concerned classification, it appeared to make it quite unnecessary. As the indicator was arranged by a continuous number, from one to any number representing the last book added, it seemed to be the best method, as it certainly was the easiest, to arrange the books by accession numbers. Such was the magic of the indicator that the Library Association actually passed a resolution commending it to local authorities, the worst

[1] See Brown, J. D., *Manual of Library Classification*, pp. 83–96, 1898. See also Sections 61–65 above.

[2] In his *Handbook of the Public Libraries of Manchester and Salford*, pp. 190–96, Manchester, 1877; reprinted in *The Library World*, v. 24, pp. 97–101, 1921–22.

Shelves.

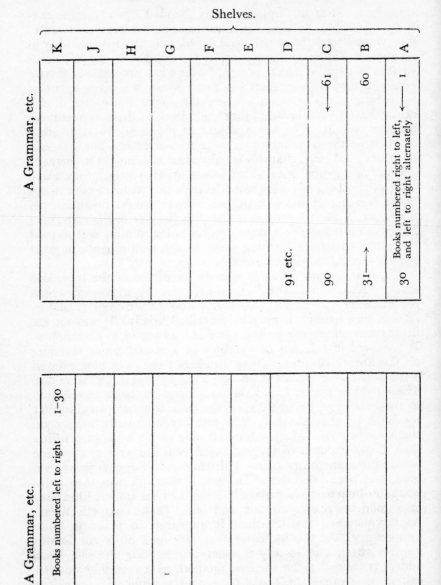

A Grammar, etc.

K J H G F E D C B A

61
60
1

91 etc.
90
31 ⟶
30

Books numbered right to left, ⟵
and left to right alternately

A Grammar, etc.

Books numbered left to right   1–30

A B C D E F G H J K

Shelves.

blunder in its history, and by so doing put back the calendar of technical library progress by thirty years.

313. The full value of classification was not properly realized until James Duff Brown did the greatest service that has been done in modern times to public libraries by experimenting with the open access system at the Clerkenwell (now Finsbury) Public Library. This meant, of course, the throwing open of the shelves to readers, and some form of shelf classification is essential to such a method. This, as we have seen, occurred in 1895, and in conjunction with J. Henry Quinn, he devised a classification which was used in the pioneer open access libraries. The Quinn-Brown system was superseded in 1898 by the Adjustable System which Brown published as an appendix to his *Manual of Library Classification and Shelf Arrangement*. That classification has now been superseded by the Subject system. The *Manual* has long been out of print, but the little book was a landmark in technical librarianship. It owed much to Edward Edwards, and its author had no formulated theory of classification; but he was the first to give a terse and comprehensive outline of the work that had been done in classification, and made it an accessible study. It is not too much to say that as much to him as to Dewey is due the good order which is usual in British libraries to-day as is the general use of the open access method.

314. Contemporaneously the problem of classification had been engaging American librarians; with more rapid and better results than in Europe. Dewey, as we have already seen, made a revolution in library arrangement with his Decimal Classification, which first saw the light in 1876. There was this difference, too, between the English and the American librarian. The former in his reach after distinction usually designed some piece of mechanical apparatus, an indicator, adjustable shelf book-rest, or similar article, showing an intense occupation with the mere machinery of libraries; his American colleague, on the other hand, devised for the same purpose a new classification or a set of cataloguing rules. It is significant that of the four schemes of classification now in most general use in libraries—the Decimal, Expansive, Library of Congress and the Subject—three are American in origin, and now we have from America Bliss's great work. They are only the merest fraction of the total number of schemes that have been proposed across the Atlantic. It is a point worthy of speculation as to whether or not the presence of scientific methods of book arrangement and the absence of mechanism and barriers were not largely responsible for what was formerly the higher estimation in which the American librarian was held and the better financial conditions which his libraries enjoy as compared

with the English librarian and his library. All these differences are fortunately ceasing to exist.

315. It was some time before the Dewey classification got any real hold upon British librarians. In the eighteen-nineties, however, L. Stanley Jast, then librarian of Peterborough, came out as a champion of the scheme, and at much the same time Basil Anderton and the late T. W. Lyster were also its advocates. But generally there was a great fear of the difficulty and complexity of Dewey, a fear founded partly upon ignorance of the scheme itself, and partly upon the fact that until 1900 there were hardly any trained library assistants in England to apply it. This led to the issue of a number of broad classification schemes in which some such arrangement as follows constituted the whole scheme:

A Religion and Philosophy.
B History.
C Travel.
D Social Science.
E Science.
F Fine Arts.
G Useful Arts.
H Literature and Language.
J Poetry and Drama.
K Fiction.
L Miscellaneous.

—classifications which did not classify, and by their incoherence were expected in some way to make things easier for librarian and reader. Some think that it was unfortunate, too, that Duff Brown, the most influential librarian of the time, never viewed the Decimal Scheme with any kindness, holding it to be too American, and producing schemes of his own, which, good as they undoubtedly are, offer no ultimate advantages over the American scheme.

316. Closely allied to the advocacy of classification for English libraries, was the controversy which has been dignified by the name of the battle of the catalogues. This was begun in 1897 in England by a paper by Brown and Stanley Jast entitled *The Compilation of Class Lists*,[1] read before the Library Association in January 1897, in which it was advocated that catalogues should themselves be arranged in the order of the classification scheme, with adequate indexes; and the advantages of this type of catalogue, now widely accepted by librarians, were explained. The

[1] In *The Library* (1st Series), v. 9, pp. 45–69; in the same v. is the first counter-attack by Robert K. Dent, "The New Cataloguer and Some of His Ways," pp. 174–8; and further articles by Brown and Jast, and by W. E. Doubleday, follow. These set the plan for the "battle," which lasted for some years.

controversy engendered a great deal of heat and a certain amount of light, on a subject which before had not received adequate attention. At this stage in the history of librarianship it is not necessary to pursue the matter; but the discussion did much to popularize classification study.

317. The publication of E. C. Richardson's lectures, *Classification, Theoretical and Practical*, 1901, which have been referred to so often in this book, gave the study a new meaning and put heart into it. The Library Association later promoted courses for the study of library matters, and the late Franklin T. Barrett, and afterwards Mr. Jast, both lectured on the subject of classification at the London School of Economics; and now it is a cardinal subject in all librarianship courses.

318. It has been shown that the theory of classification enunciated by Richardson has not been universally accepted. When I first read a paper upon it before the Library Association, in 1907,[1] E. Wyndham Hulme stated that "he had come to the conclusion that the final order of the larger groups or families of literature could be changed at the wish of the classifier, without affecting the value of the classification, which depended upon the accuracy and sufficiency of the division and definition of the ultimate sub-classes. Book classification was not a science. It was an art, like that of fitting a child's puzzle together. You must be familiar with the pieces before you could put the puzzle together. It was therefore impossible for any satisfactory system of book classification to proceed from one person, for no librarian however well-informed could affect even a nodding acquaintance with all branches of literature." This interesting pronouncement its author amplified in a series of articles entitled *Principles of Book Classification*,[2] which he did not publish in book form and apparently did not complete. There are enough of them, however, to show his theory and its main applications, and as I have dealt with the question in earlier pages, it is unnecessary to discuss it again. Apart from certain other objections it may be admitted that Hulme's theory of classification is difficult, if not impossible, to teach; it is individualism in method triumphant. However, it has helped to draw attention to the Library of Congress system, which is supposed, in some way, to be constructed on the theory enunciated. It has also attracted later workers in classification, who put forth schemes of their own. Thus, Lawrence A. Burgess produced what he called *The "Form Table" Scheme of Book Classification*,[3] and Lionel Roy McColvin proposed *A New Bibliographical Classification*,[4] in which "the prime aim has been

[1] *Lib. Assoc. Record*, v. 9, 426–42; ibid., v. 9, 468, 1907. [2] *Ibid.*, v. 13–14, 1911–12.
[3] *Library World*, v. 27, p. 180, et seq., 1925. [4] *Ibid.*, v. 28, p. 107, et seq., 1925–26.

to show not the theoretical relationship of things, but the use, made by man of things and knowledge," and both are based on such considerations as Hulme advances. It is impossible to criticize these new attempts, as the first is published only in outline, and the second not at all so far as actual tables are concerned.

319. From the time of its advocacy by Brown and Jast the classified catalogue has taken some sort of root in England, although here, as in America, the dictionary form with all its attendant and inherent deficiencies is the more popular form. In fact, in recent years there have been few printed library catalogues of any kind. Most of those we can study are at least twenty years old. Amongst such complete classified catalogues the best perhaps is that of Newcastle-upon-Tyne Public Libraries, and the last noteworthy one that of Bolton Public Libraries. Each was issued as a series of separate class-lists. Most libraries which have adopted this form have been able to produce only one or two class-lists, but some of them have been good. *The Classified Catalogue of the Finsbury Public Libraries*, Pt. 1, General Works, Pt. 2, Philosophy (1915), Bristol Municipal Public Libraries' *Reference Library Catalogue: Sociology Section* (1913), Coventry Public Libraries' *Catalogue of Books in Natural Science, Useful, Fine, and Recreative Arts* (? 1914), Norwich Public Libraries' *Music and Music Literature* (1924), and Hampstead Public Libraries' *Catalogue of Works of History and Historical Material* (1923), are examples that are evidence of the appeal of the classified form. To them may be added the *Bulletin of Additions* of the Glasgow Public Libraries (3 issues, various dates), although it is a self-contained Dewey catalogue of general character on a large scale with indexes and other apparatus, and except for the fact that it is not a catalogue of a whole library stock, might have been mentioned under complete catalogues; and the same Libraries' *Guide for Young Readers: Woodside District Library* (1921), a classified (Dewey) catalogue of children's books preceded by an index of authors and titles and completed by a subject index.

320. In America the *Catalogue of the A.L.A. Library* published in 1893 at the suggestion of Melvil Dewey, made the classified catalogue a household word amongst librarians.. It was re-issued in a greatly revised form in 1904 as the *A.L.A. Catalogue: 8,000 volumes for a popular library* (Washington: Government Printing Office). This was a dictionary and a double classified catalogue within one cover. In the dictionary section the class-marks of both Cutter and Dewey were added to the entries; while there were separate sections classified by Dewey and by Cutter respectively. Supplements in Dewey form to this catalogue appeared in 1912 (*A.L.A. Catalogue*, 1904–11, 3,000 titles, edited by Elva L.

Bascom, Chicago), and in 1924 (*A.L.A. Catalogue*, 1912–23, an annotated list of 4,000 books, Chicago). The other American classified catalogue which is best known to English librarians is that of the Carnegie Libraries of Pittsburgh,[1] which is a fully annotated and most desirable Dewey catalogue. The great occasional class-lists of the Library of Congress are standard examples of the application of the classification of that library.

321. The stocks of living libraries make rapid growth and are subject to continuous change; to-day it has become an economic impossibility for most libraries to issue a printed catalogue which must be revised and reprinted at very short intervals if it is to represent the stock; and as we have suggested, the abandonment of the complete printed catalogue has been almost general. Brown offered a solution of the problem in the form of his *Select Catalogue and Guide* to the Islington Public Libraries, 1910, a classified catalogue on his own Subject system, with indexes, of what he regarded as the basic stock of the libraries, of those books which it would seem would always be required by the public and therefore would be maintained permanently. This appears, in modern circumstances, to be the best approach to a general printed catalogue where the cost forbids a complete one. The average library depends upon either the sheaf or the card catalogue, both of which forms have been brought to a high degree of effectiveness, as we shall have occasion to show later. This catalogue is sometimes supplemented by a bulletin, issued periodically, containing entries of additions to the stock. The contents of such bulletins are usually set out in alphabetical author order under main class headings; and only a few have the closer classified arrangement which is the essence of a classified catalogue. Amongst bulletins in various forms, issued at various times, although most of them have now ceased publication, may be mentioned those of Coventry, Croydon, Finsbury, Ipswich and Norwich, all of which have a common ancestor and have Dewey class-marks; those of Aberdeen University Library, and of the John Rylands Library, Manchester, which are both fine publications and have Dewey arrangement; that of Islington, which uses Brown's Subject class-marks; and that of Edinburgh, which uses those of the Library of Congress. There are many similar American bulletins, and without implying any appraisal or criticism of these or of others, those of the following libraries may be noted—Brooklyn, Grand Rapids, New York, Pittsburgh, and Pratt Institute (Brooklyn).

322. It only remains to look at the present position of classification in England. The Dewey Decimal Classification far

[1] In three series running to twenty-five parts, 1907–1914, Pittsburgh.

outstrips its competitors, and is used by two-thirds of public libraries and a number of institutional ones. About fifty libraries use the Brown Subject Classification. The Library of Congress scheme, which is a "large library" scheme, is nevertheless in use in twenty-eight libraries, of which the National Library of Wales is the largest. The schemes used in non-public libraries are varied and some home-made. In the Library Association *Manual on University and College Library Practice*, Dr. Offor disparages Dewey, commends Bliss, but leans towards the home-made scheme. Some school libraries use the Cheltenham scheme, but in the *Guide to School Libraries*, issued by the Incorporated Society of Assistant Masters in Secondary Schools, the balance is held between Dewey and Bliss. Business and commercial firms, as well as some notable intellectual institutions, are making full or part use of the Universal Decimal scheme. In several places in his interesting *Special Library Methods*, 1940,[1] John L. Thornton discusses the varying schemes used in learned society and other special collections. There is no uniformity there.

This account is only approximately accurate, as I said in the first lines of this chapter; and, indeed, it is a rather humiliating one, showing a conservatism that is astonishing. It does suggest, however, the hold that the Decimal Classification has won in England despite its outworn categories and frequent cross-division and its too general want of balance. The scheme has the one vital quality of "reviseableness," if I may be allowed to coin a rather ugly word, and its other advantages are great.

323. As for the future of classification in England, prudence forbids any other prophecy than may be inferred from the fact that the public is demanding more and more of the librarian information, and the manipulation of materials in producing it, which can only be revealed through the means of classifications becoming ever more minute and more scientific. Whether this will come by the continued revision and expansion of the standard schemes which become gargantuan in size, or whether the synthetic methods, complex and difficult as they appear to be, of Ranganathan, or of Farradane, will prevail, the future must reveal. A Classification Research Group, established as the result of the Royal Society's Scientific Information Conference, 1948, has been at work since 1952, its members drawn mainly from scientific and technical libraries. It makes slow progress, as may be expected in a field where every worker is inclined to have his individual point of view, and where the aim is to agree upon principles of synthetic classification which, in the words of its Honorary Secretary,

[1] Grafton.

Brian C. Vickery, will be of practical use, to those who make, use and teach classification."[1] Vickery himself has devoted several scholarly articles to the impact of classification on indexing. He has produced a volume, *Classification and Indexing in Science*, 1958, which is practical and most readable and ranges more widely in the structure of schemes as well as in indexing than its title indicates.

323.1. It may be added that Bernard I. Palmer is Chairman of the Research Group, whose proceedings are reported in the *Journal of Documentation* and amongst its members, or associated with it, are E. J. Coates, R. A. Fairthorne, J. E. L. Farradance and A. J. Wells, a fact worth remarking as each is also a writer who gives severe study and clear thinking to matters of importance to the more advanced student of classification.

[1] *Library Association Record*, v. 55, pp. 187–8, 1953.

DIVISION THREE
THE PRACTICAL WORK OF CLASSIFICATION

CHAPTER XXI
CLASSIFICATION AND LIBRARY ADMINISTRATION

324. Every librarian when placed for the first time in charge of a library will, if he is wise, face the question of the arrangement of that library before he engages in any other important work in connexion with it. Even if his library is not in actual existence, and has yet to be built, he will settle with most considered care the two points: 1, whether or not the library shall be classified, and 2, if he decides in favour of classification, by what scheme it shall be done. It is rather late in the day to advance arguments in favour of the classified as against the unclassified library: no modern librarian who has any sound knowledge of the purpose of libraries and of the tasks they have to perform will hesitate for a moment in deciding in favour of classification. But when he has decided to classify, he is confronted immediately with a series of important practical problems the solution of which is vital to the future of his library.

325. The first concerns the design of the library building. It is necessary to say that a classified library requires more room than one which is unclassified, and a more simple mode of planning. In an unclassified library additions of books can be made to the shelves at any part that may be convenient: such adding cannot alter the significance of an order which does not exist; and usually the empty shelves stand ready for new books at the end of the collection; because in the ordinary unclassified library the books are arranged in a straight numerical order, the first book received being numbered 1, the second 2, and so on without limit and without reference to any characteristic of the books.

326. In the classified library it is desirable to leave spaces at the end of every subject on which a number of books have been written, and to the literature of which frequent additions may be expected; or, at least, spaces should be left at the end of each class, in order that additions may be accommodated without too much movement of the general arrangement. This is a mere

economy of time. Theoretically—seeing that books which are arranged by subject are independent of the shelves—the space may be left at the end of the whole collection; but this would involve the pushing up of thousands of volumes in a library of moderate size whenever books were added, and in practice that would be out of the question. It is clear, then, if space must be left at the end of each class, that more shelves must be provided than would be necessary in the unclassified library.

327. Another point of elementary importance is the relation of the classification to the method of administering the library. An open-shelf library without classification would be absurdly impossible and confusing we know. So also is it difficult to administer an open shelf library that is housed in several rooms, unless there is a larger staff than most libraries can afford: the ideal library is one large room containing the whole of the classified collection. Even with an adequate staff, the library, if divided up amongst a number of rooms, is likely to be less effective in various ways than is the other. There is loss of time in getting from room to room; and the point for us as classifiers is that either there must be one class in one room and another in another and so on; or, there must be several parallel classified collections, one in each room. Neither method is economical nor desirable in a general library, and even in seminar libraries, each confined to a subject, there are grave difficulties arising from the fact that the boundaries of knowledge are most indefinite, and the inter-relations of subjects so many, that a student of one subject will often require books belonging, on their predominant classification, to some other subject.

328. These considerations apply in a library which, as it were, is a one-piece institution, but, to use a phraseology now somewhat harmless, a public library system is a complex of branch libraries, each with at least three sequences nowadays, of books for adults, for children and of periodicals for either or both. All central libraries have reference departments which in all larger towns are the principal departments of the system; some branch libraries, as in the London "district libraries," have them too. There is the further complication that library stock is of different sorts: books, periodicals, pamphlets, manuscripts; and many have to maintain special collections.

A further simple consideration is that the primary classification of books is by the characteristic of size. It is obvious that large books, quartos and folios, for example, cannot stand side by side with octavos and smaller books on the same shelf without a loss of vertical space that few libraries can bear. Further, books are published in unequal proportions as regards size; one cannot forecast with accuracy how much space will be required in a given time for each size of books. The shelves, therefore, of a classified library should be adjustable, so that, as the number of any one size of books grows, the shelves may be made wider or narrower vertically, as the case may be, to accommodate them. I am presuming, you will observe, that the books will be arranged, before any other classifying is undertaken, in at least two series by the sizes, 1, octavos and smaller books, and 2, quartos, folios and larger books. In reference libraries it is better to have three sequences:

1. Octavos and smaller books.
2. Quartos.
3. Folios.

In lending libraries folios are few, and the two series I have named will usually be sufficient. The problems of size classification are dealt with later (Section 367).

329. In older libraries, or others where readers do not go to the shelves, there usually is no close classification, although this is not always the case, and some of them possess classified catalogues. Usually such libraries have been arranged in the simple numerical accession order mentioned above. It may be thought, too, that if there is a classified catalogue the purpose of classification on the shelves is achieved by its means and shelf classification is superfluous, seeing that only the staff have access to the shelves. Consider, however, the daily quest of readers, not for a book on a given subject, but for all the books upon it; and consider, too, the time that is wasted if the librarian is suddenly required to assemble all the books he has on the French Revolution, or Radium, or the Einstein Theory. He must classify his books to the extent of the subject every time he has to answer such a requirement. Would it not be better to do it once and finally for all subjects by the simple act of classifying the whole library? The fact that we have too many separate sequences in a classified library does not invalidate classification. There is a wide difference between the consulting of a dozen or more *groups* of books for the whole of those dealing with a subject and the searching hopefully through a whole unclassified collection or series of collections.

330. It is now sufficiently clear that classification has a very decisive bearing not only upon the arrangement of the books on the shelves, but upon the planning of the library building, the character of its apartments, the type of shelves to be used, and on the method of working. So important is a right decision at the outset that no apology should be necessary for emphasizing the fact. A library is a most complex machine, in which changes

present disheartening difficulties if they are not foreseen; and the better its organization from the point of view of the public, the greater are the difficulties any change involves. Consider an example. For complete service a library has books which are classified on the shelves: the classification symbol is written, or stamped, on the back of the book, on the back or front of the title-page, and on the board label inside it. The library has also name catalogue, classified catalogue, shelf list, accessions register: the symbol appears on all of these; in fact, all except the first depend for their arrangement upon it; and the classified catalogue has an average of from three to five entries for each book, and, if card charging is used, as is the most general practice, the class-mark is written on the book card. To alter the class-mark of one book only would mean the alteration of at least twelve records; and in a system of libraries each of which has a complete card catalogue of the books in the system, this number is multiplied accordingly. If, therefore, it becomes necessary to change a library, or even a whole class, the cost in labour and money is really formidable. Preliminary thought, a careful regard for the probable future of the library, and the choice of a classification which, because of its flexibility and adaptability, will meet all reasonable possibilities, are economic necessities. Never be misled into a position of the librarian who thinks some inferior scheme, easy to apply, "will do for the present." Look well ahead.

331. We are on more delicate ground when we come to make choice of the classification scheme we are to apply. There is no guiding rule here adequate for all places and every type of reader. One can readily believe that in some special libraries the Dewey scheme would be found inadequate or even lacking in the necessary scholarship. Objections similar or different might be discovered to any other classification scheme that we know. The choice, however, must be made, unless you intend the onerous and chancy task of constructing a scheme of your own. I do not attempt to deter the possible Dewey or Cutter who may read these pages from such an experiment; because I do not believe for a moment that the ultimate classification, impossible of improvement, has been reached. Even with the challenging individual achievements of Bliss and Ranganathan before us, I would ask you not to attempt any such thing without much searching of heart, and a recognition of the fact that sound authorities—Wyndham Hulme amongst them—are of opinion that no great general scheme hereafter can be the work of only one person. In any case the task is more than herculean; and most of us, I imagine, will be content to avail ourselves of the schemes designed by other men. Each of the three or four leading

classifications has its individual virtues, and the choice of any
of them can be justified on a number of grounds. It is unnecessary
at this stage to offer any advice in the matter; but it is good sense
to point out that there would be very distinct advantages to
readers if all libraries were arranged similarly; if a reader entering
the reference libraries at Liverpool, Birmingham, Glasgow and
the British Museum could be sure that the arrangement of subjects
in each was identical and that if he had mastered the arrangement
of one he had virtually mastered the arrangement of them all.
(This, of course, can only be so approximately, because, classing
being an art and not an exact science, no two libraries could
possibly reach identical placing of all books. That difficulty is
insuperable until a central cataloguing bureau classes all our
books for us.) There may be a virtue in adopting the scheme
which is most popularly used, in order that your library may
form, as it were, one more branch of the great national library
of which every library in every town may be considered to be a
branch. There are counter-arguments. It is said, for example,
that the adoption of a uniform system of classification throughout
all libraries would eradicate or stultify the individual initiative
of librarians. There is value in the argument; but the librarian
whose initiative is circumscribed by his classification has very
little initiative; and the public advantages of uniformity outweigh
it, as I think, entirely; quite apart, of course, from the salutary fact
that the purpose of libraries goes rather beyond the preserving of
the initiative of librarians.

332. This would seem to lead to the conclusion that we should
all adopt the Dewey classification, because that happens to be
the most widely used. This may be so; but dogmatism on this
matter is obsolete. The arguments in favour of and against
uniformity are, however, to be noted. In these chapters it will
be convenient to draw most of our examples from Dewey's scheme,
because of the commonness of its use. Moreover, a knowledge
of this scheme, whether we ourselves apply it or not, is an
indispensable part of the librarian's equipment.

333. When the choice of a scheme has been made, it should
be studied root and branch; its outline, hierarchy, method of
sub-division, common sub-divisions, mnemonic features, indexing,
and its notation and the manipulations it permits should be
thoroughly grasped. In spite of all our precedent study, this is
no easy task. For the amateur classifier the way is beset with
pitfalls, confusions, absurdities; most of which are due to the
practice of classing by minute sub-divisions of the classification
without reading back from them to the main heading in which
the sub-division appears. Another prevalent mistake is to crowd

books on subjects for which there are headings in the sub-divisions into the main class; for instance, I have seen books on the history of an English county placed under the headings for the general history of Europe, and have seen even worse elementary mistakes. Then notations are frequently misread: I do not mean that correct figures are copied incorrectly, but that historical numbers are mistaken for geographical ones; and there are many other instances. A study of the scheme in its entirety would prevent such errors as these; and, what is more important, suggest the full possibilities of a scheme, which are often greater than appear on the surface.

334. Then there arises the question: Should the chosen scheme be used as it stands, or only in part? If our library is not a large one, is it necessary to go, say, further than the three-figure position of Dewey (to "more than three figures," in ordinary classification jargon)? Would not further sub-division mean unnecessary minuteness with the corresponding disadvantage of a long class-number? Further, even if there is a real advantage in minute classification, is this not neutralized in practice because readers cannot understand or cannot remember the figures of a long class-mark? Librarians who advocate a limited use of a classification scheme, do so on grounds which should now be negligible. In few libraries, they urge, is there sufficient librarianship in the staff to make this possible; the library has not enough classifiers equipped for the task. If I may instance my own circumstances: at Croydon, which is medium-sized and not one of the great libraries of the country, in 1939–40 we added about 20,000 volumes. It is manifestly impossible for one man to classify this number of books in a single year, and to carry out the multifarious other duties that fall to a librarian. The argument was once upon a time a good one; it is not so to-day. Every fair-sized library has now at least one or two good classifiers, and, if it has not, it should get them.

335. The arguments in favour of the limited use do not seem to be adequate. As for the public: it is not quite so unintelligent as some librarians appear to think: it can usually understand six or seven figures or letters, even decimal figures or letters divided alphabetically. When it is unable to follow a classification, it is because the guides and indications with which the library should be furnished are lacking or are inadequate. The practical point is that the classification should be carried as far as is necessary to define and segregate the subject matter of the books. Sooner or later, if the library grows, the full classification will be needed, and we know what is involved in alterations. Cutter's maxim is: "Be minute, be minute, be not too minute," which is not

altogether conclusive, because it is difficult to say what being too minute means. The more positive rule, "Classify a book in the most specific head in the main tables that will contain it" is preferable; because if this is observed it must bring the whole classification into play. In brief, use the classification as it stands unless there are quite unusual reasons in favour of a different course, as might be the case in an old cathedral or similar library, which is complete and will never be increased in size.

336. Modifications are sometimes made in schemes, and this question deserves thought. It is curious that the librarian mind is so constructed that it likes "nibbling at classification schemes" —to use the phrase of James Duff Brown. In part this is due to the weaknesses of one kind or another that a librarian can see in the scheme he has chosen; few schemes, indeed, do not seem capable of improvement in some way when we have tested them. I do not recommend modifications beyond those which are permitted, or are provided for, by the maker of the classification. Dewey, for example, shows us three ways of treating biography: at 920, or with the subject with which the person written about was identified, or as a separate class arranged alphabetically under the names of the persons biographed. Other examples can doubtless be found.

337. The modifications which are usually made—which, if they are to be made, should be provided for at the outset—concern works of and about Literature, and History and Travel worry some librarians into mauling a scheme. Dewey has the great and difficult class, Fiction, arranged as part of Literature, first under the language, then under the form (Fiction) and then chronologically. As we know, all the divisions of his Literature are similarly arranged. In a library where the readers are of the student type and need literature in a systematic order this arrangement of Dewey is probably to be preferred to any modification of it. In a general library, readers have as a rule no systematic view or systematic need of literature; and, so far as Fiction is concerned, for one reader who definitely wants to read Jane Austen, Hardy, D. H. Lawrence or Virginia Woolf, three vaguely want "something to read." Moreover, how many of our general readers know if William Faulkner and Henry James—to use names at random—are English or American authors; and how many have any notion of their dates? It seems, therefore, quite legitimate to remove all fiction from the Literature class, and to make a separate class of it arranged alphabetically according to the names of the authors. Other modifications sometimes made have the purpose of bringing together works on History and Geography: on the ground that the students of a given country

or town want both its past and present characteristics together. Sometimes this is done by classing all geography at the history number; sometimes by using the history number plus some individualizing sign for travel; thus

> 942·21   History of Surrey.
> 942·21(T)   Travel in Surrey.

And the use of these numbers ranges the books on travel in Surrey immediately next to those on the history of the county. In the Subject Classification of Brown this is done by using one number only for a place, which is divided into history and travel by the addition of a number from the categorical table; thus

> U830·10   History of Surrey.
> U830·33   Travel in Surrey.

338. If any librarian possessed the knowledge and industry necessary to make Dewey (shall we say) a really one-place classification he would do a great service to classifiers; but his scheme would no longer be Dewey, but a new classification, to be studied as such. Meantime, it must be said that to write a history of all the modifications of this or that scheme which have been made to answer the convenience, and sometimes the vanity, of librarians would occupy an inordinate space, and would not serve any purpose except occasionally to show the futility of the work. Those described are the most common.

CHAPTER XXII

THE RULES FOR CLASSING BOOKS

339. Forty years ago L. Stanley Jast asserted that "it is one thing to have a satisfactory classification and another to have a satisfactory classifier." Although satisfactory classifiers are now available, the implications of the assertion remain. It is quite safe to say that few persons can classify in a practical manner who have not studied how to do it in relation to the actual working of a library. If classification were a recognized science with laws as immutable as the accepted laws of Nature, it would be a relatively simple task to set out precepts and even codes for practical classing. It is not; it is an art in which, in hundreds of cases in a year, an exercise of personal judgment is required. All rules are conditioned by that fact. This most important rule is hardly a rule at all.

1. *Place a book where it will be most useful.*

It can be seen at once that this involves a number of considerations. Useful for whom: the general reader, the student, the client who is no reader at all and whom we wish to attract? Again, if it seems a useful place to-day, is that because of some temporary turn of thought or fashion or is the attraction to a place real and likely to last? The answer, in a rough way, is that if here, as elsewhere, we follow the guidance of those who are the professional workers in the subject we are classing, we are more likely to serve the best interests for the longest time. In addition to this major precept, there are a few rules which Dewey, Brown, Cutter and later writers have evolved, and these can be cast into brief paraphrase, and then studied in detail: there is no more important part of our study than this part. These are the *rules for classing*:

1. Place a book where it will be most useful.
2. Class by subject, then by form, except in pure literature, where form is paramount.
3. Place a book at the most specific head that will contain it.
4. When a book deals with not more than three divisions of a subject, place it in the one that is most prominently dealt with, or—if the treatment is of equal importance—in the one dealt with first. When the book deals with more divisions of the subject than three, place it at the general heading which covers them all.
5. When two headings clash, make a decision as to which is to prevail.

6. When a book appears on a subject which has no stated place in the classification scheme, determine the heading to which it is most nearly related, and make a place for it there.

7. Avoid placings which are in the nature of criticism.

To these seven essential rules may be added one or two working principles, which are hardly rules, but which deserve attention:

1. Consider the predominant tendency or purpose of a book.
2. Where one subject affects another, or an author influences another, place under the subject or author influenced.
3. Books pro and con any subject go together at the subject.
4. Always have a reason for your placing of a book.
5. Index all decisions.

340. Since we class a library by subjects, in the nature of the case the rule we have numbered 2 is of crucial importance. *To class by subject and then by form* means only, first determine the subject of the book by the main tables and place it there; then add to that subject class-mark the appropriate common subdivision number or other qualifying symbols to indicate the method in which the subject is presented. The difficulty is that we cannot always determine what the subject is without some examination and thought; and even then, the chances of error are greater in this work than in any other known to us. The art of classing is complicated at every stage by the complex character of books, which are so often one thing in appearance and another in actuality. This explains, in part, Jast's assertion which is quoted above. No ordinary course in classification itself can equip a classifier fully, because that equipment implies a knowledge of the subjects treated in books, and although we may have educated classifiers, we cannot have omniscient ones. The main, the crucial, problem of classification is the *subject of the book* to be classed; and there is no royal road to determining that in some cases. Some sixty per cent of books, however, are on specific, easily recognized topics, and on these the classifier can work fairly rapidly. For the remainder we can only suggest a simple common-sense procedure. The classifier takes the book in hand, reads the preface and the list of contents, and runs through the index in some cases. Only very elusive works refuse to yield their subject and their purpose to this simple method, providing always, as already suggested, that the classifier recognizes these things. Bliss instances an example which appears to me to illustrate, as does Jevons's steam-engine book, the point just made: "If the book on Scotland is not mainly geographic and historical, but consists of descriptive and narrative chapters together with a melange of literary and scientific observations and reflections on the national traits and institutions, also considerable social philosophy in the

last chapters, the judgment is indeed complex and the decision may be uncertain." But surely, from first to last, this is a book on Scotland.

341. The first warning is: Never class a book by the face value of its title-page: the results of doing so would be ludicrous, as certain quite hoary jokes in literature, and in classing itself, prove. The shepherd who bought Ruskin's *Notes on the Construction of Sheepfolds* was acting on the same principle as the classifier who places by title only, and reached a similar result. Such a warning is scarcely needed by the careful student. The more difficult book is that which has a metaphorical or allusive term for its title, a form of title to which Ruskin again was specially addicted: *Unto this Last, Time and Tide, The Eagle's Nest* and *Fors Clavigera*, convey absolutely nothing to a classifier at sight, and some of them have to be read, at least in part, before the subject can be discovered.

342. Even more difficult are those books which cause some classifiers to confuse subject and form. It is here that we must consider always the dominant key of a book, and ask ourselves why it was written—not critically, of course, but merely inquiringly; who is the author and what his purpose. Supposing we have a book entitled *The Nutrition of Animals showing the effects of vegetable diet upon health and habit.* Is it, we ask, a book on the nutrition of animals or one on vegetarianism? We read some of it, and see that it deals with the eating and digestive processes of herbivorous animals in great detail perhaps; but it is clearly a book with a purpose, and that is not the physiology or biology of animals, but the advocacy of a vegetable diet for man. The subject of the book for the classifier is vegetarianism, although he may refer from animal nutrition in his catalogue to the place chosen, and should do so. Jast has given a further example which is more subtle, Haddon's *Evolution in Art*, he remarks,[1] "has been classed in Anthropology on the ground that it is a work on 'life-histories of designs,' written by and from the point of view of a biologist." The classifier reached this conclusion from his knowledge of the fact that Haddon was a well-known exponent of Evolution, and naturally concluded that this was one other contribution to his special subject. "But," Jast continues, "this is to confuse what is clearly treatment with topic. It is design treated biologically, and in Design in Fine Arts it should certainly go. Drummond's *Natural Law in the Spiritual World*, about which nobody could make any mistake, is a similar example, only it is Natural Theology this time treated biologically."

343. It will be clear now that the assumption is made that books on specific topics, if placed under those topics, fulfil the

[1] Library Classification. In Greenwood's *British Library Year Book*, 1900–01, p. 33.

simple but all-important rule that "books must be placed where they will be most useful." The modern classifier has a much easier mind on this matter than the older classifier; because he remembers always the extra classifying power he has at his disposal in the classified catalogue. He will make references under Evolution for Haddon's book; and under Natural Law for Drummond's, in the assurance that the student of biology who may need these particular books will be certain to find them although they are shelved apart from his subject.

344. The primary rule of the most useful place, which is really a part of the fundamental rule of classification: "*characteristics chosen for classification must be essential in relation to the purpose of the classification*," helps us to determine what is the subject of one or two difficult books. Take these titles:

> A Bibliography of Road-making.
> The Law of Public Libraries.
> Book-keeping for Grocers.

Are these books on road-making, libraries or grocery, or books on bibliography, law and book-keeping? The bibliography of road-making will not help the engineer to construct or the surveyor to administer roads in a direct sense; the librarian will get little of library methodology from the Law of Public Libraries; nor does book-keeping for grocers deal with the practice or policy of the grocer. Nevertheless 99 per cent of bibliographers will never have occasion to need a bibliography of roads, and lawyers and book-keepers will require the respective books on law and book-keeping named in much the same proportion. On the other hand, the road-maker, the librarian, and the grocer may frequently need these books; they are on his subject, are likely to be most constantly useful to him. These are cases where, from the point of view of the subject, the right place may be disputed, but the "use" of the book determines what we shall do. Such books as *The Influence of Malory on Tennyson* would go under Tennyson, *Trigonometry for Airmen* under Aeronautics, and so on. So it is usually ruled that the law, history, bibliography and book-keeping of a subject go with the subject. This rule applies in an ordinary sense. There are special libraries, or there may be special circumstances, in which the alternative subject may be preferred.[1] Again, references in the catalogue would be made from these subjects to those at which the books have been shelved.

---

[1] Alternative schedules appear in some schemes and are frequent in Bliss, and in the Colon scheme may be used at will, but it is usually *subjects* that are placed alternatively in schedules; *books have one place only;* that is to say, wherever we put the books in a schedule other books on that subject must go there.

345. The procedure to be adopted may be summarized to this point: Take a book in hand and ask yourself these questions:

(*a*) What is the subject?
(*b*) What is the form in which the subject is presented, or its method of treatment?

Then turn to your classification scheme and consider:

(*a*) What is the main heading, embracing the subject?
(*b*) What is the division?
(*c*) What is the specific place?

This, or a similar procedure, should be used in the application of any of the popular classification schemes. In all of them subdivisions may really stand for relations and points of view and not for the concrete subject; or the subject may be treated with one purpose at one heading and with a quite different one at another. Thus in Dewey we can get some remarkable results, as the following books illustrate:

Dewey
numbers

1.	} 394·1	{ Drinking Customs of the World.
2.		The Cellar Book.
3.	641·87	Light Wines for Autumn Dinners.
4.	663·5	Whisky Distilling.
5.	613·81	The influence of Whisky on Hearing and Seeing.
6.	614·345	The Control of Whisky Production.
7.	178·1	The Moral Evils of Whisky Drinking.

On the face of it, they all deal with drinks, but, according to Dewey, the first two deal with Social Customs, the third with Domestic Economy, the fourth with Chemical Technology, the fifth with Hygiene, the sixth with Public Health, and the seventh with Temperance as a branch of Ethics. Similar instances might be multiplied. The main heading is the only check in placing such books, and when a place is selected the classifier should always read upwards to the containing heading and satisfy himself stage by stage that the book really belongs to it.

346. We have already dealt with the reasons why a book should be classed in the most specific head that will contain it. Such specific classing is an ultimate economy, in that it makes for the accurate separation and definition of topics. A library which classed all its histories of England at one number, for example, and failed to sub-divide by periods and places, would have so large and miscellaneous an assortment of volumes under the number that the effectiveness of the collection would be impaired gravely. The matter need not be stressed further here.

347. The composite book; that is to say, the book dealing with a number of subjects, requires a brief treatment. It was this type of work which led the early thinkers on classification to despair of applying it to books. Here, again, the classed catalogue rescues those topics from neglect which are necessarily out of sight when a book dealing with more than one subject is placed, as it must be, at only one of them. If the book includes subjects in many branches of knowledge, it is clearly to be put in the Generalia class, and common sense must determine whether it is worth the labour and expense of analysing and classing its contents in the catalogue; often it is not; but sometimes, when the book is of a character that its chapters add something important to the subjects, it is well worth while. Very occasionally the most important contribution to a subject is in a book which cannot be classed at the subject. Dr. Kelley's study of classification deficiencies is based on that indubitable fact. It is, however, most undesirable to load a catalogue with superfluous and irritating entries of chapters on matters which have been dealt with already as well, or better, in monographs. While the general work must go in Generalia, be satisfied that it really is general: many supposedly general works have a dominant subject in them: are really better at, say, science, history, or what not. The book which deals with two or three subjects is a more simple problem. It is placed at the subject which is treated most fully in the book, with catalogue references from the other subjects. When the subjects appear to be of equal importance the first treated may serve as the arranging subject. It is better to use the general heading for a book which deals with more than three divisions of a class. The following are examples of such composite works considered here from the point of view of the Dewey classification:

PRINGLE, ANDREW. Practical Photo-micrography. 1902.

[Dominant subject is microscopy, in Dewey a sub-division of Biology, but Photo-micrography is also an application of Photography, a Fine Art (Class at 578+778).]

RIVERS, W. H. R. Medicine, Magic and Religion: the Fitz-Patrick Lectures before the Royal College of Physicians of London, 1915–16. 1924.

[Dominant subject is Medicine, as may be gathered from the audience addressed, but it is also a definite treatise on Primitive Religion. A difficult book which appears to me to fall into General Medicine and to need references from General Religion and Magic (610+200+133).]

PORRITT, NORMAN. Religion and Health: their mutual relationship and influence. 1905.

[In this a practical physician studies the bearing of personal faith on personal health. Medicine is the attracting subject (613+248).]

WICKSTEED, P. H. Dante and Aquinas: the Jowett Lectures, 1911. 1913.

[Dante's religious system, which must arrange with Dante's works, and Mediæval Philosophers (851·15+189·4).]

CROCE, BENEDETTO. Ariosto, Shakespeare, and Corneille. 1920.

[The bulk of the book deals with Shakespeare and that is its dominant interest in an English library—i.e., Shakespearian criticism, which ranges with Shakespeare's works. Note, however, that the mere number of pages does not always determine the importance of a subject. References are necessary from Italian Poetry and French Drama (822·33+851·22+842·41).]

ROMANES, G. J. Essays. Edited by C. Lloyd Morgan. 1897.

[If the essays were placed individually, references would be required from Natural History, Instinct, Woman, Mind, Recreative Arts, Philosophy and Medicine. It has thus too wide a range for any specific subject placing (042 General English Essays).]

Other examples are legion, and there are many books in which the variation of subject is much more subtle than these show. Even in these it will be seen that there is room for difference of opinion as to the rightness or advisability of this or that placing.

348. The most exasperating book is that which, from the indeterminate nature of the subject, appears to have an equal right to go into two places in the classification. The first books on the Einstein Theory were examples of the type, as were the earlier books on Aviation. Was Einstein physics, mathematics, mechanics, or what? It was first put into electricity; then gravitated to gravitation and only by degrees by most of us was recognized as a general physical theory. Were airships to go at Engineering or Pneumatics? I know the first books on Airplanes got under "gases," as aeronautics were placed there in the days when heavier-than-air machines were still an unrealized dream. In all doubtful cases a decision must be made, and the place chosen must be indexed. There is no more important work for the classifier than to index every decision he makes in regard to subjects which are new to him and to the classification. The new subjects should be written in the index of all the copies of his classification, in order that any future book on the subject may be placed consistently. It is probably better to put all the books on a subject in a wrong place, so long as that place is indexed, than to put some in the wrong place, and later, acting on better knowledge, to place subsequent books in another and the right place. In the first method the books on the subject are at least all together, and the reader will forgive many theoretical mistakes if he gets that important advantage. It is therefore necessary throughout to be sure of what has been done previously, so that the desired consistency may be assured. Although we do not accept, because it derides every *real* purpose of classification,

Dewey's view that it does not matter much where a book is placed so long as that place is definitely indexed, we do accept the view that it is even more confusing to have several places for books on the same subject.

349. Akin to this type of work is the book on a new subject. Neither the Einstein Theory nor aircraft were entirely new things; but, at the time of its appearance, Radium was; and there was no place for it in the classifications. Some theorists placed it with radio-activity as a sub-division of electricity, and others chose other places. Finally its relationship to the Chemical Metals determined its place; and the classifier took the nearest heading, added a new figure to his notation, and placed it there. This is the procedure to be followed with all new subjects. The flexibility of modern classification and notation enables us to insert subjects at any point in the classification without dislocating the sequence. Care should, of course, be exercised in order that the best place is chosen for the addition, and it is important that new headings should not be made when the connotation of existing headings really includes the subjects that appear to be new. The index may be able to do what we seek by a new sub-division.

350. Naturally, in all classing we use every reference book that may serve as a tool in the work. It is elementary that a well-equipped cataloguing room has good dictionaries of languages and of as many subjects as possible, collections of other library catalogues and, as important as anything, the principal schemes of classification and such codes as are available. The best introduction to any scheme is that which the author has prefixed to it, and Bliss, Brown, Dewey and Ranganathan are generously supplied that way and each gives detailed instructions as to application. It is, therefore, a matter for wonder that so many library students seem unable to get access to any but the scheme used in their own libraries and, by an exclusiveness which belies library spirit and purpose, outside students are sometimes denied the reference use even of that scheme. Every library, save the smallest, should possess all the schemes which are described in this book. It is surely unnecessary to point out that we supply books for tinker, tailor, soldier, sailor, and the rest. Jast wondered if a well-written *Manual of Burgling* ought to be excluded —and this being so, it is illogical to withhold books on our own calling. The library that does not possess Bliss's two books on organization and Ranganthan's *Prologomena* is without the means for its staff and other readers to make a proper study of classification. As for the schemes named, they are expensive, but they are not "mere" books; they are tools as much as a card-cabinet or a book-case, and do not cost more than these! The only separate

and extensive code is Merrill's *Code for Classifiers*, in which librarians of great experience have set out class by class their agreed procedure in applying the Dewey scheme; a new edition of this is much to be desired. Elementary drill in this sort of classing is provided by the writer's *Introduction to Library Classification*, but there the answers must be provided by a qualified teacher. Fortunately we have to-day a number of good teachers. Bliss devotes two suggestive chapters to the Art of Classifying Books.[1]

350.1. Since 1950 the work of classing current books has been helped greatly by the punctual weekly appearance of the *British National Bibliography*, under the editorship of A. J. Wells. This gives a classified list of the week's books in which the Dewey notation used is made fully comprehensive by the application to it of Ranganathan's phase, facet and focus methods. In any case, this work provides an invaluable standard of reference.

[1] *Organization of Knowledge in Libraries*, Chapters VI–VII.

CHAPTER XXIII
BOOK AND WORK NUMBERS

351. When books have been classed to their most minute subject, it is necessary to have some final arrangement within that subject. Or, to put the matter as a question: if we have forty books on such a subject as relativity, what is the order in which these shall be arranged after classification? This problem has led to a certain amount of minor discussion. In the arrangement of scientific and technical books, a chronological arrangement has occasionally been preferred, on the ground that the last book added to the shelves contains or is influenced by the knowledge contained in all works standing before it. Alternatively, an inverse chronological order has been advocated, which places the newest book on the subject first in order, on the theory that this is the book that the average reader will require rather than an older book. Both of these methods are serious and practical ones. Another that has been tried appears to be fantastic; that is, an arrangement in order of difficulty, beginning with the elementary, proceeding to the popular, and thence to the technical treatise. Equally fantastic, because equally difficult and controversial in its carrying out, is an arrangement in order of merit.

352. All these methods may in theory be applied to the arrangement of entries in catalogues as well as to the arrangement of books upon the shelves. For the arranging of books in chronological order, it is doubtful whether there is a better method than that of adding the date number by means of the time symbol of the Universal Decimal schemes to the class-mark of any classification whatsoever. Thus, a series of treatises on psychoanalysis might be marked 131 "1916", 131 "1917", 131 "1923", and 131 "1924". There is nothing to be learned by the classifier, except that the date is always enclosed in inverted commas.

353. An ingenious contribution to chronological arrangement is the Biscoe Date Table, which will be found in the Appendix to all editions up to and including the 13th of the *Decimal Classification*. This is as follows:

A—Before Christ	H—1810 to 1819	N—1870 to 1879
B—0 to 999	I—1820 to 1829	O—1880 to 1889
C—1000 to 1499	J—1830 to 1839	P—1890 to 1899
D—1500 to 1599	K—1840 to 1849	Q—1900 to 1909
E—1600 to 1699	L—1850 to 1859	R—1910 to 1919
F—1700 to 1799	M—1860 to 1869	S—1920 to 1929
G—1800 to 1809		

Undated books are marked with the letter of the supposed date
—M indicating a book published any time between 1860 and 1869.
All other books are numbered with the letter and the year number,
ignoring centuries, as in this example in the Dewey notation:

580·2   Q05 Balfour. Manual of Botany. 1905.
614·132 P99 Return on Infant Mortality. 1899.

The *Subject Classification* (Section 40) contains also a much more
extended date table.

354. The average library, however, arranges books in author
order, and several numbers, more or less ingenious, have been
proposed in order to secure absolute or approximate alphabetic
arrangement. The simplest is the number invented by William
Stetson Merrill of the Newberry Library, Chicago, in which the
alphabet is divided up into 100 numbers as follows:

01 A	34 Gill	67 Pek
02 Agre	35 Goe	68 Pfi
03 Als	36 Got	69 Pif
04 Ap	37 Greeno	70 Po
05 Ash	38 H	71 Pow
06 B	39 Hat	72 Q
07 Ban	40 Hesi	73 R
08 Bax	41 Hiu	74 Rey
09 Beno	42 Hov	75 Robi
10 Bix	43 I	76 Row
11 Bou	44 Ini	77 S
12 Brim	45 J	78 Sanch
13 Bum	46 K	79 Schar
14 C	47 L	80 Schwar
15 Carr	48 Lang	81 Sevi
16 Chan	49 Law	82 Simons
17 Ci	50 Leo	83 Soo
18 Clo	51 Lit	84 Steb
19 Cond	52 Long	85 Stratt
20 Crom	53 M	86 T
21 D	54 McL	87 Thau
22 Day	55 Marc	88 To
23 Dicke	56 Mau	89 Trum
24 Doy	57 Merr	90 U
25 E	58 Min	91 Ull
26 Elg	59 Moo	92 Upt
27 Erm	60 Mu	93 V
28 F	61 N	94 Ven
29 Fel	62 Nev	95 W
30 Fit	63 Nol	96 Wats
31 Forr	64 O	97 Wha
32 G	65 P	98 Wit
33 Gay	66 Parkm	99 X—Z

355. A much more elaborate and universally approved method is what is known as the Cutter Author Marks, a device of Charles Ammi Cutter. In the introduction to his *Expansive Classification* he explains the principle which has guided him in making the number. It is that one or more letters of the author's name are written, after the class mark, according to the following:

CONSONANTS, except S, one letter.	S, two letters.
VOWELS, two letters.	SCH, three letters.

To the initial or initials thus written, is added a number which is short if the name occurs at the beginning of the alphabet and progresses in length as the names progress along the alphabet. We thus get symbols of this kind:

Abbott	Ab2
Beard	B34
Smith	Sm51
Schneider	Sch57

This number may be expanded decimally to accommodate names falling between any two running numbers. Writing of this number, Cutter's friend, William E Foster, of Providence,[1] says: "In connexion with the *Expansive Classification* should be mentioned the preparation of a succession of alphabetical 'tables' for ready and convenient use. These tables, which he designated 'alphabetical-order tables,' were at first limited to two-figure numbers, and comprised two parts, namely, 'the consonants except S,' and 'the vowels and S.' Gradually, in using these tables in his own library he began adding a third figure in exceptional instances as the need arose (in such cases as fiction or biography). Later, from 1899 to 1901, he began systematically expanding this into a three-figure table. Meanwhile, Kate E. Sanborn (late Mrs. Gardner M. Jones, of Salem, Mass.) had also been preparing a set of tables, carried to the third figure. This work appeared in two parts also, the vowel-table first, in 1892, and later, the consonant table, in 1895. The third edition of this work (1899) bears the title 'C. A. Cutter's alphabetic-order table, . . . altered and fitted with three figures by Miss Kate E. Sanborn.' This work was, as indicated by the word 'altered,' quite distinct from Mr. Cutter's 'three-figure' table, above mentioned, since Miss Sanborn had not used Mr. Cutter's two-figure table as the basis for this work, but had made a new one."

It may be said that the Cutter numbers cannot be applied in the Cataloguing Room without direct references to the printed tables which Foster describes.

[1] *Library Journal*, v. 28, p. 699, 1903.

356. Of the other alphabeting numbers may be mentioned those which Brown gives at the end of the tables of his *Subject Classification*, and an ingenious book-mark devised by Stanley Jast and described by him in *The Library World* (v. 3, pp. 120–3 and pp. 150–2). In this scheme the author number consists of the first two letters of the author's name, names commencing with the same two letters being distinguished by the figures 1, 2, 3, etc. Thus La Fontaine LA, Lamartine LA1, and so on, other authors being numbered in the order of their arrival in the library. In fiction and pure literature generally the first *three* letters of the author's name are used. The various works of an author are distinguished by using the initial letter of the title after a point, and other works commencing with the same letter are numbered 1, 2, 3, etc. Thus Shakespeare's *Macbeth* is marked SHA.M, *The Merchant of Venice* SHA.M1, *A Midsummer Night's Dream* SHA.M2.

357. In writing all these numbers either in catalogues or on the shelf it is usual to make them into a fraction formed of class number and author or date. Thus Freud's *Psycho-Analysis* would be written $\dfrac{131}{F25}$ for the Cutter mark, $\dfrac{131}{FR.P}$ for the Jast, and $\dfrac{131}{31}$ for the Merrill arrangements respectively.

Sections 30–44 of the introduction by Brown to his own scheme will be found profitable reading on several of these book-marks.

CHAPTER XXIV

THE APPLICATION OF CLASSIFICATION TO SHELVES

358. Assume now that we have a large collection of books to arrange. What is the best way to proceed in the light of the experience of other classifiers? The simplest task is that of the librarian whose new collection has not been arranged by some inexperienced person, or according to some poor or little-known system. In the latter case it is best to treat the collection as an unclassified one, ignoring altogether the previous arrangements, which may tend to confuse us both by their virtues and their defects. Begin from first principles.

359. Go over the collection and arrange the books in the main classes of the scheme adopted, for example, the ten main classes of Dewey, if you are using that system, writing the first figures 0–9, as the case may be, inside the first boards of the books. Write in pencil, so that corrections, which are frequent as a rule, may be made easily. Then break up each class, so made, into the first hundred divisions of the classification, adding the second figures to the numbers; and then proceed, in like manner, to the first thousand divisions, adding the third figures. Many classifiers are able to proceed thus far without referring to the classification scheme for guidance, and, without attaching too great an importance to memory, the good classifier will memorize at least the first three figures (the first thousand places) of his classification scheme, as being the most economical part of his classing equipment; but, even if one is not blessed with a memory that can compass so much of the scheme, the method described should be followed to the first two figures at least.

360. From this will be gathered an important, albeit simple, point in working. It is this: *always class a book mentally before appealing to the tables of the scheme.* Such a method not only strengthens the classifier's knowledge of his scheme as well as his memory; it also compels him to think out the subject of his book with care, from its class to its division, and thence to its sub-division.

361. Now arrange the books on your shelves according to the two or three numbers which you have applied to them. This, of course, is a merely mechanical process which may be carried out by an untrained assistant. The final classification of the books, with the scheme book by book, can now proceed in the most favourable conditions. If the classing has been carried by the

mental method to three places, it will be evident that whole groups of headings can be used together. Sometimes the specific numbers for a whole shelf of books can be found on a single page of the tables. Thus, the preliminary arrangement, which may have seemed to you to be tedious and unnecessary, becomes the most rapid way of working. Even expert classifiers work in this manner when they have large numbers of books on miscellaneous subjects before them. In short, class your books as closely as possible without appealing to the scheme, as this leads to efficient and rapid work.

362. The classification symbol ultimately chosen must be written on some permanent part of the book. End-papers and fly-leaves wear out or become dirty, and are always removed by the bookbinder when the book is rebound: these should not be used for any permanent record. Probably the best position is the back or front of the title-page; I, myself, use the back, and have a definite place for the class-mark and cross-references on a process stamp which is impressed on the back of the title-page, as shown below. Even here it is advisable that the number be written in good lead pencil. It is quite permanent enough in this position, as many numbers of more than thirty years' standing, which are as good to-day as when they were written, prove. Nothing is more unsightly than ink alterations in books; but, it may be suggested, if ink is used, when revisions must be

1	Lib.	No.	10
2	Class ✕	✕	11
3	V.	P.	12
4	Cut	Cata.	13
5	Sta.	Ann.	14
6	Pl.	Subj. I.	15
7	Bk. C.	Check	16
8	Acc. Bk.		
9	Sh. Reg.	Apprd.	17

1. Library in which book is placed. 2. Class mark. 3. Vendor. 4. Initials of assistant who cuts leaves. 5. Initials of assistant who stamps. 6. Initials of assistant who book-plates. 7. Initials of assistant who writes book card. 8. Initials of assistant who writes entry in accession book. 9. Initials of assistant who writes entry in shelf register. 10. Accession number. 11. Cross-references. 12. Price. 13. Initials of cataloguer. 14. Initials of annotater. 15. Initials of assistant making entry in subject-index. 16. Checking of work. 17. Final check by chief cataloguer.

made that they be made boldly and efficiently. Many people write corrections over original figures so that only they can tell what number is intended.

363. In the largest libraries the classifying is done by a person who is wholly a classifier; but in the average library the classifier and cataloguer are one and the same person, and, especially where additions of books to an existing collection are concerned the two operations are carried out at the same time, by the methods explained in detail in the next chapter.

364. The processes through which a book passes on its way to the shelves belong to the subject of library routine. Suffice it to say that at various stages the class-mark is entered in the accession book, written on the charging card, and entered in the shelf-register. It is also carried on to the board-label of the book; and finally stamped or written on the back of the book in the manner to be described later.

365. The arrangement of a library for service involves a careful regard for rapidity of work with the minimum of staff. In a library in which the public is not admitted to the shelves, one has to remember that every book issued has to be fetched from its shelf by the staff, and, when the books drawn run to a thousand and more in a day, there would be great fatigue for the staff if the books most frequently in demand were not placed as near as possible to the charging desk. Thus, Fiction would be on the nearest shelves, and other classes would be near in the order of their popularity: thus, Travel, History, and Biography would be closer to hand than, say, Religion, Philosophy and Philology. The ideal arrangement of a library is, of course, in the exact order of the scheme—as, from 0 to 9 in the case of Dewey; but in practice we have seen that such an arrangement is rarely practicable. This altering of the ideal order of the classes is called "broken order."

366. In an open-shelf library the same problem occurs, but in a different form. Here the problem is to give due prominence to the classes, and so to arrange that there is the minimum of congestion of traffic. Fiction is, therefore, distributed so that the fiction readers are spread over the widest area that is convenient for them; and usually is placed on the shelves around the walls of the room. The arrangement of the remaining classes may very well be in the exact order of the classification; in fact is much better so, as readers can follow the unbroken sequence of the class-numbers quite easily, but are liable to be puzzled by the various broken orders which occur necessarily in some libraries owing to rigid shelf sizes and other accidental causes.

367. The order of the books on the shelves, then, is the numerical order of the class-marks, from 0 to 9, but, of course, as we saw, the primary arrangement of books is by size, and octavo, quarto, and folio sequences, as necessary, must create

parallel classifications from the very beginning. In each of these the order is, as suggested, that of the class-marks. When, however, the books are arranged in that order, there is a final order necessary to individualize the books which bear that class-mark. Thus the books on Evolution are arranged chronologically by the date of publication or alphabetically by the names of authors. There are other arrangements, as the inverse chronological order which places the newest book first in each heading, and an order of merit has been suggested, which places the best book first, or the best book with which to begin the reading of the subject; but these methods have few advocates, and for all practical purposes the alphabetical and chronological arrangements are the only ones that matter. Which of these is to be chosen will depend upon the type of library and the sort of people who will use it. In research and student libraries there is much to be said for the chronological order; but, in general libraries, certainly in municipal libraries, the alphabetical order is to be preferred.

368. In a closed library it is possible, when once the books have been placed on the shelves in their correct order, that a very simple indication of that order by means of a guide card to each class in addition to the writing of the number on the backs of the books will be a sufficient guide for the staff to the location of any particular book. In open-access libraries a much more extensive treatment of the shelves is necessary, and, indeed, it may be desirable even in a closed library. The public needs a number of clues to and indications of the arrangement. These are

1. A catalogue.
2. A subject index.
3. A guide to the shelf arrangement as a whole.
4. Class guides.
5. Bay guides. (Sometimes called "tier" guides.)
6. Shelf guides.
7. Individual book guides.
8. Cross references (dummies).

Postponing the catalogue and subject index and their correlative, the shelf-register, for separate treatment, we may consider the guides.

369. The best guide to the whole shelf-arrangement is a plan, showing the positions of the book-cases, and giving the numbers and names of the main classes contained in them. Such a plan should be bold, and may be made more effective if each class is coloured differently upon it; and it should be framed and placed in the most prominent position available. Small reproductions of such plans, say, of postcard size, are sometimes published so that readers may possess their own copies. The following is an example:

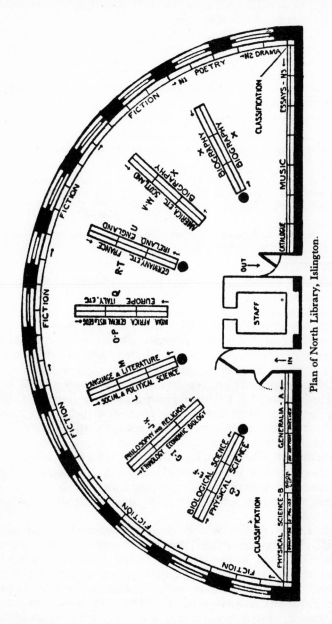

Plan of North Library, Islington.

This standard layout, devised by James Duff-Brown, is still found in several libraries, but there is very great flexibility in lending library arrangement today.

370. A class guide is one that is placed at the top centre, or at the end, of a class on the book-case. Sometimes it is merely a bold statement of the class number and subject, as

> 300 SOCIOLOGY.

or it may set out the main divisions of the class, with references to parallel sequences, as

---

300 SOCIOLOGY.

300 General Works.	360 Associations and Institutions.
310 Statistics.	
320 Political Science.	370 Education.
330 Political Economy.	380 Commerce, Communication.
340 Law.	
350 Administration.	390 Customs, Costumes, Popular Life.

See also the Quarto and Folio collections for books on Sociology too large to be shelved here.

Such class-guides take various forms. The most common is the framed card, hung on the top of the book-case at the beginning or about the middle of the class; but sometimes, as at Islington and elsewhere, swinging guides like inn signs placed at the top ends of the cases. An effective system of signs is one in which at the ends of the book-cases, the letters are in white on glass which is black otherwise; and these glass signs are lighted from behind at night. Whatever form may be chosen, it is well to avoid ugly black and white printing for these labels. Colour is being used far more freely than it used to be in our libraries, and it can be introduced into labels with real effect. E. A. Savage used white letters with red initial letters on sage green cards for the guides at Wallasey Libraries, and the effect of the labels, which were artistic in the form of letter as in the colour, was good. Obviously much artistic taste and ingenuity can be, and is, given to such signs; it is worth while to have such detail as perfect as possible.

371. Large classes which occupy several bays of shelving require closer guiding; and the most convenient unit to guide is the bay. (A bay, in the jargon of library furnishers, is a vertical set of three-feet shelves; it was formerly (wrongly, no doubt) called a "tier." Tiers of shelves in precise meaning are horizontal lines of them.) Much ingenuity has also been expended on such guides, and many forms are in use. Those most in favour attempt to set out exactly what may be found in the bay, and

probably the best form of bay-guide is that designed by Jast and described by James Douglas Stewart in *The Library World*, v. 7, pp. 113–18, 1904–05. This consists of a frame containing a card on which each shelf is shown and on each shelf the subjects of its books. The frame is fixed on a block of wood placed on a shelf at about the sight-level of the average person. An illustration will make the method clear.

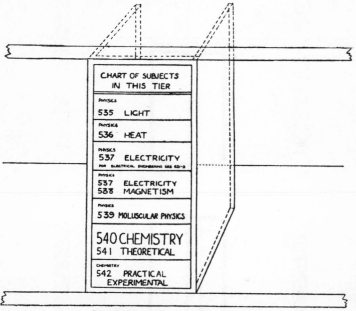

Bay Guide. Designed by L. S. Jast.

Such guides are not cheap; moreover, they occupy in each bay the space of about three books, and that becomes a real loss of space in a large library.

372. To obviate this loss Jast designed another bay guide, consisting of a frame, glazed on both sides, so that the plan of the shelf can be shown on one side, and notes on characteristic books and useful references can be shown on the other; and this frame is hinged to the left upright of the bay and can be swung forward when the books behind it are required. An illustration of this is given on page 240.

373. A third guide, devised by Savage for the Wallasey Libraries, which attempts to give similar information, consists of a stout narrow card (7 in. by 3 in.) eyeletted at the top, and suspended on a brass hook on the left upright of the bay. On

this the particulars of the bay-contents are typed. This "guide" can be lifted off by readers if they desire. A modification of this guide in the Central Lending Library at Croydon was found to be effective. The illustration given on page 241 shows its appearance.

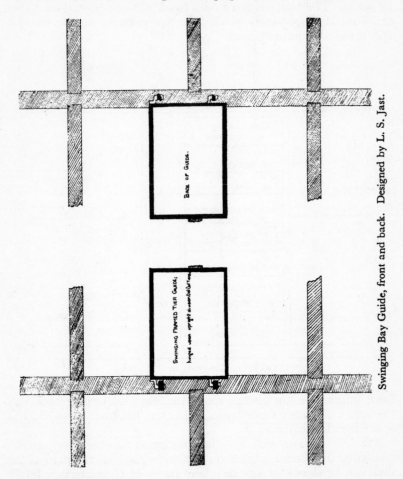

Swinging Bay Guide, front and back. Designed by L. S. Jast.

374. Various other methods of bay-guide have been used, the best-known being a book-cover, projecting when placed on the shelf beyond the other books, and having some such word as EXPLANATION lettered boldly upon it. Inside this cover the arrangement of the bay, with notes, is given. This guide, which was described by Savage in *The Library World*, v. 8, pp, 261–6, 1905–06, has its uses, but it involves rather more effort (although only slightly more) on the part of the reader using it.

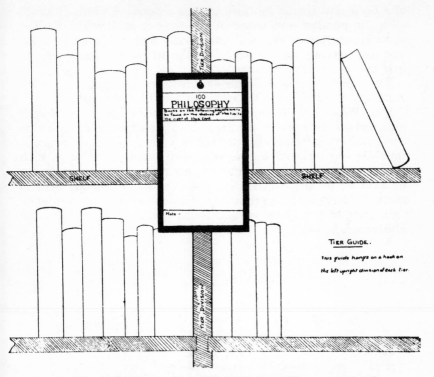

Card Bay Guide, place on hook at about the level of the eyes, on the left
upright of the tier.   Designed by E. A. Savage.

375. A subject-guide, as distinct from a bay-guide, is a most
useful thing. That is to say, a guide placed amongst the books
to indicate where a new subject begins. It should be in the shape

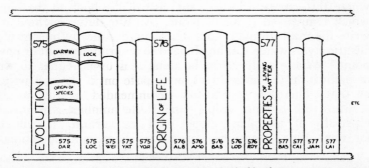

Subject Guides inserted in shelf of books.

of a book, but should be distinctly *not* a book. A block of wood, with the number and name of the subject on it will serve the purpose; and the reader will understand that between one block and the next are all the books on the subject indicated on the first block; as shown on page 241.

The Newberry Topic Guide—a thick strong card covered with cloth and lettered down the edge—is a form of this guide.

376. What are commonly called shelf-labels, are guides attached to the edge of the shelves to indicate subjects. These are usually printed labels attached in various ways. Sometimes, they are even pasted to the edges—a foolish practice as such guides must frequently be removed. Sometimes they are protected by xylonite or talc, which clips upon the shelves, or are held in metal holders which clip similarly. Sometimes they are combined with book-rests. These various forms may be judged from the illustration below.

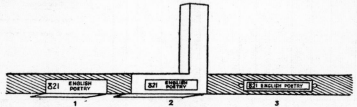

Shelf Labels:
1. Shelf label in xylonite holder.
2. Metal label holder combined with book-rest.
3. Ordinary brass screw-on label holder.

If the subject-guide, or a form of it, is used, these shelf-labels are unnecessary, and those that are fastened to the shelves and involve work in moving them, are undesirable.

377. Every book should bear its class-mark on the back of the cover. The best method is to stamp it in gold-lettering and, where this can be afforded, the visit of the book to the binder which is involved is worth while. An alternative method is to write the mark through gold or coloured paper by means of an electric stylus which can be plugged to an ordinary light or power point.[1] Where neither can be done, it is usual either to write or paint it on the book direct, or to paste on a tag and write it on that. There are several inks recommended for this purpose. A white ink is most visible, and if the number is varnished, especially if aeroplane dope used as varnish, it will last for some time. Tags are various in shape, and sometimes a

[1] This pen was, I believe, invented by Gaylord Bros., an American firm. A similar stylus is marketed by the Woollston Co., Nottingham.

different colour is used for each class, on the ground that mis-placements are readily detected by means of the colours. It has been found that a small white round tag (Dennison's $\frac{A}{85}$ gummed tags for example) will serve quite satisfactorily for all classes.

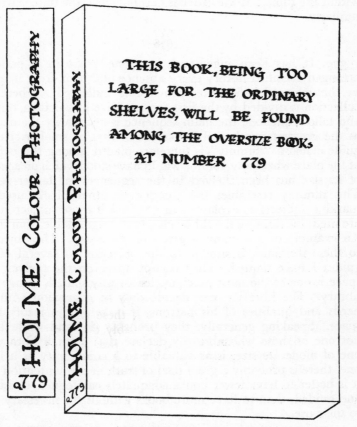

A "Dummy" book: a cross-reference from Octavo shelves to shelves
for oversize books.

The position of the number is worth a word. Usually it is placed $1\frac{1}{2}$ inches from the bottom of the book; but as this is on the part of the book which is held in the hand while it is being read, some librarians prefer it as near the top of possible. A further argument used is that the reader looks for the book first by the class-mark, then by the author, and finally by the title; and these particulars should appear in this order on the book.

378. The author mark should appear immediately under the class-mark on the book, in fraction form; thus

$$\frac{576}{D45}$$

That is, assuming that an alphabetical arrangement is made within the topic. If the order is chronological the date is written similarly

$$\frac{576}{1876}$$

379. It has been ingeniously suggested that in a perfectly arranged classified library every absence of a book from its place in the main classification sequence is indicated. Where the collection is divided by the first factor of size into octavo, quarto, and folio sequences, the main sequence is necessarily the octavo, as the greatest number of books are of that or smaller size. A guide called a "dummy" is therefore placed among the octavos at the place where any volume would have stood which on account of its size has been shelved in the sequences for larger books. This dummy resembles the wooden or other blocks used for marking subjects as explained in 375, but if those subject-guides are used, the dummy should be clearly distinguishable from them. An example of a dummy is given on page 243. The objection to these dummies is similar to the objection to several of the guides I have named. They occupy space on the shelves, and space is one of the most precious, least-easily spared, things in a library. The librarian can decide only in connexion with the needs and qualities of his patrons, if these guides justify their space. Speaking generally, they probably do; and while I am not one of those who absurdly declare that a small library, or one of moderate size, is as valuable to a community as a large one, there is probably a great deal of truth in the contention that it is better to have fewer books adequately catalogued, classified, and guided, than to have more books without the necessary keys to their use.

CHAPTER XXV
BOOK-DISPLAY

380. Any open-shelf library is a book-display in the widest sense; our best advertisement of our capabilities as librarians are reflected there. The larger, more adequately lighted, appropriately decorated and conveniently, even comfortably, furnished our public rooms are the finer is the book-display. "Our light and learning radiate from the books on our shelves," was a remark by Frank Pacy which, conservative as he was, enshrines the truth. If, therefore, in the pursuit of readers we neglect in any way that for which we pursue them, the book itself, then is our work vain. This seems a necessary argument in a book devoted to a cultural side of librarianship which nevertheless is a librarian's technique, ancillary to his main vocation, which is to gather wisely, make accessible and exploit fully in the interest of readers, and in some cases to conserve, books and other literary material. By now we have demonstrated how classification serves these purposes.

381. It has become the custom of late to use the term "book-display" in the special sense of advertising books on selected subjects or of some definite interest by making exhibitions of groups of them with accompaniments. It is, of course, not new. L. Stanley Jast devoted much thought and time to book-display methods forty years ago, in some of which I took a modest part. It was not novel then because it was practised, in their own fashion, by booksellers for a half-century. Some might even urge that the best book-display is that the Charing Cross bookseller makes when he places outside his shop a tilted shelf with the fascinating label, "All these books 6d. only," the attraction for every bookman being possibilities of literary treasure at inordinate cheapness, although Charing Cross Road is not peopled by booksellers likely to be caught unawares. At Wallasey Ernest A. Savage took from the business window-dresser the plan of window display, and two of his branch libraries were in shops in the windows of which, some invitingly open at attractive illustrations and others being nice copies with striking titles well in view, he put alluring selections of the books he wanted people to borrow. Mr. Savage has written a book which is mainly on book-display which reflects the individualistic ingenuity and enterprise in book exploitation which he has always shown.[1] In the more recent

[1] *Manual of Classification and Book Display*, 1946. (Allen and Unwin's "Library Manuals").

libraries, of which Baltimore is the major example but the newer branch libraries at Leeds amongst others furnish nearer examples, windows on the ground floor of the library building or flanking its main entrance have been built for displaying books. It is too true that the older libraries conveyed to a stranger in their buildings no sign of their purpose, and the desire to-day to produce distinctive buildings for libraries recognizable as such may take many forms, but those must be most appropriate which show at once that they have business with books.

382. It will be outside our province to enter far into the field of library advertising to which, as a subject, book-display belongs. It needs no demonstration that if the librarian is to perform one of his services, which is to create readers, he must lure them, if that be not too smug a term, into reading what he believes they ought to read and otherwise might not read. The simplest form of display is that of the shelf, or book-case, of the latest additions. Theoretically, it is done to enable students to examine the recent works on their subject, and it does achieve this; but in cold fact its more usual value is to assure our clients, who seem always doubtful of the fact, that the library does acquire new books. If the books are available for use, in an ordinary popular library, they, and the display therefore, usually vanish in a few minutes; if they are reserved for issue on a particular day, on that day readers who are at leisure will queue to snap them up and when the others arrive later their annoyance is often vocal; and, if readers are allowed to reserve them, the resentment of the others is again often real. A frequent form of display is that of titles of new books in attractive little periodical lists or bulletins which some of our smaller libraries issue with carefully chosen type and sometimes bizarre effects, such as the inversion of titles, omission of punctuation and other means of giving what the advertising expert calls "attention value." It has the purposes of, and sometimes accompanies, the new book-display, but it creates an immediate demand for copies of these mint new books which we are unable to satisfy. No popular library can supply at the peak of ordinary demand any successful book to every reader who wants it, and these lists merely stimulate our embarrassment.

383. What, however, is meant by Book-Display is, in theory, defined by Bliss in his account of a *Group* of books:

"Individuals from several classes may form a group; they may come from, and they may enter, other groups. Groups are composite, selective, accidental, local, and temporary; they are not relatively permanent *totalities*, as classes are. But classes may be grouped and regrouped, and so may subject-matters, studies, and sciences; again so may books, documents, maps, etc. Arbitrary bibliographic classifications differ little from mere groupings of books, etc. Such groups frequently need to be regrouped for uses, as interests require. But by logical and natural classifications such grouping is facilitated and economised."[1]

This is somewhat heavily worded, and simply means that from a well-classified library it is possible to bring together, on shelves or tables or in troughs, a temporary selection of books from any or from several classes to serve or stimulate interest in a special occasion. The active librarian has his finger on the pulse of public thought, watches world activities, keeps a calendar of the anniversaries of great men and events, knows what is occupying Parliament or his own area, and so on; and while they are hot news he endeavours to illustrate them by book-displays. He is also concerned to keep before his readers good books, from the classics to works on subjects that would be neglected by most people. The suggestibility of the general reader is very great; he prefers the judgment upon books of other people to his own so long as it is not obtruded upon him unsought and without tact. The best illustration of this is the crowd round the shelves or slopes attached to most open-access discharging desks where the returned books are put while awaiting re-shelving. "A lot of foolish people, taking the books which have been chosen by people as foolish than themselves," it has been said. No doubt the astute librarian uses these slopes for the occasional display of books of worth. It must not be done too often.

384. A whole book can be devoted to the ingenuities of library staffs in making displays. They can be of one book on a special stand, with some sort of poster label bearing an illustration, portrait or other illustration and some brief statement of why the book is shown. It is clearly useless to display a book about which such a statement cannot or need not be made. A country involved in war, biographies of a man whose centenary or other anniversary occurs, and so on, may occupy a book trough, well set out with good space about it to individualize the display. Larger groups, as, for example, a display of "the best-sellers of the Victorian era," may occupy a whole room. Engaging invitations to people, "Why not learn a Language?" with the books upon it shown or, to come to one not specially connected with classification but the most popular of all, "Books the librarian has read and recommends," are the sort of thing contemplated. (This is a whimsical success when one remembers that the average reader credits the librarian with having read every book in his library!) The field is without limit.

[1] *Organization of Knowledge in Libraries*, p. 332.

385. These displays are, of course, not confined to the library premises. Joseph L. Wheeler, whose *Library and the Community*, 1924,[1] is the best book on the subject, writes with enthusiasm of getting shopkeepers to permit the use of a window for displays occasionally. We do not think this concession can be expected from the only stores in this country where it would be effective, but an empty shop may often be available and the opportunity should not be missed. Displays can be made at local bazaars, exhibitions, societies, and in many other places where people meet.

386. Such displays should be appropriate, be planned with care, make use of suitable staging, background, good and efficient labelling and use colour with taste. It is in the setting-out that the difficulty may arise. Home-made labels, ill-drawn diagrams, ineffective wordings are all to be feared and, sometimes, avoided, although some libraries have an assistant who is an artist; for, whatever may be said, an ill exhibition does far more harm than good in this country, and I suppose in every other. Then the display should be such that the return in library effectiveness is likely to repay the cost in time and labour involved. Some of the warmest advocates of this sort of work, and I count myself amongst the most experienced and constant of such, have found that the making of settings, labels, and posters is a very engaging occupation which can consume much valuable time, often the best paid we have. Wheeler advocates the work being done by the least costly employees who can be taught to do it, which is sensible enough.

387. The most successful displays are always staffed unobtrusively and what is displayed is available for immediate borrowing. This cannot always be done and—where the displays are mere exhibitions of library rarities—a quite desirable form of exhibition—must not be. A show of books which readers cannot get easily may be merely tantalizing, may irritate rather than please.

388. As the subject can be made elastic enough to cover the whole of book distribution activities, I content myself here with drawing attention to the special furniture, tilted shelves, display troughs, stands, book-supports, pictorial posters and frames, draperies, etc., etc., which have been devised to make display effective. J. P. Lamb of Sheffield has done specially good work in this matter. Several illustrations of the gadgets that have succeeded are given in Gilbert O. Ward's *Publicity for Public Libraries*, 1924.[2]

---

[1] A.L.A., Chicago. See also Bibliography, p. 335.
[2] N.Y.: H. W. Wilson, Chapter XII.

389. One word may be said. Common sense and courtesy to the solid reader would suggest that not too many shows should be made at a time. They mean the removal of important books from their proper place on the classified shelves, and thus may be missed by readers who really need them more than the fortuitous recruit to reading who may be won by book-display.

CHAPTER XXVI

THE CLASSIFIED (CLASS) CATALOGUE AND THE SHELF REGISTER

390. An essential part of the equipment of a library of any kind is a shelf register. It is the shelf-inventory, as it were, showing the position of every book and is the principal means by which the laborious, usually difficult, and rarely completed, work of stock-taking is carried out. It is usually entered up at the time of the cataloguing of the book by the cataloguing staff, and is, therefore, the most current of the systematic records or (if you prefer the phrase) catalogues of the library. It takes several forms, but the one which is generally in use, and the only one I need describe, is that on loose sheets which are kept in a box or in a loose-leaf binder—I prefer the latter. An example will show the ruling of such a shelf register sheet. One such sheet is given to each subject. In the right top corner is written the class-mark of the subject and the name of the author and the title of each book are written in the first two columns as it is received. The narrow columns on the right are for stock-taking; as each book is checked a tick ($\checkmark$), as shown, is placed against its entry. Entries of withdrawn books are ruled through as required. Such a shelf register is ruled for ten years as a rule, but in a busy library the sheets have to be rewritten at more frequent intervals than that owing to the inevitable withdrawals, alterations, and additions.

391. In some libraries the shelf register is hung in its binder at the beginning of a class so that the public can use it. There is no real objection to this plan which, in libraries where the catalogues proper are not kept completely *au courant* with the additions, may serve a most useful purpose; but the shelf register is primarily a staff tool and the public use of it would mean frequent renewal.

392. *The Catalogue.* The principal, the indispensable, key to a library is the catalogue; and whatever form that catalogue may take it must provide some means of showing what books are available on every subject so far as that is humanly possible. It is therefore necessary to give as much thought to the form of catalogue as to the scheme of classification itself. The pros and cons of the various forms need not now be discussed: there are advantages and disadvantages in every form of catalogue. For the classification student the points that really matter are these:

						575	
Author.	Title.	1944	1945	1946	1947	1948	etc.

Ruling of a Shelf Register Sheet.

In the dictionary catalogue subjects are arranged alphabetically, and the endeavour is made to enter every book *under its specific alphabetical name.* Thus a book on (say) the Rose, would not, as in the subject catalogue, be placed first under the class heading Botany, and then at the specific place under that heading; but would be entered directly under Roses; thus we get

>Flowers, Cultivated.
>>Thomson.   Flowers in their Seasons.
>>Woodward.   Garden Flowers.
>>*See also*   Sunflowers, Sweet Peas,
>>   Roses, Violets.

Also   Roses.
>>Hole. Book of the Rose.
>>Thomson. Rose Grower's Manual.
>>Twentyman. Roses in Suburban Gardens.

Of these two examples, the first is the only form of main-class subject entry given in the average dictionary catalogue; and the second is the specific subject entry which is the principal form of subject entry in such a catalogue. In the classified catalogue what may be regarded as a precisely reverse method is used.

Here the entry is made under the main class heading, and the sub-entries are arranged in the strict order of the classification itself; so that the more general book precedes the more special, in one table which naturally exhibits the hierarchy and the family relationships of books. Thus Botany would be entered in some such manner as follows:

590—589.   BOTANY.

580	GENERAL.
	Arber. Agnes, Herbals: their origins and evolutions, 1470–1670. Illus. Por. 1912.
580·016	BIBLIOGRAPHY.
580·016	Vesque, J. Catalogue de la Bibliothèque de Joseph Decaisne. Por. 1883.
581	PHYSIOLOGIC AND STRUCTURAL BOTANY.
581	Baillon, H. Natural History of Plants. 8v. Illus. Q. 1871–88.
581	Bose, J. C. Plant Response as a Means of Physiological Investigation. Illus. 1906.
581·6	ECONOMIC BOTANY.
581·6	Oliver, F. W., and others. The Exploitation of Plants. 1917.
581·9	GEOGRAPHIC BOTANY.
581·9	Boulger, D. C. Plant Geography. Illus. 1912.
581·9	Meyer, F. J. C. Outline of the Geography of Plants. 1846.
581·94	*Geographic Botany, Europe.*
581·94	Kruse, Friedrich. Botanisches Taschenbuch enthaltend die in Deutschland, Deutsch-Osterreich, und der Schweiz, etc. 1887.
581·942	*Geographic Botany: England.*
581·942	Carter, H. G. Genera of British Plant. 1913.
581·94221	*Geographic Botany: Surrey.*
581·94221	Brewer, J. A. (*Ed.*) Flora of Surrey. 1863.
582	PHANEROGAMIA.
582	Bary, A. de. Comparative Anatomy of the Vegetative Organs of the Phanerograms and Ferns. Illus. 1884.
584	PHANEROGAMIA MONOCOTYLEDONÆ.
584	Armstrong, S. F. British Grasses and their employment in agriculture. Illus. 1917.
585	PHANEROGAMIA. GYMNOSPERMÆ.
585	Veitch, James, and Sons. Manual of the Comferæ. Illus. 1900.
586	CRYPTOGAMIA.
586	Groves, James, and Webster, G. R. Bullock. The British Charophyta 2 v. Illus. 1920–24.
587	CRYPTOGAMIA: PTERIDOPHYTA.
587·3	*Cryptogamia: Pteridophyta: Filicinæ: Ferns.*
587·3	Bower, F. O. The Ferns (Filicales): treated comparatively. v. 1. Illus. Q. 1923.
588	CRYPTOGAMIA: BRYOPHYTA.
588	Braithwaite, R. The British Moss-Flora. 3 v. Illus. Q. 1887–1905.
588	Cooke, M. C. Handbook of British Hepaticæ. Illus. 1904.
589	CRYPTOGAMIA: THALLOPHYTA.
589	Harvey, W. H. Phycologia Britannica. 4 v. Q. 1846–51.
589·2	*Cryptogamia: Thallophyta: Fungi.*
589·2	Berkeley, Rev. M. J., and Smith, W. G. Outlines of British Fungology. 2 v. Illus. 1860–W1.
589·3	*Cryptogamia: Thallophyta: Algæ.*
589·3	Gray, S. O. British Sea Weeds. Illus. 1867.

I have condensed the catalogue from which my example is drawn. There would probably be many entries under each number in an actual catalogue, and the repetition of the class numbers would not then seem so overdone as it seems here. The example is sufficient for the reader to see the "genealogical" arrangement of the entries. The whole family of botanical books in all its chief relationships is shown by this method and cannot be shown by any other.

393. A classified catalogue consists of three indispensable parts: these are, an outline of the classification scheme; the main tables; an index. To these an introduction may, and in my view should, be added, in which the method and best way of using the catalogue should be explained.

394. The outline of the classification sometimes gives all of the scheme that is used in the catalogue; and it will be found on examination that rarely is the whole of a classification scheme used or anything like it, not because the books are not classified to the fullest extent, but because books on many subjects named in the full tables do not exist or are not "carried in stock." It is more usual to make the outline extend to three places of Dewey, or a proportionate number of places of any other scheme.

395. The main tables set out the classification with the entries of the books in the strict order of the scheme, the main classes being equivalent to the chapters in a book, the divisions and sub-divisions to the paragraphs and sentences. This is the principal part of the catalogue, and it will be as full or brief as circumstances dictate; and it will contain all the analytical and added entries necessary to reveal the subjects in books of general or composite subject matter.

396. A classified catalogue must have a subject-index, and should also have an author-index, and sometimes also has a title-index. Sometimes these are in separate alphabets; but they can be combined in one; and there are several advantages in combining them; anything that reduces the number of references that readers have to make is to be desired.

397. It will be best to take an example of an actual book, and show how it is treated in classified cataloguing. The entry slip as it leaves the hands of the cataloguer may be as follows:

708·2 CHANCELLOR, E. BERESFORD. Walks Among London's Pictures. By E. Beresford Chancellor. XVL, 531 pp.

914·21 Chancellor, E. B. London; Art Galleries; English; Walks among London's pictures.

The principal entry in all forms of cataloguing is made under the name of the author, and in very much the form given in this example, which conforms to the Anglo-American cataloguing rules. The class-mark is written at the beginning of the entry, as that is the symbol by which the main entry of the book is to be found. At the foot of the slip for the use of the staff only is a reference to the second subject of the book (914·21 London), and the various index references. This can be copied on to separate slips by another person than the cataloguer but in my experience it is better that all reference and index slips be made out at the time of the actual cataloguing of the books. This book is seen to require in addition to the main entry, one reference slip, and separate index entries under

> Chancellor, E. B.
> London: Art Galleries.
> Art Galleries: English.
> Pictures: London.
> Walks among London's Pictures.

The reference under 914·21 would be merely a repetition of the main entry in which the class-mark 914·21 would be written above the mark by which the book is shelved; i.e. 708·2.

398. Seeing that references are a part of the main tables, they are written on slips of the same size as the main entry. Index entries, which are much more numerous and are usually very brief, can be written on much smaller slips. The reference shown above gives a clue to the method of treating *analytics*; that is to say, entries for subjects in books which deal with more than one subject and therefore analyse the book. The following will show the points:

914·21

708·2 Chancellor, E. Beresford.

Walks among London's Pictures.

This is the cross-reference from the secondary subject (London). It is arranged under the heading which bears the London number (914·21), but at the side the number at which the book is shelved is printed. The reference thus takes its place in the sequence as follows:

914·21 LONDON: DESCRIPTION.

914·21 Ashton, John. The Fleet: its river, prisons and marriages. Illus. 1889.

914·21 Baker, H. B. Stories of the Streets of London. Illus. 1899.

708·2 Chancellor, E. Beresford. Walks among London's Pictures.

914·21 Cook, Mrs. E. T. Highways and Byeways in London. Illus. 1903.

The following are the index slips, in the order of their importance:

1. | Chancellor, E. B. Walks among London's Pictures.   708·2

2. | London: Description.   914·21

3. | Art Galleries. English.   708.2

4. | Pictures: London.   708·2

5. | Walks among London's pictures (Chancellor, E. B.)   708·2

There will be variations from the wording given, in accordance with the cataloguing code and the type of indexing employed. For example, the author entry (1) could for the sake of economy —always of consequence in cataloguing—be reduced to "Chancellor, London's Pictures", and the initials also be omitted from (5), exceptions to this being made only in the case of two or more authors with the same surname. If these entries and all similar entries for other books are sorted into one alphabetical sequence, the resultant index will yield an answer in one reference to almost any inquiry concerning a book.

399. When the catalogue copy is being prepared for the printer, the slips for main entries, references, and analytics are arranged in the strict order of the class-marks; and within that class-mark alphabetically by names of authors if there is more than one book. They are pasted on large sheets of paper, and the main headings (that is, the names of main classes) are brought out in heavy type, and the divisions and sub-divisions in heavy type proportionately to their importance. The index entries are pasted up alphabetically also on large sheets. The condensed page of a classified catalogue given in section 392 will give some idea of its appearance.

400. The physical form of the catalogue is no less important than its method of internal compilation. The printed form has hitherto been under discussion in these pages, and the examples given are for use in a printed catalogue. No doubt the ideal catalogue from the point of view of the reader is the printed one:

it has the book form which everyone understands, and portability; but, as every modern librarian knows, it is an economic impossibility in the average library to-day, and it presents, besides the difficulty of cost, the additional one of being incomplete in a growing library even at the date of publication. The classified catalogue, issued in the form of separate class-lists, is certainly more manageable than the complete alphabetical catalogue, seeing that each class can be revised and reprinted separately as need arises; but so rapid is the growth and so many are the changes in the stock of a modern library that some form of inclusive manuscript or flexible catalogue is necessary.

401. Many forms have been tried and more have been suggested; examples being, the slip, the placard, the sheaf, and the card forms. Of these only the last two—the sheaf and the card —have anything like a general acceptance. We are not concerned with the pros and cons of this question except as they are affected by classification; and a very brief description of these two forms will suffice.

402. The sheaf catalogue is a variation, and was probably the forerunner, of the loose-leaf ledger. It consists of separate sheets of tough paper held together in book-form by means of an expanding and locking cover. In its earliest form the sheets and the cover had slots at top and bottom through which a cord was passed tying them together; thus

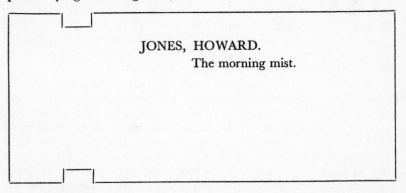

JONES, HOWARD.
The morning mist.

403. The later forms are holed or slotted at the narrow end, and the holes and slots fit on to metal rods which hold the sheets into the cover when it is locked by means of a key. Two examples of the sheaf sheet may be given. This is the latest form of the Staderini sheet as I saw it in use in 1926 in the Marucellian Library in Florence.[1]

---

[1] The Dante entry I have made myself, and it probably does not represent the cataloguing method of the Library.

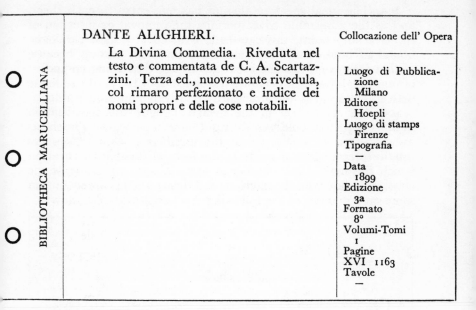

BIBLIOTHECA MARUCELLIANA

DANTE ALIGHIERI.

La Divina Commedia. Riveduta nel testo e commentata de C. A. Scartazzini. Terza ed., nuovamente rivedula, col rimaro perfezionato e indice dei nomi propri e delle cose notabili.

Collocazione dell' Opera

Luogo di Pubblica-zione
  Milano
Editore
  Hoepli
Luogo di stamps
  Firenze
Tipografia
  —
Data
  1899
Edizione
  3a
Formato
  8°
Volumi-Tomi
  1
Pagine
  XVI 1163
Tavole
  —

404. The common British form, perfected by the late Arthur W. Lambert, is an ordinary blank sheet perforated and slotted, as:

WEISMANN, AUGUST.

575
WEI

Essays upon heredity and kindred biological problems, by August Weismann. Edited by E. B. Poulton, Selmar Schonland and A. E. Shipley. 2 v. 1891–92. Oxford: Clarendon Press.

Size $7\frac{7}{16} \times 4\frac{7}{16}$ *in.*

405. The ideal sheaf catalogue[1] has one entry to each sheet, and as the adjustable cover permits the removal or insertion of sheets at any point, this catalogue is in effect a card catalogue bound in book-form. It is more popular with readers because of that form, and has the great advantage that being composed of thin tough paper it occupies less space than the card catalogue with its thick cards and necessarily relatively cumbrous cabinets.

406. On each sheet of the sheaf catalogue the classification number is written boldly in the right-hand top corner. The sheets are arranged in the order of the numbers. Main classes are usually preceded by a guide in the form of a coloured sheet on which the main class number is written, and the name of the class, and under this the divisions and their numbers are set out; in some such manner as the following (reduced) examples show:

300
SOCIOLOGY

This class is divided as follows:—

300 Sociology: General.
310 Statistics.
320 Political Science.
330 Political Economy.
340 Law.
350 Administration.
360 Associations and Institutions.

370 Education.
380 Commerce and Communication.
390 Customs, Costumes, Popular Life.

Each of these divisions is guided by a similar sheet of any colour, setting out its own sub-division; thus:

330
POLITICAL ECONOMY

This division is sub-divided as follows:—

330 Political Economy: General.
331 Capital, Labour, Wages.
332 Banks, Money, Credit, Interest.
333 Land, Ownership, Rights and Rent.
334 Co-operation.
335 Socialism and Communism.

336 Finance, Public Funds, Taxation.
337 Protection and Free Trade.
338 Production, Manufacture, Prices.
339 Consumption, Pauperism.

---

[1] The best discussion of the methodology of this form is to be found in James Douglas Stewart's *The Sheaf Catalogue*, London, 1909.

THE CLASSIFIED CATALOGUE 273

In some cases projecting tabs are pasted on the outer edge of the guide sheets, to serve the purpose of a thumb index.

407. The more widely used card catalogue, which is the special invention of librarians, is too well known to require description. Here it is popular, and in America catalogue and card catalogue are practical synonymous terms. As in the case of the sheaf catalogue a single card carries a single entry, and thus perfect mobility and expansibility are obtainable. Moreover, for ordinary bibliographical purposes, its universality, as compared with other catalogue forms, has been brought about by the standardizing of the card. A card 5 by 3 inches (12·7 by 7·7 centimetres) is now recognized as the international standard. A further and inestimable advantage has arisen from the fact that several great bibliographical institutions now print their cards for circulation amongst other libraries. Of these the Library of Congress is the most important, as it issues printed cards for every book deposited for copyright purposes with the Library, and therefore for all American books that matter as well as for British books which are subject to American copyright.[1] Amongst others may be mentioned the Concilium Bibliographicum, of Zurich, a card catalogue of current zoological literature.[2] Any librarian can subscribe the very small sum charged for these cards and incorporate them in his own catalogue; any slight variations in cataloguing form, etc., as between his own cards and these are easily adjusted or are negligible.

HERBART,[1] JOHN FREDERICK.

Outlines of Educational[2] Doctrine, by John Frederick Herbart. Translated by Alexis F. Lange.[3] Annotated by Charles de Garmo.[4] New York: Macmillan, 1904.

1. Author. 2. Title. 3. Translator-Editor. 4. Editor.

---

408. Modern card catalogues are usually made on "the unit-card principle", a method which, as can easily be demonstrated,

[1] Library of Congress Catalogue Division, Card Distribution. Handbook of Card Distribution, 1902.
[2] The best account is by W. E. Hoyle and Clara Nordlinger in *The Library Association Record*, v. 1, pp. 709–18, 1899. See also *The Library Jnl.*, v. 28, pp. 661–63, 1903, and *Public Lib.*, v. 13, pp. 42–43, 1908.

applies equally to the sheaf catalogue. A single catalogue card is made for each book, and this is duplicated in order to serve all additional entries, cross-references, joint-author cards, etc. The example on p. 259 will illustrate the principle.

Entries for this book will be required in a dictionary catalogue under all the words I have underlined as well as under the subject. Instead of making slips for each of these the cataloguer has five copies of this card, and merely writes the arranging names or word on the top line as the entry requires; thus for the editor

DE	GARMO, CHARLES.
	HERBART, JOHN FREDERICK.
	Outlines of Educational Doctrine, by John Frederick Herbart. Translated by Alexis F. Lange. Annotated by Charles De Garmo. New York: Macmillan. 1904.

and so with every added entry.

Another example may be given:

	NICHOLSON, HAROLD.
	Byron: the last journey, April, 1823–April, 1824, by Harold Nicholson. Constable. 1924.

for which an entry will be required under *Byron, George Gordon, 4th Lord,* as well (possibly, but not necessarily in this case) as one under the title. One catalogue entry as above, with the added words on the top line, will serve all purposes. It is in this manner that the Library of Congress cards and those of other card-distributing agencies can be made to serve in any catalogue.

409. The classified catalogue, in systematic form, rarely stands alone; it has usually a companion in the shape of a "name" catalogue. That is to say, the catalogue assumes two forms:

1. A name catalogue in which books are entered under the names of their authors, persons written about, editors (when of sufficient importance) and series.

2. A classified catalogue in strict order of the classification scheme with all the necessary analytical entries.

There is also, in most cases,

3. A subject index, for which the printed index of the classification scheme itself may suffice in some libraries; or it may be printed separately, or may be on cards. When on cards, it is sometimes inserted in the name catalogue, each card falling into the one great alphabet of which that catalogue consists.

410. Here, again, the unit method of cataloguing is the most expeditious, economical, and least liable to mistakes. The cataloguer merely writes on the card all the indications that are necessary to the person filing the cards. An example of the somewhat complex entry required for the cataloguing of a biography will indicate the value and success of the unit method.

The first three cards file in the alphabet of the Name Catalogue; the fourth and fifth under 927·594 (Biography of French Painting: the shelving number) and 759·4 (French Painting, the secondary subject). I am not concerned with the cataloguing form involved in my examples: any code will be subject to the same or quite similar treatment. What I am concerned to demonstrate is that one operation of cataloguing, skilfully carried out, can be made to serve, as the secondary process of duplicating the cards and

I. Original card, being entry for Name Catalogue under "Watteau"

927·594   WATTEAU, JEAN ANTOINE, 1684–1721.

French painter.

STALEY, EDGCUMBE.

Watteau and his school, by Edgcumbe Staley. Bell. 1902. Great Masters in Painting and Sculpture.

O

II. Author card: Name Catalogue

STALEY, EDGCUMBE.
927·594   WATTEAU, JEAN ANTOINE, 1684–1721.
French painter.

STALEY, EDGCUMBE.
Watteau and his school, by Edgcumbe
Staley. Bell. 1902.   Great Masters in Painting
and Sculpture.

O

III. Series card: Name Catalogue

GREAT MASTERS IN PAINTING AND SCULPTURE.

927·594   WATTEAU, JEAN ANTOINE, 1684–1721.
French painter.

STALEY, EDGCUMBE.
Watteau and his school, by Edgcumbe
Staley. Bell. 1902.   Great Masters in Painting
and Sculpture.

O

IV. Subject card: Classified Catalogue: Same as Card I
V. Subject card: Cross reference: Classified Catalogue

759·4
927·594   WATTEAU, JEAN ANTOINE, 1684–1721.
French painter.

STALEY, EDGCUMBE.
Watteau and his school, by Edgcumbe
Staley. Bell. 1902.   Great Masters in Painting
and Sculpture.

O

adding the analytic headings, references, etc., is merely intelligent clerical work.

411. The Subject Index when it is made on cards may take this character:

VI. Subject Index card: Name Catalogue

For books on this subject see cards in Subject Catalogue numbered as below.

FRENCH REVOLUTION. 944·04

O

The general problems of the index have already been dealt with sufficiently in Chapter VIII.

412. The principal function of the classified catalogue, our main consideration here, is the analysis of books into their components. All the way, hitherto, we have insisted upon the need for the placing of a book at its dominant subject (or form as the case may be) and for referring from its other possible subjects. Such "referring" has no meaning apart from the catalogue: it is in the catalogue that the references are made, as the examples we have just considered demonstrated. The question arises: how far shall references be indulged in? Common sense is the only guide. Some librarians have been known to give analytic entries for the *Encyclopædia Britannica* and similar works which are themselves indexes or are schematic in character; and such books as G. J. Romanes's *Essays*, noted in the previous chapter, have been referenced under the dozen or so subjects with which they deal. In the former case analysis has been carried too far; in the latter it may be justified in the library where exhaustiveness in every subject is required in the catalogues, either because the library aims at universal comprehensiveness, as might be expected, or hoped for, in a national library, or because the stock of books is small and every book must be made to yield its full value. It may be urged that in all libraries this detail is desirable; but it can be answered that to congest the catalogue with masses of

entries for inconsiderable contributions to subjects is expensive, space-wasting, and frequently irritating to the reader. A cross-reference under any heading should mean that the work mentioned there is a real addition to knowledge. In this matter the classifier must exercise his judgment.

413. The adequate, even exhaustive, guiding of the card catalogue is essential to its success. Common as the form is in libraries, and increasingly as it is becoming known to the public, it is by no means attractive to the public. It must be understood, a defect which it shares, of course, with every systematically constructed book or article; but it also involves the, to some, distasteful physical exercise of turning over the cards one by one until what is sought is found, or found to be absent. Our aim must be to make it as simple as may be. Every drawer of a card-cabinet bears label-holders, and these should contain labels with the inclusive class-numbers written boldly on them. The guiding of the cards in the drawers is accomplished by means of cards from ¼ to ½ an inch taller than the cards used for entries. In order to make them distinctive the cards have been made in colours, and the ends of the projection have been curved. We thus get a guide occupying the width of the drawer, as shown:

300 SOCIOLOGY

A "Single," or Main Class, Guide Card.

Not much ingenuity is required to perceive that such guides can be adapted effectively by colour and by shape or size. This has been done, so that we get schemes in which the guide cards are divided into sizes to represent classes, divisions, sub-divisions, sections, etc. The guide shown above is called a "single," as its projection (or "tab" as it is usually called) occupies the whole width of the drawer. Guides with a tab half the length are called halves, a third the length, thirds, and so on. The diagram shows this:

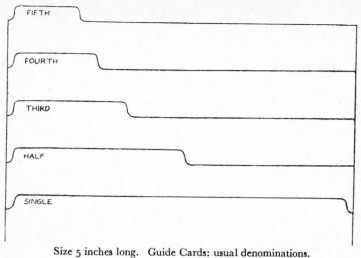

Size 5 inches long. Guide Cards: usual denominations.

Singles can be used for Main Classes; Divisions can be shown by Halves; Sub-divisions by Thirds; important Sections by Fourths, and Sub-sections by Fifths. Or, Singles of a distinctive colour can be used for Main Classes, Singles of the general colour for Divisions, and smaller guides proportionate in size to the character of the sub-division. The illustrations exhibit the two commonest methods of guiding that are in use.

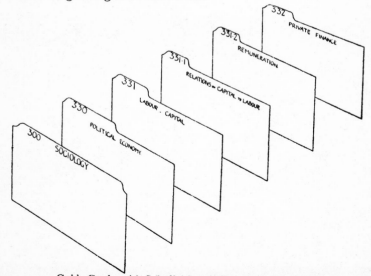

Guide Cards: with Sub-divisions indicated by size of tabs.

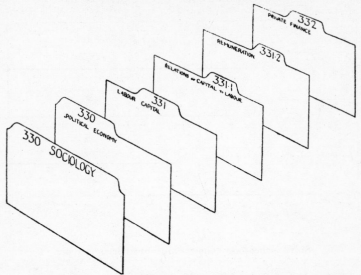

Guide Cards: with Sub-divisions indicated by size and position of tabs.

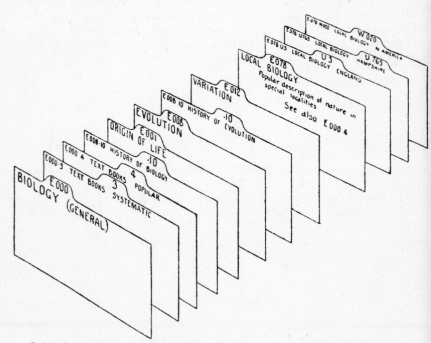

Guide Cards: from a catalogue section arranged by the "Subject Classification."

On each guide are written the subjects it covers. Thus the Main Class guide shows the main divisions, the divisions the sub-divisions, the sub-divisions the sections.

Main Class Guide (Single)

300 SOCIOLOGY

3 SOCIOLOGY.
300 General.
310 Statistics.
320 Political Science.
330 Economics, — Political Economy.
340 Law.

350 Administration.
360 Associations and Institutions.
370 Education.
380 Commerce. Communication.
390 Customs, Costumes, Popular Life.

Divisions Guide (Half)

370 EDUCATION.

37 EDUCATION.
370 GENERAL.
371 Teachers, Methods, Discipline.
372 Elementary Education.
373 Secondary, Academic, Preparatory.
374 Home Education, Self-Education and Culture.

375 Curriculum.
376 Education of Women.
377 Religious, Ethical and Secular Education.
378 Colleges and Universities.
379 Public Schools. Relation of State to Education.

Sub-divisions Guide (Third)

371

TEACHERS, METHODS, DISCIPLINE.
371 GENERAL.
371·1 Teachers, Personal, Professors, Masters, Instructors.
371·2 School organization, Records.
371·3 Methods of Instruction and Study.
371·4 Systems of Education.
371·5 Government, Discipline, Authority.

371·6 School Premises and Equipment.
371·7 School Hygiene.
371·8 Student life and Customs.
371·9 Education of Special Classes.

Sections Guide (Fourth)

```
          ┌─────────────────┐
──────────┤      371.9      ├──────────────────────────────
          └─────────────────┘
```

EDUCATION OF SPECIAL CLASSES.

371·9 General.
371·91 Physically defective.
371·92 Mentally defective.
371·93 Morally defective Delin-
       quents.
371·94 Other abnormal classes.
371·95
371·96 Special Ranks.

371·97 Special Types.
371·98 Special Nationalities.
371·99 Co-education of Races.

414. Judgment is also to be exercised as to the extent to which guiding is to be carried. The ideal is to guide every subject on which literature exists in the library; i.e., if there is only a single card on a subject it should be preceded by its guide. This would mean that some catalogues would consist of almost as many guides as of book-entry cards. On the other hand, novices consulting the card catalogues are prone to suppose that only such subjects as are guided are represented in the library.

415. From the examples given it will be possible for the librarian to work out a system of guides to meet his individual needs. The guides used at the Institut International de Bibliographie (Chapter XIV, Section 198) are also to be studied; they are less elaborate than those in use in England and America, but they are quite effective. Several manufacturers of cards have printed guides or have them elaborated by means of celluloid protectors, and have made tabs by means of which ordinary cards can be transformed into guides. The practical librarian will, of course, make himself familiar with all such aids.

416. Nearly every American book on cataloguing is in effect a book on the card catalogue—in the United States the terms appear to be synonymous. There is only one British book on the subject—Sayers's and Stewart's—*The Card Catalogue*, London, 1913 but James Ormerod has published a useful pamphlet entitled *Style in Card Cataloguing*, 1939; and it is also dealt with admirably in James Duff Brown's *Library Classification and Cataloguing*, London, 1912.

CHAPTER XXVII

SPECIAL CLASSIFICATION

417. In this and the succeeding chapters attention must be given to a few types of special classification which are of more common application. A special classification has been defined already (Sections 20, 27) as a map of a part of knowledge or of subject, and in practical experience it is soon found that for certain parts of the stock of a library the ordinary classifications are not sufficiently minute as they stand, and if expanded according to their own principles would be too cumbrous in their notation for the liking or convenience of most librarians. In any case, the province of special classifications in libraries is dealt with too sketchily by the standard classification schemes, and expansions or modifications to meet varying circumstances have been made in great numbers. A reference to H. G. T. Cannons' *Bibliography of Library Economy*, 1876–1909, shows there registered schemes for the arrangement of

Anthropology.	Law.
Architecture.	Library Economy.
Biography.	Local Collections.
Book Arts.	Mathematics.
Chemistry.	Medicine.
Children's Books.	Music.
Countries.	Naval Subjects.
Education.	Numismatics.
Fairy Tales.	Philosophy and Religion.
Fiction.	Photographs and Paintings.
Folk Lore.	Psychology.
Forestry.	Recreative Arts.
Government Documents.	Science.
Greek and Latin	Shakespeariana.
Classics.	Sociology.
History.	Typography.
Illustrations.	Zoology.

and there have been many others.

418. I have set out this formidable list deliberately as showing that in thirty-three years scores of librarians had not only proposed special classifications or modifications of older ones, but had actually written about them; and it is probable that other modifications not written about were even more in number. It is almost axiomatic that a special library must have special classifications,

because in a special library the extreme ramifications of the subject specialized are sought and no classification scheme of a general character has set these out exhaustively. It has been shown, however, that a properly constructed general classification has in it the possibilities of expansion to any degree. This is true of most classifications, and is readily seen in the Decimal Classification, but the length of the notation for such a subject as the one cited by James Duff Brown—the Prayer Books of the Unitarian Church in Islington, London—which was 264.288421, which only carried the subject as far as London, i.e., Prayer Books plus Unitarian plus London, has become so great that there would naturally be some hesitation in using it. But such a notation would be necessary were we using the Dewey Scheme to classify a special collection of prayer books—a very possible sort of special collection. If a mixed notation of seeming complexity but real simplicity is not objected to, it will be found that the Brussels Expanded Dewey is competent to classify almost any special collection that can be contemplated.

419. I have, however, to deal with facts as they are, and must now proceed to discuss the arrangement of such outstanding matters as the local collection; prints and photographs; deeds; and lantern slides and negatives. Other matter which is subject to classification is dealt with under the heading "The Vertical File."

420. *The Local Collection.* The dominant interest of any general library must be the past and present of the place in which it is situated. This is at any rate true of the rate-supported library, and on occasion it may be equally true of an institutional or other privately owned library. Much literature exists upon the character and scope of the local collection, and all that need be repeated here is that a general library must collect everything in literary form, whether manuscript or printed, written about its own town or written by those who have lived in it. Further, all libraries should have a select collection on the county, but except in the greater counties which might be divided for this purpose, only one library, and that the largest and most accessible, should collect literature on the county as a whole. An ignoring of this principle has introduced an entirely unnecessary but very costly element of competition into collecting for these libraries, and in some counties we have libraries less than ten miles apart which are both competing in the same field to the great detriment of each other, and without any corresponding public advantage.

421. How far local collecting should go beyond literature depends upon whether a town possesses an art gallery and

museum or not. If these exist many such articles as prints and coins may be left to them. A library, however, will endeavour to fill the gap in so far as local material which is not specifically museum material is concerned when these sister institutions are absent. Even in their absence, however, it is not the business of the library to collect local biology, botany and zoology, let alone archæological objects. There is much to be said, however, for the collecting of prints, photographs, and such engraved things as tokens, all of which have a direct documentary interest. So far as prints are concerned, there is a distinct cleavage between those which have an artistic and those which have a merely record or historical interest, and it is usually held, in any case, that the art gallery should take those where the predominant interest is artistic and the library the others.

422. Briefly, if any classification should be special, it is that of the local collection. The whole subject of the county or town can be shown by a single symbol; as, for example, S for Surrey, or M for Middlesex; an economy which is seen immediately when we remember that the mark for Surrey in Dewey at its shortest is 924·21, and in Brown U83.

423. We have, therefore, to make a parallel classification distinguished from all other classifications used in the library by some such symbol as those given. The main problem to be settled is which will be the most convenient arrangement of material on the county, by subject or by locality; that is to say, will the greater number of readers inquire, for example, for all books on the churches of Sussex, or for all books on Chichester, including its cathedral and churches. Or, again, will people ask for the history or sport in a certain ward in the town, or for the history of sport in the town as a whole? It will be seen at once that, as in all classification, either alternative is possible. James Duff Brown has discussed this matter in paragraph 14 of the Introduction to his *Subject Classification*, but without settling the matter conclusively. It is one which each classifier must decide for himself, but my own preference is for a topographical arrangement with a subject sub-division. This appears to me not only the more practical method as established by a rather long experience, but also because the essential characteristic of a local collection *is* topography.

424. The question then arises: what shall be the topographical unit? The simplest arrangement would be one of the places having a definite name on the map of a county, or the district or wards of a town, arranged alphabetically and numbered in that order. Thus, for a topographical arrangement of Hampshire, we might have:

Hoo	Hampshire—General.	
Ho1	Rivers, Canals	⎱ traversing whole
Ho2	Mountain ranges	⎰ area.
Ho3	Hampshire North.	
Ho5	,, South.	
Ho7	,, East.	
Ho9	,, West.	
H10	Aldershot.	
H11	Alice Holt Forest.	
H12	Allington.	
H13	Alresford.	
H14	Alton.	
H15	Alverstoke.	
H16	Amesbury.	
H17	Amport.	

It will be seen that there is a breaking away from pure Topography at Ho1 and Ho2, but this is the most convenient manner of dealing with the subjects covered by these numbers. The two figure basis of the notation would allow for all possible numbering contingencies, as these numbers could be decimalized if necessity arose. This brings us only to the locality, and subject sub-division could be obtained by adding to this topographical number the subject number from the classification generally used in the library written in brackets. Examples with numbers added from Dewey and Brown would be as follows:

	Dewey.	Brown.
Artillery at Aldershot	H10(358)	H10(B887)
Alice Holt Forest—Birds of	H11(5982)	H11(F6)
The Priory at Amesbury	H16(726)	H16(J86)

The curves prevent any confusion between the two classifications which have been combined.

425. While this method is extremely simple, I find it objectionable in some degree because it divides districts which are contiguous on the map. A better way, it appears to me, would be to divide the county into its hundreds, and then to arrange the component places in the hundreds alphabetically. Again, however, the hundreds themselves could only be arranged in contiguity to every one of the hundreds which are so upon the map; but there would be more connexion between the members of each topographical unit than there would be in the mere alphabetical arrangement explained in the last paragraph. In our new "hundreds" basis classification, we should get an arrangement[1] such as this:

[1] The list from which this excerpt is made is in the Victoria County History of Hampshire, v. 5, pp. 437-50.

Hoo–09	HAMPSHIRE General (as in paragraph 326).
H10	Alton, Upper Half.
H101	Chawton.
H102	Coldrey.
H103	Froyle.
H104	Hartley Maudiff.
H105	Holybourne.
	etc.
H11	Alton, Lower Half.
H115	Binsted.
	Dockenfield.
H116	Headley.
H117	Kingsley.
H12	Bishop's Sutton, Upper Half.
H121	Brighton.
H122	Medsted.
H123	Wield.
	etc.

Subject sub-division would also be made as in the last paragraph.

426. The arrangement of a single town could be upon a similar principle, wards or historic divisions, such, for example, as the ecclesiastical parishes, being made the basis of the scheme. Thus:

C 09	CROYDON—General.
C 10	North.
C 11	South Norwood Ward.
C 12	Upper Norwood Ward.
C 13	Norbury Ward.
C 14	Bensham Manor Ward.
C 15	Thornton Heath Ward.
C 30	South.
C 31	South Ward.
C 32	Central Ward.
C 50	East.
C 51	East Ward.
C 52	Addiscombe Ward.
C 53	Woodside Ward.
C 70	West.
C 71	Waddon Ward.
C 72	Broad Green Ward.
C 73	Whitehorse Manor.
C 74	West Thornton Ward.

427. The late Robert K. Dent proposed a special subject classification for Aston Manor, which is interesting and worth quoting.

LOCAL BOOKS[1]

"A general classification as an extension of the Dewey system, where Local Collections are kept separately from General Topography, and are on an extensive scale."

Call all Local Books x, and where there are two or more district collections kept separately (as here, Aston and Birmingham), call one xi and the other x2.

[Contributions to Local History not provided for in the ensuing tables may follow as xii.]

X10. General History of the Town.

X12. CHURCHES AND CHURCH HISTORY.

X12. General. X12. 1, Episcopalian. X12. 2, Roman Catholic. X12. 3, Baptist. X12. 4, Congregational. X12. 5, Jewish. X12. 6, Methodist (various). X12. 7, Society of Friends. X12. 8, Unitarian and English Presbyterian. X12. 9, Minor Sects.

X13. GOVERNMENT, POLITICS AND PHILANTHROPY (SOCIOLOGY).

X13. 1, Local Government. Sub-divided: 11, Health. 12, Libraries. 13, Education. 14, Fire Brigade and Watch Committee (Police, Magistrates, etc.). 15, Street Improvements and Public Works, Drainage, etc. 16, Water. 17, Gas. 18, Electricity. 19, Trams.

X13. 2, PARISH AND UNION AFFAIRS (Workhouses-Asylums, etc.). X13. 3, Political Associations and Parliamentary Elections (Local). X13. 4, Philanthropical Associations. Sub-divided: Medical and Nursing; Relief of Distress; Education of the defective.

X14. LOCAL DIALECT.

X15. SCIENTIFIC ASSOCIATIONS (also here class Schools and Educational Institutions other than Council Schools).

X16. LOCAL MANUFACTURES.

X17. FINE ARTS: ASSOCIATIONS; GALLERIES AND MUSEUMS; DESCRIPTIONS OF FINE WORK DONE IN THE LOCALITY.

X18. LOCAL LITERATURE: 1, Books locally printed. 2, Books by local authors not locally printed (if desired). 3, Libraries (non-municipal). 4, Literary Institutions.

X19. Local Topography and Biography. 1, Guide Books. 2, Lives of Local Worthies. 3, Maps and Plans. 4, Street Lists, Directories, Voting Lists, etc. 5, Local Prints, Views, etc. 6, Local Portraits.

In the Dent scheme a topographical sub-arrangement might be worked out, but for small towns this may not be necessary, although on occasion it would prove to be convenient.

From the foregoing examples it will be seen that the local collection usually has an arrangement special to itself; but

[1] *Library Assoc. Rec.*, v. 9, pp. 107-08, 1907.

pamphlets, cuttings, broadsides, and other small literary matter while arranged by this special classification should be filed in accordance with the methods described in the next chapter.

428. The best treatment of the various questions relating to local literature from the point of view of classification is to be found in *The Camera as Historian*, by H. D. Gower, L. S. Jast and W. W. Topley (Sampson Low, 1916), a work primarily intended to give practical instruction in the work of photographic survey and record. The chapters on classification, which are by Jast, contain the most extensive treatment of a single county that we possess; a matter which may be overlooked in view of the special focus of the work as a whole. A simple treatment is to be found in Berwick Sayers's *Library Local Collections*, 1938, and a more extended one is to be found in John L. Hobbs's *Libraries and the Material of Local History* (Grafton, 1948). The most recent scheme is A. J. Philips's *Outline of a Scheme for the Classification of the Local Collection and for all Material with a Topographical Basis* (the author, Laird's Rest, Hythe End, Wraysbury, nr. Staines, Middlesex, 1953), which also contains a mature, interesting account of practical experience in making the collection.

CHAPTER XXVIII

THE VERTICAL FILE. PAMPHLETS, ARTICLES, CUTTINGS

429. The work of the librarian would be greatly simplified if his stock were confined to volumes of books. These indeed, as the foregoing pages have abundantly shown, present many problems, from our point of view, but in the main there is a ready and recognized solution for them once the art of classification is understood. The modern librarian, however, is the custodian, and oftentimes also the collector, of many varieties of literary and graphic material which are not books.

430. The most nearly related of these to the book is the pamphlet, a form of literature which tends to increase. The standard

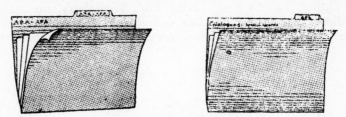

Early Form of Folder for a Vertical File

definition of a pamphlet is an unbound work of less than one hundred pages, although we know in practice that many pamphlets are bound. Then, much important information does not become available in books for many months or even for two or three years; it is only to be found in newspapers or periodicals. In order to make this accessible it is in most cases necessary to collect newspaper cuttings and odd pages from magazines and periodicals. It is frequently necessary, too, to preserve either permanently or temporarily handbills, broadsides, trade cards, and all sorts of fugitive matter which is published in single sheets. There is also the collecting of illustrations and prints, maps, manuscripts, deeds, indentures, and sometimes negatives and lantern slides. This statement does not exhaust the whole of the material which becomes subject to treatment at the hands of the librarian. In the mass, and without the most careful classification and cataloguing, it forms a chaos in which little can be found to any purpose. Properly filed, classified, and indexed it may become an active reinforcement to the book stock of the libraries.

431. The modern special library, works, business, or professional, which is now the auxiliary of so many firms and institutions, depends for most of its current effectiveness upon pamphlets, clippings, and similar material. The essence of the work is classification and indexing. It is, therefore, necessary that we should explore the possibility of this large field of classification work.

432. I have headed this chapter "The Vertical File" in order that I may lead up to what is regarded by the best authorities as the most

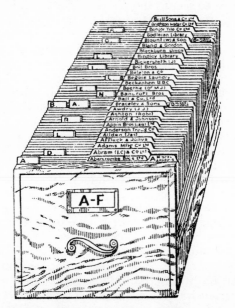

Open Drawer of a Vertical File.

practical and rapid method of treating the material under discussion. At this stage in business knowledge a very brief description of the vertical file itself will suffice for most readers. An examination of the catalogue of any firm which deals in office appliances and stationery will show at least one example of a vertical file. The file is so called from the fact that it consists of a number of folders which stand on their ends in some sort of receptacle—cabinet, drawer, or box—and may be consulted much in the manner in which a card catalogue is consulted. The folder is so called because it is a long sheet of paper, usually manilla paper, which is folded practically in half, but one of the "halves" being a little longer than the other. This folder is used, in the manner illustrated, to hold papers, clippings, or any other loose, unbound material. The folder usually stands on its edge with the shorter "half" in front. The back of the folder then projects sufficiently to enable the writing on the projection of a brief description or title of the contents of the folder or the classification symbols, or other indications. This is the original type of folder. Without fastening fittings, inside or out, it is usually called the loose-leaf folder. Other folders are furnished inside with flexible metal prongs and a metal strip slide; the papers are punched and fitted over the prongs on the strip which hold the slides which hold the prongs flat and so secure the papers. The method, then, involves the process of punching, fitting and securing which takes some time; it is best adapted for the arrangement of papers in inverse chronological order, so that the most recent are on top. There are many variations and refinements of the method, a popular form being the suspended folder, of which the Twinlock examples may usefully be mentioned. The folder has prongs and slide, and its top two edges are reinforced by white metal strips which at each end have a slot or hook projecting laterally about half an inch. These slots fit on to parallel wires or metal rails which are fitted into the vertical file and so the folder is suspended, can be moved forward or backward and opened easily for consultation without the withdrawing of the folder. Plastic tabs move along the front strip to any position and are the labels. The result is pleasing, and for papers which it is imperative to keep together, serves well. The form of folder I have used is the loose-leaf and found it to work well in the hands of careful filers, and it certainly has greater mobility and can be revised, weeded out and reinforced with greater ease. The matter is one for personal choice not for argument; but it is perhaps not superfluous to remark that the modern librarian watches every development made by commerce and professional workers in the apparatus of filing and indexing.

433. We have now envisaged an instrument of very comprehensive character, which used fully and on a considered plan could be made into a singularly complete receptacle for all the material which is not in book form in the library. That is to say, folders of quarto size will hold every news-cutting, letter, broadside, and pamphlet which a library receives. They can also be made, with certain careful adaptations but without altering the size of the file and not breaking the sequence, to hold small maps, deeds, and illustrations. If all this material is placed in a series of folders, which are classified minutely and arranged in the order of the classification, we have a file of infinite mobility and simplicity, which is parallel with the whole of the book stock, may be catalogued in precisely the same way, and any material in it will usually be found by one reference from catalogue to file. Such a file is maintained wholly or in part in several libraries. The

International Encyclopædia of the Institut International de Bibliographie was in the main a file of the type described.

434. It will be necessary to deal with each of the forms of material we have named both with and without reference to its treatment in the vertical file.

435. The first consideration is the one that we have already hinted at: has the matter to be filed permanent or temporary value? It is quite clear that the treatment we give to temporary material should not be costly, or as costly as that which we give to permanent material. Our ideal will be one coherent system of filing in which these two qualities in our stock are recognizable. In this workaday world the average librarian is compelled to discard as much fugitive literature as he acquires, or very nearly as much. A file must be a living, growing entity, or it may be of little effect.

436. To deal first with pamphlets. The accepted definition of a pamphlet as a literary work consisting of less than one hundred pages is convenient, but it implies that such pamphlets are not, and ought not to be, bound. The rule appears to be too rigid. If a pamphlet is large enough to bear a binding which will take visible lettering on its back, and its subject-matter has permanent interest to warrant it, there is no reason, except that of cost, for not binding it. The ideal arrangement, surely, of all library material is on the shelves in one sequence. I am inclined to think, for example, that all local pamphlets should be separately bound; thus they are better preserved and may be more safely handled. When none of these considerations applies, the following methods come under consideration:

437 (1) *Binding in Groups.*—Some librarians, with quite modern ideas, are of opinion that the best method of treating a group of pamphlets is to classify them and then to bind several pamphlets dealing with one subject, or with cognate subjects, into a volume, and thus form a series of bound collections of pamphlets which can be made to stand in an approximate classified order on the shelves, while the individual pamphlets are discovered by the author and subject catalogues in which the volumes are analysed. The advantages and disadvantages of such a system are too obvious to the practical librarian to need enlarging upon. It will clearly be understood that I am speaking of pamphlets which are classified into groups before binding, and that our bound volume is limited to a subject or to closely cognate subjects. It would be against bibliographical common sense to bind pamphlets into volumes because they were pamphlets and irrespective of their subject-matter.

438 (2) *Filing in Boxes.*—Akin to this method, but without its

main disadvantage, is the filing of pamphlets in boxes, which approximate to book shape, using here, too, a classified order. There are many types of pamphlet boxes which have book shape, to be obtained from stationers, and have xylonite or other transparent label holders on the back of them to carry the class marks.

439 (3) *The Coloured Band Method.*—The ingenious John Cotton Dana, one of the most original and stimulating of modern American librarians, in his *American Library Economy*[1] describes lucidly, with examples, a method of filing pamphlets loosely on shelves. He expresses the view that the success of the vertical file is so great that librarians tend to include in it material un-fitted for the method. Such material he considers to be "large pamphlets, pamphlets in long sets or series, and pamphlets not definitely of value in the study of subjects of to-day." These it would be too costly to place in the vertical file because such placing would involve the use of folders and catalogue cards, and the work consequent upon employing these. He, therefore, proposes that pamphlets shall be made of a uniform size of 9 inches by placing those which are less than this size in 9-inch envelopes. The pamphlets are then sorted into their main classes and on each main class is pasted a band of coloured paper running along the lower part of the back of all the pamphlets, each class having a distinctive colour. The number of colours will depend, of course, upon the number of classes used. Sub-division of each is obtained by pasting another coloured band above the first, and further division by other bands to the full extent that the back of the pamphlets will allow. Thus, presuming the pamphlets to be 9 inches high and the space needed for the band $\frac{1}{2}$ inch, there are 16 possible locations of each pamphlet. If 10 colours are used it is possible to make 160 distinctive divisions. It is quite clear that if each colour represents a subject or sub-division of section, pamphlets when assembled on the shelves by the colours will automatically be drawn into their class, division and sub-division. The scheme has possibilities, especially for application to trade catalogues and similar fugitive pamphlets which are subject to frequent change or renewal. To describe all its features would require space greater than we can give. A reference to the author's own description of it is well worth the trouble involved.

440. (4) *The Vertical File Method.*—There may be other methods than those described of handling pamphlets, but none of them has any general vogue. There remains to be considered the vertical file. Here the pamphlets are arranged in folders, and the folders are placed in classified order in the file. Each pamphlet is marked with its classification number, and sometimes a folder

is given to each pamphlet, or sometimes several pamphlets on the same subject go into one folder. E. A. Savage, who used the method extensively at the Coventry Public Libraries, and was undoubtedly aware also of Dana's method, tells me that the single pamphlet in the folder was in the end the only practical method, where it was customary to lend out the pamphlets to enquirers who often wanted to use them away from the library building.

441. *Articles.*—The question of the preservation of periodicals is a difficult one for a library, but it is specially difficult for the medium-sized or small library. When revising Brown's *Manual of Library Economy*, I laid it down as a rule that periodicals which are indexed in such works as the *Library Association Index to Periodicals* should be bound and preserved permanently as part of the library stock. I am more doubtful now of the wisdom of being so generous in the matter. In fact, I fear that it is impossible for the average library to preserve anything like the number of periodicals which are so indexed. Moreover, in the smaller library, and perhaps even in the larger one, the bound periodical is far less effective than the separate articles forming it would be if they were properly handled. In a large number of cases, therefore, I would not hesitate to recommend the cutting up of magazines and reviews and the preserving of such articles as appear to warrant that course. The articles are treated as if they were pamphlets, sometimes being bound into classified volumes or, if dealt with separately, each is sewn into some sort of a cover; a manilla cover for preference.

445.[1] NEWSPAPER-CUTTINGS are the commonest source of current information. Thousands of items of interest, numberless small facts, biographical hints, as well as nearly all commercial information, are in newspaper paragraphs which never get into books, and may be lost if they are not dealt with at the time of their appearance. This is easy to recognize in connexion with references in the newspapers to matters concerning the town in which the collecting library is situated. Newspaper-cuttings, then, form a large part of the filing problem, and as we have suggested already, in commercial libraries they form the greater part of it. In order to obtain the best results it should be made the business of some particular person or persons to examine all newspapers, and to extract cuttings according to definite principles of selection. Few libraries or other institutions, I imagine, would collect cuttings for all subjects in the classification, but cuttings on such trades and industries as are peculiar to a town or important in it are obviously desirable. All references to the town itself in papers other than local papers should also be sought for, but the assistance

[1] The author has deleted matter covering sections that were numbered 442-444.

of a press-cuttings agency might be enlisted in this matter, as the local collection is probably the most important part of any municipal library and it is essential that nothing that matters should be missed. Other desirable cuttings it is difficult to specify, but one may say that all references to the dominant interest of the day in every branch of activity and thought, and biographical, historical, and similar articles, should be preserved when they are not too obviously a rehash of material which already exists in better shape in books.

446. Economy of time and labour forbid too careful a scrutiny of articles to see whether they are completely original or not. Experience will assist the selector in choosing the right type of article for filing. Here, as elsewhere, however, there should be a rough secondary classification of all material into (*a*) temporary and (*b*) permanent, and whatever after-treatment the cuttings receive it should be possible to recognize that a cutting has only a temporary value or otherwise.

447. The treatment of cuttings has also been as various as that of pamphlets. The oldest method still survives, in which the cuttings are simply pasted into a newspaper-cuttings book, if one may judge from the stationers' shops where such books are still to be bought. As such a method is the negation of all order, it need not be more than mentioned. A more sensible method is to mount cuttings on sheets of stiff paper, and to fasten these in classified order into loose leaf bindings on the principle of a large sheaf catalogue. There can be no doubt, however, in the minds of all who have used it of the superiority of the vertical file in this connexion. In this, cuttings which have only a temporary interest can be placed in folders of a different colour from the others. Temporary cuttings need not be mounted as a rule, unless they are likely to be subjected to much of handling. Cuttings which are to be filed permanently may be mounted on sheets of paper, which need not be thick or cost much. These sheets should bear the title and class mark of the cutting, as well as the source from which it has been taken. The sheets I use are 11″ by 8½″ in size, are of a stout paper with a good writing surface, the heading is as shown, and there are spaces for entry words, class marks, etc., both on top and at the side to permit the filing of the sheet either on its side or upright.

448. It will, of course, be realized that the source of all cuttings must be shown, as this is the authority on which the information they convey is given. (One may say, incidentally, that all information given by librarians should be qualified with the name

of the book or other material from which that information is taken; that is to say, no librarian should himself pose as an authority on anything apart from his books, although, indeed, individually he may be an expert on some subject).

449. THE UNIVERSAL ENCYCLOPÆDIA.—I think it will be recognized that a vertical file covering the whole classification

Author

Title or Subject

Source

Sheet on which cuttings are mounted.

might be a universal encyclopædia of the greatest value, expansible and always current. The model of such a file was that of the Institut International de Bibliographie at Brussels, where in a long series of drawers the vertical files covered universal knowledge. To make such an encyclopædia perfect would be a very drastic and expensive process. It might involve in the first place the cutting up of every existing encyclopædia, and the filing together of the articles from all of them on each subject. Thus, to mention one subject, one would get the articles on psychology not from the *Encyclopædia Britannica* alone, but also those from *The Encyclopædia Americana*, Larousse, Meyer, Nelson, Chambers, and so on. These would form the basis of the encyclopædia, which, would be reinforced by pamphlets, magazine articles, and, finally, newspaper-cuttings and other fugitive material on psychology. It is probable, however, that most librarians will be content to leave their encyclopædias in their unique detachment; a contentment with which I agree personally. That, however, does not invalidate the desirability, and sometimes even necessity, of filing material which is auxiliary in the various forms that have been described.

450. MISCELLANEOUS.—Attention is given in Chapter XXXI to the classification of library economy. Generally speaking, such a classification is applied to the letters and administrative papers of libraries. Many of the papers, however, which come into this category have also a very important interest from the point of view of the vertical file. It may be desirable to make a distinction between letters which have a mere formal character and those which have a subject interest. Librarians send out every day letters which deal with subjects, information that has been sought for and is conveyed to readers, and so on. Copies of all such letters sent out and received may very well find a place in their classification in the vertical file. Of course, letters dealing with the merely administrative side of the library belong to the private office and we deal with them elsewhere.

451. It is probable that the ordinary collections of illustrations, which are used for bulletin work and for circulation to schools, such as are common in American libraries and are becoming more so in England (there are collections, for example, at Birmingham, Cardiff, Chelsea, Islington, Manchester, Croydon, and many other places) can best be filed in the vertical file. When mounted, however, they are in bulk very heavy and, to facilitate reference and to prevent damage to the edges of the mounts, it is desirable to place stout dividing boards (plywood or millboard, for example) at frequent intervals in the drawer to give support. This file can also be used for deeds, the majority of maps, and lantern slides. All these subjects require separate treatment, which is given below.

452. THE CLASSIFICATION OF THE VERTICAL FILE.—There are few more severe and searching tests to which we can put a classification scheme than that of applying it to such a file as we have been considering. Classification is here pushed, by the nature of the material to be arranged, to the extremity of minuteness. The difficulties that arise are so real that some librarians have abandoned the systematic order provided by the ordinary schemes, and have preferred the alphabetical arrangement of subjects, as in a dictionary catalogue (with authors and titles omitted). Such is the arrangement described by Dana in *The Vertical File*, a chapter in his *Modern American Library Economy*. Whatever may be said for the method—which, after all, is the grouping of material

first into minute classes and then the re-sorting of these classes into the simple order of the alphabet, and is, therefore, classification of a kind—alphabetical order cannot give the full advantages of a systematic classification. Those advantages appear to be worth the extra labour involved. The labour is great, because of the minuteness of the material, as the following articles, clipped from a single issue of *The Observer*, will demonstrate:

> Ervine, St. John. An Unlovely Theatre [The Memorial Theatre at Stratford-on-Avon].
> Garvin, J. L. America's "Grey Cardinal" [Colonel House].
> Fox-Strangways, A. H. Music in 650 B.C.
> The Squirrel and the Nut: memory in animals.
> The Bloomsbury Site: the University [of London].
> Squire, J. C. The Georgian Parson.
> Wireless on Trains.
> "The Complete Peerage": the sport of pedigree hunting.
> The Crystal User: is he a handicap to progress?
> Sherwell, Arthur. The Unreformed Public House.

Here it will be observed that the dominant subject of each clipping is fairly obvious, as Theatre, Aeronautics, Biography, Musical History, Animal Intelligence, London University, etc.; but there would be a mass of other material under each heading, and closer order is essential. The classification of Ervine's article ought to show the subject, place, and date of the theatre in question, and there is the question of the relationship of this particular theatre to Shakespeare. The index references would be simple enough:

1. *Author.*   Ervine, An Unlovely Theatre.
2. *Title.*   Unlovely Theatre, An. Ervine.
3. *Subject.* Theatres: Stratford-on-Avon. Shakespeare Memorial.
4. *Secondary Subjects.*   1. Shakespeare: Memorial Theatre, Stratford-on-Avon.
                           2. Stratford-on-Avon, Shakespeare Memorial Theatre.

Few cuttings would be worth so exhaustive a treatment; and the desideratum is a filing which shows the bare essentials—the simplest *sure* means of locating this article. It would appear that these are what I have called the subject and secondary subjects, which can be noted, using Dewey thus:

792 Theatre   42·48 Warwickshire

that is to say, 792·4248, which is quite indefinite; and, again:

822·33 English Drama: Shakespeare

which is more indefinite still; and, as it stands, the Dewey classification provides no further sub-division. The former of the two
placings might be preferred, but much further sub-division is
necessary. To deal with the same subject (Theatre: Warwickshire) in the Seventh Expansion of Cutter, we get:

Vu Theatrical history   45 England

that is to say Vu45 and no further sub-division, which is even
more indefinite than Dewey; and, not to pursue the point too
far, in Brown's *Subject Classification*, we get:

N241 Theatres   U615 Stratford-on-Avon

that is to say N241U615, which is much more satisfactory in this
special example, but as it marks all the theatres in a given place
and not any particular theatre the notation would not be minute
enough in most cases. The student may apply similar experiments in placing the other articles I have named above and
I think will see that the ordinary library classification, without
expansion, is not quite a satisfactory medium for arranging very
extensive files of cuttings, although it may serve for rigidly
selective ones. If the schedules of the Universal Decimal Classification are examined, it will be found that these, with their
apparatus of auxiliary signs, will meet the case. A study of the
entries given above will show that their satisfactory classified filing
requires minute sub-division of subjects, and very detailed
chronological, geographical, and similar tables. These the
Universal scheme provides; but many librarians prefer, and
always will prefer, to enlarge their own schemes sufficiently to
meet their needs. With the knowledge we now have of the
possibilities and limitations of the various schemes which are
described in the earlier pages, this is a practical task, although it
is one full of chances and pitfalls.

453. The index to the printed tables of the classification is the
natural subject key to files which are arranged by the classification
itself. This is adequate for all ordinary purposes, but, here again,
the introduction of extensions and modifications often makes it
an incomplete and not altogether satisfactory one. If a fuller
index is found to be necessary, one on cards is that most easily
managed. Entries made in it should be sufficient to guide any
reasonable enquirer in one reference to the file sought. Only
signed articles, likely to be of interest on account of their author,
should be indexed under their name, but this, and all other
articles should be indexed under the subject word and, very
occasionally, its synonyms. The *A.L.A. List of Subject Headings*
and the *Library Association Subject Index to Periodicals*, in company

of course with the indexes to the classification scheme itself, offer good guidance in the choice of entry words.

454. Some librarians prefer to incorporate the cards of their file index with their main card catalogues of books. This has distinct advantages, but has the grave defect of congesting the catalogue with matter of a relatively minor character which needs continuous revision. A cutting or an article may be invaluable at times, but it cannot have the importance generally of a book.

454.1. See also paragraphs 465-6.

CHAPTER XXIX

PRINTS, ILLUSTRATIONS, LANTERN SLIDES AND NEGATIVES

455. All the material named in the heading requires careful and minute classification; in fact, more minute classification than any other material with the possible exception of newspaper-cuttings. Local prints and photographs form part of the Local collection, and it would be of distinct advantage—at least in theory—if they could be arranged by precisely the same classification; but it is at least arguable that this is not possible.

456. First, however, a few words may be devoted to the questions of the mounting and filing of these prints. In the volume by Gower, Jast, and Topley, alluded to above (Section 428), this matter receives exhaustive treatment, and anyone about to form a collection should turn to that work. In summary, all prints and photographs should be placed on mounts of uniform size, as this expedites handling and simplifies storing. "Nature" paper mounts, as free as possible from chemicals, and especially from hypo-sulphite of soda, which is an agent most destructive of photographs, are to be preferred to inflexible, thick cardboard mounts, sunken or otherwise, as the latter are liable to crack and break at the corners. Photographs should be mounted with a dry mountant, and prints should be pasted on with the greatest care with an acid-free paste. The size of the mount which the organizers of the Photographic Survey and Record of Surrey found to be most convenient is $12\frac{7}{8}''$ by $10\frac{5}{8}''$, and ninety per cent. of photographs and prints will go on these; but for larger pictures $16\frac{5}{8}''$ by $13\frac{3}{4}''$ has been found to be a useful size.[1] Of course very large pictures, which come but rarely into the hands of the classifier, require mounts of sufficient size, but even here it is well to have standard sizes, so that an arrangement into groups may be made. Mounts of grey, sage green, and vandyk brown are more effective, durable, and less likely to show stains than white ones.

457. The filing of the mounted prints has been done in several ways. The use of the mounts described above implies that "separate" filing is the ideal, and that the mounting of photographs or prints into bound albums is undesirable from almost

---

[1] These sizes are those into which the sheets of the paper manufacturer cut without undue waste.

every standpoint. The separate mounts, however, are sometimes bound by the loose-leaf method, which permits of insertion and classification; the photographic survey collection of Sir Benjamin Stone, at Birmingham Reference Library, is treated in this way. Or the prints may stand on their edges in file boxes, resembling the ordinary transfer cases used in connexion with vertical files. Or they may be filed, also on their edges, in vertical files, precisely in the manner in which cards stand in a card catalogue. These appear to be the most satisfactory methods now in vogue, though doubtless there are others. Of these, where there is prospect of growth—and collections of illustrations often expand enormously—it would appear that the vertical file is the best method; and, as illustrations in mass are very heavy indeed, steel cabinets with drawers having hard steel wheel (or ball) bearings are in my experience suitable. For the standard mount ($12\frac{7}{8}''$ by $10\frac{5}{8}''$) cabinets intended in commerce for the filing of foolscap folders will serve. If there is the likelihood of much handling of the collection, the mounts may be inserted in folders, at least one folder being allotted to each subject having a specific number. The folder protects the print and has the additional advantage that it provides a uniformly projecting edge on which classi-fication and other arranging numbers and words may be written. As for ordinary illustrations filed in drawers strong dividing boards are desirable at close intervals to support the prints or folders.

458. To confine ourselves first to the classification of local photographs. These have been arranged in several ways; as follows: (1) under the name of the photographer with card index references from the locality and subject; (2) the order of accession merely, with all other references in the card index; (3) in alpha-betical order of subjects; (4) in alphabetical order of locality; and (5) in systematic order; indexes of various kinds being added to (3-5). It is not likely that any reader will use (1) or (2), and (3) presents so many possibilities of cross-division and confusion that few will venture upon it. Here, again we encounter the problem of place versus subject. Jast, working on long ex-perience, is of opinion that photographs deal with such minute subjects that the locality characteristic becomes secondary, and classification *by subject* is to be preferred; in *The Camera as Historian* he states his case at some length. He provides the full tables of a classification of the county of Surrey, which can be adapted easily to any other county; and one virtue—in my eyes a vital one—of his scheme is that it can be used in exactly converse sense; can be used with the locality characteristic as primary and the subject characteristic as secondary.

459. The following are the main classes

(01-47) Topography.
         Art.
49   Literature.
50   Geology.
51   Palæontology.
52   Zoology.
53   Botany.
537 Horticulture and Agriculture.
54   Architecture.
55   Antiquities.
56   Meteorology.
57   Passing Events.
58
59
(60-99) County divided by Boroughs, Urban and Rural Districts, etc.

460. The notation, it will be observed, is a/decimal one. We have here two arrangements for Topography: (01-47) and (60-99). The first (01-47) is a series of numbers obtained by marking the squares on the quarter sheet of the 6 inch Ordnance Survey map. This map, as is well known, is divided into a series of squares and each of these squares is given a number lying in the series 01-47 used decimally. This is used for marking landscapes, views, etc., where the interest is definitely topographical, and for the topographical sub-division of subjects. The second series of topographical numbers (60-99) is primarily for marking local literature, and is the Jast alternative for the topographical classification described in Chapter XXVII. It is also to be used for such subjects as Passing Events, where the unit of the Ordnance Map square is not quite so apposite as that of the actual town or village in which the event occurs. The two sequences cannot be confused, as the numbers differ, but if the second sequence were used for a subject it would create dire confusion to use the first as well; one or other must be chosen and adhered to. A section may be quoted to show the working of the notation.

55   ANTIQUITIES
         Prehistoric.
551 Palæolithic age.
552 Neolithic age.
553 Bronze age.
554 Iron age.
         551-4 sub-divided like 01-47, and further divided as under:
              1 Camps.
              2 Dwellings.
              3 Interments.
                   etc.

Historic.

555 Coins, medals.
556 Legal.
557 Domestic.
557.2 Trade, e.g., trade signs.
557.4 Communication.
etc.

A print on a Palæolithic camp at Abinger, near Dorking, would receive the class mark 551(331)1 (i.e., 551 Palæolithic age, 331 Dorking district—number from the map square—and 1 camp); and a Carnival at Godalming would be 577(81); i.e., 577 Passing Events—carnivals, 81 Godalming, the number in this case being taken from the second topographical sequence. It will be noted that the topographical numbers are always written in brackets, as is the style in the Universal Decimal Classification, in order to distinguish them from subject numbers.

461. After much experience, I am inclined to the view that this order should be reversed, and that a topographical arrangement with subject sub-division would be a more satisfactory working scheme. This reversal the Jast scheme admits readily; its application merely means the reversal of the numbers with the following results:

	Jast.	*Reversed.*
Palæolithic camp at Abinger	551(331)1	331(551.1)
Carnival at Godalming	577(81)	81(577)

The *subject* is enclosed in curves in the reversed example to prevent confusion.

462. The classification is equipped with special tables for marking material which requires minute division, and such tables are essential to the marking of every sort of print. Thus, 489, Portraits and other biographical material, has this table:

Portraits.
A   of the subject.
B   of his parents.
B2   father
B3   mother
B4   grandfather
B5   grandmother
C   Other members of his family.
D   His wife.
D2   Second wife [and D3 for the third, if necessary].
E   His children.
F   His friends, schoolmasters, etc.
G   Caricatures.
H   Personations (for actors, etc.)
J   Pets.

K Birth place.
L Later residences, except
M Death-place.
N Incidents in his career.
P Scenes associated with him.
Q Grave.
R Monuments, memorials, statues.
S Memorial objects.
T His sketches, drawings, etc.
U Institutions founded by him.
V
W
X
Y Autographs, facsimiles, bookplates.
Z Other.

The sub-arrangement of all prints is shown by what approximates to an author-mark consisting of the first three words of the subject. Hence a portrait of Tennyson is 489 TEN, and of his mother 489 TEN.B3, and his house (and death-place) Aldworth 489 TEN.M. Similar tables are provided for details of ecclesiastical buildings, castles, etc., all of which can usefully be used with this or any other scheme.

463. OTHER PRINTS.—Other prints and illustrations are collected in large numbers by some librarians; for example, in all modern children's libraries illustrations having definite subject interest, from discarded books, periodicals, prospectuses, advertisements, and catalogues. The mounting and filing of these are done by the same methods that are used for local prints; but here the classification scheme used for newspaper-cuttings will generally be preferred (see Section 445). Nevertheless, such tables as Jast proposes for the marking of portraits and churches, etc., are absolutely necessary. It may also be pointed out that from the beginning of the collection the classification should be used to its minutest detail, otherwise there will be much re-marking at a later stage. All that has been said of the filing of Local Collection prints applies here.

464. LANTERN SLIDES AND NEGATIVES.—Lantern slides are clearly as susceptible to classification as any other kind of picture and, indeed, demand some form of it. The best method of filing, both for safety and rapid reference, is in drawers like cards in the card cabinet; but drawers of the right size are needed in order that the slides may fit in accurately and that undue movement be impossible. Suitable cabinets are sold by firms which specialize in photographic equipment and lantern slides. The standard slide cabinet drawers have *internal* measurements of about $10\frac{3}{4}''$ by $3\frac{1}{2}''$, and are divided into four compartments. They hold 75

slides comfortably, from which figure it is possible to compute the number of drawers required for a collection. The classification that is ideal is that which would serve for news-clippings, that is to say, any sufficiently minute bibliographical classification, and certainly the U.D.C. can be used here. The classification of slides premises that the title and class marks and any other necessary indications are written on the masking of the slides; thus—

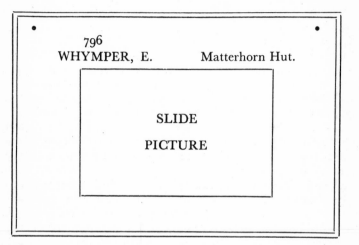

and the slide must be indexed, under subject at least, as are books or other pictorial material.

464.1. The chief difficulty about lantern slides is the fact that they are used not as subject units, but rather as units in a lecture-subject; they are illustrations to lectures. In theory, and to some extent in practice, if slides are arranged in perfectly classified order, then a set to illustrate a lecture on any subject can easily be built up. The work, however, of building up and then of demolishing directly after the delivery of the lecture takes times and is often unnecessary. It seems that in many cases the law of convenience is served best if the slides are kept in lecture sets and any other form of arrangement abandoned. This decision is made reluctantly, but seeing that the placing together of things which are used together is the essence of practical classification, it seems to be a satisfactory one even from the point of view of the classifier. In this arrangement a subject index is even more necessary.

464.2. Some libraries have collections of negatives as part of their local collection, or it may be that they make their own lantern slides. As is the case for lantern slides, suitable cabinets of drawers for the filing of negatives can be obtained. Negatives can be classified in the same manner as lantern slides, and in order to preserve the unprotected film it is advisable that they should be inserted into folders or envelopes before being filed in the drawers. On these can be written the class mark. This mark should also be written in black ink on a corner of the film of the negative where there is a lantern slide corresponding to the negative, a reference to the whereabouts of the negative should be written on the lantern slide. This is very useful, as casualties amongst lantern slides in a much used collection are liable to be many.

465. Film records, micro- and other, now form a familiar part of reference, and in some cases even lending, library stock. Microfilms can be stored in tin containers, and these are often square in shape and can be filed in cabinets as if they were broad catalogue cards. They are so small that a large collection occupies very little space. They can of course be classed and indexed as other items. Larger films are usually stored in flat, circular metal containers and laid horizontally on shelves, the titles being shown on their edges and the containers placed so that these are visible.

466. Gramophone records are stored vertically on very narrow shelves and usually in the cardboard or manilla envelopes in which they are sold. Usually the ordinary method of classing and cataloguing is not used; the catalogues of the recording firms have been found to be as economical a method for use as any yet devised. Records of the band or tape variety are stored in much the same manner as films. These subjects are under frequent discussion; one of the most useful guides to their manipulation is R. L. Collinson's *Cataloguing, arrangement and filming of special material in special libraries*, Aslib, 1950, and I have found suggestive and interesting the brief accounts and good sketches of various filing equipment in *Planning the library . . . problems of library design, book storage and shelving*, Roneo, 1950.

CHAPTER XXX
DEEDS AND OTHER SIMILAR MANUSCRIPTS

467. This is not the place to dwell upon the importance of a good system for the collecting, conserving, and recording of the documents, mainly handwritten, which are the original record of public, private, and commercial transactions and are the sources of most authentic history. The high authority of the Master of the Rolls, who has named many places including selected libraries as repositories where such documents may be deposited and consulted, lies behind recent efforts. Much devoted study, energized by such pioneers as Henry Hall, Cuthbert Johnson, and Hilary Jenkinson, has been dedicated to their acquisition, repair, and arrangement. In every county and in some towns there is some sort of organization approximating to a records society and the Church has lately become more conscious of the importance of its registers and other documents. These with others find a centre in the British Records Association which has given special attention in a series of reports from its own committees to these matters.

468. The Association's *General Report of a Committee on the Classification of English Archives*,[1] 1936, should hereafter form the basis for the arrangement of any considerable collection, and may afford hints even where the documents are few in number. The scheme proposed has six main classes which can be set out, with the divisions mentioned in the report although not arranged in a schedule:

1.—Public, Central Administration:

> The sub-division of these documents includes such locally important documents as
>> Commands of the Army,
>> Local Registries of the Supreme Court,
>> Local Establishments of the Ministry of Health,
> all of which being part of Government or Central administration are classed with such archives as are preserved at the Public Record Office. "The boundaries of the various groups within it, derived from the living and defunct administrations, are already fixed and their character well known from official publications" such as the *Guide to the Public Records* by M. S. Giuseppi and the First Report of the Royal Commission on Public Archives, 1912.

[1] See our Bibliography, page 337.

2.—Public, Local Administration:

> Courts and Court Officers.
>> Sheriff and their courts—County, Hundreds, Tithings Court Rolls.
>> Escheator and Coroner.
>> Justices of the Peace and Quarter and other Sessions Clerk of the Peace.
>
> Statutory Authorities.
>> Earlier.
>>> Boroughs.
>>> Improvement Commissioners.
>>> Sewers Commissions.
>>> Boards of Guardians, Unions.
>>> Highway Boards.
>>> School Boards.
>>
>> Modern.
>>> County Councils.
>>> Urban.
>>> Rural.
>>> Parish
>>>> etc.

3.—Semi-Public Administration:

> "The private satisfaction, advantage or profit of individuals" is their cause.

> I. Statutory and Chartered Bodies.
>> National.
>> Local.
>>> Docks and Ports.
>>> Public Utility Companies or Trusts.
>>>> Roads.
>>>> Light.
>>>> Water.
>>>> Transport.

> II. Endowed Institutions.
>> Colleges and Universities.
>> Schools.
>> Hospitals.
>> Other charities.

> III. Learned and Professional Societies and Corporations [London mainly, but there are local bodies of similar function.]
>> Inns of Court.
>> Law Society.
>> General Medical Council.
>>> etc.

> IV. City Companies of London and Similar Bodies.

4.—Private Administration.

    Manorial administration and land ownership.

        Manorial Records.

        Muniments of Title.

    Household administration.

    Personal correspondence and papers concerned with Family
        and Social Relations.

    Tenure of Office in a public, or semi-public, capacity.

    Commerce and the Conduct of Business.

    Private Bodies.

        Artistic.

        Literary.

        Scientific.

        Social.

    Other public work of private bodies, including Learned
        Societies.

5.—Archive Groups resulting from Ecclesiastical Administration:

    Ecclesia Anglicana.

        Provincial.

        Diocesan.

        Archidiaconal.

        Peculiars or Immediate Jurisdictions.

        Ruridecanal.

        Parochial.

        Capitular.

        Monastic.

    Other Ecclesiastical Authorities.

    English Roman Catholics.

    Nonconformist Bodies in England and Wales.

    Moravian Church in England.

    Foreign Protestant Refugee Churches in England.

    Communities of Orthodox Greek Church in England.

    Anglo-Jewry.

    Registers of Births or Baptisms, Deaths or Burials, and
        Marriages.

    Statutory Bodies concerned with Ecclesiastical Matters.

    Ecclesiastical Commission.

    Welsh Church Commission.

    Governors of Queen Anne's Bounty.

    Representative Body of the Church in Wales.

    National Assembly of the Church of England.

    Religious Societies.

        S.P.C.K.

        C.M.S.

        B. and F.B.S.

        L.M.S.

        S.A.

6.—Documents of Historical Interest artificially collected.

469. Each of these may be developed with a notation which any reader of this book may formulate but already, in its Second Report, the British Records Association provides a detailed classified list of the documents to be found in parish archives, and in the Fourth a classification of conveyancing documents of the seventeenth, eighteenth, and nineteenth centuries.

470. Most public or general library collections of deeds fall into the Sixth of the above main classes and for these no complete arrangement has been devised. Hilary Jenkinson has expounded his views of archive arrangement, in general, in his *Archive Administration*. He asserts that "the only correct basis of arrangement is exposition of the Administrative objects which the archives originally served." In the Record Office, therefore, the archives are arranged according to "the various *Courts* (the Chancery, the Exchequer, etc.) under which mediæval archives are grouped, and the *departments* (Admiralty, Home Office, and the like) which supersede or are added to these in modern times." These have often changed in name and sometimes in function, and I gather that the characteristic which forms an Administration is all those qualities which an Administration possessed when it was active; that is to say, a class name may be given to any group of documents which form, according to our author's definition, "the archives resulting from the work of an Administration which was an organic whole, complete in itself, capable of dealing independently, without any added or external authority, with every side of any business which could normally be presented to it."

471. These classes are divided into independent administrative organizations, for example, Exchequer of Receipt, with sub-divisions representing the administrative functions of these organizations; for example, issue, and, finally, sections (called here classes) representing the original or newly made series, for example, Issue Rolls.

472. For further description of this very interesting method of treating national archives, reference should be made to the book from which we have quoted, which is the fruit of scholarship and long and successful practical experience. The method, as a classification is not always easily applicable to such deeds as the average library is likely to accumulate. Much depends upon the purpose of the collection and the questions it is intended to answer. In the Public Record Office the purpose is national history in all its characteristics; but in the ordinary library the purpose is local history. In local history it would appear that the government source of the document is a quite subsidiary matter, whereas its date in relation to a certain locality is all important. If, however, in spite of the difficulties we can work out a local

classification and use the B.R.A. scheme as its sub-divisions, we may reach a standard and practical classification.

473. Meanwhile, for those who have small collections it seems to me that an acceptable and practical method is to arrange local documents in the same way as local prints; with this distinction, however, that the first interest in the document is topographical, the second interest is subjectival, the third interest is chronological, and the fourth is personal. I would, therefore, arrange local deeds first by the locality to which they belong, then by the subject with which they deal, then by the date they bear, and the final arrangement within the minute group thus reached would be alphabetical by the names of the principal persons named in the documents. The following examples will suffice to show the method proposed:

> Woking. Land Taxation, 1799. Collection of the Land Tax, 1799. $S99^1(333)^2$ "1799"[3]
> ——— ——— ——— 1800–04. Five Annual Redemption Returns, 1800–04. $S99(333)$ "1800-4."
> ——— ——— ——— 1814–25 Two Annual Land-Tax Redemption Returns. $Soo(333)$ "1914-25."

The final arrangement, by personal names, is only necessary where two deeds bear the same mark.

474 Hilary Jenkinson[4] also describes the methods of filing and storing in vogue. I quote: "Different shapes and forms of documents lends themselves to a greater or less degree to boxing and enveloping, and in some instances it may be necessary to choose between cleanliness and air, in which case air must have the first place. As a rule, however, it is possible to meet both. At the Public Record Office parchment deeds, for example, are loosely folded and slipped each into a stout, square, flapless envelope, numbered with the same number as the deed: a box, the dimensions of which in section are slightly larger than those of the envelopes, receives them in the fashion of cards in a card-index: a loose lid with a deep brim closes it. For loose small documents of irregular size, or for small rolls, larger boxes of similar construction but having the lid hinged are used. A good plan is to have the end of the box, opposite to that on which the lid is hinged, itself hinged at the bottom; the result is that when the lid is raised a few inches the hinged end falls down, and if the documents are all labelled with tagged labels facing outwards the one required can generally be extracted without taking the box off

---

[1] Local collection classification number for Woking.
[2] Dewey number for Land.
[3] Date in " " as in Brussels marks.
[4] *Manual of Archive Administration*, Ed. 2, 1937. London: Lund.

the shelf. The dimensions of the box and shelf are, of course, made inter-dependent for economy of space in storing The material of these boxes is *stout* mill-board with strong binder's cloth for all joints or as a complete covering "

475 Other methods I have seen in vogue have been the tying up of deeds dealing with a particular subject, or upon allied subjects, into bundles, literally with red tape, and the storing of the bundles in numbered boxes. Each deed in this method is found by referring from the catalogue slip to the box. The virtue of this second system is that it is better than no order all; there is little more to be said for it.

476. As for the method of the Public Record Office, that described first is clearly an elementary form of vertical filing. If for the box with its loose lid and the shelf at which it rests is substituted the drawer in the vertical file, it would seem that precisely the same result can be obtained with an economy of furniture and space. At any rate, I have experimented upon this assumption myself, and my own method, which, admittedly, has not been used on a large scale, is to place documents loosely folded in stout manilla envelopes of uniform size, and to place these envelopes in order in the vertical file. There are, of course, documents which require special care, having valuable but fragile wax seals attached to them, or coins or other impediments to mass filing. These must be treated separately according to the circumstances; probably they are best in independent boxes with the seals placed in cotton wool in little cloth bags—a method which aims at protection, and has no other charm from the point of view of the classifier.

CHAPTER XXXI

CLASSIFICATION OF LIBRARY ECONOMY

477. All general library classifications have divisions devoted to the arrangement of the material of library economy. Primarily these classifications are intended for the arrangement of books and other literary material. The librarian, however, needs to give careful consideration to the filing of his correspondence and administrative papers, and to the arrangement and indexing of his stationery and stores. Few modern librarians would be content with a haphazard mode of treating these important matters.

478. To deal with correspondence first. The prevalent method until twenty years ago was the letter-copying book. The working of this method is merely by using a copying ink for the writing of the letter and then transferring an impression from the copy to the absorbent pages of the letter book. This method does not permit of a classified arrangement, as the letters are copied into the book in the order in which they are written, irrespective of subject-matter, and they can only be found by means of full and complicated indexing. One advantage the copying book has over other methods is that manuscript alterations in the letter despatched are recorded in facsimile in it. It is difficult to see any other virtue in this obsolete method.

479. The essential principle of filing letters is that an actual copy of a letter shall be filed with correspondence which has called it forth or which arises from it. There is no better method than by making carbon copies. The filing can be done in various ways, either in binders, Stolzenberg files, or by the loose-leaf method which we describe in the chapter on the vertical file (Chapter XXVIII). Whichever method is adopted, the librarian the choice of three methods of arrangement—alphabetical order of correspondents; alphabetical order of subjects; systematic classified order.

480. Alphabetic order of correspondents is certainly the easiest system initially, but the difficulties it presents when the whole correspondence on a particular subject is needed are too great to commend it for use in any but the smallest library, and even there it would be a very indifferent method.

481. Alphabetic order of subject, on the lines of the subject headings in a dictionary catalogue, is a much more commendable method. The folders would arrange in very much this order:

Additions.
Administrative rules.
Advertisements: Library Magazine.
Aids to reading.
American Library Association.
Annotation.
Announcements.
Application forms.

and so on. Cross-references would be made by inserting guides in the file directing from synonyms and cognate subjects to the word under which the letters were filed. The method would not do away with the need for a name index as a clue to the correspondents. An examination of the index to any library economy classification will show that the weakness of this alphabetical method is that cognate subjects are separated, as is the case with alphabetical subject classification of books.

482. Systematic classification of library economy now prevails, accompanied by card indexes. Schemes have been proposed by Charles Madeley,[1] L. Stanley Jast and James D. Stewart, in addition to the expansive tables for this purpose incorporated in every general scheme from Dewey to Bliss. Of the separate schemes the most recent is *The Tabulation of Librarianship*,[2] 1947, by Stewart. It is a detailed arrangement for the literature, papers, processes, stationery and stores. The notation consists of a single letter base with decimal divisions and a useful introduction and relative index complete a useful work. An older scheme is Jast's *Classification of Library Economy and Office Papers*,[3] 1907, which in some features (as the outline on Table IV shows) the *Tabulation* resembles.

483. The librarian will consider carefully, however, whether he will introduce for his office papers another classification than that by which he classifies his books. There is a distinct advantage in a uniform system of classification throughout the library. On the other hand, such uniformity is practically impossible. As a case in point the classification of the local collection, as we have seen, cannot be done by any general scheme of classification at present in existence except by means of modifications and expansions that would produce gigantic notations.

484. The difficulty of the sections for classifying library economy in Dewey and similar schemes is that they are primarily intended for the classification of books and literary material.

---

[1] *Classification of Office Papers: with a scheme for Museums and Library Work*, L.A.R., v. 6, pp. 367–87, 1904.
[2] Grafton.   [3] Grafton, o.p.

They do not specifically provide for administrative correspondence and papers, although, of course, there are bound to be letters on such matters as ordering, checking, and collation of books. At present there is much to be said for the Stewart or Jast scheme, partly because the revisions and additions that it continually needs can be made without mauling a larger scheme.

485. I used Jast's scheme for over thirty years and found these conditions to apply; an extract from his introduction to the tables is worth repeating here, as its principles apply with some modifications to the other schemes mentioned:

"*Correspondence.*—Correspondence should be treated like other material and arranged by subject. In the case of a public library most correspondence is far more valuable under subject than if arranged alphabetically or by date. For example, a library is running a course of lectures, all its correspondence dealing with that course will go in 244, and be kept together; all its quotations (other than books) will go in 514, its accepted quotations in 5145, and, if wished, this material may be sub-divided like the main classification, and all quotations for, let us say, shelving, 514381, will then arrange together; so again quotations for second-hand books will go in 6236, and here will gradually collect a mass of valuable memoranda, which in an ordinary way would not be worth keeping, merely because it would be lost in a mass of other material. Another advantage of the subject arrangement of letters is that a great deal of ephemeral material can be automatically weeded out, or destroyed at once, as it will usually be found that either the whole of the material coming under one number is worth keeping or not worth keeping, that is, as a group. In the latter case, a manilla sheet, bearing its appropriate number, should be inserted in its proper place in the file with an instruction not to keep, as e.g.—

---

444 Staff. Examinations. Papers of Candidates.
These are not to be kept.

"A small library with comparatively little correspondence would not probably use the full scheme, but as familiarity with the scheme increases the tendency will probably be, even in this case, to divide pretty minutely, the advantages of close classification being very great. If an assistant is told off to do the classifying and filing, it will not be necessary for the librarian to mark the class number on his letters; he will probably find it easier to write the subject heading in pencil as a guide to the classifier. The classifier then adds the number in the upper left-hand corner, and the date in the right-hand corner, to show the order within the folder, thus:

---

579   6N14
Reports out.

The date number analysed is 6 (for 1906) N (for November), 14 (for 14th). The main objection to classifying correspondence is that a letter may be filed where it cannot be found when it is wanted, but this is a danger to some extent of even an alphabetical arrangement. It may be entirely obviated by having an alphabetical index of correspondents and entering the number at which each letter is filed under the name of its writer. This should be on cards or slips and will serve as an address register as well as an index to the correspondence. There is practically no more trouble in keeping this record than in indexing an ordinary letter book. It is presumed that copies of all replies are taken on loose sheets and filed with the original letters.

Jones, Edward,
Public Library,
Castleborough.

*06A*912, *My*579, —, *So*5, *O*579, —, *N*579.

Sample Entry, Index to Correspondence.

"The figures and letters in italics are in red ink and indicate year and month. The dash indicates repetition of preceding reference.

"*Receptacle Numbers.*—Some numbers are intended not to mark material but receptacles. Thus a folder marked 4243 will contain letters, memoranda, and other material to be submitted to the chairman. This material, therefore, only temporarily rests in 4243, on its way to be permanently filed in various other numbers. Similar receptacle numbers are 551–555, etc."

486. These classifications apply not only to letters and documents, but also to library supplies. Cupboards and shelves are marked with the containing numbers from the classification tables, and in or on these the various articles are stored in classified order, each package bearing the classification number. By this means the frequent difficulty in finding this or that form of supply is removed.

487. As in all forms of classified arrangement, the key to the files and store cupboards and shelves is the index. The printed

subject index attached to the scheme used is a sufficient guide to any folder or article. It is necessary, however, to support this index with a card index of names. This card index is in practice the address register. I would advocate keeping in this card index not only the name and address of each correspondent and the dates on which letters have been sent to or received from him, but also his telephone number, telegraphic address, monomark, cable code or any other particular concerning him which makes his identification and communication with him more rapid. Every letter that leaves the library should bear upon it the classi-fication number of the subject with which it deals, with a request that the person written to will refer to that number in replying. By this means the work of classification and filing can be kept up to date.

488. One of the main difficulties in dealing with correspondence is the greater or smaller importance of the letters, and the desira-bility or otherwise of preserving them. James Duff Brown held that the filing of most correspondence was a waste of time, and was caused largely by the fear of the librarian that he would lose something that might doubtfully be useful. Few will hold such a view, but there certainly are many letters which are purely formal and without interest. It is very difficult, however, to say when even the barest written acknowledgment may not assume importance. The best method of dealing with correspondence files is to file everything and to weed out at very frequent intervals; at least once a year.

APPENDIX

BIBLIOGRAPHY

CONTENTS

THE purpose of this Manual has been to give as full an account of library classification as a well-equipped librarian, who does not seek to be a specialist in the subject, may be expected to possess. The list that follows subserves that purpose. It is by no means exhaustive. The fine bibliography which is so important a part of E. C. Richardson's *Classification*, and the long lists in Cannons's exhaustive *Bibliography of Library Economy* and its supplement, *Library Literature*, are so thorough in their different fields that it is unnecessary for any other person to traverse them. The modern student finds much of his material in the current library journals, amongst them the *Communicationes* of the Fédération International de Documentation, the *Journal of Documentation* of Aslib, which has a regular round-up of library technical literature, including classification, the papers in Aslib *conference proceedings*, the regular section in *Library Science Abstracts* (Library Association) and, for many classification studies, *Abgila*, the journal of the Indian Library Association (Delhi) may be consulted. Students reading for Library Association examinations would do well to study the volumes of the *A.A.L. Guide to Professional Examinations*, edited by A. J. Walford, and anything else that Dr. Walford writes on cataloguing and classification. All I have done here is to give an entry to every book or other work that has a vital relation to the study or that I have found to be specially useful; and to express briefly their scope or any opinion I may have formed about them where this seemed worth while or necessary. The interested reader might usefully compare it with the much more selective list in H. E. Bliss's *Organization of Knowledge in Libraries* with its careful appraisals.

I. PURE CLASSIFICATION.
1. Logical Principles, Terms, etc.

Any recognized treatise on Logic may be consulted for the basic principles of formal classification and there is advantage for the beginner in the reading of an elementary book on scientific method. The simplest of such works is Huxley's *Introductory* (Macmillan), and I have found J. Arthur Thomson's *Introduction to Science* (Home University Library) very useful.

In making the following selection of logic text-books I am well aware that some are out-moded; for example, the modern logician tells us quite rightly that Jevons was an estimable writer in his day but that he has been surpassed and extended by moderns and some of his views are no longer acceptable. So far as our study is concerned there is no need to challenge the assertion, even if it were possible to do so, but I still think that Jevons gives the best simple explanation of the logical process of classifying used by the maker of book-classification schemes, untrammelled by refinements which are perhaps necessary in more modern logical study. In my view Jevons's *Principles* is what I describe it to be.

COHEN, Morris R., and NAGEL, Ernest. An Introduction to Logic and Scientific Method. 1934. Routledge.
An American text-book; ch. 10–12 deal attractively with general classification principles.

FOWLER, Thomas. Elements of Deductive Logic. 1896. Ed. 10, 1905. Oxford Univ. Press.
Ch. 8 deals with the general subject.

—— —— Elements of Inductive Logic. 1869. Ed. 6, 1904. Oxford Univ. Press.
Pp. 52–89 is one of the best writings on natural and artificial classification.

JEVONS, W. S. The Principles of Science: a treatise on logic and scientific method. 1874; several editions since. Macmillan.

Pp. 673–730 contains what is probably the most useful logical treatment of classification. The chapters on Terms, the Predicables, etc., in his *Elementary Lessons in Logic* (Macmillan) can also be commended as an introduction.

JONES, W. H. S. How we Learn: a short primer of scientific method, for boys. 64 pp. 1916. Camb. Univ. Press.

JOSEPH, H. W. B. An Introduction to Logic. Ed. 2, 1916. Oxford: Clarendon Press.

A full and good treatment, by a modern scholar, of the traditional view of logical theory in such manner as to refute Jowett's criticism "that Logic is neither a science nor an art, but a dodge." Ch. 1–7 should be read.

MILL, John Stuart. A System of Logic. 2 v. 1843, many editions since, including a 1 v. small print edition. Longmans.

Ch. 7: "Of the nature of classification and the five predicables."

READ, Carveth. Logic: deductive and inductive. 1898. Ed. 3, 1924. Simpkin.

One of the best elementary treatises, comparable with Jevons's *Elem. Lessons* but more modern and rather more difficult.

STEBBING, L. S. A Modern Introduction to Logic. Ed. 2, 19.

Steers between the traditional and modern teachings; by a most accomplished writer. May well follow and supplement the older books.

II. CLASSIFICATIONS OF THE SCIENCES.

1. General.

BLISS, Henry Evelyn. The Organization of Knowledge and the System of the Sciences. 1929. New York: H. W. Wilson Co.

A detailed and scholarly study of the methods used by intellectual workers in the various fields for the analysis and synthesis of knowledge in all forms. Its ultimate aim is to deduce the most practical, permanent, and valid arrangement, in order that it may become the basis of a bibliographical system. See his *Org. of Knowledge in Libraries* and his *Bibliographic Classification* which are its outcome.

COMTE, Auguste. The Positive Philosophy. Trans. by Harriet Martineau. 1853.

Ch. 1 of vol. 1 gives what is useful in our study. Comte is challenged by Spencer, who in turn is countered by Karl Pearson, and Bliss finishes the progression. A fair account of Comte's classification is to be found in J. S. Mill's *Auguste Comte and Positivism*, ed. 4, 1891; and extracts from Martineau's translation and brief accounts of many philosophical systems are to be found in the capital selection of extracts which forms Benjamin Rand's compilation, *Modern Classical Philosophers*, 1908 (Constable).

FLINT, Robert. Philosophy as a Scientia Scientiarum, and a History of Classifications of the Sciences. 1904. Edinburgh, Blackwood.

An excellent critical and descriptive view of knowledge systems. It covers in a brief way a similar field to the two earlier authorities—William Whewell's *History of Inductive Sciences*, ed. 3, 1857, London, and C. W. Shield's *Philosophia Ultima, or, Science of the Sciences*, ed. 3, 1888, New York.

MALISOFF, William Marias. Meet the Sciences. 1932. N.Y.: Williams & Wilkins.

A sound survey of the sciences, which the author assembles in the order—abstract, natural and human. It is condensed and severe but not beyond the lay reader.

PEARSON, Karl. Grammar of Science. 1892. A good reprint in Dent's "Everyman" series.
A classic.

SPENCER, Herbert. The Classification of the Sciences. In v. 2 of his *Essays*. 1897. Williams & Norgate.

2. Linnæan Classification.

FOWLER, Thomas. Elements of Inductive Logic. pp. 50–87.
A useful bibliography of Linnæus will be found in B. D. Jackson's *Linnæus: the Story of his Life adapted from the Swedish of T. M. Fries*, pp. 387–407. London: Witherby, 1923.

3. Biology.

The simplest reference under this heading would be: "Consult any systematic text-book." The following are samples in Biology and its two great divisions, Botany and Zoology, and are not necessarily the only or even the best text-books in these subjects.

GEDDES, Patrick, and THOMSON, J. Arthur. Biology. 1925. Home Univ. Library. Thornton Butterworth.
Deals at considerable length with the classification of books on Biology, with illuminating remarks on the shortcomings of accepted library schemes and suggestions.

REES, Abraham. Cyclopædia. 1819. Article on "Classification," v. VIII. Longman. *o.p.*

4. Botany.

BALFOUR, J. H. Manual of Botany: the structure, physiology and classification of plants. Illus. 1875. Later editions. Edinburgh: Black.
Pp. 405–23, deal with nomenclature and the systems from Linnæus to Hooker, and are followed by very full details of the classes.

BENTHAM, George, and HOOKER, *Sir* J. D. Handbook of the British Flora: a description of the flowering plants and ferns indigenous to, or naturalised in, the British Isles. Ed. 7, 1937. London: Reeve.
Classification or systematic botany, pp. xl–xlii. Bentham and Hooker's divisions are followed by Dewey in the arrangement of 583–589.

RENDLE, A. B. The Classification of Flowering Plants. 2 v. v. 1, ed. 6, 1930; v. 2, 1925. Cambridge Univ. Press.

SACHS, J. VON. History of Botany, 1530–1860. 1906. Oxford Univ. Press.
This is continued to 1900 by J. Reynolds Green's *History of Botany*. 1909. Oxford University Press.

See also an article by Monica Cant, "Some Notes on Botanical Classification," in *The Library Assistant*, v. XIX, pp. 52–57.

5. Zoology.

ARISTOTLE. De Partibus Animalium. Trans. by William Ogle. 1911. Clarendon Press.

Book I. on the method of science, classification, etc.

NICHOLSON, H. A. Synopsis of the Classification of the Animal Kingdom. 1882. Blackwood. *o.p.*

CLAUS, C. Elementary Text-Book of Zoology. Trans. by Adam Sedgwick. v. I, 1892. Sonnenschein.

Chapter IV a useful history of classifications.

IMMS, A. D. A General Text-Book of Entomology: the anatomy, development and classification of insects. Ed. 3, 1934. Methuen.

Pp. 199, *et seq.*

6. Crystallography.

JEVONS, W. S. The Principles of Science (see above).

Pp. 359–363 deal with classification in crystallography—a very perfect form of natural classification.

III. LIBRARY CLASSIFICATION.

1. Bibliography.

BLISS, Henry Evelyn. The Organization of Knowledge in Libraries. Ed. 2. 1939. N.Y.: H. W. Wilson Company.

Bibliographical notes (11 pp.) are devoted to a few specially relevant books and articles, and they form a discriminating account of the best that has been written on our subject, given with candour, tempered with appreciation and charity.

BURTON, Margaret, and VOSBURGH, Marion E. A Bibliography of Librarianship: classified and annotated guide to the Library Literature of the World (excluding Slavonic and Oriental Languages). 1934. Library Association.

Pp. 79–96 deal with cataloguing and classification.

CANNONS, H. G. T. Bibliography of Library Economy: a classified index to the professional periodical literature in the English language relating to library economy, printing, methods of publishing, copyright, bibliography, etc. 1876–1920. 1927. Chicago: A.L.A.

This monumental volume is supplemented by the serial Library Literature. A volume covering 1921–32 appeared in 1934 (A.L.A.); this was succeeded by a volume for 1933–35 (H. W. Wilson Co.), 1936, and thereafter yearly volumes appeared for 1936, 1937 (Wilson). All these supplementary volumes include books as well as articles and are in dictionary form. Good summaries are a feature of the later volumes.

LIBRARY ASSOCIATION. The Year's Work in Librarianship, 1928–50. L.A.

A bibliographical summary of librarianship, bibliography and archives which includes in most volumes a critique of classification. Will appear hereafter in five-yearly volumes, the first to cover 1951–5.

—— Library Science Abstracts. 1950. Quarterly.

PETZHOLDT, Julius. Bibliotheca Bibliographica. 1866. Leipzig.
Outlines of principal schemes, 1347–1862.

RICHARDSON, E. C. Classification, Theoretical and Practical: together
with an appendix containing an essay towards a bibliographical
history of the systems of classification. 1901. Ed. 3, 1930. N.Y.:
Wilson Co.

NOTE.—Current lists appear regularly in *The Library Journal* and
synopses and in some cases articles appear in *The Wilson Bulletin* (both
N.Y.). An annual of wide range, which was available until 1939, is
the work known as "Vorstius," or the *Internationale Bibliographie der
Buch und Bibliothekswesens mit besonderer Berücksichtigung de Bibliographie*,
1926—, a classified list of general library economy edited by J. Vorstius
and E. Steinborn.

2. General Monographs.

BLISS, Henry Evelyn. The Organization of Knowledge in Libraries
and the Subject Approach to Books. 1933. Ed. 2, revised, 1939.
N.Y.: Wilson Co.

BROADFIELD, A. The Philosophy of Classification. 1946. Grafton.
A critical review of principles, mainly destructive but suggestive. Advanced.

BROWN, J. D. Library Classification and Cataloguing. Illus. 1912.
Grafton. *o.p.*

This was a re-writing of his *Manual of Library Classification*, 1898, the first English
monograph on the subject. The cataloguing part of it, under revision that
made a new and larger book, is embodied now in H. A. Sharp's important
Cataloguing (Grafton).

HULME, E. Wyndham. Principles of Book Classification. *L.A. Record*,
v. 13–14, 1911–12. Reprinted as a pamphlet in the A.A.L. series.

An unfinished series of articles which are a scholarly venture in theory, based
on the assumption that classification of books and knowledge are entirely distinct in purposes and should be so in method. A valuable lead up to the more
complete and satisfactory theories of to-day.

KELLEY, Grace Osgood. The Classification of Books: an enquiry into
its usefulness to the reader. 1937. N.Y.: Wilson Co.

Well worth study. As a result of general and special experience, Dr Kelley
concludes that classification does not reveal all the material on subjects and,
indeed, may even obscure the main work on a subject. See also her admirable
chapter in *The Acquisition and Cataloguing of Books*, edited by W. M. Randall,
1940, Univ. of Chicago Press, pp. 163–86, in which she reviews her classification
experience and relates it to library effort generally. The quotation at the back
of our title page comes from this.

MANN, Margaret. Introduction to Cataloging and the Classification
of Books. 1930. Ed. 2, revised, 1944. Library Curriculum
Studies. A.L.A.

The American official students' text-book; lucid and very practical, as is all
this fine teacher's work.

PALMER, Bernard Ira, and WELLS, Arthur James. Fundamentals of
Library Classification. 1951. Allen & Unwin.

An English restatement influenced by the C.C. principles and focusing them
effectively on Dewey classing.

PHILLIPS, W. Howard. A Primer of Library Classification. 1937. Rev. ed., 1951.

A neat, compact, brief text-book which every student should possess. It is modelled on the earlier editions of our own *Introduction* from which it differs in some particulars.

RANGANATHAN, S. R. Prolegomena to Library Classification. 1937. Madras Library Association; London: Edward Goldston.

Dealt with in chapter XIX. and elsewhere. A restatement of the rules on "canons", done with ingenuity, scholarship and some novelty. Inspired to some extent by Bliss, but mainly directed to the exposition of the interesting "Colon" scheme. See also works listed under Colon C. (below).

RICHARDSON, Ernest Cushing. Classification, Theoretical and Practical (see above).

An outstanding book on general principles which has had great influence. Admirable bibliography.

SAVAGE, E. A. Manual of Book Classification and display for public libraries. 1946. Allen & Unwin.

The brief study of classification is individual and is built upon the principles of E. W. Hulme (above) and on the L.C. Classification to some extent. Readable, vigorous and challenging even to extravagance.

SAYERS, W. C. Berwick. Canons of Classification. 1915. Grafton. *o.p.*

The author's earliest tentative views on the subject. Better written than his later books but, in many of its ideas, superseded.

SAYERS, W. C. Berwick. The Grammar of Classification. Ed. 4, 1935. Assoc. of Assistant Librarians.

—— —— —— An Introduction to Library Classification, Theoretical Historical and Practical: and a Short Course in Practical Classification: with readings, questions and examination papers. Ed. 9, 1954. Grafton.

A student's text-book which supplies not only the teaching but also the "drill" in classing which is a necessary part of the study. Contains every type of question that has been set in examinations for thirty years.

3. Accounts or Descriptions of Classification, contained in General Works on Library Economy, etc.

BOSTWICK, Arthur E. The American Public Library. Illus. 1910. Ed. 3, revised, 1923. Appleton.
Pp. 162–176.

BROWN, J. D. Manual of Library Economy. Illus. 1903. Ed. 6, revised by Berwick Sayers, 1950. Grafton.

An account appears in each edition.

BURGESS, L. A. Canons of Classification: a revaluation. In *The Library World,* v. 34, pp. 3–6, 1931.

"Courteously but rather trenchantly disparages the theoretical value of the principles and canons of both Dr. Richardson's volume and Mr. Berwick Sayers's *Canons* and *Manual*."—*H. E. Bliss*. Mr. Burgess is a sound student of our subject and has been helpful to the present writer.

CIM, Albert. Le Livre: historique, fabrication, achat, classement, usage et entretien. 5 v. 1905. Paris: Flammarion.

V. 4 deals with classification very fully with outlines of many schemes as far as Brunet as his followers.

CONSTANTIN, L.-A. Bibliothéconomie: ou, nouveau manuel complet pour l'arrangement, la conservation et l'administration des bibliothèques. Manuels-Roret. 1839. Ed. 2, 1840. Paris.
Chapter XXVIII (pp. 95–165) deals interestingly with classification as applied to catalogues.

DANA, J. C. A Library Primer. 1899. Ed. 3, 1920. Illus. Boston: Library Bureau.
Ch. XVI (pp. 97–131) deal with classifying and cataloguing, author-numbers, and the shelf-list.

EDWARDS, Edward. Memoirs of Libraries: including a handbook of library economy. 2 v. Illus. 1859. Treubner. *o.p.*
V. II, book III, contains a most valuable history of book classificatory systems to about 1850. The work on which all subsequent histories in English appear to have been based.

FERGUSON, John. Some Aspects of Bibliography. 1900. Edinburgh: George P. Johnston. *o.p.*
Pp. 12–22, but the whole of the meagre 102 pages is valuable.

GRAESEL, Arnim. Handbuch de Bibliotekslehre. 1890. Ed. –, 1902. Leipzig.

—— Manuel de Bibliothéconomie. . . . Traduction de Jules Laude. 72 figs. et 13 tableaux. 1897. Paris. H. Welter.
Edition francaise revue par l'auteur et considerablement augmentee. Pp. 480–500, "Systèmes bibliographiques anciens et modernes," contain brief accounts of the German schemes of Hartwig, etc.

GREVE, Dr. H. E. Openbare Leesmusea en Volksbibliotheken. 1906. Amsterdam: Mass & van Suchtelen.
Standard Dutch manual of library economy. Sections 214–40 deal with cataloguing and classification.

HUTCHINS, Margaret, JOHNSON, A. S., and WILLIAMS, M. S. Guide to the Use of Libraries: a manual for college and university students. 1922. New York: Wilson Co.
Pp. 9–76 are a good example of the way to explain classification systems and their application to shelves and catalogues for lay readers.

KEPHART, H. Reference List on Classification *In the* United States Commission of Education. Annual Report, 1892–3, v. 6, p. 861.
A bibliography.

MAIRE, Albert. Manuel Pratique du Bibliothécaire. 1896. Paris.

MEEL, J. VAN. Bibliothèques Publiques: traité théorique et pratique. Illus. 1924. Antwerp: Veritas.
Pp. 138–49. Simple, useful general account of the why and how of classification.

MOURAVIT, Gustave. Le Livre et la Petite Bibliothèque d'Amateur: essai de critique, d'histoire et de philosophie morale sur l'amour des livres. N.D. Paris: Aubry.
An excellent enthusiastic work on the book arts with good descriptions of the French schemes of classification. Quoted in Section 147 of this book.

OTLET, Paul, and WOUTERS, L. Manuel de la Bibliothèque Publique. Illus. Ed. 2, 1923. *Publication no. 133 de la collection de l'Institut International de Bibliographie.*
Section 25, pp. 69–123. Elementary and admirable.

RANDALL, William M. *Ed.* The Acquisition and Cataloguing of Books. 1940. Chicago, University Press.

Pp. 163–86, Classification of books in retrospect, by Grace O. Kelley; pp. 187–219, Reclassification and Recataloguing, by Maurice F. Taube.

RANDALL, William M., and GOODRICH, Francis L. D. Principles of College Library Administration. 1936. Chicago: A.L.A.

Brief, interesting suggestions appear in the half-dozen pages dealing with our subject; i.e., the need for adaptation of schemes to local service, because while "the librarian will always take special care to secure consistency in practice," (p. 123), "consistency at the expense of usefulness is vicious" (p. 96); accepts the principle that, in spite of theoretical considerations, books used together may rightly be placed together (pp. 156–7); it also deprecates the use of untrained workers for the processes of cataloguing and classification. See also Woledge and Page, below.

ROEBUCK, G. E., and THORNE, W. B. A Primer of Library Practice. 1904. Ed. 2, 1914. Grafton.

Pp. 106–122. Elementary.

ROUVEYRE, Édouard. Connaissances Nécessaires à un Bibliophile: accompagnées de notes critiques de documents bibliographiques. 10 v. Illus. 1877. Ed. 5, 1899. Paris: Rouveyre.

V. ix deals with classification on much the same lines as Cim (above)—mainly with French schemes, of which it gives good outlines. Adverse to the Dewey classification.

SAWYER, Harret Price (*Ed.*). The Library and Its Contents: reprints of papers and addresses. *Classics of American Librarianship: edited by Arthur E. Bostwick.* 1925. New York: H. W. Wilson Co.

Pp. 201–295 form a section on classification consisting of reprinted articles from American library and literary journals; by Cutter, Cole, Fletcher, Foster, Langton, Gifford, Martel, Collar, Rathbone, Hunt, and Bay; and ranging in date from 1886 to 1917.

WOLEDGE, G., and PAGE, B. S. A Manual of University and College Library Practice. 1940. L.A.

Pp. 63–66 are merely a brief series of interesting indications, by Dr. R. Offor that the scheme used should accord with the order in which the faculties use books; that the D.C. is defective, the L.C. is better, and Bliss is better still. There should, he thinks, be no hesitation in altering ("amending" is the word used) any scheme freely, so long as index references are kept. The author seems to prefer the attractive experiment of home-made schemes, a method which in these days is surely most uneconomical and undesirable.

4. Particular Schemes.

Bacon.

BACON, Francis, *Viscount St. Albans.* The Advancement of Learning.

There are various editions. That by Spedding in his complete edition (Works of Bacon), v. 4, 1858–61, *o.p.* is the one I prefer from the literary standpoint. A student's edition is that by W. Aldis Wright (Clarendon Press, 4s., several reprints), which contains a folding chart of the Baconian classification.

Bliss's Bibliographic Classification.

BLISS, Henry Evelyn. A Bibliographic Classification: extended by systematic auxiliary schedules for composite specification and notation, 4 v. (in 3 v.). New York, 1953. W. H. Wilson Company.

The fully expanded work which is dealt with in our text.

—— A System of Bibliographic Classification. 1935. Ed. 2, revised, 1936.

This work (343 pp.) is an extended outline of the scheme, with auxiliary tables and indexes. The introduction is noteworthy.

Incorporated Association of Assistant Masters in Secondary Schools. Guide for School Librarians. 1937. Oxford Univ. Press.

Ch. 4, Classification and Cataloguing, by C. A. Stott, is a useful descriptive study of Dewey and Bliss in relation to their possible use in school libraries.

Introductory studies and reviews of the B.C. from the pen of L. A. Burgess appear in Phillips's *Primer* (above) and the present writer deals with it in his *Introduction* (above). See also references in the text.

Brown's Subject Classification.

BROWN, J. D. Subject Classification: with Tables, Indexes, etc., for the Sub-division of Subjects. 1906. Ed. 3, revised and enlarged by James Douglas Stewart, 1939. Grafton.

The complete work, with descriptive introduction which is a valuable contribution to the methodology of classification. The third ed. has been handled by its Editor with a wise conservatism, although there has been considerable extension through insertion of new subjects, his effort being to continue the use undisturbed of numbers for existing subjects. The index has been expanded. The printing of the schedules is now in the orthodox one-column-to-page form which is a distinct improvement.

BISHOP, W. W. [Review] in *The Library Journal*, v. XXXI, pp. 836–38, 1906.

BLISS, H. E. Organization of Knowledge in Libraries, ch. XIII.

ISLINGTON PUBLIC LIBRARIES. Select Catalogue and Guide: a classified list of the best books on all subjects in the Central, North and West Libraries. 827 pp. 1910.

A class catalogue on the scheme edited by J. D. Brown.

SAVAGE, E. A. The Subject Classification. In *The Library World*, v. IX, pp. 48–53.

NOTE.—Useful descriptive accounts appear also in Phillips's *Primer* and Berwick Sayers's *Introduction* (above).

Brunet.

BRUNET, J. C. Manuel du Libraire et de l'Amateur de Livres, 9 v. in 8. Ed. 1860–80.

V. 5 contains the classification.

BLISS, Henry Evelyn. Organization of Knowledge in Libraries (see above).

CIM, Albert. Le Livre (see above).

FLINT, Robert. History of the Classification of the Sciences (see above).

MOURAVIT, Gustave. Le Livre et la Petite Bibliothéque (see above).

ROUVEYRE, Édouard. Connaissances Nécessaires (see above).

Cutter's Expansive Classification.

CUTTER, C. A. Expansive Classification. Pt. I. The First Six Classifications. 160 pp.. 1891–93. Boston. C. A. Cutter.

See the seventh expansion below. The first six, here catalogued, are preceded by various introductions on the principles and practice of the scheme.

—— Expansive Classification: Seventh Scheme. Ed. W. P. Cutter. Boston.

This, the final expansion left unfinished at Cutter's death, was carried on by his nephew, but has now been abandoned. The various divisions have undergone complete revision at the hands of specialists.

—— Expansive Classification. In *Transactions and Proceedings of the Second International Library Conference, London,* 1897. pp. 84–88. 1898.

An exposition of the system written by its author at a time when it was practically unknown in England. It has the synopsis of a special scheme arranged for a Shakespeare Collection. Perhaps the best introduction to the system.

—— Suitability of the Expansive Classification to College and Reference Libraries. In *The Library Journal,* v. xxiv, c. pp. 41–49; Discussion, c. pp. 154–56. 1899.

(1) A series of eulogies of the system; (2) an exposition of its application to libraries generally, which is really an argument in favour of its notation; and (3) its application, with examples, to college collections. Makes comparisons with the Decimal Classification.

AMERICAN LIBRARY ASSOCIATION. Catalogue of the A.L.A. Library: Five Thousand Volumes for a Popular Library. 1893. Washington: Government Printing Office.

The entries on pp. 145–256 are arranged according to the Expansive system, and are followed by sample pages of author and subject indexes respectively.

BLISS, H. E. Organization of Knowledge in Libraries.

Ch. XI is a searching criticism.

BROWN, J. D. Library Classification and Cataloguing. Pp. 63–68. 1912. Grafton.

A brief introduction and outline.

—— Manual of Library Economy.

A useful practical introduction and an outline is given in every edition.

RICHARDSON, E. C. Classification. Pp. 201–7.

A brief bibliography of the scheme, an outline, and a history, with random examples illustrating the notation; eulogistic.

Decimal Classification.

SHURTLEFF, Nathaniel B. A Decimal System for the Arrangement and Administration of Libraries. 1856. Boston.

A rare work; the only original copy to which I have had access is in the Wigan Public Library, but typed copies are in the Library Association and the Croydon Public Libraries. See section 168.

Dewey's Decimal Classification.

DEWEY, Melvil. Decimal Classification and Relative Index for Libraries, Clippings, Notes, etc. Ed. 14, revised and enlarged, 1942; Ed. 15, The Standard Edition, 1951. Forest Press, Lake Placid Club, Essex Cty., N.Y.

Edition 14 contains an elaborate introduction, in phonetic English, detailing the history and application of the scheme, three summary tables, the main tables, the relative index and an index supplement, and index tables for geographical, form, language and philological divisions; edition 15 is a most drastic reduction to "essentials". See account in text.

—— A Classification and Subject Index for Cataloguing and Arranging the Books and Pamphlets of a Library. 1941. N.Y.: Brick Row Book Shop.

A limited edition in exact photographic facsimile of the pamphlet in which Dewey, who had used it for three years, put out the first version of his scheme for the criticisms of his librarian friends. The copy was preserved by E. C. Richardson. The plan in its essentials is seen to have sprung full-grown, with its classes, divisions and sections, the normal meaning of zero and the use of form numbers.—*C. E. Peters.* Not in phonetic English. Reviewed in *Library Journal*, v. 66, p. 636, 1941.

—— Abridged Decimal Classification and Relative Index for Libraries, Clippings, Notes, etc. 1894. Ed. 3, 1921. New York: Forest Press, Lake Placid.

The tables are divided generally into three-figure places, with occasionally a fourth and fifth figure. The use of this without reference to the full edition is difficult and rarely satisfactory.

AMERICAN LIBRARY ASSOCIATION. DEWEY, MELVIL. *(Ed.)* A.L.A. Catalogue: 8000 v. for a Popular Library, with Notes, 1904–11.

Pt. 1, Classified; pt. 2, Dictionary. Pt. 1 is in strict classified order, with annotations. The prefatory matter includes a brief explanation of the system, and three summaries, i.e., of the 10 main classes, the first 100 divisions, and the first 1000 divisions.

BLISS, H. E. Organization of Knowledge in Libraries.

Ch. X. is a searching example of the adverse criticism which its author has valiantly delivered against the most popular of schemes.

BROWN, J. D. Library Classification and Cataloguing. pp. 54–61. 1898. Grafton.

Outline and an elementary explanation.

—— Manual of Library Economy. London: Grafton.

Outline in each edition.

HOYLE, W. E., and NORDLINGER, Clara. The Concilium Bibliographicum at Zurich and its Work. In *The Library Association Record*, v. i, pp. 709–18. 1899.

Describes the card catalogue of zoology issued according to a greatly extended Dewey scheme.

JAST, L. Stanley. Classification in Public Libraries with Special Reference to the Dewey Decimal System. In *The Library*, v. vii, pp. 169–78, 1895.

—— The Dewey Classification in the Reference Library, and in an Open Lending Library. In *The Library*, v. viii, pp. 335–50, 1896.

—— The Dewey Classification, and Some Recent Criticism. In *The Library*, v. ix, pp. 340–45, 1897.

—— Classification in British Public Libraries. In *The Library Association Record*, v. v, 1903.

Jast was one of the pioneers of the decimal system in this country. Although his papers are comprehensive, he deals largely with notation in the first paper, but in the later ones he meets the critic on the grounds of theory. The third paper replies to criticisms in Lyster's *Some Observations*. The last sums up the advance of a decade. This and Lyster's article are well worth reading as early accounts of the effects the D.C. produced in England.

LYSTER, T. W. Notes on Shelf-Classification by the Dewey System. In *The Library*, v. ix, pp. 329–39, 1897.

The results of the writer's experiences of the working of the system in a large library, with many ingenious suggestions on the problems of classification. See also his "Observations on the Dewey Notation and Classification," in *The Library*, v. viii, pp. 482–90, 1896.

NEWCASTLE-UPON-TYNE CENTRAL PUBLIC LIBRARY. Catalogue of Books on the Fine Arts, 1900.

May be regarded as typical of a series of unannotated class lists issued by the Newcastle Libraries, in which a strictly classified section is preceded by an author list and summary of the class, and is completed by a subject index. In the later class lists, which are upon Mathematics, Useful Arts, Education, etc., the Brussels geographical bracket is utilized.

PITTSBURG, U.S. CARNEGIE LIBRARY. Classified Catalogue.

Perhaps the most elaborately annotated complete catalogue in existence. Combine Dewey numbers and Cutter author-marks in the notation.

RICHARDSON, E. C. Classification, pp. 193–200.

A brief bibliography, an outline, and a brief good commentary on the system, and a few random examples of the notation.

Universal Decimal Classification

of the Institut International de Bibliographie—later, I. de Documentation, and now Fédération International de Documentation.

MANUEL DU RÉPERTOIRE BIBLIOGRAPHIQUE UNIVERSEL. 1896. Brussels.

—— Ed. 2, 4 vols. in 2 vols., Brussels, 1927–33, with title: Classification Décimale Universelle.

—— Ed. 4, *in Progress*, in English, with title: Universal Decimal Classification, v. 1, General Introduction, 1936; v. 2, facsimile 2 54, Chemistry, 1939; v. 2, part 3—55, 56, 57, 58, 59, Geology–Zoology; 1943. British Standards Institution.

The first fascicule, now translated as the General Introduction, is the best account of the methods and purpose of the scheme. An abridged ed., *Manuel Abrègè du Rèpèrtoire Bibliographique Universel: organization, travaux, mèthodes, tables abrègèes de classification*, was published in Brussels in 1905.

The earlier and extensive account of the I.I.B. and the scheme are to be found in the *Bulletin* of the Institut, 1896.

—— BRADFORD, S. C., Editor. Universal Decimal Classification: abridged English Edition. 1948. British Standard Institution.

All text-books, Sayers's *Intro.*, Phillips's *Primer*, Bliss's *Org. of K. in Lib.*, etc., describe it. The following is a very selective list of available literature.

BRADFORD, S. C. Documentation, 1948. Ed. 2, with introductory by J. H. Shera, 1953. Crosby, Lockwood & Son.

Has an excellent study of the U.D.C. as its basis.

FEDERATION I. DE D. Communicationes, 1934 and Quarterly.

The F.I.D. serial of transactions and papers, which give correct revisions and other work on the scheme.

POLLARD, A. F. C. 025.4 : 535. The Decimal Bibliographical Classification of the Institut International de Bibliographie. 1926. Cambridge University Press.

025.4 : 535. The Decimal Bibliographical Classification of the Institut International de Bibliographie. 1926. Cambridge University Press.

"Partly translated for the formation and use of a Universal Bibliographical Repertory concerning Optics, Light, and Cognate Subjects."—*Sub-title.* An introduction explains the whole system. The tables of the general classification are given in outline with those parts expanded which deal with optics, etc. The common sub-divisions and signs of combination form the third section, and the whole has an excellent index. A most valuable and much needed introduction to the system as a whole.

SCIENCE MUSEUM, SOUTH KENSINGTON. Classification for Works on Pure and Applied Science in the Science Library, 1908. Ed. 3, 1936. London: Stationery Office.

The schemes selected, with full expressions of classes 5–6, and somewhat more briefly 7; but giving an outline of all classes and brief descriptions of the form divisions and signs of combination.

The Journal of Documentation (Aslib) and the Conference Proceedings of Aslib devote considerable space to the U.D.C.

Library of Congress Classification.

LIBRARY OF CONGRESS CLASSIFICATION. 4to, 1901. (In progress.) Washington: Government Printing Office.

The schedules of each class are issued separately; in a few cases sectional parts of a class form an independent publication. Nearly all the classes have now been published. They vary in length and price; under a regulation adopted in 1942 presentation copies are no longer available. The following is a list of the current editions at November 1950:

Outline of the Library of Congress Classification. 1942. (Reprinted 1948.)
Library of Congress Classification Schedules:
A. General works: Polygraphy. 3rd ed., 1947.
B. Philosophy and Religion.
   Part I, B–BJ: Philosophy. 2nd ed.
   Part II, BL–BX: Religion. 1927. Out of print.
C. History: Auxiliary Sciences. 2nd ed., 1948.
D. History: General and Old World. 1916. (Reprinted 1946.)
   D501–725. European War. 2nd ed., 1933.
   D731–829. World War, 1939–45. 1947.
E–F. History: America. 2nd ed., 1913. (Reprinted 1946.)
G. Geography, Anthropology, Folklore, etc. 3rd ed. In preparation.
H. Social Sciences. 3rd ed.
J. Political Science. 2nd ed., 1924 (Reprinted 1944.) Out of print.
L. Education. 3rd ed. In press.
M. Music. 2nd ed., 1917. (Reprinted 1942.) Out of print.
N. Fine Arts. 3rd ed., 1922. (Reprinted 1942.) Out of print.
P. Philology and Literature.
   P–PA: Philology. Classical Philology and Literature. 1928.
   PA.   Supplement: Byzantine and Modern Greek Literature. Medieval and Modern Latin Literature. 1942.

PB–PH: Modern European Languages. 1933.
PG: Russian Literature. 1948.
PJ–PM: Languages and Literature of Asia, Africa, Oceania, America;
       Mixed Languages, Artificial Languages. 1935.
PJ–PM: Supplement: Additions and Changes to January 1, 1936.
P–PM: Index to Languages and Dialects in the Volumes P–PA,
       PB–PH, PJ–PM. 1936.
PN, PR, PS, PZ: Literature—General, English, American, etc., 1915.
       (Reprinted 1946.) Out of print.
PQ.   Part 1: French Literature. 1936.
PQ.   Part 2: Italian, Spanish and Portuguese Literatures. 1937.
PT.   Part 1: German Literature. 1938.
PT.   Part 2: Dutch and Scandinavian Literatures. 1942.
Q.   Science. 5th ed., 1950.
R.   Medicine. 3rd ed. In press.
S.   Agriculture, etc. 3rd ed., 1948.
T.   Technology. 4th ed., 1948.
U.   Military Science. 2nd ed., 1928. Out of print.
V.   Naval Science. 1910. (Reprinted 1946.)
Z.   Bibliography and Library Science. 3rd ed., 1927. (Reprinted 1946.)
     Out of print.
L.C. Classification—Additions and Changes. Quarterly. List 1 (March 1928).
     Subscription $1.50 a year; foreign subscription, $2.00 a year; single copy
     40 cents. (Lists 1–72 [1928 through December 1948] may be purchased
     from the Card Division of the Library of Congress at $14.55 for the
     set. List No. 70 [April–June 1948] is out of print.)
Subject Headings Used in the Dictionary Catalogs of the Library of Congress. 5th
     ed., 1948. $6.50.
Supplements: July 1947–December 1949. 1950. 45 cents.
                January—(Issued monthly. To be used with the 5th edition
                and the Cumulated Supplements.) Subscription $2.00 a year.
Subject Sub-divisions. 6th ed., 1924. (Reprinted 1936.) Out of print.
Subject Headings with Local Sub-divisions. 5th ed., 1935. Out of print.
Literature Subject Headings and Language Subject Headings. 5th ed., 1926. Out
     of print.
Notes and Decisions on the Application of the Decimal Classification. Quarterly.
     First series, No. 1–15—February 1934–April 1942. Published irregularly.
     Second series, No. 1—July 1942- Quarterly. Subscription 30 cents a
     year; foreign subscription 40 cents a year; singly copy 10 cents. To be
     purchased from Card Division of the Library of Congress.
LACY, DAN L. C. : a Sesquicentenary Review 2 v., 1950; v.2, Organization
     of the Collections, has a useful history of cataloguing and classification at
     L.C., pp. 235–58.
All L.C. publications, except as noted, are distributed by the Superintendent
     of Documents, Government Printing Office, Washington 25, D.C.

LIBRARY OF CONGRESS. Reports of the Librarian of Congress for the
Fiscal Year ending 30 June, 1901, and annually since.

Each issue contains a brief report from the Chief Classifier on the progress of
the system, with notes on its methods, problems and practical working.

—— Account of the Catalogues, Classification and Distribution Work.
In *The Library of Congress Bulletin,* vii, 28 pp. 1904.

—— Manual: Constitution, Organization Methods, etc. In *The
Report of the Librarian of Congress,* 1901. Illus. 1901.

An admirable account of all the activities of the Library, including an historical
sketch, with excellent illustrations.

GROUT, C. W. Explanation of the Tables used in the Schedules of the
Library of Congress Classification: accompanied by an historical

and explanatory introduction. 1940. 4to. 108 pp. Columbia School of Library Service.
A mimeographed thesis.

HICKS, F. C. Library of Congress Classification and its Printed Catalogue Cards. In *The Library Journal*, v. xxxi, pp. 255–56. 1906.

RICHARDSON, E. C. Classification: Theoretical and Practical, pp. 136–40.
Outline of main classes and divisions with brief description.

The chapters by Mortimer Taube in Randall's Acquisition and Cataloguing of Books (see page 325, *ante*) on "Reclassification and Recataloguing" deals with the turning over of a library from Dewey to the L.C. scheme. The books by Bliss, Phillips and Sayers all deal with the system. The L.C. promises at some propitious date to produce a manual "for the use of our subject headings and our system of classification."—*Report of L. of C.*, 1942.

Lund and Taube.

LUND, John, and TAUBE, Mortimer. A Non-Expansive Classification System: an introduction to Period Classification. In *The Library Quarterly*, v. VII, pp. 373–94, Chicago, 1937.
This article is of unusual interest. Academic users of libraries have always criticized subject arrangements of books, mainly because the details of knowledge change and what are main subjects to-day become sections to-morrow, or the converse. Its argument is dealt with in our text.

Ranganathan's Colon Classification[1]

RANGANATHAN, S. R. Colon Classification. 1933. Ed. 5, v. l, 1957. Madras Library Association, Triplicane, Madras.
—— Classification and Communication. 1951. Delhi Univ.
—— Classification and International Documentation. 1948. Int. Fed. for Documentation.
—— Classification, Coding and Machinery for Search. 1950. Unesco/NS/SL/3.
—— Elements of Classification. 1945. Poona, N.K. Publishing House.
The beginner's book.
—— Library Classification: Fundamentals and Procedure: with 1,008 Graded Exercises and Rules. 1944. Madras L.A.
—— Philosophy of Classification. 1951. Copenhagen, Ejnar Munksgaard.
—— Prolegomena to Library Classification. 1937. Madras L.A.
—— (Editor). Depth Classification and Reference Service and Reference Material. 1953. Delhi, Indian Library Association.
All R.'s works from his *Five Laws of Library Science*, in which it is briefly foreshadowed, lean upon the C.C. and here are given only those directly upon classification. The order in which they may be read I have ventured to indicate in par. 306.1 where also are indicated some of his main students in this country:

[1] The English agents for the works published in India are Messrs. G. Blunt & Sons, Ltd., Great Russell Street, London.

see Index below under Freeman, Foskett, Mills, Palmer, Vickery and Wells. As is inevitable in a continued advocacy, there is much repetition in the successive volumes, but the methods involved also progress continuously and reference to *Abgila*, the journal of the Indian Library Association, is an essential part of the study of those who would keep in currency with them.

Other Schemes.

BURGESS, L. A. The "Form Table." Scheme of Book Classification: a new proposal. In *The Library World*, v. 28, pp. 180–182, 197–201, 214–215, Feb.–April, 1925.

FARRADANE, J. E. L. A Scientific Theory of Classification and Indexing and its Practical Applications. In *The Journal of Documentation*, June 1950. VI 2, pp. 83–99, *et seq. See* par. 307.

MCCOLVIN, Lionel R. A New Bibliographical Classification: some preliminary chapters. In *The Library World*, v. 28, pp. 107–109 124–127, 143–145, 181–183, Dec., 1925–April, 1926, *in progress*.

PERKINS, Fred. R. Rational Classification of Literature for Shelving and Cataloguing Books in a Library: with alphabetical index. Ed. 2, 1882. San Francisco: Francis, Valentine.
The introduction is interesting and useful.

IV. CLASSIFIED CATALOGUES.

BISHOP, W. W. Practical Handbook of Modern Library Cataloguing. 1914. Ed. 2, 1924. Baltimore: Williams & Wilkins. London: Balliere.

GARRISON, F. H. John Shaw Billings: a memoir. Por. 1915. New York: Putnam.
Pp. 213–77, "The Surgeon-General's Library and catalogue", describe the conditions of the production of one of the finest of dictionary catalogues, and have many incidental references to classification.

ORMEROD, James. Style in Card Cataloguing. 32 pp. Ed. 3, 1939. Birmingham: Cambridge.
An excellent set of model cards with practical text.

RANGANATHAN, S. R. Classified Catalogue Code. 1934. Madras L.A.
—— Theory of Library Catalogue. 1939. (*Ibid.*)
Together by far the largest contribution to the subject.

SAYERS, W. C. Berwick, and STEWART, J. D. The Card Catalogue, etc. Illus. 1913. Grafton.

SHARP, H. A. Classification and Cataloguing. In his *Cataloguing: a text-book for use in Libraries.* Ed. 4, 1948, pp. 422–31. Grafton.

STEWART, J. D. The Sheaf Catalogue. Illus. 1909. Grafton.

TAYLOR, Margaret S. Subject and Form Catalogues. In her *Handbook of Classification and Cataloguing for School and College Libraries*, ch. 7. 1939. Allen & Unwin.
Simple, practical work.

WALFORD, A. J. Cataloguing for Examination Purposes. In *The Library Assistant*, v. 36, pp. 68–76. 1943.
A formal article which crams much value into small space. See also the preliminary note to this Bibliography.

V. PRACTICAL APPLICATION.

BROWN, J. D., and Others. Open Access Libraries: their planning, equipment and organization. Illus. 1915. Grafton.

Chapter V, Classification and Shelf-Guides, by H. T. Coutts. Pp. 105–141.

DELISLE, Léopold. Instructions Élémentaires et Techniques pour la Misè et le Maintien en Ordre des Livres d'une Bibliothèque. Ed. 4. N.D. Paris: Champion.

The learned author has produced a most attractive little introduction to book arrangement; its technique is very elementary.

JAST, L. Stanley. Library Classification. *In* Greenwood, Thomas (Ed.), *British Libraries Year-Book: a record of library progress and work.* Illus. 1900.

Pp. 20–36. The best introduction to classifying available at its date in any English work. The practical hints rest largely upon the introduction to Dewey's *Decimal Classification.*

MERRILL, William Stetson. Code for Classifiers. Ed. 2, 1939. Chicago: A.L.A.

A valuable series of definitions and rules based mainly on the D.C. hand recording, where they diverged from it, decisions made in the L.C. system. Class by class the scheme is considered with examples and suggested solutions drawn from the experience of many classifiers. A new edition would be welcome.

RANGANATHAN, S. R. Fundamentals. *See* entry for R. above and par. 300 in the text.

SAYERS, W. C. Berwick. Introduction to Library Classification (see above).

Part III is a course in the actual classifying of books, consisting of a first lesson giving the rules for classifying and nine other lessons dealing with the classes of Dewey in sequence; with numerous readings and exercises.

Book-Display.

BRISCOE, Walter A. Library Advertising. 1927. Grafton.

LEYLAND, Eric. Wider Public Library. 1938. Grafton.

McCOLVIN, L. R. Library Extension Work and Publicity. 1927. Grafton

SAVAGE, E. A. Manual of Book Classification and Book-Display for Public Libraries. 1946. Allen & Unwin.

See also his "Books to Lend: a talk on Book-Display in Popular Libraries," an article in *The Library World*, v. XL, pp. 107–13, 1937.

HILTON SMITH. Aids to Readers. In W. E. Doubleday's " Primer of Librarianship." 1931. Allen & Unwin.

See also his "Aids to Public Library Readers," *Library Assoc. Record*, v. VIII (new ser.), pp. 263–74, 1930.

FLEXNER, Jessie. Circulation Work. 1927. A.L.A.

WARD, Gilbert O. Publicity for Public Libraries. 1924. N.Y.: Wilson Co.

WHEELER, Joseph L. The Library and the Community: increased book service through library publicity based on community studies. 1924. A.L.A.

Consult the indexes of the library journals for articles which appear with great frequency, which is not strange, as the question really covers much modern library enterprise.

VI. A BRIEF SELECTION OF SPECIAL CLASSIFICATIONS.

Examples only of the schemes which are not merely selections of general schemes or slightly adapted versions of a part of them. Many other schemes are given or described in the papers of the Association of Special Libraries and Information Bureaux, and in the American *Special Libraries*. A great many I do not know, of course. These below I do. An interesting, general work which deals briefly in passing with various schemes is John L. Thornton's *Special Library Methods*. 1940. (Grafton).

Book Arts.

NEW YORK, GROLIER CLUB. The Classification used in the Library. 1910.
A small decimal scheme.

Catholic Books.

LYNN, Jeannette Murphy. An alternative Classification for Catholic Libraries. 466 pp., 1937. Chicago: A.L.A.

Children's Books and Schools.

FEGAN, Ethel S., and CANT, Monica. A Library Classification for Schools: the Cheltenham Classification. 1937. Cambridge: Heffer.

Education.

BOARD OF EDUCATION. Scheme of Classification adopted for the arrangement of the Books on the Shelves in the B. of E. Library. 1909. London: H.M. Stationery Office.

Fiction.

BURGESS, L. A. A Fiction Policy. In *The Library Assistant*, v. 36, pp. 76–81. 1943.
Presents a thematic scheme, which has a two-letter alphabetical notation with sub-divisions of "merit" and further suggested qualifications. Perhaps the most effective scheme of its kind.

Law and Legislation and Public Administration.

DABAGH, Thomas S. Mnemonic Classification for Law Libraries. 1936. California Univ. Press.

GLIDDEN, Sophia Hall, and MARCHUS, Dorothy. A Library Classification for Public Administration Materials. 512 pp. 1942. Chicago: Public Admin. Service and A.L.A.
An extensive alphabetical decimal scheme described in its foreword "as a

standard guide for libraries in the field." Revised and extended from Anderson and Glidden's *System of Classification for Political Science Collections.* 1928. Univ. of Minnesota Press.

KAISER, J. B. Law, Legislative and Municipal Reference Libraries: an introductory manual and bibliographical guide. 1914. Boston Book Co.

NEW YORK STATE LIBRARY. Classification of Legislation. 1903. N.Y.S.L. Legislation Bulletin 22x.

Library Economy.

STEWART, J. D. Tabulation of Librarianship. 1947. Grafton.

JAST, L. S. A Classification of Library Economy and Office Papers. 1907. Library Supply. *o.p.*
A decimal scheme, flexible and practical.

Local Collections.

GOWER, H. D., JAST, L. S., and TOPLEY, W. W. The Camera as Historian. 1916. Sampson Low.
Referred to in our text.

GUILDHALL LIBRARY, LONDON: SMITH, Raymond. Classification of London Literature. 1926.

HOBBS, J. L. Libraries and the Material of Local History. 1948. Grafton.

PHILIP, A. J. Outline of a Scheme for the Classification of the Local Collection and for all Material with a Topographical Basis. 1953. See par. 428.

Maps.

THIELE, Walter. Official Map Publications. Ed. A. F. Kuhlman. 1938. A.L.A.
Has ch. on classification, cataloguing and care of maps and a tentative classification scheme.

Manuscripts, Deeds, and Archives.

BRITISH RECORDS ASSOCIATION. Reports from Committees:
1. On the Classification of Archives. 31 pp. 1936.
2. Classified List of the Varieties of Documents which may be found in Parish Archives. 11 pp. 1936.
3. Archives of Religious and Ecclesiastical Bodies and Organizations other than the Church of England. 22 pp. 1936.
4. On the Cataloguing of Deeds. 41 pp. 1938.
This valuable series gives instructions and schemes for the classifying and registering of all sorts of deeds and is the best manual on the subject.

JENKINSON, Hilary. A Manual of Archive Administration, including the problems of War Archives and Archive Making. 1922. Oxford: Clarendon Press.
The standard work on the whole question. A large section, however, is devoted to classification.

Medicine.

BARNARD, Cyril C. A Classification of Medical Libraries: with introduction, local list, index of parasites and general index. 1936.
Lund.

Music.

DICKENSON, G. S. Classification of Musical Compositions: a decimal-
symbol system. 38 pp. 1938. Poughkeepsie: Vassar Coll.

McCOLVIN, L. R., and REEVES, Harold. Music Libraries. 2 v.
1937–8. Grafton.

Ch. III, pp. 25–39, deals with the classification of music and gives a suggested
scheme in which Dewey's 780 is completely and efficiently remodelled.

Patents.

PATENT OFFICE LIBRARY. Key to the Classification of the Patent-
Specifications of Germany, Austria, Denmark, and Norway.

VII. THE VERTICAL FILE. INDEXING.

BROWN, J. D. Manual of Library Economy. Ed. 5, pp. 311–26.
1937. Grafton.

BROWN, G. F. Indexing: a handbook of instruction. 1921. Grafton.

CLARKE, A. L. Manual of Practical Indexing: including arrangement
of subject catalogues. Ed. 2, 1933. Grafton.

COPE, E. A. Filing Systems: their principles and application to
modern office requirements. 1913. Pitman.

DANA, J. C. (Ed.): American Library Economy, v. 2. List of Subject
Headings for Information File. 1917. The Colour-and-Position
Method for Filing. Pt. I. 1918.

KAISER, J. Systematic Indexing, Card System Series, v. 2. 1911.
Pitman.

WHEELER, M. T. Indexing: principles, rules and examples. 1905.
Ed. 2., 1913. N.Y. State Library.

INDEX

The numbers are those of sections, not pages.

The following abbreviations are employed:

C.	= Classification.
C.C.	= Ranganathan. Colon Classification.
D.C.	= Dewey. Decimal Classification.
E.C.	= Cutter. Expansive Classification.
L.C.	= Library of Congress Classification.
S.C.	= Brown. Subject Classification.
U.D.C.	= Universal Decimal Classification.